CHICANO SAN DIEGO

CHICANO SAN DIEGO

*Cultural Space and the
Struggle for Justice*

Edited by
RICHARD GRISWOLD DEL CASTILLO

The University of Arizona Press | *Tucson*

The University of Arizona Press
© 2007 The Arizona Board of Regents
All rights reserved .

LIBRARY OF CONGRESS CATALOGING-IN-PUBLICATION DATA

Chicano San Diego: cultural space and the struggle for
justice / edited by Richard Griswold del Castillo.
    p. cm.
  Includes bibliographical references and index.
  ISBN 978-0-8165-2568-3 (pbk. : alk. paper)
    1. Mexican Americans—California—San Diego—History.
2. Mexican Americans—Civil rights—California—San Diego—
History.   3. Civil rights movements—California—San Diego—
History.   4. Social justice—California—San Diego—History.
5. Mexican Americans—California—San Diego—Social
conditions.   6. Community life—California—San Diego—
Social conditions.   7. San Diego (Calif.)—Ethnic relations—
History.   I. Griswold del Castillo, Richard.
F869.S22C47   2007
305.868'079498–dc22   2007023268

Publication of this book is made possible in part by the proceeds of
a permanent endowment created with the assistance of a Challenge
Grant from the National Endowment for the Humanities, a federal
agency.

Manufactured in the United States of America on acid-free,
archival-quality paper containing a minimum of 50% post-
consumer waste and processed chlorine free.

12 11 10 09 08 07   6 5 4 3 2 1

*For the thousands of immigrants who have died,
and continue to die, crossing the U.S.–Mexico
border each year in search of a better life and a
piece of the American dream*

CONTENTS

ILLUSTRATIONS

CHICANO SAN DIEGO

INTRODUCTION: A BORDER REGION AND PEOPLE

Richard Griswold del Castillo

San Diego is known throughout the world for its beautiful beaches and mild climate, and civic boosters like to say that they live in "America's finest city." Not highlighted in the tourist promotions is the fact that the San Diego region is also home to several million Mexicans and Chicanos, people whose descendants founded this city more than 230 years ago. Except for advertising the restaurants and shopping opportunities in "Old Town" and suggesting possible trips to Tijuana, just across the U.S.–Mexican border, such publications give little attention to the historic and contemporary importance of San Diego's Spanish-speaking population. A person scanning bookstore and library shelves or surfing the Internet will find very little of value written about the ethnic Mexican people in this area. They have been rendered invisible by long-term political and historical forces. This book seeks to give voice to the rich heritage of the Mexican-origin people who live in this important border region. The story that emerges in these pages is that of a long struggle by people of Mexican descent to have their society and culture respected and their views heard.

This work responds to a larger problem that pervades our local, regional, and national consciousness: the tendency to ignore, discredit, and discount the Mexican heritage in the United States. This constructed invisibility and devaluation begins with school textbooks, where aside from mention of the Mexican War in 1846 and César Chávez in the 1960s, virtually no mention is made of the Mexican American presence in U.S. history or of the importance of their culture. It also is a sad truth that few positive representations of the Mexican heritage appear in the electronic and print media. The lack of understanding of the political, economic, and cultural importance of the Mexican people in the United States is based on ignorance, which starts in the schools and pervades public life.

This book and others like it is a small step toward educating ourselves about the realities of our multicultural and globalized world as we enter the twenty-first century.

A famous philosopher once said "all history is local," meaning that the largest theories and generalizations in history are based on interpretations of local events. So it is that the master narratives of U.S. history have been largely based on the experiences of Euro-Americans in the eastern regions of the United States. To understand the issues of the American Revolution, we study the history of Boston or of Washington, DC; and we study Charleston to understand the origins of the Civil War.

Chicano San Diego, then, seeks to add to a larger understanding of American history by telling a new story, that of the Mexican and Chicano peoples in San Diego, California. It is a story that has local, regional, and even national significance because it revises and challenges predominant interpretations and seeks to incorporate perspectives and experiences that traditionally have been excluded, omitted, and devalued.

San Diego, California, is located in the extreme southwestern part of the United States, bordering on Tijuana, Baja California Norte, one of the largest metropolitan regions of Mexico outside of Mexico City. San Diego County's population in 2000 was more than 2.8 million and has been growing by about 2 percent every year as people have been attracted here by the climate and jobs. Mexicans and those of Mexican descent comprised about 26 percent of the total, or 750,000 people, in 2000 making them the largest nonwhite ethnic group in the county (fig. i.1). In the 2000 census African Americans comprised about 6 percent of the total and American Indians less than 1 percent. The city also has the largest population of people of Filipino descent in the United States (almost 100,000), and there are sizable groups of Asians, including Vietnamese, Hmong, Korean, and Chinese.[1]

San Diego's history has been heavily influenced by the military, especially the U.S. Navy and Marine Corps, which have constructed bases throughout the county. Today, the county of San Diego has seven military installations with more than 148,000 employees. Defense spending in San Diego is more than 11.7 billion dollars a year, and almost 146,000 civilian jobs have been created to support the military.[2] Besides this, hundreds of thousands of former military families live in San Diego. One of the fastest growing groups in San Diego is seniors more than sixty-five years of age. Almost 500,000 seniors lived in the county in 2000, and

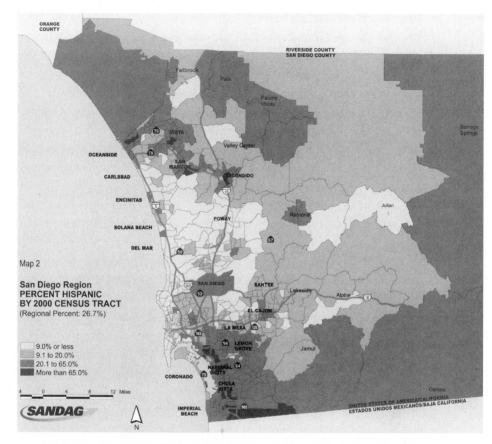

FIGURE i.i. Map of San Diego, 2000 census tract by percentage of Hispanic population. (Courtesy of SANDAG, "Mapping the Census," p. 7)

at that time this population had been increasing at a rate of more than 10 percent per year.[3] This combination of military personnel and retirees has been the basis of a conservative, Republican-dominated elite that has sought to develop San Diego as a tourist attraction with minimal attention to the needs of marginalized groups.

Yet San Diego has been and remains a special place for the Latino peoples of California,[4] having been founded as the first Indo-Hispanic settlement in California in 1769. The Spanish-Mexican pioneers developed the first agriculture and stock raising in the area and organized systems of government, law, and land tenure that influenced the later development of the modern city of San Diego. When the Americans took over the region after the Mexican War, the Mexican population of San Diego was a diverse collection of Hispanicized Indians, mestizos, Spaniards, Afro-Mexicans, and other ethnic groups. This ethnic and racial diversity within the Mexican population, with its attendant mixture of cultures and languages, has been a defining characteristic of *la raza* (the people of Indo-Hispanic heritage). A complex terminology of identification has developed to try to capture this diversity: the terms *Chicana/o* and *Mexican American* are used to refer to those individuals of Mexican heritage, while the terms *Hispanic* and *Latina/o* generally describe membership in a larger Pan–Latin American culture. Regardless of the term we use to identify ourselves, our language, culture, and history are products of the mixture of European with indigenous and African peoples.

Certain forces have made the Chicano/Latino experience in San Diego different from that of Latinos in other regions. One difference emerges from the region's geopolitical setting. The fact that San Diego is on the international border, adjacent to a major Mexican metropolitan area, Tijuana, gives our region a special dynamic. Ties to Mexico are historic and ongoing. Geographic proximity has constantly reinforced the "Mexicanidad" of the barrios and *colonias*, not only through immigration but also through the influence of the media, tourism, and the establishment of binational friendships and family ties. San Diego has a greater proportion of Mexican-origin people than southern California's great metropolitan center, Los Angeles. San Diego's other Hispanic groups, from Central and South America, Puerto Rico, and Cuba, are less influential in molding the local Hispanic society and culture than is true elsewhere. Together with the Mexican inhabitants of Baja California Norte, the Chicano/Mexican population in this binational region numbers almost three million, a sizable linguistic and cultural bloc whose growing presence will play a major role in the future of the region.

There is a paradox underlying San Diego's history. Unlike the typical border city, San Diego has developed with its back to Mexico, as local economic and political leaders on the U.S. side have consistently ignored the ways in which the region is connected to Mexico through historical, cultural, and increasingly, economic factors. The result has been that most European-origin San Diegans do not think of themselves as living in a border city. They do not recognize the importance of the Mexican presence across the international line or within the city. The tourist-oriented economy of San Diego and the relative prosperity of the region (compared to other border cities) has acted to insulate white San Diegans from their dependence on Mexicans and Chicanos for continued economic prosperity and for the cultural distinctiveness that makes San Diego an attractive tourist destination. This historical amnesia has had consequences for the development of Chicana/o society and culture here.

Another important factor shaping the special regional character of Chicanos and Latinos has been the nature of the English-speaking, non-Hispanic population that has dominated San Diego's political and economic development for the past 160 years. The "Anglos," themselves a diverse ethnic group, have controlled San Diego since 1848 and until very recently, the Mexican-origin population has been of little consequence in public life. Until just a few years ago, there had never been an elected city or county official of Mexican, Hispanic, or Mexican American heritage. San Diego's economy has been dominated by the U.S. Navy, aerospace, and tourism, sectors that have offered limited opportunities for Latinos living within San Diego. It is not surprising to find, from the most recent census, that Hispanic families have the lowest median family income of any ethnic group in San Diego county ($26,453) or that, with the exception of American Indians, Hispanics have the lowest percentage of college graduates of any group in San Diego County (10 percent). Part of the puzzle in understanding why this is so resides in our collective ignorance of the lessons of the past.

A recent book, *Under the Perfect Sun: The San Diego Tourists Never See*, takes a critical view of San Diego's history and is a first step in uncovering the reasons why Mexicans and Chicanos in San Diego have remained marginalized.[5] Mike Davis, in particular, reveals how the city has been controlled by an almost hereditary elite who have dominated the development and exploitation of the human resources of the region. Davis and his coauthors give some attention to the underclass of ethnic minorities and radicals who have unsuccessfully opposed the elite but do not give significant attention to the historic Mexican and Chicano presence in the city. Thus, even among sympathetic writers, the role of Mexicans and Chicanos in shaping San Diego has remained hidden. One consequence of *Chicano San Diego* will be to provide the ethnic Mexicans who live here, especially the youth, with a sense of belonging and of pride in their participation in the rich history of this region.

That's not to say that scholars have totally ignored the Chicano population. As early as 1990 Larry Herzog documented the plight of Chicanos in the 1970s in *Where North Meets South*. Subsequently, Leo Chávez brought the plight of undocumented Mexican immigrants out of the shadows and into the public light in his study *Shadowed Lives*. More recently, Carlos Vélez-Ibáñez offered a participant observation–based account of some of the events associated with the rise of the Chicano Movement in San Diego in *Border Visions*.

But these efforts have largely been "snapshot" contributions to a mosaic whose contours have remained uncharted. Moreover, the limited images they present have been continually overshadowed by the representations of undocumented immigration in the region, which have served to perpetuate the historic image of Mexicans in the U.S. borderlands as nothing more than commodity labor.

This anthology illuminates the emergence, experiences, and struggles of Chicanas/os in San Diego. In so doing we seek to advance knowledge about Chicanos in what historian David Gutiérrez calls "the third space"[6] by building upon the paradigmatic contribution made by Vélez-Ibáñez in his sweeping overview of the Mexican experience in the U.S. borderlands. Our work follows his lead thematically, theoretically, and methodologically. Thematically, our anthology embraces and empirically underscores Vélez-Ibáñez's vision of U.S. Mexicans as being "engaged in the process of cultural creation, accommodation, rejection, and acceptance."[7] We elaborate on this theme by documenting the struggle of Chicanas/os for social justice in a space where they have encountered and continue to confront oppression. Theoretically, we seek to unmask broader assumptions about Chicanas/os in the city, to use Vélez-Ibáñez's terms. Methodologically, we follow him by combining traditional narratives with autobiographical treatments that provide insight into Chicanos' contemporary lived experience from the bottom up. Such an approach enables us to reveal U.S. Mexicans in San Diego as more than just commodity or immigrant labor and instead as a people who have been creating a home, a cultural place and space, and struggling for social justice on their own and in conjunction with their counterparts across the border. They have historically always been "Mexicans without borders," a term Vélez-Ibáñez coined to describe the people who live in the third space. While the geopolitical border has shifted, other racial, political, cultural borders have emerged. Chicanas/os in San Diego have been challenging these less visible borders. The point is that borders as limiting and delimiting national and ethnic boundaries have been fluid through our history.

The chapters in this book are the result of the collaboration of scholars and activists, males and females, San Diego natives and migrants from other parts of the Southwest and even Europe. Although it is a multidisciplinary anthology, several common themes tie the essays together. Some of the chapters in this book are historical narratives focusing on the mestizo settlers of this region as they attempted to survive in a forgotten and neglected outpost of the Spanish Empire and later the Mexican Republic. Other chapters are personal testimonies and reflections based on the experience of living in this dynamic border region. These personal stories are linked to the history of larger struggles of Chicana/o and Latina/o peoples throughout the Southwest.

The chapters are organized in roughly chronological order, beginning with a brief overview of the indigenous and early Spanish settlers in San Diego and ending with a first-person account of human and civil rights struggles along San Diego's border with Mexico. Each chapter develops the themes of political and cultural struggle to overcome colonial submergence and how Mexicans and Chicano communities have engaged in creative elaboration of a third space, a place that is uniquely their own. The final chapters tell of Chicana/o efforts to preserve their space by engaging in political actions during the Chicano Movement, by creating a vibrant artistic renaissance, by forming organizations to oppose gentrification of their barrios, and by protesting and speaking out against the brutal treatment of undocumented immigrants.

In compiling this book, we have collectively been aware of how much our effort is a preliminary one. There is much more research and writing to be done on many of the topics raised in these pages. This anthology is a baseline survey of the Chicana/o history of San Diego, not intended to be exhaustive in coverage or groundbreaking in theoretical analysis. We hope our work here provides a beginning for others who will elaborate on this rich history.

As suggested, much of this book is the result of personal experience and draws heavily on oral histories and newspaper accounts. There are relatively few published accounts of the struggles of Mexican-origin people in San Diego. As might be expected, there is much more scholarship treating the founding of San Diego and its Spanish and Mexican periods up to 1848. The first two chapters of this book draw from the most important scholarly resources for this period, the most thorough being the multivolume *History of California* by Herbert Howe Bancroft. But this venerable survey suffers from a historicism that obscures and distorts the major themes that are important to understanding later Chicano history, most notably the importance of *mestizaje* (the mixture of indigenous, Spanish, and African elements) in the daily lives of Spanish-speaking San Diegans and their struggles to achieve political and cultural autonomy. Additionally, the older sources also occasionally reveal disturbing cultural prejudices and anti-Mexican stereotypes. The first two chapters in this book therefore are a reexamination and reinterpretation of a well-established historical narrative.

Subsequent chapters, treating the ethnic Mexican experience from after U.S. annexation up to 1940, have had to draw on a limited body of scholarship, mostly published articles appearing in the *Journal of San Diego History*. An early pioneer in attempting to rescue the Chicano history of San Diego was Mario T. García, a well-known historian who in his youth taught at San Diego State University and researched the ways in which the San Diegan Californios experienced the American conquest and colonization after 1848.[8] Another important contribution to the Chicano history of San Diego has been the research of Frank Norris, who wrote the first history of Logan Heights, a middle-class Anglo-American neighborhood that became a barrio.[9] We also relied on Robert Alvarez Jr., whose father was a plaintiff in the first successful anti-segregation lawsuit in California in 1930. Robert wrote an account of that event which later was made into an important documentary film.[10] Other published historical interpretations of the Chicanas/os' community struggle to gain a voice in San Diego have been written by Isidro Ortiz, who studied challenges to voting restrictions that denied Chicanos representation; by Gilbert Gonzáles, who studied the farmworkers who courageously confronted economic exploitation in the Imperial Valley; and by Richard Griswold del Castillo, who researched the ways in which Chicanos, Mexicanos, and Anglos interpreted a violent racial episode, the San Ysidro Massacre.[11] Of necessity, the contemporary history of Mexicans and Chicanos in San Diego relies on oral histories, personal reminiscences, and scattered unpublished sources. Tragically, the archives of some of San Diego's most important Chicano artists, organizations, and leaders are not available to the general public because they have not been valued by libraries as resources. Herman Baca, founder of the Committee for Chicano Rights in the 1960s, has a huge archive that he allowed us to consult. Salvador Torres, a renowned artist who helped develop Chicano Park, also had a massive document collection, but because of lack of local interest, his archive was given to the University of California in Santa Barbara. We hope that this book will provide librarians and others with an impetus for accessing and preserving the many documents that remain scattered in private collections and which will be important in writing the next generation's history.

This book has as its audience, first, the Mexicans and Mexican Americans who live in this region. Most of them have come here from elsewhere, as migrants either from southern Mexico or from other parts of California and the Southwest. For them, the San Diego–Tijuana region is a foreign country, a place that has no history, a region where people are connected only by the happenstance of geography. We hope that this historical overview will serve not only to provide them with a sense of belonging to a larger tradition and heritage but also to motivate them to contribute to its development and manifestation. Another audience for this book is the non-Hispanic peoples of the region, many of whom are also migrants from other countries and places in the United States. We hope that this account will provide them with a new perspective on living in an area with a large Spanish-speaking population, a perspective that will enable them to relate to these people in constructive and positive ways. Finally, we hope to reach with our history people who live elsewhere in the United States and Mexico. They may have only a vague idea of where San Diego is located and who lives there. We sincerely hope that as a result of this book they not only will understand the region and its Hispanic peoples in a fuller way but also will come away with a greater appreciation of the richness of the Mexicano and Chicano heritage.

A brief introduction to the authors of the chapters will help orient the reader to the collective and individual resources that have been part of making this book. Richard Griswold del Castillo is a historian who teaches Chicana and Chicano history at San Diego State University (SDSU). His research interests have been focused on the nineteenth-century Southwest, in books such as *The Los Angeles Barrio, 1850–1890* and the *Treaty of Guadalupe Hidalgo: A Legacy of Conflict*. Richard helped in the development of the chapters dealing with San Diego's history up to the 1940s and coordinated the overall book project. Isidro Ortiz is a political scientist who also teaches in the Chicana and Chicano Studies Department at SDSU. He has been researching community organizations and development and has co-edited a number of books, including *Chicano Studies: a Multidisciplinary Approach* (with Eugene García and Francisco Lomelí) and *Chicanas and Chicanos at the Crossroads: Social, Economic, and Political Change* (with David Maciel). Isidro's understanding of how community organizations work has been valuable in writing the crucial chapter on the Chicano Movement in San Diego. Roberto Martínez is a community activist, the former director of the American Friends Service Committee in San Diego, responsible for monitoring and acting on incidents of abuse of the human rights of immigrants along the U.S.–Mexican border. Roberto's rich experience in community organizing and in publishing annual reports summarizing the abuses suffered by Mexican immigrants made his contribution to this book especially valuable. Roberto developed the chapter dealing with the struggles of the Mexicano and Chicano communities in San Diego for human rights. Rita Sánchez is a professor of Chicano Studies and English at Mesa College who received her degree from Stanford University. She has had lots of experience in the arts, having owned and operated the first Chicano art gallery in San Diego and having organized a large number of art shows. Rita's research in family history has resulted in a book, *Cochise Remembers: Our Great-Grandfather, Charles Henry Coleman*, and many articles on family history. She is also author of "The Five Sanchez Brothers in World War II," a history of her uncles, her father, and her family during World War II. Her enthusiasm and experience in the local arts scene gives an important background for the chapter on Chicano arts in San Diego. María de la Luz Ibarra is an anthropologist who teaches Chicana and Chicano Studies at SDSU. She has written numerous scholarly articles about the lives of Mexican immigrant women who are domestic workers, and she is currently working on a book manuscript about this subject entitled, "Creen que no tenemos vidas." María's experiences growing up in a migrant camp in San Diego's north county combined with her academic training have given her special insights in writing about migrant women in San Diego. Emmanuelle Le Texier is a professor of political science at the Institut d'Etude Politiques in Paris, who got involved in researching barrio issues during her Fulbright visit to California in 2002. She has published several articles in France on Latino politics. Emmanuelle has a fresh and unbiased view of the ways in which Mexican Americans have mobilized. She represents a new generation of international scholars who are researching the U.S.–Mexican border and its communities. José Rodolfo Jacobo is a doctoral student at SDSU. His love of U.S.–Mexican border history has resulted in a number of important projects: a coauthored book entitled *Juan N. Cortina and the Struggle for Justice in Texas* (with Carlos Larralde) and a co-edited book of poetry and photographs entitled *The Giving Gaze*. Like María, Rudy grew up in the farm labor camps of north county as the son of a bracero worker. His interest and personal experiences in the Bracero Program give him special expertise in writing the chapter on San Diego during the 1950s.

In preparing this book, we have been helped by many individuals and institutions. Our thanks go to the librarians at SDSU, who assisted us in tracking down rare and important documents. Also, the photo resources of the San Diego Historical Society and the photo archives of *La Prensa* were valuable, as were the archives of Herman Baca, head of the Committee on Chicano Rights. Additionally, the California Council for the Humanities helped support the construction of a Web site for use by high school students interested in the Chicano/Mexicano history of the region. We encourage teachers to use this Web site to supplement their teaching of California and U.S. history (go to www.rohan.sdsu.edu/dept/mas/chicanohistory/index.html). Finally, we want to give our appreciation to the many students who have encouraged us in our endeavor by helping us shape our vision of the region and its distinctive history and dynamic. Ultimately, this book is a challenge to them to go beyond our work and write more about their communities and families.

1

NATIVES AND SETTLERS: THE MESTIZO HERITAGE

Richard Griswold del Castillo

This is a story told by the Kumeyaay people of how they first came to live in what is today San Diego, California:

> Many years ago all the peoples were united as one and together they traveled west out of the sunrise led by a chief whose wife had died and who had only one daughter. Among the assembled people, was a young boy who, during the migration west, fell in love with the chief's daughter. Before long the young boy and the chief's daughter made love. When they reached what is today Borrego Springs, the final part of the desert, the boy climbed a mountain (called Hahpowugh) to hunt some deer. After killing a buck, he watched from a distance the birth of their child.
>
> When the chief looked at the newborn baby and the girl, he told the boy that he had to give the meat of the deer to the people because of the baby's birth. That night all the people feasted, with songs and dances. During the height of the festivities the chief proclaimed that his heart would not let him continue the journey west and that they should continue without him. So all the people split into different groups, called by the Spanish the Cocopahs, the Luiseños, the Diegueños, and the Cahuillas. The chief stayed behind at the rock near what is today Vallecitos, turning himself to stone.[1]

This Kumeyaay origin story, dating from prehistoric times, tells of migration; of familial obligation toward the community; and of the people being divided, abandoned by their leaders, and having to develop their own direction. These mythic themes echo through the ages, foretelling, perhaps, some of the concerns of native, Mexican, and even Chicana/o history.[2] The indigenous, Spanish, and Mexican settlers of this place that later was named San Diego had to find their way despite their isolation and apparent powerlessness. They learned as a people to shape a resilient and enduring society, one that survived many hardships to become our common heritage.

The indigenous people of San Diego are an important part of the story. For hundreds of years they profoundly influenced the society and culture of the Spanish-speaking settlers who first arrived in 1769. The Kumeyaay natives provided the labor force that built the Spanish and Mexican missions, presidios, and ranchos. The native Indians contributed elements of their language to the newcomers' description of the topography and intermixed their language with Spanish to form regional dialects. The Kumeyaay resistance to enslavement by Spanish and Mexican officials altered the Europeans' expansionist plans. The small minority of native peoples who became part of the Spanish colonial settlement helped raise the food and the children of the Euro-American settlers. Because of class prejudices, farming and domestic service became Indian work. The native knowledge of medicinal plants and uses of herbs added to the folklore of the new settlers. Some natives intermarried with, and others were raped by, the Spanish and Mexican settlers. Their children, mestizos of the frontier, had a mixed cultural legacy. Indeed, because most of the Spanish and Mexican settlers were mestizos or mulattos from southern Mexico, and because Spanish surnames and language became common among many of the local Indians, except for dress, it was hard to tell the Spaniards and Indians apart. By the nineteenth century the native peoples had become part of the visible and invisible Hispano-Indian culture of the San Diego border region.

After the end of the Mexican War in 1848, the Mexican Americans, later Chicanos, would have even more in common with the native peoples. Like the Indians before them, the Chicanos would be conquered in war and be given a treaty that offered them no real protection. As a subjugated people, they would be compelled to adapt to a new language and economy. Like the native peoples, they would be forced to live in segregated areas and would be discriminated against because of their race. And just as the Spanish had reduced the native people to a subordinate laboring class, so too the Anglo-Americans would relegate the Mexican Americans to working-class occupations.

The ironic coincidences between the histories of the native peoples and of Mexican Americans in the twentieth century should not, however, lead us to oversimplify or romanticize the extent of their communalities. The native peoples

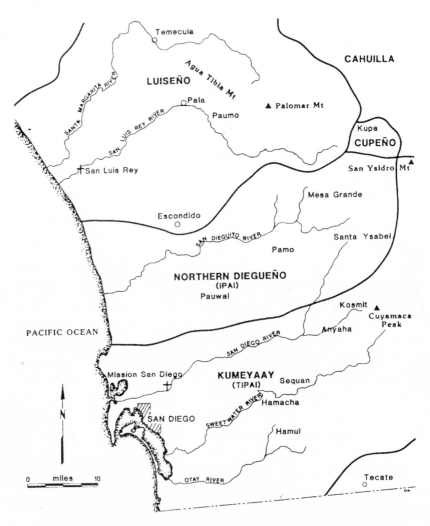

FIGURE 1.1. The Indians of San Diego County. (From Carrico, *Strangers in a Stolen Land*, p. 12. Reprinted courtesy of Richard Carrico.)

have had their own historical and cultural identity, separate from that of Chicanos. Their prolonged history of conflict and coexistence with the Spanish-speaking settlers requires an introductory understanding of the indigenous peoples.

The first boundaries that the future progeny of the Mexicans in San Diego faced were those that separated the indigenous from the Mexican/Spanish cultures (fig. 1.1). The early history of these two groups was one of conflict as well as convergence, and the emerging mestizo settlement contained Indian as well as Spanish influences even while each group struggled to establish its own cultural space and sense of justice.

The Kumeyaay Culture

The first settlers of the San Diego region were migrants who entered from the north, perhaps as much as 13,000 years ago. These game hunters eventually evolved into more sedentary peoples who supplemented their diet with acorns and grasses. Anthropologists call these early peoples the San Dieguito and La Jollan, after the locations of their excavated settlements.[3]

The ancestors of the present-day native peoples of San Diego are descended from the mixture of these early peoples with another wave of Yuman-speaking migrants who crossed the desert from the east, coming from Arizona or perhaps northern Mexico. This group eventually dispersed over present-day Imperial and San Diego counties and became known to the Spanish as the Diegueño Indians. Farther to the north, another band of peoples entered as migrants. They were related to the Shoshonean-speaking people from the desert. The Spanish called them the Luiseños and Cupeños.

The people most closely tied to the Hispano-Mexican settlers in San Diego's Mission Valley called themselves Kumeyaay. The Kumeyaay themselves were a large band spread throughout what is present-day San Diego County and into northern Baja California, comprising two divisions speaking dialects of the same language. To the north, from Escondido to the coast, lived the Ipai, or northern Diegueño. The Tipai, or Diegueño Kumeyaay, lived in present-day Mission Valley and southward into northern Baja California. The Kumeyaay lived in hundreds of small, semi-permanent *rancherías*, or village camping spots, migrating with the seasons to the mountains during the annual harvest of acorns and grain grasses, which were their staple foods. They were very successful in maintaining a dense population in comparison to natives in other regions of North America. Probably between nineteen and twenty-five thousand Kumeyaay people resided in San Diego at the time of first Spanish contact.[4]

These peoples remembered their history in family and clan gatherings where they created an oral tradition that survived from generation to generation. The stories were memorized and sung, and often were directed toward the Great Spirit. Each band had one singer who knew all the songs and stories and who taught them to the others. For example, one story, the legend of Takwish, was told through 1,050 songs that were sung from sunset on Friday until sunrise on Sunday.[5] There were probably hundreds of such stories, each encapsulating the "soul" of the people and transmitting their identity and heritage to the next generation.

Unfortunately, over the four hundred years of Western colonization that began with the entrance of the Spanish, many of these stories have been lost. They were, properly speaking, the authentic history of San Diego prior to the arrival of the Europeans. Surviving remnants of this rich heritage are jealously guarded and not readily available to non-Indian peoples. It would be interesting to know what the Kumeyaay thought about the newcomers who began settling in their midst—to have their stories about the events and personalities that were influential to them. Some indigenous accounts of the mission system, largely critical of the treatment of the Indians, have been passed down, and a few fragments have been gathered by historians and ethnographers, but these do not reflect the intricacies of the native imagination.[6] Most of what we know of the indigenous culture is filtered through the lens of Western religious or academic institutional thinking.

By all accounts the native peoples revered the souls of things, animals, and plants in the natural world. Some have called this belief system animism: revering nature, talking to it, and taking life from it with respect. Key to the preservation among the Kumeyaay of rituals and beliefs regarding the natural world was the shaman, a religious leader who was also expert in folk medicine. The shaman interpreted the dreams that were bestowed by the Great Spirit to connect people with one another and the natural world.[7] Inherited from their ancestors along the lower Colorado River was a belief in the power of individual dreams and visions. The importance of dreams in the Kumeyaay culture served to emphasize individual spirituality above communal ritual.[8] Besides mediating with the spirits, the shaman, or *kwisiyai*, preserved a vast knowledge of medicine, including spiritual incantations and uses of various herbs. Similar to later *curanderos* among the Mexicans, the shaman was a practitioner of holistic medicine—a true cure was possible only by bringing the body and the soul into harmony with the natural world. In this process the shaman used breath and touch in addition to plants and animals. Much of this lore was part of the culture of the members of the band. In her autobiography, Delfina Cuero mentioned many of the medicinal uses her people made of the local plants.

The shamans as well as others could gain powers from the spirit world through dreams. Cuero told of a relative who obtained knowledge of healing methods through a dream.[9] For the Kumeyaay, the most sacred spot was the mountain they called Kuuchumaa (Tecate Mountain). It was here that the shamans performed their initiation rites and where they learned from the spirits what powers they had been granted. Important Kumeyaay shamans were cremated and buried on the top of Tecate Mountain.[10]

One building important in the spiritual life of the people was the sweathouse, a structure that provided the spiritual cleansing necessary for successful under-takings. Groups of men would spend time in the sweathouse singing or discuss-ing daily concerns. Most often the sweathouse was associated with ceremonies of a spiritual nature, mostly purification. Women were strictly forbidden from entering these sweathouses.[11] Later on, Chicanas and Chicanos would adopt the sweathouse ritual of purification and modify it to relate to their understanding of their indigenous roots, continuing an ancient tradition.

The Diegueño peoples were the only bands of indigenous peoples in California to trace their origins directly to the Pueblo peoples in the greater Southwest. The Kumeyaay did not have corn, beans, and squash agriculture as part of their heritage, but they did know the use of the metate and mortar to grind grains and plants, and the techniques of making coiled and sewn baskets.[12] Climatic conditions, namely the absence of rain during the summer months, made the cultivation of corn difficult in the San Diego region. In any case the availability of local plants made such innovation unnecessary. The consumption of acorns as a primary food of high nutritional value was unique to the indigenous peoples of Alta and Baja California. Although oak trees grew on the lands of vari-ous peoples of the greater Southwest and northern Mexico, only the California bands developed the techniques that made them available for food. To make acorns edible, they have to be leached of their tannic acids through immersion in water or mud. The Kumeyaay used coiled baskets for the leaching process, while the Luiseño and Cahuilla used a sand basin or earthen depression. The invention of leaching processes probably originated with the California Indians.[13]

Despite the lack of maize agriculture, the Kumeyaay may have practiced a kind of ecological and plant management with regard to both oak trees and grasses whereby they increased the locations of food-producing and medicinal plants.[14] Interplanting ensured the survival of some food resources during drought. The Kumeyaay elders also reported planting cuttings from oak trees and hybridizing them to produce more acorns. The result was stands of oak trees near villages.[15] The Europeans, used to row-type agriculture, did not recognize the native grain fields as such, although one Spanish document recorded the harvesting of non-European grain grasses by the local Indians.[16]

First Encounters with the Spanish

In the last part of the eighteenth century, the Spanish crown decided to finance the settlement of Alta California primarily for strategic political reasons, namely, to establish a viable claim to this area in order to oppose the encroachment of the Russians and other European powers. Additionally, California ports could provision the valuable Manila galleons as they made their way south to Acapulco laden with riches from Asia. Of course, the Catholic Church wanted to expand its missionary endeavors as far north as possible. Baja California had already been colonized with a string of missions and presidio outposts before the first settlements were founded in California.

On September 28, 1542, only twenty years after the conquest of the Aztec capital, Tenochtitlan, a Spanish expedition led by the Portuguese navigator Juan Rodríguez Cabrillo discovered a "landlocked and very good harbor," which he named San Miguel since it was the feast day of that saint.[17] Cabrillo and explorers who followed him had been sent to discover a suitable port for the Manila galleons as well as to search for a northwest passage between the Pacific and Atlantic. Anchoring near the mouth of the harbor, Cabrillo's men explored the bay with a small boat. A shore party rowed toward a congregation of Kumeyaay who had assembled, but as the Spanish neared land, most of them ran off. Only three natives remained to inspect the strange newcomers. Cabrillo's men gave these three some gifts, and in sign language the Indians communicated that they knew of other strange men like them who had been seen inland. Later that night, an expedition from one of Cabrillo's ships landed on shore, intending to fish. The Kumeyaay regarded this as a threatening act and began attacking the party with arrows, wounding three of the Spaniards. This was the first conflict between

Europeans and the native people of California. It would certainly not be the last. Significantly, it had to do with food and territory.[18]

The next meeting between the Kumeyaay and the Spanish, sixty-one years later, was less violent. On November 10, 1603, the Spanish-Basque explorer Sebastián Vizcaíno reached San Diego Bay with his expedition of three ships, two hundred men, and three Carmelite friars. Since his flagship was the *San Diego* and the feast day of this saint was on November 12, only two days hence, he renamed the harbor San Diego. The expedition stayed ten days, during which time they refitted their ships, buried those crew members who had died from scurvy, set up a tent church, and sent an expedition inland to scout the territory. During their stay, their contact with the local Kumeyaay was limited to exchanges of gifts.[19]

Two centuries would pass before the Kumeyaay would meet another group of strangers. The first of four Spanish colonizing expeditions arrived on April 11, 1769, when the ship *San Antonio*, commanded by Juan Pérez, anchored in the bay. That same day, as remembered by Kumeyaay elders but not noted by the Spaniards, an earthquake shook the mountains and the sun was partially eclipsed, portentous signs, perhaps, that the world as they knew it was about to pass away.[20]

The Colonization of California: San Diego's First Settlement

The Spanish sent four expeditions to converge on San Diego, two by land and two by sea. This early contingent of soldiers, sailors, some Indians from Baja California, some tradesmen, two priests, and a doctor brought the Euro-Hispanic population to a few more than one hundred. When they arrived most of the sailors were sick with typhus, a disease transmitted by lice and fleas. Unfortunately, San Diego's climate is well suited for such vermin, and within the next few weeks more than half of the men died onshore in a tent camp set up for them.[21] On May 14 the first overland expedition of soldiers arrived at San Diego, commanded by Captain Fernando Rivera y Moncada. Father Juan Crespí and a contingent of Christianized Indians from the southern missions accompanied the soldiers. They had marched overland up the Baja Peninsula from Loreto. Soon after the arrival of the second contingent, the commanders decided to abandon the beach and find a more permanent settlement. It was Pedro Fages who picked the new location, a hill overlooking the bay and the nearby river.[22] Finally, on July 1,

1769, Father Junípero Serra and Captain Gaspar de Portolá's expedition arrived. Besides the contingent of soldiers, they also brought forty-four Christianized natives from Baja California. Only 126 of the total of 219 explorers and settlers who had arrived in the last three months were still alive. On July 16, 1769, Father Serra presided over a mass celebrating the official "birthday" of San Diego.[23]

The Spanish-speaking settlers of San Diego who arrived in 1769 were barely able to survive in this desert outpost far from their civilization. The natives resisted conversion and attacked the Spanish settlement again and again. During the first year of colonization, most of the Spanish colonists died of disease, starvation, and wounds. Thus, it was not foreordained that this enterprise would succeed. The harsh life endured by the early soldier-colonists bonded them into a tightly knit community—one that would become the nucleus of a civil settlement in the Mexican era.

Who were these first Spanish-speaking settlers in San Diego? Given their high mortality rates, a better term than *settlers* might be *survivors*. We may never really know with exactitude who they were. The names of the military and religious leaders as well as a few of the artisans and doctors are well known to historians, but no one can be sure about the names of the soldiers and sailors who made up the bulk of the expedition. The records of those who died after the landing in San Diego were later destroyed when the Indians attacked and burned the mission in 1775. (Later, Father Serra reconstructed some of these records from memory.[24]) For the next decade San Diego would be a transient presidio with very few of the soldiers remaining very long, a foreshadowing, perhaps, of the military future for San Diego. The leaders of the founding expedition, Padres Serra and Vizcaíno and Captain Portolá were Spaniards of different ethnic stocks. This has led some to suppose that the whole expedition was composed of fair-skinned Spanish conquistadors. Notwithstanding the practical impossibility of determining the ethnicity of the surviving soldiers, there is evidence to suggest that the majority of them were mestizos and mulattos with the Spanish Iberians being mostly the priests and officers.

The Mission Presidio

Lieutenant Pedro Fages had chosen the site for the San Diego settlement well. From the site, near the top of a barren hill, it was possible to see the entrance to the bay and inland up the river valley for several miles. The presidio site was near a river, providing a source of fresh water for domestic and agricultural needs.

Also close by was a Kumeyaay village named Cosoy, located where Old Town San Diego now stands. Inevitably, as the Spaniards constructed the wooden structures that would serve as the mission and the infirmary, the Kumeyaay grew curious and wandered into the camp. Every day larger and larger crowds gathered to inspect the Spanish and their clothing and material goods. The natives entered and a few items were stolen. Finally, violence erupted on August 15, 1769, when some natives entered the mission shed and attempted to take some clothing from the infirmary. The soldiers used their weapons and the natives shot back a volley of arrows, killing a young boy and injuring a priest, a solider, a blacksmith, and a Baja California Indian. When the dust cleared, three Kumeyaay warriors lay dead.

As a result of this skirmish, Serra ordered that a log stockade be constructed around the mission. Hence, the first mission was to be located inside the presidio grounds. The possibility of retaliation scattered the residents of Cosoy village, preventing the priests from making the necessary contacts for conversion. For more than a year they did not convert a single Indian.[25] Raids by the Kumeyaay continued, and the Spanish began to die from wounds and from starvation. In January 1770, when Portolá returned to San Diego from Monterey, he found only twenty colonists left. Many had died and others had been ordered back to Baja California.

It is sometimes a mystery to modern students why some of the first founders of European colonies in the Americas suffered from starvation. The problem, at least in the case of San Diego's first Euro-Hispanic settlers, was a lack of familiarity with the ecosystem, as well as a lack of good trading relations with the local Indians. With each skirmish there were fewer and fewer natives willing to approach them to trade for food. The soldiers were used to wheat and meat and, if necessary, maize (corn). When game grew scarce and the corn crop, planted in the riverbed, was eaten by birds, they had to try to barter with the Indians to survive, at least until the next provision boat appeared. Ironically, the Spaniards were reduced by hunger to entreating a few friendly natives for food in order to survive. (Several decades later the tables would be turned when starving Kumeyaay had to beg food from the Mexican settlers.) Even hunting was a limited source of food. The scarcity of shot and gunpowder and absence of large game meant that hunters could not be expected to feed a garrison. Thus, the chronicle of San Diego's early history was one of waiting and hoping for the next supply expedition.[26]

The next few years saw a consolidation of the Spanish colony in San Diego.

More soldiers and priests came and went. Father Serra left and was replaced by Father Mugáregui in 1774. Before Serra left, he received permission to move the mission out of the presidio and several miles upriver. There were several considerations in this move: first, Serra wanted to remove the neophytes (newly converted Indians) from the corrupting influence of the soldiers. Father Jayme, in his letter of 1772, complained about the soldiers raping the Indian women.[27] This, in turn, led to the Indians avoiding contact with the priest. There were very few converts, and Serra wanted to increase the yield of souls by moving away from the cause of the problem. Another reason for the move was to find suitable agricultural lands near the mission. On more than one occasion, a flood washed away the crops or a drought dried them up. The new location would provide a more dependable water supply for agriculture. The military commanders also wanted to be rid of the massing of Indians around and inside the presidio. No mention was made of the possibility that the new mission might be difficult to defend, being so far from the presidio.

The friars moved their mission in August 1774 to a site near the Kumeyaay ranchería called Nipaguay. With a small number of neophytes, they set about building a small church out of the tules and willows that grew in the area. The neophytes dug a well to provide drinking water, and the friars planned to construct a dam farther upriver to develop irrigated farming. Within a year Serra's hopes began to be realized. The mission now had ninety-seven neophytes, but this was still fewer than any other mission in California at the time.

A Mission under Siege

The new mission at San Diego was vulnerable to attack, and the surrounding Kumeyaay did not wait long to attempt to get rid of the intruders. On November 4, 1775, around midnight, an estimated one thousand Kumeyaay Indians attacked the mission, burning most of it to the ground and killing Father Luis Jayme along with several other Spaniards. The cause of the uprising apparently was the actions of two brothers, Carlos and Francisco, both newly baptized neophytes who had been punished for having stolen a fish from an old woman. Carlos was the chief of the local ranchería. Because they resented their treatment by the padres, they ran away from the mission and began to organize an uprising of the surrounding rancherías. When they learned that about half the presidio garrison had been sent north to San Juan Capistrano, they saw a chance to wipe out the Spaniards once and for all. In the Spanish investigation that followed, some accused the resident neophytes of helping the attackers, but they denied it, insisting that they had been forced to go along with the attackers.[28]

For the next fifty years Mission San Diego de Alcalá functioned as the southernmost outpost of the Franciscan chain of missions. Spanish laws required that those natives who resided in and near the missions elect an *alcalde* (mayor) and several *regidores* (councilmen) each year to govern themselves. The padres opposed this and complied only nominally. The soldiers protested that the padres were allowing the Indians to ride horses in violation of the laws, but the padres protested that there were no other vaqueros available.[29] The conversion of natives proceeded slowly due partly to the problem of the multiplicity of dialects spoken by the various Kumeyaay rancherías. Father Jayme had managed to learn enough of the predominant Kumeyaay dialect to translate a catechism into the native tongue, but it was destroyed in the 1775 attack. The mission fathers, following the lead of others in Mexico and California, sought to teach native children the Spanish language as well as Christianity.

Evaluating the Mission System

One of the major controversies surrounding the Spanish colonization of the Southwest regards the treatment of the Native Americans. A wide range of historians and anthropologists as well as Indian activists agree that the mission system throughout the Southwest, whatever its rationale at the time, resulted in the deaths of hundreds of thousands of Native Americans.[30] The mission system in California was perhaps the most intrusive of all. The missions in Texas were abandoned early on; the ones in New Mexico provoked a violent and successful rebellion that curtailed their activities; and in Arizona, the missions were few and scattered. In California the twenty-one missions significantly disrupted the Native American economy and lifeways, although it is important to remember that only about one-tenth of all the natives in California were missionized. The indigenous population decline in California due to concentrating the natives, exposing them to new diseases, and depriving them of their traditional foods can only be estimated. In California the missions grew to include about 20,000 neophytes at their peak. The mission annals in the period from 1769 to 1834 recorded 62,600 deaths but only 29,100 births.[31] There were periodic neophyte rebellions, and thousands of Indians ran away to escape the harsh treatment and near-starvation rations given them by the priests. Armed expeditions sent out in pursuit rounded up additional candidates to repopulate the missions. In addition, many natives who were not in the missions died from diseases such as syphilis and influenza. The total California native population is estimated to have declined by more than 100,000 during the Spanish and Mexican eras, and most of the decline was because of the influence of the missions.[32]

With regard to Mission San Diego de Alcalá, the statistical data gathered by Bancroft and Cook illuminate the mission's effect on the Kumeyaay population. The pattern of much of what they report for San Diego was duplicated in the other missions. In the 1790s the number of neophytes at San Diego had increased to 1,523 souls, making the mission the most populous in California at that date. (Mission San Luis Rey, in present-day Oceanside would later gain that honor.) Unlike at some of the other missions, the priests at San Diego de Alcalá allowed some of the neophytes to live in their home villages, many of which were relatively near the mission. The padres regularly "released" neophytes from the dormitories when food supplies were low, to allow them to forage for food. For this reason Mission San Diego had a comparatively good demographic record in comparison to the other missions.[33] Unfortunately, even at San Diego, the death rate was high, with more than 59 percent of those baptized, both children and adults, dying within a year. Later, this death rate would increase to 75 or 80 percent of baptisms per year. Deaths regularly outstripped births. By 1820, at the beginning of the Mexican period, about 35 percent of the total neophyte population could be expected to die within a year.[34]

The cause of many of these deaths was disease aggravated by malnutrition, this despite the glowing reports of mission prosperity chronicled by the mission padres. By the early 1800s Mission San Diego had grown to be one of the wealthiest in the chain, with thousands of cattle, sheep, and pigs and a harvest that was surpassed only by Mission San Gabriel. Despite this reputation for abundance, the neophytes who worked to make it possible were badly fed. Cook found that the average nourishment per person per day in Mission San Diego was 955 calories—a starvation ration. He computed the average for all the missions as 1,405 calories per person per day, still below an adult requirement. Meanwhile, a soldier in the San Diego presidio consumed an average of 3,410 calories and the average adult Spanish settler's diet may have approached 4,000 calories.[35]

As was true elsewhere, large numbers of neophytes ran away from the restrictive controls of the padres. Usually, the padres required that unmarried men and women in their charge be segregated at all times and that single women be locked up at night. Attendance at mass and at work details was obligatory. Up to 1817 San

Diego had 316 runaways, the second largest number in the system, topped only by Mission San Gabriel with 595. Running away was often provoked by hunger and by punishments that were regularly inflicted by the *mayordomos* (overseers) under the direction of the padres. As can be judged by the number of runaways, life at the mission was not entirely idyllic.

From the Spanish, and later Mexican, administrative point of view, the missions were successful in generating food to feed the Spanish colonists, in generating some foreign trade, and in pacifying a sizable number of natives. As the defenders of the missions point out, the attitudes toward crime and punishment were a product of the age and were not especially cruel for that time. Despite the material wealth generated by the missions, a wealth in land and livestock that would later be appropriated by Californio rancheros, the missions also decimated a sizable portion of the native population and alienated some of those who survived. Even the Hispanicized Indians, those who had converted, were not to be entirely trusted. Undercurrents of distrust and fear of revenge emerged periodically in the Mexican era, a legacy of the mission system. Except for a small garrison of soldiers stationed at the mission, all of the soldiers and their families lived within the presidio walls.

The Presidio Settlement

About 1800 a few retired soldiers began to build small adobes on the river plain below the presidio. By that date about 160 persons lived in and around the presidio, and it had been completely rebuilt with adobe walls and an interior adobe chapel. Population growth was slow but was augmented periodically by new garrisons of troops and their officers. By 1811 the population had grown to 237, about a hundred of them children.[36] In 1800 eight orphans arrived from Mexico, part of a government effort to populate their northern outpost. The priest from the mission periodically celebrated marriages within the presidio chapel, but these were rare events, given the lack of marriageable women. In the Spanish colonial period, only three soldiers officially married local Indian women: Joseph Antonio Ruiz Leiva married Clara Sinusin, a mission Indian, in 1779; Joseph Villalobos married Ana María Alilidonza, another San Diego mission Indian; and Maximo Rosas wed Antonia, a neophyte from San Gabriel mission. Of course, there were unofficial unions, rapes, and illicit liaisons, which were illegal under Spanish law but not frequently punished.[37]

Because of the proximity of the mission, the presidial settlers did not develop ranchos or farms, instead purchasing their food from the local padres. The crown budgeted 14,000 pesos per year for presidial supplies, and for much of the Spanish period the presidio was in debt to the mission. To supplement their diet, and perhaps to make a little money, some of the soldiers and their families had livestock and small gardens near the presidio. Despite various reported construction projects, the presidio appeared to outside observers as a crudely built place. In his 1793 visit to San Diego, British explorer George Vancouver wrote that he thought the presidio was "the least of the Spanish establishments . . . there were neither works, guns, houses, nor other habitations nearer than the presidio, five miles from the port, and there they have only three small pieces of brass cannon."[38]

The greatest danger was not from foreigners but from the continuing attacks by the local natives. In 1797 Indians attacked a presidio official as he was returning from official business in Los Angeles, and the same year Indians attacked mission vaqueros at San Miguel, a mission in Baja California. Every month the presidio soldiers had to respond to rumors of attack, hunt for fugitives from the mission, or administer punishments to neophytes. The only prison in San Diego was an adobe building located within the presidio walls, and it regularly housed neophytes sentenced to hard labor for various offenses and a few wayward soldiers.[39]

As for politics, the most interesting intrigue involved foreigners and news of a rebellion in Mexico against Spain. In 1811 Comandante Francisco María Ruiz discovered a "seditious" paper being circulated among some of the troops, probably propaganda from the Hidalgo rebellion in Mexico. He discovered that sixty men had formed a conspiracy to overthrow Spanish authority and promptly arrested five of the ringleaders, including the father of Pío Pico, later a Mexican governor of California. Two of them were eventually released, but three others died in irons within the presidio jail. The last prisoner was released ten years after this event.[40]

By 1821 San Diego's presidio had begun to spill over onto the flat lands below. The presidio had a population of about one hundred men, and twenty-five more were stationed at the mission. A reinforcement of fifty-five troops from Mazatlán had arrived in 1819. In the subsequent decade, soldiers and their families built adobe houses outside the presidio walls, the nucleus of what is today Old Town San Diego. Many had gardens or small farms located in the San Diego River valley.[41] There was no money in circulation, so people bartered with one another to get what they needed. Children began to be a visible subpopulation, and for a few years, retired military men staffed a school. José Antonio Carrillo taught a class there in 1813.[42]

On April 20, 1822, news of the proclamation of Mexico's independence from Spain arrived. The officers, soldiers, and civilians took oaths of allegiance to the newly independent government, and the friars and neophytes were required to make a similar oath. There were no reported protests to this change of allegiance. Within a few months the male *gente de razón* population of the district began involving themselves in the politics of the new government. While Mexico's independence made no apparent difference in the daily lives of the people of the region, profound social and economic transformations were soon to radically alter the Californio way of life.

Mexican San Diego, 1821–1848

During the two decades following Mexican independence, the settlers of Alta California became more independent in spirit as they developed a stronger regional identity. Along with thousands of other pioneers who lived in Mexico's far northern frontier, the colonists at San Diego cultivated an intense sense of loyalty to family and place, especially when confronted by outsiders who threatened their way of life. This strong identification with family and place was a cultural development that shaped the twentieth-century history of the Mexican Americans and Chicanos in San Diego.

Ironically, the landholding Californios of this era owed their prosperity and independent spirit to the policies of the central government of Mexico, whose secularization laws led to the redistribution of the mission lands. Under the new laws, the native people who had worked for the missions were supposed to be emancipated. In fact, Californio land hunger and the failure of the missions to assimilate the natives meant that the ex-mission Indians became a landless, exploited, and homeless population. The mission lands passed into the hands of several hundred Californio families. Among the native people, who outnumbered the Mexican population by at least ten to one, sporadic resistance against the settlers and ranchers continued.

Mexican San Diego became an important center for the Californios' assertion of regional independence and rebellion against arbitrary authority. In 1825 the Mexican government selected José María Echeandía as the new governor of the territory of Alta California; after traveling by ship to the port of San Diego, Echeandía decided to stay at the presidio. With Echeandía's residence in San Diego a rivalry between north and south began. The politicos of the north resented the south's emergence as the de facto seat of government. Nevertheless, for the next few years San Diego was the unofficial capital of the province, and the governor carried out all his official business there.

Soon after his arrival, Echeandía ordered the first celebration of Mexican Independence Day on September 16, 1827. Sixteen cannon shots were fired from the presidio, Mexican flags were displayed on the presidio fortifications, and a formal ceremony took place in the plaza at 9:30 in the morning. After that the entire population proceeded to the church to give thanks. This was followed by a fiesta hosted by the governor.[43]

Governor Echeandía gave the local San Diegans opportunities to participate in territorial government. On February 18, 1827, he ordered the first election ever held in the town—to select a *diputación*, or provincial assembly. Several local men took office along with others from throughout the province. Later the governor convened this new diputación in Monterey, where it met sporadically to discuss new policies and laws. San Diego was not yet large enough to have its own town council, or *ayuntamiento*; nevertheless, the young men of the region were able to influence territorial policy through their contacts with the governor and because some local men, like Juan Bandini and José Antonio Estudillo, were appointed by the governor to official posts.

In 1830 the Mexican central government appointed Lieutenant Colonel Manuel Victoria to succeed Governor Echeandía. From the start, Governor Victoria was not popular with many San Diegans. He removed the territorial government from the presidio and went to live in Monterey, where his actions were influenced by the norteños. Juan Bandini, a Peruvian immigrant who had come to San Diego in the 1820s, was perhaps the most active leader of the anti-Victoria movement. Other prominent San Diegans shared Bandini's sentiments, and in 1831, about a dozen conspirators led by Pío Pico and Bandini took over the San Diego presidio and issued the "Pronunciamiento de San Diego," California's first political document of rebellion. Probably written by Juan Bandini, it set forth in the florid literary style of the day the reasons why people should join in rebellion against Victoria. It accused Victoria of "criminal abuse" and claimed that the signers were motivated by "love to country [and] respect for the laws," which Victoria was accused of breaking. Listed as grievances were the governor's suspension of the government of Santa Barbara, the execution of several people in violation the procedures of law, and the banishment of several prominent Californios. Victoria was termed a despot.[44]

In December 1831 the Californios from San Diego and Los Angeles fought a battle with Governor Victoria's army and forced him to agree to resign.[45] Thereafter, the political struggles among Californios, between families, and between the *norteños* and *sureños* complicated the political situation for many until José Figueroa, the new governor appointed by Mexico City, arrived. But the new governor did not particularly like the Californio leaders from San Diego, whom he termed a "clique of conceited and ignorant men." As a result San Diego's political influence declined.

Secularization and the Ranchos

During the 1830s the intention of the Mexican government was to convert the mission properties into Indian pueblos. This policy, which envisioned free settlements of Hispanicized natives, ultimately was subverted by the local Mexican frontier settlers, many of whom regarded the Indians as incapable of self-management or property ownership. The initial secularization of the mission lands and emancipation of the neophytes proceeded rapidly under Governor Figueroa, and subsequent Mexican governors finished the legal process. Secularization affected about 18,000 Christianized natives in California. At the beginning Governor Figueroa took the unusual step of traveling to some of the missions to explain the benefits of emancipation to the natives in person. At San Diego he spoke to 160 families but only ten agreed to accept their freedom, and these ten families were not enough to form a pueblo. So Figueroa appointed Santiago Argüello as the commissioner in charge of Indian properties at San Diego.[46] Eventually, more ex-neophyte families accepted their changed status and established the Indian pueblo of San Dieguito, near the mission. Others near Mission San Luis Rey moved to an existing native pueblo at Las Flores. And another Indian pueblo grew up in San Pascual, near present-day Escondido. Each of these new pueblos was instructed to select its own alcalde, or mayor. Thus, the first elected government in the San Diego region, ironically, was instituted among the Kumeyaay pueblo dwellers in the Mexican period. Those natives who agreed to live in these pueblos were informally allowed to use the lands they needed for dwellings and agriculture. The Californios declared the rest of the ex-mission lands abandoned and open to petition for ownership.[47]

That so few natives embraced the pueblo structure attests to the failure of the missionization program to assimilate them into the body politic. Many were only too happy to leave and return to their former lives, but others whose villages had disappeared because of disease or war were now homeless, lacking even the nominal protection of the mission padres. The homeless Christianized Indians were at the mercy of the Spanish-speaking population and became the peons, vaqueros, servants, mistresses, and disposable laborers of the Mexican pueblos and presidios. By 1834 Mission San Diego had been secularized along with five other missions in California. Mission San Luis Rey, the most populous, had its properties administered by Pío Pico. At Mission San Diego, there were more than five thousand neophytes, but most of them departed after the priests left. An estimated two thousand moved closer to the newly constructed pueblo of San Diego, where they found occasional work as servants and laborers. For the rest of the Mexican period, the Christianized ex-neophyte native population greatly outnumbered the Mexican mestizo population within the San Diego district.

During the decade that followed, Californios petitioned the Mexican government to claim hundreds of ranchos formed out of lands that had been declared "abandoned" by mission commissioners. Many of these commissioners ended up owning the very lands they administered. Who benefited from this era of rancho creation within present-day San Diego County? Certainly not the majority of the population. Rancho grantees were limited to a few who because of political influence or long service to the mission or presidio were in a position to claim the land and the cattle on it. To be successful, individuals had to do more than claim the lands. They also had to have the interest and ability to manage a cattle ranch, since that was the only means of earning a living from the land in semiarid Southern California.

The following listing is of San Diego's Mexican land grants (see fig. 1.2, numbers in parentheses refer to map):

Agua Hedionda Rancho (stinking water), 13,331.01 acres, granted to Juan Marrón in 1842; near Carlsbad (1).

Buena Vista Rancho, 1,184 acres, granted to Felipe, an Indian, in 1845; city of Vista (2).

Cañada de San Vicente, 13,316.13 acres or 3 square leagues, granted to Juan López in 1845; near Lakeside (26).

Cuca Rancho (a root used as a substitute for coffee), 2,174.25 acres, granted to Juana de los Ángeles in 1845; Palomar Mountain (3).

Cuyamaca Rancho (rain above), 35,501.32 acres, granted to Agustín Olvera in 1845 (the grant was not confirmed by the courts); near Julian (4).

El Cajón Rancho, 48,799.85 acres or 11 square leagues, granted to Doña María Antonia, wife of Miguel de Pedrorena, in 1845; city of El Cajon (5).

FIGURE 1.2. Map of the ranchos of San Diego County. (Taken from "Map of the Ranchos of San Diego County." Courtesy of Fidelity National Title Group, originally published by R. W. Brackett Co., 1939.)

Guajome Rancho (home of the frog), 2,219.41 acres, granted to Andrés and Manuel, two Luiseño Indians, in 1845; east of Mission San Luis Rey (8).

Rancho Guejito y Cañada de Palomia (small gravel or pebbles), 13,298.59 acres or 3 square leagues, granted to María Orozco in 1845; near Escondido (9).

Jamacha Rancho (wild squash vine), 8,881.16 acres, granted to Doña Apolinaria Lorenzana in 1840. (Lorenzana also was the grantee of Rancho Cañada de los Coches); Sweetwater Valley (10).

Jamul Rancho (slimy water), 8,926.22 acres, granted to Pío Pico in 1829 and run by Andrés Pico, 1836–38; purchased by María Amparo Ruiz de Burton and inherited by her daughter, Nellie Burton de Pedrorena; near Jamul, Dulzura (11).

Janal Rancho (spongy ground), 4,436 acres, a former Indian ranchería adjoining Otay Rancho, granted to Antonio Estudillo in 1829; adjoining Otay lakes (12).

La Cañada de los Coches (glen of the hogs), 23.39 acres, granted to Apolinaria Lorenzana in 1843; east of San Diego near Flyn Springs (6).

Las Encinitas Rancho (little live oaks), 4,431.03 acres or 1 square league, granted in 1842 to Andrés Ybarra; city of Encinitas (7).

Los Peñasquitos (small cliffs), 8,486.01 acres, granted to Captain Francisco Ruiz, the San Diego presidio commander, in 1823; he gave the rancho to Francisco Alvarado in 1837 as compensation for the latter's taking care of him in his advanced age; north county, San Diego (13).

Los Vallecitos de San Marcos Rancho, 8,877.49 acres, granted to Francisco Alvarado in 1840; city of San Marcos (14).

Rancho de la Misión de San Diego de Alcalá, 58,875.38 acres, granted to Santiago Argüello in 1845; site of the former mission (15).

Monserate Rancho, 13,322.90, granted to Ysidro Alvarado in 1846; Fallbrook area (16).

Rancho de la Nación, 26,631 acres, granted to Don Juan (John) Forster, an Anglo who had married Isadora Pico, sister of Andrés and Pío, in 1845; National City (17).

Otay Rancho (brushy, place of reeds), 6,657.98 acres, granted to Doña Magdalena Estudillo in 1829 and regranted to Pío Pico in 1846; present-day Otay Mesa (18).

Pauma Rancho (bring water), 13,309.60 acres or 3 square leagues, granted to Antonio Serrano in 1844; near Palomar St Park (19).

Peninsula de San Diego Rancho, 4,185.46 acres, granted to Pedro C. Carrillo in 1846; Coronado and North Island (20).

El Rincón del Diablo Rancho, 12,653.77 acres or 3 square leagues, granted to Juan Bautista Alvarado in 1843; San Marcos (21).

San Bernardo Rancho, 17,763.07 acres or 4 square leagues, granted to Captain Joseph F. Snook, one portion in 1842 and another portion in 1845. Snook married the daughter of Juan Bautista Alvarado of San Diego; Rancho Bernardo. (22)

San Dieguito Rancho (St. James of La Marca), 8,824.71 acres or 2 square leagues, granted to the Silva family and then taken possession by Juan Osuna in 1836, near present day Rancho Santa Fe (23).

San Felipe Rancho, 9,972.08 acres, granted to Felipe Castillo, an Indian, in 1846, east of Julian (24).

Rancho San José del Valle and Rancho Valle de San José (aka Warner Ranch), 26,688.93 acres and 17,634.06 acres, granted to Silvestre de la Portilla in 1836; Portilla had abandoned the land by 1840, when Antonio Pico received a portion of the rancho but later abandoned it. Juan (John) Warner was granted the whole area in 1844; present-day Warner Ranch (25).

Rancho Santa Margarita y Las Flores, 89,742 acres, granted to Andrés and Pío Pico in 1841; these lands conjoined with Las Flores Rancho, which they had acquired from the Indians; part of present-day Camp Pendleton (27).

Santa María Rancho, 17,708.85 acres or 4 square leagues, granted provisionally to Narciso Botello in 1833 and, because Botello failed to fulfill the requirements, regranted to Joaquín Ortega in 1843; present-day Ramona in the Santa Maria Valley (28).

Santa Ysabel Rancho, 17,719.40 acres or 4 square leagues, granted to Joaquín Ortega and his son-in-law Edward Stokes in 1..5844; near Julian (29).

The Mexican government made twenty-nine rancho grants, totaling more than half a million acres, to persons living in the San Diego area between 1823 and 1846.[48] A significant number of the initial rancho grantees were women, Indians, and foreigners. Evidently, it was neither socially nor legally impossible for them to acquire lands. Indeed one scholar has found that out of the seven hundred rancho land grants made by the Mexican government, fifty-five (13 percent) were to women.[49] In San Diego this was exactly the percentage. There were four women grantees: Magdalena Estudillo, Apolinaria Lorenzana (two grants), María Juana de Los Ángeles, and María Antonia Pedrorena. There were three native grantees: Felipe, owner of Buena Vista Rancho; Felipe Castillo, owner of Rancho San Felipe; and Andrés and Manuel, the initial owners of Rancho Guajome. In addition, several naturalized foreigners received rancho grants—namely, Juan José (John) Warner, Joseph Snook, and Edward Stokes—showing that neither ethnicity nor even recent naturalization was a barrier to ownership. As might be expected, the majority of the first grantees were Mexican men. In terms of tradition or bonding with the land, it is worth noting that an overwhelming number of the grants, twenty-four out of twenty-nine, were made during the last six years of effective Mexican sovereignty in California, that is, between 1840 and 1846.

A few points should be made regarding the relationship between Mexican land grants in San Diego and social and political status. The grants ranged from very small, such as Rancho La Cañada de los Coches with twenty-three acres, to immense, such as Rancho El Cajón with 11 square leagues, or more than forty thousand acres. Twenty Californios possessed more than one square league, or about four thousand acres apiece; and a select group of three owned more than forty thousand acres. These big landholders included two naturalized Mexicans, Joseph Snook and Juan José Warner; a woman, María Antonia Pedrorena; and four Californios, Pío and Andrés Pico, Agustín Olvera, and Santiago Argüello. Notably absent from the list of large landholders are individuals who played key roles in the political affairs of the region; important merchants, such as Juan Bandini or Henry D. Fitch; and any member of the Estudillo or Carrillo families, both of which held important offices in the Mexican provincial government. Of course, members of these families held grants in other areas of California. Evidently direct ownership of rancho lands in San Diego was not necessary to achieve honor and status in Mexican California. Some members of the Californio political and cultural elite were economically dependent on extended family members who owned land and cattle and actually worked the ranchos. In that sense family connection, not landownership, was essential to the careers of many of Californio leaders.

The Pueblo of San Diego: Independence and Decline

By 1830 there were probably fewer than four hundred persons living in the civilian settlement that grew up near the San Diego presidio. The people did not yet have self-government but were ruled by the district's military commander. The presidio itself gradually fell into disrepair, especially after the secularization of the mission, and was abandoned. Former soldiers and their children were the first settlers of what later came to be called Old Town.

One European visitor described the settlement in 1827 as "a shapeless mass of houses, all the more gloomy because of the dark color of the bricks of which they are rudely constructed. Under the presidio on a sandy plain are seen thirty to forty scattered houses of poor appearance, and a few gardens badly cultivated."[50] Subsequent American visitors were not much kinder in their appraisal of the local architecture—not realizing perhaps the limited construction materials that were available. Many of the town dwellers also maintained fields and temporary residences in Soledad Valley some distance from the pueblo. In any case, agriculture was seen as the task of the Indian workers.

In 1833 a group of San Diego Californios petitioned the governor to formally declare the settlement a pueblo with the right to self-government and exemption from military rule. Governor Figueroa approved the petition and so did the diputación. Pending approval by the Mexican president, the San Diegans were instructed to hold their first municipal elections. This led to the creation of the ayuntamiento, an institution of local democracy with a long history in Spain and Latin America. The selection of town officials was indirect, through electors who were adult, male residents of the town. The electors, in turn, voted for the alcalde who was mayor and judge, a number of regidores, who assumed various positions within the town government, and the *síndico procurador*, who acted as the town constable and attorney.[51] On December 18, 1834, the first municipal election took place, and on December 21 the electors met and selected the new town officials. The alcalde was Juan María Osuna, a retired soldier who had been born in the San Diego presidio and who, two years later, would be granted Rancho San Dieguito. The regidores were Juan B. Alvarado and Juan María Marrón, both of whom would shortly receive land grants, and Henry D. Fitch, a New England sea captain turned merchant who had married Josefa Carrillo, a member of a prominent Californio family.[52]

For the next few years the *pobladores* of San Diego held elections for their local officials. The families whose members served in elected and appointed posts had the names of Argüello, Machado, Moreno, Bandini, Fitch, Estudillo, Osuna, Alvarado, Carrillo, and Pico. Together, they would arbitrate the official affairs of everyday life and struggle with provincial politics. The most pressing local issue was the control of Indian depredations, which increased after the final secularization of the missions. The settlers expected their government to do something to provide schooling for children and to adjudicate disputes and crimes.

Because of a decrease in population, a change in central government policy, and an erosion of political influence in Monterey, San Diego lost its town government in 1838. For the rest of the Mexican era, Los Angeles would be the official seat of municipal government (the *cabecera*) and San Diego's affairs would be administered by a *juez de paz* (justice of the peace) and later by a sub-prefect.

A major consequence of San Diego's being given pueblo status was its eventual acquisition of vast communal lands. In May 1846 Governor Pío Pico confirmed San Diego's ownership of 48,000 acres including water rights. It was the largest such concession ever given to a Mexican town in California. The grant, a legacy of the Mexican government, was a rich resource that subsidized much of San Diego's municipal development well into the twentieth century.

The end of self-government for San Diego had been caused in part by factional rivalries. In the 1830s San Diego's leading families, in alliance with those of Los Angeles, struggled with rival families in northern California for control of the provincial government. Besides the considerable importance of family honor, the San Diegans wanted to have a customshouse that would allow foreign ships to put in there without being required first to travel to Monterey to pay duties. Many San Diego Californios saw loosening Monterey's control of trade as a key to the future economic prosperity of their region. Underlying the numerous intrigues and revolts of this era was the sureños' desire to achieve more economic and political independence.

The last gasp of San Diego's attempt to salvage regional pride and political influence began in the spring of 1837, when Juan Bandini, Santiago E. Argüello, and Pío Pico led about forty men before the town council and persuaded it to endorse El Plan de San Diego. This document, written by Juan Bandini, proclaimed that everyone should reject the new governor, Juan Alvarado, who represented norteño interests. The San Diego Californios led an opposition movement for the next year until they lost a battle against Alvarado in April 1838 and the governor arrested many of the conspirators.[53]

During the 1840s there were probably fewer than two hundred people living in San Diego pueblo. The decline in population had been due to a number of factors. The most notable problem had been an increase in Indian depredations on the surrounding ranchos, which had led families to leave the pueblo either to defend their kinsmen's stock and lands or to seek a more secure life farther north. The soldiers had left, and without an official customshouse, trade was not thriving. The political humiliations endured by San Diego's Californios during the 1830s led to a less than optimistic feeling about the future. The bright and ambitious left for greener pastures.

Pío Pico's life during this time is a good example of what happened to many Californio residents of San Diego. Pico and his brothers and sisters had grown up in San Diego, the children of José María Pico, a corporal at the presidio. As a young man he traveled throughout California but always regarded San Diego as his home. As we have seen, he was a leader of various rebellions in San Diego against the norteños. During 1837 his rancho at Jamul was raided more than once with great loss of cattle and life. Alvarado imprisoned him briefly after the failed rebellion in 1838. Since San Diego seemed to offer no future, Pico moved to Los Angeles in the 1840s along with Juan Bandini, Agustín Olvera, and many other members of San Diego's elite. Eventually, they and the Angeleños challenged Monterey once more and in 1844, they succeeded in getting Pío Pico chosen as the last Mexican governor of Alta California and in moving the capital to Los Angeles.

Indian Relations

From the beginning the San Diego settlers had lived surrounded by thousands of natives, most of whom regarded the Mexicans with fear and suspicion. As previously mentioned, the secularization of the missions and the disbandment of the military garrison made conditions ripe for Kumeyaay raids and retaliation. Complicating matters was the fact that thousands of ex-mission Christian Indians drifted in and out of the Mexican settlements, working as servants and laborers. When not living in the mission or pueblo, they rejoined relatives in the hinterlands. Sometimes the Mexicans recruited local Indians to serve as auxiliaries in the armies that the San Diegans raised during their civil wars with the norteños.[54] Many Kumeyaay servants were intensely loyal to their Mexican employers, often saving their employers' lives by warning them of impending attacks. Other Mexican settlers regarded all Christianized Indians with suspicion, as possible conspirators in league with the marauding bands in the backcountry.

The mission system and mistreatment by the soldiers had created motives of revenge among some Indians. The pueblo government, the ex-mission administrators, rancho mayordomos, and masters of households frequently punished Indians with lashes, chains, and forced labor. This too added to the reservoir of hostility. But a more common reason for attacks on Mexican settlements was starvation. A series of Indian attacks, retaliatory raids, kidnappings, and massacres in the San Diego backcountry in 1836 and 1837 pointed out the vulnerability of the Mexican settlement.

The Indians were not united in their opposition to the Mexicans. Former neophytes and even gentile bands often joined with the Californios in their wars against the Indian raiders during these years. But for many Mexicans, the loyalty of the Christianized Indians was always problematic. Historian Hubert Howe Bancroft aptly summarized the condition of these years: "Notwithstanding the fragmentary nature of the records, it is evident that in all these years the frontier ranchos were continually ravaged by Indians and that there was no security for either life or property."[55] As a result, historians have concluded that the Californio rancheros of San Diego were near collapse when the Americans took over in 1848. Their cattle had been depleted and much of the pueblo population had scattered to defend the ranchos or to find more secure residences.[56]

Since the majority of San Diego Californios received their land grants during the 1840s, they would have had only a short time to build up their herds before the outbreak of the Mexican War in 1846. This event dramatically changed their economic environment. While persistent Indian raids slowed rancho development in the Mexican era, the native menace would be less important in bringing about the decline of the Californios than the impending American invasion.

Foreigners and Otherwise

The first foreigners to live in San Diego came primarily for economic reasons but stayed because they fell in love. They were merchant seamen and trappers and traders. For most of the Mexican era, there was a thriving business in smuggling, and each year more and more foreign ships visited the port of San Diego. Gradually, a small number of foreigners married into the local families and became Mexican citizens. Over the years the foreigners who stayed in San Diego provided some excitement for the small settlement. Their influence in political and economic affairs grew steadily throughout the Mexican era.

One notable incident involving a foreigner was that of Henry Delano Fitch and his love affair with Josefa Carrillo, which was the scandal of the decade. Fitch fell in love with Josefa while visiting San Diego on business in 1826. A year later he eloped with her and they were married in Valparaiso, Chile. Upon his return, Fitch was arrested and put on trial for kidnapping. After a long investigation and imprisonment, he was finally released and sentenced to the penance of hearing high mass on his knees with his wife and lighting candles for three consecutive *días festivos* (feast days).[57]

Despite the initial hostility of his in-laws, Henry Fitch went on to become a respected member of the Mexican pueblo, being elected to several local offices. He worked mainly as a merchant and was a *compadre* of Miguel de Pedrorena, a Spanish merchant who lived in the pueblo. Fitch did the first survey of the pueblo lands, which resulted in the Mexican grant. He and Josefa had nine children before he died in 1849. Other foreigners who fell in love and married Mexican women were Tomás Ridington, who married Juana Machado; Joseph Snook, who married María Alvarado; and Cave Johnson Couts, who married Ysidora Bandini.

Several important San Diegans were not, properly speaking, Mexicans. Miguel de Pedrorena was a Spaniard who had come to San Diego from Peru. He married into the Estudillo family and eventually owned Rancho El Cajón and Rancho San Jacinto Nuevo. Despite his landholdings he was described by his contemporaries as poor but proud. He and Juan Bandini, a Peruvian of Italian background whose parents had come from Spain, were close friends and both were enthusiastic about the possibilities of American annexation. As already noted, Bandini was one of the leading politicos of San Diego during the Mexican era. The foreigners, both American and non-Mexican, without exception backed the Americans during the Mexican War and served as intermediaries between the native population and the new conquerors. While culturally Mexican and having close family ties to the Californios, they had little commitment to supporting the Mexican political system.

The End of an Era

The Mexican era in San Diego lasted only some twenty-five years but brought some radical changes: the destruction of the mission system and decommissioning of the presidio garrison, the creation of a ranchero class, and the development of local democracy and regional politics. The smallness of the San Diego settlement, which never numbered more than five hundred individuals, made for a society where the details of everyone's life were common knowledge. San Diego's families were also joined by blood and marriage to other families throughout Alta and Baja California, and this mitigated against provincialism. Mexican San Diego developed a lively political life but lost the struggle to free itself from the dominance of the provincial government in Monterey. Toward the end of the Mexican era, San Diego's village settlement was depopulated and the outlying ranchos were struggling, victims of Indian depredations. By the 1840s, the growing importance of foreign merchants and landholders in San Diego and California was a sign that revolutionary changes were about to take place.

2

THE AMERICAN COLONIZATION OF SAN DIEGO

Richard Griswold del Castillo

In 1848 California became part of the United States after the signing of the Treaty of Guadalupe Hidalgo ending the Mexican War. During the hostilities, Mexican San Diegans put up a heroic resistance against the American invaders. Many Mexicanos were not willing to give up their independence without a fight. There followed a colonization of the conquered territories by Anglo-American immigrants and, in the case of California, by immigrants from all over the world, which led to the rapid submergence of the Californio way of life. Mexican Californians became a distinct numerical minority and lost control of their local governments and lands, so that within a generation they had disappeared as far as the new colonists were concerned. Mexicans and Indians became irrelevant to Euro-Americans' plans for economic development and progress. Despite guarantees to the contrary, the Mexicans who were now citizens of the United States were treated as foreigners who were not entitled to the same rights as whites.

In San Diego, the process of colonization followed similar patterns as elsewhere but at an accelerated pace, since there were so few Mexican San Diegans and most of the town's leaders favored incorporating themselves into the American project. Mexicans in San Diego were confronted by new political, cultural, economic, and racial boundaries. These new limits challenged their way of life, yet the Mexicans managed to cope with the radical new economic and political realities surrounding them and to construct a new ethnic identity, neither entirely Mexican nor wholly American but a people set apart by their common experience of preserving their heritage, pride, and sense of social justice.

The Conquest of San Diego

On May 11, 1846, the Congress of the United States voted to declare war on the Republic of Mexico. President James K. Polk justified his declaration of war by saying that Mexico had attacked American troops and invaded the United States, and that the Mexican government had not been cooperative in negotiations over the Texas boundary issue. The first battles between U.S. and Mexican troops occurred in the area just north of Matamoros, a few miles north of the Rio Grande (Río Bravo), in an area that had been part of the state of Coahuila for decades. In reality the Mexican "invasion" occurred in territory that was not conclusively American soil. Many Americans at the time saw the declaration of war as a legitimate and natural expression of America's Manifest Destiny to acquire the western territories to the Pacific Ocean. Merchants and commercial men saw California's ports as necessary for a commercial expansion leading to the lucrative China trade. Strategically, the U.S. government worried that the British, or perhaps the Russians, might annex California and that this would jeopardize national expansion.

San Diego's port was well known as one of the best in California after San Francisco. For years American merchant ships had visited these ports, selling manufactured goods to the Mexican Californios. The occupation of these ports became a priority during the first few months of the Mexican War, and on July 9, 1846, Commodore John D. Sloat occupied the Alta California capital port of Monterey and turned command over to Commodore Robert F. Stockton. He then ordered Lieutenant John C. Frémont to occupy the town and port of San Diego. Sailing on the sloop-of-war *Cyane* with 160 men, the Americans arrived in San Diego harbor on July 29, 1846. According to the Americans, they got a friendly reception and the Californios offered no resistance. After a week Lieutenant Frémont set out with about 120 men from San Diego to assist Commodore Stockton in his capture of Los Angeles, leaving behind a garrison of about forty men.[1]

As was true elsewhere in California, the Mexican elite was divided over whether or not to accept the American military rule. On one hand, some of the Californio landholders had married their daughters to Americans, and family loyalty counted a great deal in their culture. Also some Californios stood to gain economically through the links they had forged with American traders, and they believed that future prosperity would be assured under a U.S. administration. On the other hand, the Mexican Californios loved their *patria chica*, their homeland, and were fearful of what these foreigners would do to them and their families. Very few had abstract political loyalties to the Mexican government, but most had a strong identity as Mexicans based on their language and culture.

Thus, the Californios experienced ambiguous and torn loyalties during the Mexican War. In San Diego many of the leading families supported the American occupation, including the Bandinis, the Argüellos, the Pedrorenas, and some of the Carrillos. At the same time many of the *hijos de país* in the countryside did not, including the Osunas, the Ibarras, the Cotas, and the Machados. Some families were split, with relatives on both sides of the issue, as was the Carrillo household. Henry Delano Fitch, a wealthy merchant, had married Josefa Carrillo, and he supplied the American troops in San Diego during the occupation. Meanwhile, other members of the Carrillo family fought against the Americans at the battle of San Pascual. Economic ties, friendships, and family loyalties were the strongest forces binding individuals to one side or the other, and inevitably, personalities and hurt feelings entered into the picture.

The American Occupation

The American occupation of San Diego lasted from July 29, 1846, until the first week in October. Eventually, events to the north would change the political situation in San Diego and lead to further warfare. On September 27, 1846, the Californios in Los Angeles revolted against the Americans and succeeded in recapturing the pueblo on October 4, 1846. Then from Los Angeles Captain José María Flores sent Francisco Rico and Serbulo Varela with fifty men to recapture San Diego. Capt. Ezekiel Merritt and John Bidwell, who were in charge of the American garrison in San Diego, feared that they would be overrun, so the Americans and a few of their Californio supporters decided to abandon the town. The Californios went to their ranchos and the Americans and a few allies boarded the whaling ship *Stonington*, which was anchored in the harbor. Others, like José Antonio Estudillo and his large extended family, proclaimed their neutrality in the affair and stayed in the pueblo. Without firing a shot the Mexicans recaptured San Diego from the Americans in early October 1846.

The Mexican partisans held San Diego for three weeks until October 24, 1846, when the American army moved to recapture it. An American soldier sneaked ashore and spiked the Mexican cannons on the hill where the old presidio had been (Presidio Hill). Then the American volunteers charged the

Mexican defensive positions. The Mexican commander, Serbulo Varela, had been ordered to send most of his men back to Los Angeles to protect that town from an expected attack and so was outnumbered. After a brief skirmish the Americans took possession of the town, and they hauled down the Mexican flag. But before it could touch the ground, María Antonia Machado rushed to save it from being trampled on. She clutched it to her bosom and cut the halyards to prevent the U.S. flag from being raised.

The Siege of San Diego and the Battle of San Pascual

Two days later, on October 26, 1846, Captain Leonardo Cota and Ramón Carrillo arrived with one hundred men and laid siege to the Americans and their sympathizers in San Diego. Stockton arrived a few days later with reinforcements. Don Juan Bandini (fig. 2.1), one of the leading Californios in San Diego, welcomed Commodore Stockton into his home, and it became the American military headquarters. During the occupation it was the site of frequent fiestas held in honor of the Americans. For the next several months, the Americans were trapped inside the pueblo. Skirmishes were daily occurrences.

Throughout the fall of 1846 a large contingent of Californios in Southern California continued to resist the American occupation. The countryside belonged to the hijos de país. In Los Angeles the Mexicans continued to hold on to their recaptured city, while in San Diego, the Americans and their supporters were besieged. During the siege the Americans built an earthen fort on top of Presidio Hill and even built a drawbridge for access to it. Eventually, more than seven hundred American troops would enter San Diego in preparation for the buildup for the recapture of Los Angeles. Nevertheless the siege remained effective. The Americans sent out Indian scouts to assess the Californio strength and received reports that there were about fifty of them located at San Bernardo (twenty miles from San Diego) but that many more surrounded the pueblo.

About a month after the American recapture of San Diego, the Mexican governor of California, José María Flores, sent Andrés Pico to the San Diego region to watch American troop movements. Pico established a base at Mission San Luis Rey and assisted Captain Leonardo Cota in preventing the Americans in San Diego from foraging the countryside for food. Pico had an informant within the city, his sister Margarita, who told him of the American movements. From her he learned that Lieutenant Archibald Gillespie had set out from the town toward the Indian *ranchería* of San Pascual, intending to join another group of Americans

FIGURE 2.1. Juan Bandini, 1800–1859, an influential
Californio politician who led numerous regional rebellions during the Mexican period. He was Governor Pico's
secretary and supported the Americans during the Mexican
War. He served as alcalde of San Diego and invested in
building a hotel. Granted a rancho in Mexico, he lived there
until 1855. (Used by permission of the Bancroft Library)

there. These were General Stephen W. Kearny's troops, which were coming
from the east after having marched overland from Santa Fe. On December 1, the
Americans had learned that Kearny's dragoons were about eighty miles from San
Diego at Warner's Pass, so Commodore Stockton mounted an escort of thirty
nine men commanded by Gillespie to march north and meet him.

Many of the Angeleños who were with Pico were anxious to fight Gillespie,
since he had earned a reputation as a Mexican hater when he had been in charge

of the occupation of Los Angeles. Early in December Pico's forces, initially num-
bering about seventy-two men, marched to San Pascual (called Kamiai by the
natives) to intercept Gillespie's troops.

Meanwhile, the American troops under Gillespie had joined forces with
Kearny's men near the present-day city of Ramona, in the Santa Maria Valley.
Kearny's men now numbered about 139, including Delaware Indians with Kit
Carson and African American servants of the officers and drovers. The Californios
under General Andrés Pico numbered about 150 men.[2]

The American commanders debated whether to engage Pico's troops at San
Pascual or bypass them and continue toward San Diego. Finally, over objections
from some of the officers, Kearny decided to scout the Californio positions and
sent out a party led by Rafael Machado. Machado succeeded in entering the San
Pascual village and learned of the Californio strength. But the American troops
grew impatient waiting for him and advanced, making enough noise to wake people
in the camp, who came out crying "Viva California, abajo a los Americanos."[3]

Early on the morning of December 6, 1846, the American force charged the
Californio camp in the Indian village of San Pascual (fig. 2.2). The two forces
fought most of the battle in fog and semi-darkness. During the long charge, the
Americans became spread out in a long file, with those on stronger mules and
horses far outdistancing others who were on tired mounts. The few gunshots
exchanged were in this first charge, as the Californios met the early arrivals some
distance from their camp. Captain Johnston was the first man to be killed. Then
the Californios raced away, being chased for about three-quarters of a mile. The
Californio troops then turned and charged at the Americans with their lances.
It had been raining off and on for several days, so Kearny's troops had damp
powder and had to fight with their sabers. The Americans also had trouble load-
ing their newly issued carbines with the small firing caps in the dark and cold.
The Californios were armed with long lances, which they were expert at using
for slaughtering cattle. In the hand-to-hand combat, the Californios had the
advantages of superior mounts, weapons, and battle preparation. In addition,
only about half of the American force was involved in the actual battle. The rest
were in reserve, guarding their supplies and baggage.

Lieutenant Gillespie was struck twice, the first time being thrown from
his horse and then receiving a lance in the chest. According to one Californio
account, Andrés Pico engaged in hand-to-hand combat with Captain Moore.
Another version put him with Leonardo Cota and Tomás Sánchez a mile away

FIGURE 2.2. *The Battle of San Pasqual*, by F. M. Moore. (Courtesy of California Historical Society, Photography Collection, FN-12646)

on a hill, observing the battle. One Californio solider recalled that Juan Lobo, a twenty-three-year-old vaquero from Mission Viejo, led the main Californio assault on Kearny's forces. During the battle the Californios captured one of the American cannons when the mules pulling it bolted and ran toward them. Finally, the Americans brought up another howitzer, which they fired at the Californios, forcing them to retreat.[4]

Nineteen American soldiers lay dead on the field of battle. Two more died later from their wounds. There may have been some American deaths from friendly fire. Lieutenant Emory recalled finding the body of Captain Johnston; he had been shot in the head, the only American to be killed by a bullet wound. There were many American wounded, including Kearny himself, who had suffered three lance wounds and temporarily relieved himself of command. The remnants of the U.S. troops retreated with the wounded to a camp on a hill near San Pascual. There they buried the dead in a mass grave and then sent a messenger to Commodore Stockton in San Diego to ask for help. For their part, the Californios had eleven wounded and one of their group, Pablo Vejar, had been taken prisoner. Juan Alvarado was wounded in the back by a rifle ball.[5]

The Battle of San Pascual in December 1846 marked the high water mark of the Californio resistance during the war. The bloodiest battle fought in California, it was a victory for the partisan forces. The next day, December 7, Kearny's troops resumed their march to San Diego, followed by the Californios, who constantly harassed them. Meanwhile, however, Pico received orders from Governor Flores to break off his battle with the Americans and return to Los Angeles. So Pico and his men departed, and Kearny's troops were able to move on toward San Diego in safety, arriving on the afternoon of December 12.[6]

Later General Kearny wrote that the battle of December 6 had been a "victory" and that the Californios had "fled from the field." One U.S. soldier, in contrast, wrote that they had been saved from decimation by the Californios' capture of the American howitzer, an act that made the Californios "consider themselves victorious, which saved the balance of the command." Later at the court-martial of John Frémont, Kearny admitted that the rescue party from San Diego had saved the Americans from disaster. Generally the navy officers, headed by Stockton, considered the Battle of San Pascual a defeat for the U.S. army. Of course, the Californios considered this engagement a victory, and news of it spread throughout the district.[7]

Kearny's defeat was a product of his overconfidence in the condition of his own men and his underestimation of the Mexicans' will to fight. When in New Mexico, Kearny had expressed his contempt for Mexicans, writing "the Mexicans are physically, mentally and morally an inferior and 'low flung' race." The Californios, for their part, did not follow up on their initial advantage. General Andrés Pico had divided his forces prior to the battle, not expecting to encounter Kearny's troops. Moreover, he knew that the Californios could not fight a conventional war because they lacked the military training, firearms, and supplies to do so. Under these circumstances the most effective tactic was guerrilla warfare. Pico wrote on April 15, 1847, some months after the battle, "The morale of the people had fallen, due to the lack of resources ... together with my compatriots we made the last efforts, not withstanding the extreme lack of powder, arms, men and all kinds of supplies."[8] The battle of San Pascual proved that despite internal dissention and division, many Californios were willing to die to defend their homeland from the American invasion.

Aftermath

During the hostilities between the Americans and the Mexicans, the local native groups were by and large neutral. They comprised the majority of the population of Southern California, and—having experienced the loss of mission lands and various injustices at the hands of Californios—their loyalty toward the Mexican government was not very solid. There were many natives who had assimilated to the Spanish language and religion, had become detribalized, and were living in and around the pueblo of San Diego. Many of them worked as servants and laborers or were casual migrants in search of food. On the other hand, some Luiseño, Diegueño, and Cupeño bands raided Californio ranchos, taking advantage of their weakened defenses. The Californios considered the raiding bands to be fighting for the Americans, but the majority were probably simply opportunists taking advantage of the wartime chaos. In the backcountry, away from the coast, the natives were subject to misinformation and manipulation by both sides.

An example of how resentments against the Californios affected the war was the infamous Pauma massacre. A few days after the battle of San Pascual, eleven Californio men and youths took refuge in an adobe house on Rancho Pauma owned by José Antonio Serrano. They were tricked into allowing themselves to be captured by Luiseño Indians led by Manuelito Cota. The Indians took all the men prisoner and then took them to Warner's Ranch. After a short captivity the captives were put to death by torture using red hot spear thrusts.

Immediately after learning of the capture of the Californios, a punitive force of twenty-two Californios led by José del Carmen Lugo set out together with a force of friendly Cahuilla Indians. They ambushed the Luiseño force, killing more than a hundred and taking twenty captive. The captives were later killed by the Cahuilla allies, according to their custom.[9] The Pauma massacre illustrates the persistence of native animosity toward the Mexicans and the possible manipulation of Indian hatreds by the Americans. It also reveals Californio beliefs that the Americans were inciting the Indians to attack them, in that Californios attributed a prime role in the massacre to the Americans. News of the massacre, along with the fact that in 1847 the Indians vastly outnumbered the Californios and Mexicans, may have worked to demoralize the Californio resistance movement in San Diego County.

Despite Californio victories at San Pascual, Rancho Domínguez, and Rancho Chico in Southern California, the U.S. forces were able to force the Californios to surrender, and an armistice was signed on January 13, 1847. With the Americans reoccupying Los Angeles and San Diego, the guerilla forces in the countryside disbanded. The war was officially over for the Californios, and their conflicts with the Americans now went underground to resurface in banditry and other forms of resistance.

The Mexican War divided the Californio society in San Diego into those loyal to the Americans and those who resisted with arms. This division persisted through the following decades, making it even harder for the Mexicans to unite politically against the American takeover. The Mexican War in San Diego was a small chapter in a much larger conflict; however, it illustrated both the resistance of the Mexican population to the American conquest and that the issue of loyalty was indeed a complex one.

The American Colonization of San Diego

The U.S. takeover of Mexico's northern territories following the signing of the Treaty of Guadalupe Hidalgo in 1848 was not immediate. The flow of immigrants into the newly conquered territories varied from region to region. Some places, like northern California, were inundated by newcomers because of the lure of gold and silver. Other regions, like southern Arizona and northern New Mexico, had relatively few English-speaking settlers prior to 1910. In San Diego the local Mexican community experienced immediate changes. The garrisoning of large numbers of military personnel meant that the Euro-Americans controlled the political and economic life of San Diego from the beginning of the 1850s. Unlike the upper-class Californios in Los Angeles, who were able to maintain their economic power for several decades, San Diego's elite had been financially impoverished by Indian raids during the Mexican era. Thus, they entered the so-called American era as a disenfranchised and impoverished minority. The majority of the San Diego Californio leaders, moreover, were pro-American, or at least content to let the newcomers rule. For the rest of the century, up to the time of the Mexican Revolution in 1910, a major theme of San Diego's Chicana/o history was the tenacious cultural survival of the Mexican people despite tremendous assimilative pressures.

The Garra Uprising

One episode that heightened the Americans' doubts about the loyalties of the newly conquered Mexicans and contributed to the latter's marginalization was the unsuccessful rebellion in 1851 led by Na'at, also known as Antonio Garra, a Cupeño Indian chief. This revolt illustrates that certain segments of the Native American population continued to resist foreign domination, regardless of whether the invaders spoke English or Spanish. It also illustrates the convoluted local loyalties, in that William Marshall, an Anglo, and Juan Verdugo, a

Mexican from Sonora, actively assisted Garra in his rebellion, and Garra claimed that several Californios had also promised to join him.[10]

The Garra rebellion was the last major insurrection of native peoples in Southern California. Thereafter, the regional Indians would be increasingly decimated in numbers and influence. Throughout the 1840s and 1850s, however, the natives continued to outnumber the combined Anglo and Mexican population of San Diego, probably by a factor of more than three to one.[11] Some natives worked as laborers and domestics in San Diego, but many others returned to their villages or founded new ones and tried to revive a semblance of their traditional way of life, augmenting their diet with agriculture, cattle ranching, and occasional raiding.

Antonio Garra was a Cupeño Indian who had received his education at Mission San Luis Rey (near Oceanside, California). His village, called Agua Caliente by the whites, was an amalgamation of native refugees: Luiseños, Cupeños, Kumeyaay, and Yumans. There they mixed elements of Hispanic culture with their native ways: Garra lived in an adobe house and the Cupeños had a vineyard and raised cattle. Unfortunately, their ranchería was located on the busiest southern overland trail to California and adjacent to a rancho owned by Juan José Warner, a Connecticut Yankee who had become a Mexican citizen and received a land grant from the Mexican government in 1844. Almost immediately, Warner and the Cupeños got into a conflict over the rights to use nearby hot springs.

The spark that set off the revolt was an attempt by U.S. authorities to collect a state tax on Indians, although the long-term causes of the uprising originated in decades of white encroachments into Indian territory. The rebellion began as a raid for food. Led by Garra, a small band of Cupeños allied with some Yuman raiders stole a herd of sheep near the Colorado River, killing five Americans. When they returned to the Agua Caliente ranchería on November 21, 1851, Garra ordered his men to kill all the whites in the region, with the exception of William Marshall, an American who had married a Cupeño woman and ran a local store. Marshall evidently aided the rebels, participating in slaying three other Americans and in attacking Warner's rancho the next day. The Cupeños took all of the livestock and movables from Warner's ranch, but Warner himself was absent and escaped certain death. These raids and killings, along with subsequent pursuit by and skirmishes with the Hispano-Anglo expedition raised to avenge the attacks, constituted the Garra rebellion. Evidently, Garra believed that other Indian groups would join him in his rebellion, but age-old animosities and memories of past battles divided them, and none of the surrounding groups joined his revolt.

On the day of the rebellion, Garra sent a letter to the former administrator of Mission San Luis Rey, José Antonio Estudillo, in San Diego, implying that the two had talked about a revolt. A translation of this letter was published by the *San Diego Herald* on November 27, 1851. It read in part: "Mr. Jose Antonio Estudillo, I salute you. Some time past I told you what I thought, and now the moment has arrived to strike the blow. If I have life I will go and help you."[12] Within an hour of the letter's publication, duels were being fought in Old Town between Anglos and Californios over the supposed treachery of all Mexicans.[13]

Juan Antonio, a rival who was a leader of the Cahuillas (near San Bernardino), eventually captured Antonio Garra and turned him over to the Americans. Ironically, whereas Garra had remained neutral during the Mexican War, Juan Antonio had allied himself with the Californios against the Americans. Some scholars, including historian George Hardwood Phillips, believe that Antonio was shrewdly using the Garra affair to protect his band from American retaliation.

After his capture, Antonio Garra publicly confessed to leading the uprising and said that José Estudillo and Joaquín Ortega had advised him and conspired with him. This statement was plausible because Estudillo personally knew Garra and many other native leaders from his tenure at San Luis Rey. Ortega had been the administrator of Mission San Diego during the secularization period and was also well known to many regional Indians.[14] After considering all the detailed evidence in the case, Phillips concluded it was entirely possible that some of the Californios had discussed rebellion against the Americans with Garra.[15] They certainly had as much reason to want the Americans gone as the Indians did.

Yet even though Garra's confession explicitly linked Ortega and Estudillo to the rebellion, the military tribunal trying Garra discounted his statement and refused to prosecute the two Californios. Perhaps the Americans were afraid of openly provoking the Californios. Ortega published a denial of Garra's accusations in the *San Diego Herald*,[16] but Estudillo never publicly responded to the charges.

The end of the affair was the trial of William Marshall and Juan Verdugo, who were executed on December 13, 1851. A summary trial and execution of several Cupeño warriors by a U.S. military "war council" took place near Los

Coyotes, an Indian ranchería in the mountains, on December 23, 1851. Finally, a military firing squad executed Garra himself at Old Town on Saturday, January 10, 1852, at 4 p.m. He was buried at the pueblo *camposanto* (cemetery), and today visitors can find a prominent commemorative tombstone there.

The Economic Decline of the Californios

After the end of the Mexican War, despite the promises of protection of civil liberties and property contained in the Treaty of Guadalupe Hidalgo, Mexican landholders in the United States were systematically stripped of their property and denied their civil rights. In the 1960s, Leonard Pitt, a historian of the Californio decline in Southern California, summarized this period: "Yankee settlers then swept in by the tens of thousands, and in a matter of months and years overturned the old institutional framework, expropriated the land, imposed a new body of law, a new language, a new economy, and a new culture, and in the process exploited the labor of the local population whenever necessary."[17] This general overview can also be applied to Mexicans throughout the Southwest in the 1848–1910 period. Each region, however, had its distinctive variation on the central theme of land loss and subjugation.

In San Diego, the Californio landholders had a short distance to fall. They were poor before the Americans arrived, largely because of Indian raids, accidents of geography, and political history. After the Americans arrived, the San Diego Californios were subject to the same prejudicial laws, racist intimations, greedy squatters, high taxes, expensive lawyers, and usurious bankers as their compatriots elsewhere in California. The land law of 1851, which required all Mexican landowners to validate their grants before the Land Claim Commission, placed a tremendous financial hardship on Mexican landholders, who had to hire lawyers to represent them against sometimes hundreds of squatter claimants. All this litigation cost money, which they could raise only by either mortgaging their ranchos or selling their cattle. The first option led predictably to forced sale while the second was of limited economic benefit.

In San Diego, due to Indian raids, very few rancheros owned cattle by 1850. According to Charles Hughes, an expert on this subject, only fifteen out of forty-five San Diego landowners had sizable herds of cattle on their property. Of those Californios who did have cattle, eleven owned almost 80 percent of the salable stock. Hence the Mexican landowners in San Diego by and large did not have enough cattle to take advantage of the high prices for beef in the goldfields.

During the boom years in cattle sales, 1850–1860, San Diego rancheros averaged only about 2,500 head a year in comparison to Los Angeles rancheros' 25,000.[18]

San Diego's land grant holders were further handicapped by their distance from the northern California market. Driving herds of cattle to the goldfields was a long, costly, and risky enterprise, and losses were high. The fact that San Diego was so far from major commercial and population centers also meant that manufactured goods and foodstuffs were expensive.

The limited value of cattle as a resource to pay new taxes, higher costs of living, and legal expenses evaporated during a two-year drought between 1860 and 1862. It decimated the herds and then torrential floods polished off the remnants in 1862.

Some Californios lost land because they joined in commercial and speculative ventures being promoted by the Yankees. In 1850, for example, Juan Bandini, José Antonio Aguirre, and Miguel de Pedrorena joined William Davis and a group of Anglo-American investors to develop a new commercial harbor center for San Diego, to be called New Town. Contrary to the stereotype of Californios being economically backward, these men speculated in real estate and development ventures. With Anglo entrepreneurs they plowed their money into attempts to make San Diego the western terminus of a transcontinental railway.[19] By the end of the decade, however, many of these schemes and enterprises went bust. The New Town development proved economically unprofitable, agricultural development remained stagnant, the mining booms in the region played out, and, most damaging of all, San Diego lost its bid to become a terminus of the western railroad. Although these reversals affected everyone, because of their precarious position, the Californio landholders were relatively harder hit. Juan Bandini had to borrow money to pay off loans, using his land as collateral. Other Californios lost the money they had invested as the commercial life of San Diego went into a depression that was not to lift for another twenty years. A slump in the price of cattle due to new competition and a decline in gold mining in the north during the late 1850s made things worse.[20]

Squatters, mostly Anglo immigrants but also some opportunistic Mexicanos, moved onto the unfenced rancho lands and laid claim to what they hoped would be declared public domain by the courts. Hughes found that more than half the landowners in San Diego in the 1850s lived on land they did not own. Their legal challenges in the courts were what drained the Mexican landholders of their ability to hold on to their lands. Eventually, the Land Commission did confirm most of the grants to the original claimants or their heirs, but this was on paper only. The real owners by this time were the banks and the lawyers.[21]

Adding to the Californios' woes were the rising property taxes on land. Under the Mexican regime, taxes had been levied on the produce of the land, not its market value. This changed under the Americans. Even if they did not have clear title to the land, the rancheros had to pay a property tax of eight dollars per one hundred dollars of valuation by 1856, a rate that was increasing yearly. Meanwhile, the state legislature exempted mining properties in northern California from taxation. This was a major injustice in the minds of Southern California's landholders and a reason most of them supported the idea of dividing ·the state in two.

The statistical evidence on landholding indicates something of the reversal of fortunes for Mexican landholders in San Diego. One example is José Antonio Aguirre. He owned $100,000 worth of real property in 1850. Ten years later, in 1860, his holdings had fallen to $20,000. The same decline can be noted in the fortunes of other Californio notables. The Estudillos lost $20,000 in property in the period, the Argüellos lost $24,000, and Juan Bandini, who died in 1859, lost almost all of his extensive landholdings.[22] Taking the Californio landed elite as whole, in 1850, the total valuation of their property was $413,471, compared to Euro-American holdings of $142,428. By 1860 the positions were reversed. The latter landholders now had $128,900 worth of property and the Californios $82,700.[23] By the eve of the U.S. Civil War the Californios in San Diego had fallen, never to rise again.

Political Invisibility

One of the pervading themes in the political history of San Diego's Mexican Americans has been their inability to develop an effective political voice. In Los Angeles the Californios were more successful in remaining prominent in local politics well into the 1870s.[24] The Angeleños had a viable tradition of involvement in local politics before the Americans arrived, and they remained a majority of the population into the 1860s. This was not the case in San Diego, where local government had been practically abolished in the 1830s. The Mexican *pobladores* living in Old Town were immediately outnumbered, both demographically and in terms of a voting population. In 1850 the U.S. census taker counted in the San Diego region a non-Indian population of 732, only 311 of whom were Californios; 421 were Anglos.

Because most of the Californios were women and children, only 78 Californios were eligible to vote, in comparison with more than 267 Anglo voters. Most of the Anglo newcomers were single men—soldiers and government employees.[25]

The last Mexican mayor of San Diego was Juan María Marrón, who was appointed alcalde in 1848. Marrón, ironically, had opposed the Americans during the war. Between 1850 and 1856, out of 150 political offices, only eight Californios were elected. The people chose Juan Bandini twice but he refused to serve, probably because he realized how impossible it was to make a difference. Antonio Estudillo also won several elections as county assessor. But very few other names emerged in electoral politics, despite the fact that many candidates ran unopposed. Mario T. García, who has studied San Diego's political life, believes that the Californios' lack of participation in electoral politics arose from their generally pro-American stance. In his words, "the Californios apparently saw no danger in the political hegemony of the Anglo population."[26] Whether from apathy, cynicism, or a false sense of security about American domination, they were content to let the Anglos run things.

But the dearth of Californios in political office did not mean that they did not participate in politics. José Estudillo, Juan Marrón, Juan Ortega, Juan Bandini, and Juan Padilla attended community meetings to oppose the property tax issue, to support railroad construction, and to advocate for the division of the state. Other Californios made public demonstrations of their American patriotism. Each Fourth of July they selected one of their own to give a public address, and most of the Mexican community attended. In fact, in 1853, the Californios took the initiative in organizing the pueblo's Fourth of July celebrations. According to García, those who considered themselves members of the Californio elite, or *ricos*, outnumbered those who were considered Mexican immigrants, or *cholos*, a term used by both Californios and Anglos to denote poor, working-class Mexican immigrants. In 1860 about 62 percent of the Spanish-surnamed population could be classified as members of the Californio elite, while 38 percent were Mexican born.[27] When added to their general pro-American sentiment, this class division further weakened the oppositional political voice of the Mexican Americans in San Diego.

There were also racial and class barriers to the full enfranchisement of the Mexican population. The institution of an eight-dollar poll tax discouraged all but the wealthy from voting. Racism, while a factor, was subtle and interacted with social status. Generally, the upper-class Californios sided with the Americans in deprecating the lower classes as filthy, lazy, and criminal. The ricos always joined in the posses to hunt down *bandidos* and other Mexican malefactors, and they enthusiastically supported swift justice for the Indian and mestizo elements of the population. In 1854, for example, José Estudillo, a grand jury member, supported the view that "the presence of Mexicans and Indians made the enforcement of the law more difficult."[28] Nevertheless, the English speakers retained racist opinions about even their "Spanish" (a designation Californios used to denote their upper-class status) compatriots. Spaniards, after all, were Catholic papists of questionable patriotism who were genetically disposed to be cruel and treacherous. Besides, the Californios, despite their protestations to the contrary, were obviously of mixed blood.[29]

Corruption was also a factor in keeping the Mexican vote insignificant. In the early years, as Hughes reports, election officials rowed out to meet incoming ships and ask the sailors to vote in local elections. Sailors who could not come ashore were offered ballots on board. Another documented practice was to have the person running for office, almost always an Anglo-American, work as an inspector of the polls. There resulted several charges of irregularities in the counting of votes.[30]

Finally, there persisted a language barrier. Despite a provision in the state constitution that all official business be published in English and Spanish, in San Diego, election notices continued to be published in English, while the tax notices appeared in Spanish. Because of its small population, San Diego did not have a Spanish-language newspaper, unlike Los Angeles.[31] The cumulative effect of these racial, social, economic, and cultural obstacles was to restrict the franchise of the U.S. citizens of Mexican descent and to silence their voice.

Mexican American Society

Old Town San Diego was a small settlement in the first decades after the conquest, a fact borne out by a review of the U.S. census. There are many problems in using this source—undercounting and misreporting were quite common. Nevertheless, the census is helpful in suggesting patterns and trends in the early social life of Mexican Americans in urban San Diego. Table 2.1 shows social data for Old Town up to 1870. Further research needs to be done regarding the population living in the surrounding countryside.

Table 2.1. **Population of Old Town San Diego, 1850–1870**[a]

Population	1850	1860	1870
Town residents	233	293	319
Rural residents	499	438	1,981
Total residents[b]	732	731	2,300
Dwellings	63	96	117
Families			
Male heads of household			
Euro-American	13	10	38
Mexican	19	8	6
Mixed[c]	4	6	5
Female heads of household			
Euro-American	0	3	0
Mexican	5	7	3
Total families	41	34	52
Families employing domestics[d]			
Euro-American	0	2	4
Mexican	0	9	0
Mixed	0	1	0
Average family size			
Euro-American	4.3	5.2	4.8
Mexican	5.8	7.2	6.0
Mixed	7.5	7.6	6.0
Euro-American female-headed	0	5.6	0
Mexican female-headed	8.2	7.0	6.0

[a] Note that these data do not include all Mexican Americans living in San Diego County, which until the late 1800s included present-day Imperial, Riverside, and San Bernardino counties, and part of Inyo County. The data reported here are for Old Town only. Provided courtesy of Alexandra Luberski, California State Parks.

[b] Taken from Camarillo, *Chicanos in a Changing Society*, 116.

[c] Euro-American husband with Mexican spouse.

[d] Includes female heads of household.

As was noted earlier, while the Mexicans outnumbered the Anglos in the early years, their majority was due to women and children; by the 1870s, however, even this weak numerical advantage had disappeared. The statistical trends challenge a number of stereotypes many people have about Mexican families. For one thing, the image of a large extended Mexican family living under one roof and employing one or more domestic servants is, in the case of San Diego, clearly not accurate. Mexican families were larger than Anglo families, but not significantly so, and very few families employed domestic servants. The largest families were in mixed households (that is, a Euro-American man married to a Mexican woman) and those headed by Mexican women. Alexandra Luberski noted that female-headed households were more inclined than other families to take in orphaned children and married daughters and their families.[32] It is surprising to note the absence of domestic servants within Mexican households (except in 1860). Most likely the use of Indian servants was much more prevalent on the ranchos. For reasons of local history, the town dwellers probably had a fear of Indian domestics.

There were a number of "mixed" families in the pueblo but intermarriage was not unusually high. In 1870 six out of thirty-four (18 percent) of Mexican households were "mixed," meaning an intermarriage of a Euro-American male with a Hispanic female. And ten years later, the proportion was five out of fifty-two households (10 percent). Compared to other "old towns" in the Southwest, such as the barrios of Los Angeles, Santa Fe, Tucson, and San Antonio, these rates of intermarriage were comparable to those in Santa Fe, New Mexico, a place with one of the highest rates of intermarriage in the Southwest for this period.[33] When compared to the total number of Mexican American families in the town, instead of to all families, the proportion of "mixed" households to Mexican-only households dramatically increases with each census, from 38 percent in 1860 to a whopping 55 percent in 1870. Why was this the case? No doubt the fact that Anglos greatly outnumbered Mexicans by 1870 contributed to it. Also we should not minimize the importance of San Diego's political climate of acceptance of the American order among many of the leading Californio families, all of whom married their daughters to Euro-Americans.

In San Diego, as in other urban areas of the Southwest, there was an increase in the proportion of families headed by women with children. But in San Diego the increase relative to all Mexican families was unprecedented. In 1850, five out of twenty-four Mexican families (excluding "mixed" households), or 21 percent, were female-headed. In 1860 the percentage rose to 47 percent; and in 1870 it stood at 33 percent. These high rates of female-headed households were exceptional. The highest rates elsewhere were among Los Angeles Mexicans in 1850, with 38 percent.[34]

To some extent the dramatic proportions of female-headed and mixed households are an artifact of the small totals involved. There were only nine Mexican families living in Old Town by 1870. Errors in taking the census probably produced more female-headed families than existed in reality. The number, however, is still high and reflects the serious social consequences of the economic decline of the Californios in San Diego. Men either died young, left their families in search of work, or abandoned their families because they were unable to provide for them. In this regard Mexican Americans in San Diego were experiencing the same social repercussions of the American takeover as Chicanos throughout the urban Southwest.

As Americans moved into Old Town in the 1850s and 1860s they built new wooden structures in the New England style and remodeled some of the older adobes. But in the 1870s many Americans began moving south into the New Town area, closer to the bay, leaving behind abandoned homes. The Mexicans, however, stayed behind. In 1871 the County Board of Supervisors moved the municipal government and its archives to New Town and the next year, in 1872, a fire ravaged many of the wooden structures in Old Town. This signaled the decline of the old pueblo as a social and political center for San Diego. Henceforth Old Town would be synonymous with the Mexican barrio of San Diego, until the influx of Mexican immigrants into the Logan Heights area during the early years of the next century.

A description of Mexican Old Town appeared in the *San Diego Union* in the 1870s:

> There are 73 houses in Old Town. . . . population of about 250. Of white families we have 37; single men 40; widows 5; widowers 2; children 125; Indians 30; Cinnamon 8; the total 272. We have the finest school house in the Pueblo, with an average attendance of 75 pupils when school is kept. The residences of our citizens are generally comfortable, even if not of the highest style of architecture.[35]

Other writers were less enthusiastic about the place. In 1865, Mrs. Ephraim Morse commented that, "Of all the dilapidated, miserable looking places I had ever seen, this was the worst." And in 1871 H. N. Kutchin wrote, "And a queer

'Old Town' it is, with its tumble down adobe houses, and narrow streets twisted together in inextricable confusion."[36]

Mexican American Culture

Despite the Anglo-Americans' sometimes negative opinions of Old Town, for the Mexican Americans living there, it was their home. Here they developed a vibrant social life based on their traditional culture. Many of the Mexican families were related, either by marriage or *compadrazgo*, godparentage, and there was a real sense of community as an extended family. As we have seen, many of the families intermarried with Anglo-American men and hence the Mexican heritage became mixed with Anglo ways in the families of Fitches, Wrightingtons (Ridingtons), Stuarts, Snooks, Fosters, and so forth (fig. 2.3).[37]

Old Town did not have a formal church until the 1850s. Before that time the residents used the mission church or the presidio chapel and held services in private chapels of the ricos, the Estudillos and Aguirres. Finally, in 1858 the priest who replaced the Mexican priest, Rev. John Molinier completed construction of a small adobe church called the Immaculate Conception of the Blessed Virgin Mary. It was located some distance from the plaza, reflecting urban planning foreign to Mexican and Latin American villages. The same year that adobe chapel was finished, Father Antonio Ubach arrived. He undertook the task of building a larger, more modern church closer to the plaza. In 1868, the parishioners, most of them Mexican Americans, laid the cornerstone for the church. Due to the lack of funds it was not completed until 1914, at which time it replaced the adobe chapel. The new Church of the Immaculate Conception in its architectural design reflected European influences.

The Old Town congregation of the adobe chapel were involved in organizing many community celebrations, religious fiestas, performances of La Pastorela (a shepherd drama performed during Christmas) and La Posada (a reenactment of Mary and Joseph's search for lodging in Bethlehem), and events commemorating La Semana Santa (Easter week). On April 2, 1872, the *San Diego Herald* reported that the Old Town community had heard a dramatic reading of the last will and testament of Judas Iscariot—a spoof on local town scandals and a chance to make fun of local celebrities. After the reading of the will, an effigy of Judas was hung on the plaza flagpole and then dragged around the plaza by a steer to the cheers of the Indians and children. The Pastorela, or shepherds' play, at Christmas gave the townspeople opportunities to incorporate political and satirical themes within

FIGURE 2.3. Juana Machado de Ridington (a Hispanicization of Wrightington) near her home in Old Town surrounded by nopal cactus about 1893. Descended from the first founding soldiers of San Diego, Juana was known as the Florence Nightingale of Old Town and frequently traveled into the backcountry with Fr. Ubach to minister to the Indians. (© San Diego Historical Society. Used by permission.)

the drama. The most influential Californios always had parts in the play, which was followed by a *baile* (dance) with food and drink.

Bullfights were a regular entertainment within Old Town until 1869, when they were removed to the outlying ranchos. The plaza was fenced in and dehorned bulls set loose. Young vaqueros on horseback demonstrated how close they could come to the bulls without being struck, but they rarely killed the bulls. Out on the surrounding ranchos, the Californio landowners continued the Mexican custom of holding annual rodeos where the Californios could display their horsemanship and other skills. These rodeos lasted many days and were accompanied by feasting and dancing at night.

Horse racing was a passion for the Californios and Anglos alike. In San Diego a group called the San Diego Agricultural Park Association built a racetrack on eighty acres of land between Old Town and present-day Mission Bay. They built stables, food stalls, and grandstands to accommodate the crowds, and regular races were held there into the twentieth century.

As Old Town lacked a parish hall located on the plaza, Juan Bandini's home became the social center for Mexican Americans in the late nineteenth century. José María Bandini, Don Juan's son, was famous for his hospitality and dancing ability, and his daughters, who married Anglo-Americans and had large families, frequently visited him in his large house. The music and dancing continued to be Mexican, *el son*, *la contradanza*, and *el jarabe*, but now mixed with American and European innovations, the waltz and various American folkdances. Traditional Californio *conjuntos* alternated with band music provided by the U.S. Army.

Women's Views of Life in San Diego

The older families that had been so prominent in San Diego's politics during the Mexican era continued to be important as intermediaries with the Anglo population. As already noted, many of them had been pro-American during the Mexican War and their daughters had married Anglo-Americans. The families of Juan Bandini, José Antonio Estudillo, Juan Marrón, María Pedrorena, Santiago Argüello, and Juan María Osuna remained important in the San Diego Mexican American community. In later years they would become less enthusiastic about the Americanization of their ancestral lands.

Two Mexican American women wrote about their lives in San Diego during this period. Their views offer us another perspective on the process of colonization. Arcadia Bandini Brennan was one of Juan Bandini's granddaughters. Her florid literary reminiscences of her childhood and extended family life in nineteenth-century San Diego reflected a pride in her Californio heritage.[38] She retells the story of how her grandmother, Ysidora, literally fell from the balcony of the Bandini house into the arms of Lt. Cave Johnson Couts while watching a military parade in 1851. A few years later they were married and were given as a wedding present Rancho Cuajome near the present-day town of Vista. Arcadia spent many happy hours at Rancho Cuajome, continuing to live in the Mexican style during the American era.

Arcadia remembered being cared for by Indian nurses and maids at Cuajome. According to Arcadia, when the family hired an Indian, they hired his whole family, and when a child was born, he or she was raised to be a playmate to the Californio children and later to be a nurse or maid. Like the slaves of the Deep South, when their mistress married, they went with her to her new household.[39]

Other details of post-1848 life on the ranchos emerged. Cuajome had its own chapel, supposedly the first one built on any ranch in California with the permission of the Catholic Church. "Many hours, I can remember Grandma would spend sitting in the quietness of the Chapel, saying her beads. Their quiet hitting together sounding clearly, because all was so still." She lamented the Americanization of customs of hospitality: "gone and most missed the real heart-felt welcome, and the Spanish-Southern hospitality. [Now] It's cold, all cold." Arcadia's Californio relatives cared little for paper money, which they were not used to: "It was mother's habit, if short of paper in the outhouse, to use some from her pocket, never bothering to notice the figure printed in the corner, and the rush would be on as soon as she was out of sight."[40]

Another important observer of San Diego life was María Amparo Ruiz de Burton, the first Mexican American author in the United States to write novels in English. María wrote two novels, *Who Would Have Thought It?* and *The Squatter and the Don* under the penname C. Loyal.[41]

María was born in La Paz, Baja California, and came to California in 1849 as the wife of an Anglo military officer, Henry Stanton Burton. María's great-uncle Francisco Ruiz had been the *comandante* of San Diego in the early 1800s. In California she studied English under a tutor and was a lifelong friend and correspondent with Mariano Vallejo, a respected Californio in Sonoma. In 1852 while María and her husband were living at an army post at Mission San Diego, together they purchased Rancho Jamul. She wrote to Vallejo of her aspirations: "I am persuaded that we were born to do something more than simply live, that is, we were born for something more, for the rest of our poor countrymen."[42] The Burtons lived on and made improvements to Rancho Jamul, and submitted its title to the Court of Land Claims. For the next few decades María would be involved in dozens of lawsuits trying to retain title to her land.

When the Civil War broke out, the Burtons moved to Washington, DC, where María wrote her first novel. After her husband died in 1864, she and her children moved back to San Diego to continue fighting for her land. She wrote to Mariano Vallejo:

> the Americans are and will be *always* the *mortal* enemies of my race, of my Mexico. [And,] I feel ... a true hatred and contempt (as a good Mexican) for this certain Manifest Destiny. Of all the wicked phrases invented by stupid people, there is not one more odious for me than that.... I see it instantly in photographs, all that the Yankees have done to make us, the Mexicans, suffer: the robbery of Texas, the war, the robbery of California, the death of Maximilian.... No friend of mine, this Manifest Destiny is nothing more than "Manifest Yankee trash."[43]

These private views shaped her next book project, a dramatization of the Californio tragedy: the loss of their lands and destruction of their way of life. When María returned to Jamul in 1870, there were between thirteen and fifteen squatters on her rancho, each claiming 160 acres. They had effectively ruined the homestead, which had been abandoned for a number of years. She continued her legal battles and moved to her rancho with her daughter and extended family of nine people. Later, on moving to New Town, she wrote her novel, *The Squatter and the Don*, published in 1885. All the while she was involved in litigation over Jamul and eventually the attorney's fees for the litigation and unpaid mortgages forced her into bankruptcy. She traveled to Chicago to find help in fighting for her rights to another rancho that had been in her family, Rancho Ensenada de Todos Santos. She died there in 1895, trying to get political support for her claims.[44]

Native Americans in the American Era

In 1852 San Diego's regional population numbered about 2,900, most of whom, about 2,200, were Indians. Small groups of Kumeyaay who had lost their villages to rancheros or disease were the first "homeless" population of urban San Diego. They set up temporary villages on vacant land near the pueblo and worked as laborers for the Anglo and Mexican population. Throughout the nineteenth century, natives lived in Old Town, employed as maids and servants, and they intermarried with the local Mexican population. A temporary Indian ranchería existed at 24th and Imperial avenues, composed of families of Indian railway workers, and another sprang up at what is today 5th Avenue and J Street.[45] Other Indians lived in brush houses at 27th and K streets in the present-day Golden Hills area, and many other temporary settlements sprang up.

Delfina Cuero, an Indian woman born in 1900, remembered moving to various locales throughout the region: Mission Valley, Mission Gorge, Lakeside, El Cajon, and Jamacha. She remembered, "Lots of people moved around then. If some rancher settled near their place, they had to go elsewhere." The search for food underlay this peripatetic existence. The family was always hungry. As she recalled, "Sometimes we found things. Lots of times we did not and we went hungry. I had to beg for food from neighboring Indians and ranchers. Some neighbors helped me sometimes. I went hungry and my children were hungry. Sometimes for two or three days we found nothing."[46]

The Kumeyaay who lived near the white settlements continued, as much as possible, many of their traditional customs of food gathering, preparation, and consumption, and preserved their ancient religion, especially in mourning ceremonies. Most Indians had Spanish baptismal names as well as names in their native language. Some were trilingual, speaking Spanish, their native language, and English. Often Kumeyaay people from Mexico crossed the border seeking work. In the 1860s, for example, a group of Mexican Kumeyaay lived in Switzer Canyon in a temporary ranchería while the men worked as laborers in various public building projects. Susan Tiffany lived in the Bandini house in Old Town around the turn of the century. She recalled that Indian women worked as maids for many homes, Anglo and Mexican. Of the Indian woman who worked in the Bandini home, she recalled that she was "an excellent cook and a faithful servant. . . . She was a genius at concocting mouth-watering tamales and green pepper dishes. . . . We had no trouble getting household help as Mexican and Indian girls who lived nearby were glad to earn the small amount we could afford to pay them."[47] A state law allowed for the indenture of Indian children into households—to work as virtual slaves while learning a trade. Indian children were sometimes procured for Mexican and Anglo families by intermediaries, and sometimes Indian children were sold by their parents because of dire economic straits. Delfina Cuero reported, for example, that she sold her son to a Mexican family when she was widowed and starving.[48]

The Euro-Americans employed both Indians and Mexicans in the same kinds of laboring jobs: as domestics, on the railroad, and on the docks. Although hardly distinguishable from Mexicans, the Indians suffered the most discrimination. In 1852 the grand jury ordered all Indians moved across the San Diego River, stating that their ranchería near town was "the hiding place of idle, pilfering Indians. None of these remnants of a degenerate age should be allowed on this side of the river."[49] And, again, in 1862 and 1887 the city council ordered that the Indians be moved away from the city limits.

Until the 1870s some Indians attended San Diego's first public school in Old Town. Complaints by the local families ended this practice, and a separate school, St. Anthony Indian School, was built for them in Old Town. In 1891 this school was moved to the ruins of Mission San Diego de Alcalá, some five miles away.

The native population of San Diego declined due to disease, the corrupting influence of alcohol, and sporadic racist murders. Intermarriage with the Mexican population increased over what it had been in the Mexican era, so that some Californio families acquired relatives from various native groups.[50]

The Mexican Barrios

By 1910, the year of the commencement of the Mexican Revolution, San Diego's Mexican population was still relatively small: about 2,200 in the county and 1,222 in the city.[51] Old Town remained a small enclave of Mexicans, most of them native-born. Scattered throughout the city were pockets of Mexican immigrants who had migrated to the city prior to the revolution in search of jobs. As yet, Logan Heights had not become a barrio. A review of the manuscript returns for San Diego in 1910 illustrates some of the characteristics of Mexican residences in San Diego. First of all, they were distributed throughout the city in small neighborhoods, with the largest concentration being in Old Town. Most of the Mexicanos appear to have been part of the laboring class. Most rented their homes and spoke some English while still speaking Spanish. The following examples, taken from the census, illustrate some of the social characteristics of the Mexican-heritage population.

Manuel Lucero and his wife, Adelaida, were both in their fifties, had been married nineteen years, and had migrated to San Diego in 1901. They lived with their seven children, including several stepchildren. Manuel worked as a laborer and spoke English, as did all the family. Helping to support the family within their home was Albert Archiaga, his stepson, who also worked as a laborer. The Lucero family owned their home and made mortgage payments on it.

Alantis Flores was a native-born San Diegan who lived with his wife, Antonia, and a boarder, Pedro Avalos, in a rented home. They had no children and Alantis worked as a cement mason. Next door to them were Mr. and Mrs. Mendoza, an older couple, recently married with no children. Mr. Mendoza worked as a salesperson for a retail furniture store and they, too, rented their home.

Another family was that of Alfred Sandoval, who had came to San Diego in 1898 and, four years later, had married Clara, a woman from Wyoming. Alfred worked as a bookkeeper for a steamship company and rented his home, where they lived with their three children, ranging from two to ten years of age. Everyone in the Sandoval family spoke English.

Finally, representative of the younger immigrant working class was Diego Galindo, age thirty-six, and his wife María, age twenty-eight. They had been married eleven years and had five children. They had migrated as a married couple to the United States in 1906 and spoke only Spanish, but their children spoke English. Diego worked as a laborer and they rented their home.[52]

Multiply these examples with minor variations and you have a rough idea of the variations in the social and economic life of the Mexican population in San Diego on the eve of one of the historic turning points in Chicano and Mexican history, the outbreak of the Mexican Revolution. The nucleus of the Mexican colony, Old Town, had been reduced to a tiny, forgotten, and isolated neighborhood. Mexican laborers lived scattered throughout the city and in small *colonias* in the countryside. In 1850 the Mexicans had been vastly outnumbered by the Native American population. In 1910 they were surrounded by a much larger Euro-American, English-speaking population of more than 72,000 people.

Overwhelmed demographically, completely forgotten culturally, and ignored politically, the Mexicans of San Diego had no idea that the twentieth century would begin with a renewed tide of immigration north from Mexico. Within a generation, the families that had been increasingly surrounded by Anglo settlements would find their neighborhoods changed by newcomers from Mexico, people who crossed the border to find safety just across the line. The catalytic event that began this exodus was the Mexican Revolution.

3

FROM REVOLUTION TO ECONOMIC DEPRESSION

Richard Griswold del Castillo

Since 1848 it has been impossible to fully understand the history of the Mexican American or Chicano people of this region without taking into consideration the Mexicanos in northern Baja California. Many Mexican American families are binational and have grown up on both sides of the border. Thousands of Mexicanos from Baja California Norte have come to live in San Diego and Imperial counties as permanent residents. Many thousands more have crossed the international frontier to work in the fields, on the railroads, or in factories, hotels, and private houses on *el otro lado* (the other side). Derogatory and racist attitudes toward Mexican immigrants also affect Mexican Americans who are U.S. citizens. Mexicano immigrants and many Chicano U.S. citizens work side by side in construction, the service industry, and agriculture, competing for the same jobs and experiencing the same kind of discrimination. With this interrelationship acknowledged, I discuss in this chapter the formative historical events in the creation of a binational Chicano/Mexicano community in San Diego, a society that is constantly evolving and changing. This chapter develops the theme of the role of the U.S.–Mexican border in the construction of a transnational community, a people who are increasingly asserting their rights as Americans.

Others have researched how the events of the early twentieth century affected Chicano communities in the U.S.–Mexican border region. Mario T. García's pioneering study of El Paso's Mexican barrios during the Mexican Revolution showed how immigrants contributed to the economic development of this city and managed to create a new kind of border society while organizing themselves socially and politically to protect their families.[1] The same kind of dynamic took place in other border cities. In San Antonio thousands of Mexican upper- and middle-class refugees fleeing the revolution took intellectual and political leadership of the community, a leadership that native-born Tejanos contested. In Los Angeles thousands of immigrant laborers established a new community in East Los Angeles while struggling against Americanization programs and economic inequalities.[2] These and other community studies of Mexican barrios from this time period indicate that the immigration from Mexico which began even before the revolution of 1910 increased the activism of the community through labor unions and mutual aid societies (*mutalistas*), and by reshaping ethnic identity to be more critical of the injustices that were daily experiences of Mexicanos in the United States. The border played a critical part in the development of community life for the Mexicans and Chicanos in San Diego during this period as well.

The Mexican Side of the Line before the Revolution of 1910

As we have seen in chapter 1, the Kumeyaay people are binational and have indigenous communities on both sides of the international boundary. Before the construction of the fence and the military policing of the boundary, the Kumeyaay people moved freely from one side to the other, particularly those groups who lived near Tecate and Jacumba (fig. 3.1).

In 1848 very few Mexicans lived in Baja California along the present-day border. It was a land of brush and desert, suitable for stock raising but little else. In the Spanish and Mexican period, the hills that today are covered by the city of Tijuana were Rancho Tijuana, the rancho land grant owned by the Argüello family, descended from Santiago Argüello the *comandante* of the San Diego presidio. Before the Mexican War, portions of Rancho Tijuana passed to Pío Pico, who had grown up in San Diego with his brother Andrés. The Argüellos continued to own most of what today is Tijuana, as well as rancho lands encompassing the present-day communities of Lemon Grove, La Mesa, and East San Diego.[3] The town of Tijuana was officially founded on July 11, 1889, formed out of a portion of the Argüello lands. The original official name for Tijuana was Villa de Zaragoza (changed to Tijuana in 1929). Initially this community was a small settlement of ranch houses.[4] Later it would grow to include a customshouse and a few trading posts. Not until the 1920s would it start to grow into the metropolis it is today.

Other portions of Mexican rancho lands immediately adjacent to San Diego County were owned by the Bandini family, and for the next 150 years, their descendants, along with the Picos and Argüellos, frequently crossed the border to visit family members or to live in one or the other country for periods of time. They were the first binational Mexican American families in the area.

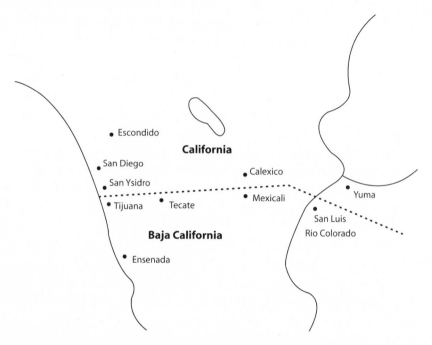

FIGURE 3.1. The U.S.–Mexican border area showing California and Baja California cities and towns. (Courtesy of Wendy Shapiro, Instructional Technology Services, SDSU)

Adjacent to the Mexican ranchos and settlement, across the Tijuana River on the U.S. side, another rancho by the name of San Ysidro was established in 1873. In 1874 the first customshouse was built, and by 1889, "Tijuana could display the baths of the Tia Juana Hot Springs Hotel at Agua Caliente, a cemetery, the customs house, a school, an adobe church, and the curio store . . . and the ranches. . . . The beginning village consisted of some twenty buildings, grouped along a sandy street on the bank of the river."[5] The people who lived on Rancho San Ysidro depended on Tijuana's small settlement for supplies, and for the next hundred years San Ysidro was more closely tied to Tijuana's economy and culture than to San Diego's.

El Valle Imperial

Mexicali, now the capital of Baja California Norte, is today a metropolis of close to a million people. Located in the midst of a vast desert, Mexicali has grown due to the development of irrigated farming in the early 1900s. The entire agricultural complex of the Imperial Valley, including the towns of Indio, El Centro, Brawley, and Calexico, developed in the twentieth century, largely as the result of the investments of U.S. railroad and land corporations along with the labor of thousands of Mexicanos, Chinese, and Hindus. Today, the people of the Imperial Valley region are vitally dependent on Mexican green card workers and Chicano laborers, who make up the bulk of the fieldworkers. Many upwardly mobile Chicanos and Mexicanos have moved to San Diego in search of better jobs and educational opportunities. Others have attended Imperial Valley College in El Centro or the San Diego State University extension in Calexico and then moved across the mountains to San Diego. There is thus a historical link between the Chicano communities of "El Valle" and the Chicano communities in San Diego.

Mexicali, Calexico, and all the other towns in the Imperial Valley owe their origin to the construction of irrigation canals that bring Colorado River water to the desert. In 1892 Charles Robinson Rockwood, an American engineer working for the California Development Company, began studying the feasibility of constructing a canal east to the Imperial Valley. Because of the topography it was cheaper to build the canal mostly on the Mexican side of the border following the old riverbed of the Alamo River, and then to enter U.S. territory near Calexico. At the time, the Mexican government had given vast land grants to American corporate interests and they supported this project. In 1901 the first water entered the Imperial Valley, and immediately a small farming community sprang up, named Mexicali.[6] On the U.S. side hundreds of settlers rushed to file for sections of land, and more than 100,000 acres were under the plow within a few years.[7] Soon the communities of El Centro, Calexico, and Brawley were born.

In 1905 a disaster took place that would change the geography of California. Engineers had constructed a new intake gate on the Colorado River to avoid the problems of silting. Spring floods that year washed away their temporary dams, however, and despite valiant efforts to stop it, the Colorado River changed course and began flowing, in its entirety, into the Imperial Valley following the Alamo Canal. The river soon created a huge lake, called the Salton Sea. The river continued on its rampage for two more years, until it was finally rechanneled by the efforts of the Southern Pacific Railroad, subsidized by the U.S. government. Thereafter, the irrigation runoff from the fields of the Mexicali and Imperial valleys flowed into the Salton Sea, making it extremely saline.

Of course, water and land were worth little unless there were workers available to clear the fields, plant, and harvest the crops. From the beginning the majority of the workers in the valley were Mexicans, although the corporations that bought up most of the land imported workers of other nationalities, such as American Indians, Chinese, Hindus, Filipinos, and Japanese. In addition, small numbers of African Americans and Anglo-Americans worked in the fields. The crops they planted and harvested were of every conceivable kind: cotton, melons, alfalfa, barley, wheat, and vegetables. Because of the good weather and abundant water, usually three crops a year were possible. The population on both sides of the international border depended on the largess of the agribusiness corporations that controlled the local economy. Noted agricultural economist Paul Taylor studied the Imperial Valley's labor conditions during the 1920s. He found that "despite the richness of soil and high financial yield of crops in good years, the agriculture of the valley is characterized on its economic side by tenant farming, absentee ownership, and a general condition of instability and impermanence."[8] That is to say, the Mexicanos and Mexican Americans in the valley lived in colonial conditions of poverty at the mercy of the farm owners. Based on racist assumptions and stereotypes about Mexicans, the white growers constantly "preferred" them over other workers because of the low wages they were able to pay. Said one grower, "Mexicans are much to be preferred to whites. Once fixed, they are permanent and reliable. I do not think they are good for other types of work."[9] During the 1920s occasional labor organizers tried to improve conditions for Mexicans in the valley, but they were jailed, beaten, and run out of town.

The Mexicans and Mexican Americans from El Valle looked west as a way out of conditions of semi-slavery. Until after World War II, however, few were able to make the move up out of the ranks of laborers and escape. Many of the most dynamic activists of the Chicano Movement came from El Valle. They brought with them a heritage of struggle and hard work.

Filibusterers and Revolutionists

Violence periodically erupted along the border, affecting the lives of Mexican Americans living in San Diego and the Imperial Valley. In 1853 William Walker, an American from Tennessee, led a group of forty-five adventurers trying to conquer Baja California and Sonora. This was the first of many efforts by soldiers of fortune to take over portions of Baja California, reflecting a continuation of ideas of Manifest Destiny and anti-Mexican sentiment. In November 1853 Walker and his men sailed by ship from San Francisco to La Paz, where they briefly took over that town. Then, forced to depart by Mexican military forces, he and his men sailed up the coast to Ensenada and captured that settlement along with several other small towns in the vicinity. Again forced out by the Mexican military, Walker and his men attempted to cross the desert to invade Sonora, but this expedition failed miserably in the dry and scorching desert. Finally, Walker and remnants of his band walked back to Tijuana and crossed the border to surrender themselves to U.S. authorities in San Diego. Walker was subsequently tried (in San Diego) and convicted of violating U.S. neutrality laws. It is said that Walker's unsuccessful invasion of Baja California so angered then-president Santa Anna, who was in the process of negotiating the Gadsden Purchase with the United States that he refused to sell Baja California.

The next major invasion of northern Mexico from California took place in 1910, when partisans of the Partido Liberal México (PLM), led by Ricardo Flores Magón, captured Mexicali and went on to take over Tecate and Tijuana in 1911. Magón's forces were composed mostly of Anglo-American radicals, Wobblies, socialists, and anarchists, who supported the ideas of the PLM enough to risk their lives in the opening battles of the Mexican Revolution. Although there were some Mexicanos in the invading army in Baja California, the whole group was branded "filibusteros" of the same stripe as William Walker, despite the fact that their leader, Magón, was well known in Mexico as a revolutionary opposed to the dictator Porfirio Díaz.

Although only about one hundred people lived in Tijuana at the time, and a good portion of them were American merchants, the PLM invasion was traumatic for border residents. In the battle for control of the small settlement, the Mexican army suffered thirty-two dead and twenty-four wounded. In the meantime the entire civilian population fled across the line to take up temporary residence in the Little Lander's Colony (today San Ysidro).[10] Joe Montijo was a boy living in Old Town San Diego when the battle took place. He remembered his father taking him to Tijuana after the battle, where he was told to select a warm jacket from among the dead. He wore his jacket, pierced with bullet holes, to school the next day.[11] Meanwhile, the children and adults living in tents in San Ysidro wondered when they would be able to go home. The *insurrectos'* control of the town was short-lived, just long enough for them to allow San Diegans to loot the stores and to collect border-crossing fees from curious tourists. During this occupation, Dick Ferris, a local promoter hired by the city of San Diego, sought to publicize the upcoming California-Panama Exposition (to be held in Balboa Park) by sending the president of Mexico a letter declaring Ferris the ruler of an independent Baja California. Meanwhile, Mexicans complained that Ricardo

Flores Magón had allied himself with Americans who "call us greasers, 'cholos,' dirty Mexicans, etc."[12] Finally, in late June 1911, the Mexican troops recaptured the town. The ultimate casualties were Magón's revolutionary credentials and American goodwill along the border.

The Magonista rebellion affected the lives of some of the native peoples living along the border. Both the Magonistas and the Mexican federal army recruited Indians from both sides of the border to fight for them. These included the Guaycure, Cocopa, and Yuma Indians as well as Indians who lived around Mexicali. General Celso Vega used Indian scouts to spy on the Magonistas, and Indian soldiers were credited with wounding the Magonista commander near El Alamo, Baja California. On the other side Captain Emilio Guerrero commanded a group of Indians within the Magonista army in Tijuana. Some believe as many as thirty Indians served in the army. After the Magonista defeat, the Mexican army pursued the Indian rebels and were reported to have executed nine to twelve men near Jamau.[13] According to one historian, the Indian involvement in this rebellion had more to do with traditional hatreds between different Indian bands than with an appeal to ideology. The alliance of various patrilineages shows that they chose the side they did hoping to exact revenge on rival groups.[14]

San Diego during the Mexican Revolution

The Magonista takeover of Tijuana and Mexicali in 1911 was a dramatic event that affected Mexican–U.S. relations and attitudes toward Mexican American border dwellers. During the subsequent years of the Mexican Revolution, which lasted until the 1930s, Mexican Americans in San Diego were affected by the increased numbers of immigrants crossing the border and by Anglo-Americans' fears about Mexican radical revolutionaries.

Throughout Southern California there was a growing need for Mexican laborers, who were hired at low wages to work in construction, light industry, and agriculture. San Diego experienced a boom in population and construction of new homes. Mexican immigrants were hired at the National City Railroad freight terminal and in lumberyards and new home construction sites throughout the city. They were needed in the waterfront district to work at California Iron Works, the San Diego Marine Construction Company, and the new tuna-packing sheds that were being built. In order to be close to their work, many Mexican families moved into Logan Heights, previously a middle-class suburb. This was the origin of the present-day Barrio Logan.[15]

During this period, Paul Taylor studied the Mexican laborers of San Diego.[16] In a sample of one hundred workers he found that Mexicans worked in a range of low-skilled to skilled jobs; low-skilled jobs included day laborer, cement worker, maintenance laborer, and the like. Semi-skilled laborers worked as gardeners, truck drivers, firemen, and janitors. Mexicans were also in skilled occupations such as carpenters, blacksmiths, and business owners. Children worked as paperboys, as junk collectors, in odd jobs, and later alongside women in the canneries. Almost one-third of the employed men were members of labor unions or employee associations. This was despite longstanding prejudice within the AFL against Mexican and black members. The white members felt threatened by the Mexican workers' willingness to work long hours for low pay, and they considered the Mexican a threat to the "American way of life."

Nevertheless, the Mexican population in San Diego continued to grow. Between 1900 and 1920 the Mexican-origin population of the city rose from 638 to 4,028.[17] Compared to the current population of San Diego, this seems like a minuscule group, but for the time, it represented a huge relative increase in the Chicano population. There was a large floating, or temporary, population as well. The downtown area between Eighth and Thirteenth had hotels, pool halls, and bars where these transitory workers spent their leisure time.[18] Many came to San Diego by boat, since travelers by rail were in constant danger of being attacked by Mexican revolutionists. Southern Pacific Railroad sent labor contractors (*enganchistas*) to Mexico and brought five hundred Mexican workers at a time to San Diego by boat. These laborers were then sent to the Imperial Valley to work in Mexico constructing the Mexicali-Sonora line.

Those Mexicanos who settled down with families and jobs in San Diego developed a community life. One of the main institutions formed by Mexicano immigrants throughout the Southwest during this time was the mutualista. This was a mutual-aid society where members gave weekly contributions and in return their families had the right to receive benefits in case of the member's death. The mutualista was also a social, patriotic, and cultural institution involving the families of the workers. In San Diego the Unión Patriótica Beneficia Mexicana Independiente was one such mutualista. The member families sponsored periodic fiestas to celebrate Mexican cultural events, such as Cinco de Mayo and Día de la Revolución (November 20). Other groups, such as La Junta Patriótica Mexicana, celebrated both American and Mexican holidays.[19]

Mexican Americans suffered the same kinds of discrimination as Mexicanos.

The *San Diego Union*, for example, did not distinguish between the two groups in their articles. All were "Mexicans." Added to the hostility that traditional labor unions felt toward Mexican workers was the stereotype of the violent border revolutionist/bandit. The *San Diego Union* helped fuel the paranoia in its reporting about the violent incidents that regularly took place along the border. For example, the headline on a March 14, 1914, article screamed, "San Diegan Murdered by Border Bandit," whereas the text stated that three suspects "were thought to be Mexican."[20] Another headline on November 12, 1910, "Death for Gringos Is Cry of Rioters," reported the news of beginnings of the Mexican Revolution.[21]

Fears of Mexican revolutionists in San Diego led to the National Guard being called out to protect lives and property along the border. More than 18,000 troops were stationed along the border in San Diego and Imperial counties. On April 24, 1914, some dynamite was found near the Sweet Water Reservoir and ten Mexican employees were fired on suspicion of sabotage. Periodic rumors circulated that Mexican revolutionists were planning to poison the water supply.[22] Accordingly, 160 soldiers were dispatched to guard Otay Dam. The city of El Cajon created its own militia, the San Diego Home Guard, to protect that community from Mexican terrorists.[23] The San Diego newspaper regularly reported about the movement of Mexicans who crossed the border back to Mexico to fight in the revolution. Fears reached such a height in 1914 that the San Diego Police Department issued orders that Mexicans in San Diego were to be kept under strict watch and were not to be allowed to have weapons or ammunition. The police conducted a series of raids of the downtown pool halls looking for seditious individuals. Throughout this period, the Justice Department employed agents to surveil Mexican nationals in the United States who were suspected of violating U.S. neutrality laws. Hundreds of reports of the comings and goings of Mexican businessmen, politicians, and workers ended up becoming part of the massive "Mexican Files." This resource gives even more detail to the fears surrounding the Mexican population in San Diego.[24]

Tijuana: The Growth of a Metropolis

During the period of the Mexican Revolution and up to the 1930s, Tijuana experienced a period of economic and demographic growth largely due to tourist enterprises owned and operated by Americans.[25] One of the first was one centering on the natural hot springs, the Tijuana Hot-Spa Hotel, built in 1885 and owned by P. L. Carle. This was followed by the construction of dog and horse racing tracks, casinos, and other hotels. Mexicano entrepreneurs opened the first bullring by 1910. When tourists visited San Diego during the Panama Exposition in 1915, they also traveled to Tijuana, which had recreational activities that were illegal in California. The Tijuana attractions—the Jockey Club, Trivoli Bar, Foreign Club, Sunset Inn, and Agua Caliente Casino—were all owned by Anglo-Americans and employed mostly American workers. This was a source of constant resentment with the Mexican labor unions and government.

A tremendous impetus for the growth of tourism was the enactment of Prohibition in the United States. Overnight Tijuana became a mecca for those who wanted to drink liquor and have a good time. By the end of the 1920s, more than 260 businesses were located in the downtown area, many of them along Revolución. These included many service businesses besides bars. Besides liquor Tijuana also had the attractions of almost unregulated prostitution and related vice establishments. This period in the city's growth engendered many negative stereotypes about Mexicans and border towns in the minds of visiting American tourists. These attitudes were generalized to Mexican Americans who lived in San Diego.

It was not until the presidency of Lázaro Cárdenas that Mexico moved to end gambling and American control of the tourist industry in Tijuana. In 1934, by presidential decree, Cárdenas outlawed gambling, and in 1937 the government expropriated American-owned property in Tijuana. Some of the casinos were converted to schools, and those Mexicanos who lost their jobs were given government employment.

San Ysidro: The Other San Diego

Bordering directly on the international line adjacent to Tijuana, San Ysidro has always been linked to Mexico. San Ysidro's early urban development came from a visionary group of people who came to settle in the valley in 1909 and founded an agricultural utopian colony called "Little Landers." They were a group of people who believed that with "a little land," people could grow their own food and provide their surpluses to others within the community. They, appropriately, christened their community with the name of the patron saint of farmers, Isidro, "a virtuous farmer who had fallen asleep and had his fields plowed for him by angels."[26]

Today San Ysidro still looms large in the dreams of many people. Undocumented immigrants fleeing the U.S. Border Patrol ask breathlessly when they come across if they have arrived—if they have crossed "la línea" and entered the land of milk and honey. For longtime San Ysidro residents who love their community and live, feel, and appreciate the social relations that make it up, their vision of San Ysidro goes beyond the limited view that some outsiders have.

Little Landers founder William Smythe described the high ideals of brotherly love and the fullest development of human potential he held for the cooperative farming venture he founded. He visualized the ideal colonist as "a man who . . . is a scientist . . . an artist . . . a man with initiative. . . . He is an independent, self-employing man. To his trees, his plants, and his vines he gives the ineffable touch of love. He is the spiritual man of the soil."[27] Smythe's idealism was reflected in the colony's symbol: a flag bearing a white star on a field of blue, the "star of hope." The Little Landers Colony prospered largely by trading with the settlements in Tijuana, but in 1916 the Tijuana River flooded and destroyed most of the houses. Most of the Little Landers departed for other locales, but a few hardy pioneers remained. Until the 1930s most of the residents were Anglo-Americans: farmers, ranchers, and workers in the booming tourist industry in Tijuana.

Ermanie Celicio was born in San Ysidro in 1912 and was one of the few Mexicans who lived in the Little Landers Colony after the flood. She recalled that "everyone was friendly. We all knew each other and everybody talked." Ermanie's father worked in various jobs for the San Diego and Arizona Railroad, which connected San Diego with the Imperial Valley; loaded and unloaded trains; and was a dealer at the Monte Carlo Club in Tijuana. She recalled that San Ysidro was where the jockeys lived and the racehorses and racing dogs were boarded. "Back then, San Ysidro was a jockey town. They kept horses and dogs here. The jockeys used to send their kids to school here."[28] San Ysidro in the 1920s was home to fifty soldiers and some Chinese farmers. No one paid much attention to the border, crossing freely back and forth.

In another interview Edward M. Cuen described what it was like to grow up in San Ysidro: "San Ysidro was a beautiful community. I think I knew everybody in town then. . . . It was just farmland, and a lot of people had cows, goats, horses, chickens."[29] Between 1929 and 1969, many things changed in San Ysidro; but the strong sense of community remained. Lydia Armenia Beltrán, who arrived in 1969, describes her reception:

> "It was a very beautiful community. We found people . . . who were very much involved with the community. They . . . told us what was going on and they said that if we worked hard and involved ourselves . . . the community would be that much better off. A little girl . . . who's now my goddaughter . . . came out and welcomed me and took me over to her house. . . . My neighbors all became my compadres. . . . Everybody's a compadre here."

Joyce Hettich, a longtime San Ysidro resident considered the unofficial town historian, remarks about interethnic relations in San Ysidro: "My experience of forty-nine years in San Ysidro is that we have all gotten along just fine." In describing relations between the Community Church and the Catholic Church, she explained how the churches would help each other out: "The Community Church minister would say to his congregation—'go over today to the Catholic Church—they're having a fundraising drive.' When the Community Church was having a drive, the Catholic Church pastor would say, 'Go over to the Community Church today, they're having a drive.'"

Today, San Ysidro is a predominantly Latino community. Mexican music is heard, and Spanish is the principal language spoken. Yet San Ysidro contains an ethnic and cultural representation that many people are not aware of. It is a community that has undergone major demographic change, particularly since the 1950s and 1960s. Andrea Skorepa, director of the Centro Familiar in San Ysidro, observed that the community became "a lot more predominantly Latino, but we've also had an emerging African American community. . . . We've gotten an influx of African Americans, Pacific Islanders, especially Filipinos."

Steven Andrew Gómez describes his own family's background and social-cultural activities: "Me, myself, being Mexican Indian, Tohono-O'odham, Yaqui, and Papago, that's who I relate to more. . . . Our entertainment is pow-wows. The gathering of the people. These are my ways. Singing [in ceremonial drums] is another way. I attend, not a church, but a circle of friends, a Native American sweat lodge, which is our church."

San Ysidro is also home to an ancient equestrian tradition going back to the Moorish days in Spain and to the Spanish-Mexican frontier days: the *charreada*, a form of rodeo with elaborate dress, highly skilled horsemanship, and beautiful lasso techniques performed by both male *charros* and female *escaramuzas*. The López brothers of San Ysidro were involved in forming an association of charros. Their char-readas drew people from as far away as Los Angeles and as far south as Rosarito.

San Ysidro's proximity to the border, which draws people from above and below the border, has been an important element in the life of the town, just as its proximity to the ocean and the salt beds once attracted Indian peoples from as far away as present-day Sonora and Arizona.

A New San Diego

As a result of the pressures of the Mexican Revolution and the growth of the economy in Southern California, new Mexican *colonias* and communities were established in Logan Heights, San Ysidro, Calexico, and Brawley. These places became the nuclei for the flourishing of Mexicano, and later Chicano, culture in San Diego. The revolutionary period fueled fear and negative stereotypes of Mexicans, and the close association of Tijuana with the Mexicans in San Diego added to Anglo-American racist prejudices. In the next decade these attitudes would be used to justify a repatriation campaign that shipped Mexicans (and many Mexican Americans) back to Mexico.

By 1930 the Mexican population of San Diego and Imperial Valley had grown due to the changes in the economy and the demand for workers. The construction of the San Diego and Arizona Railway opened up trade and travel between San Diego and the Imperial Valley, as well as with northern Baja California. Mexicano workers helped build this binational railroad and continued as maintenance workers for it up to the 1950s. The railroad was a symbol of the interconnectedness of the people of the border, a fact that would become more and more important in the lives of average Mexican Americans.

The 1920s and Mexican San Diego

During the decade following the most violent years of the Mexican Revolution, San Diego's Mexican-origin population increased due to immigration and the economic development of the region, which created a steady demand for new workers. As in other cities and towns in California, the native Californio families all but disappeared through intermarriage and being outnumbered by thousands of new immigrants from Mexico. In the 1920–1930 period, the Mexican immigrant population began to settle outside of the Old Town barrio in Logan Heights, an area of San Diego known as the "East End," a formerly upper- and middle-class residential neighborhood. From there Mexicanos commuted to work in service and laboring jobs around the city, and women found jobs in the fish canneries that were constructed along the harbor. Other settlements of immigrants grew where jobs were located, near the yards of the San Diego and Arizona Railroad and in small agricultural colonias in Lemon Grove, Escondido, and San Ysidro. The Mexican immigrant population in the Imperial Valley exploded in this period as they replaced Indian and Japanese workers. Seasonally, these workers traveled to San Diego to work in the citrus and vegetable fields.

Along with the growth and dispersion of the Mexican population was the beginning of their efforts to challenge discrimination and economic exploitation. Two major movements were the Imperial Valley strikes of 1928–1933 and the Lemon Grove incident in 1930–1931. In these confrontations San Diego's Mexicanos demonstrated that they were willing to make sacrifices, and they also wanted the power to shape their own destiny. Accordingly, they organized unions, parent associations, neighborhood groups, and mutual-aid societies that attempted to fight for justice. This was the first significant community effort by the Mexicano and Chicano people to challenge their subordinate status within San Diego and Imperial counties. It was a precursor for many subsequent *luchas* in the fields of labor, community organizing, and education.

Imperial Valley Strikes

The Mexicano communities in the Imperial Valley have historically been linked to San Diego's Chicano communities through immigration and economic development. The children of many immigrant farmworkers from the valley aspired to go to San Diego to get a college education and obtain better jobs. Simultaneously hardworking, tenacious, and socially conscious, the Mexicanos from "El Valle" became an important stimulating force within the Chicano and Mexicano communities of San Diego during the Chicano Movement of the 1960s and 1970s.

The first Chicano/Mexicano labor activism in the San Diego–Imperial Valley region stemmed from the grueling experience of the farmworkers. As the Imperial Valley's agriculture expanded, so too did the demand for workers. Initially, for the construction of the irrigation canals and the clearing of the land, a succession of groups were recruited: American Indian, Japanese, Hindu, Filipino, and Chinese laborers were the majority of farmworkers in the valley until the 1920s, when large industrial-size farms began to dominate. Thereafter, Mexicano immigrants became the major component of the labor force.

In 1927, Paul Taylor visited the Imperial Valley and reported on the conditions there. He found about 20,000 Mexican immigrants working in the fields, about half of whom had been born in the United States.[30] Working nine to ten hours a day in the spring and fall and enduring temperatures over 110 degrees in the summer, the seasonal workers suffered from low wages and an abusive system of labor contractors. As Taylor remarked, "The agriculture of the valley is characterized on its economic side by tenant farming, absentee ownership, and a general condition of instability and impermanence."[31] The seasonal rotation of crops meant fluctuating demands for workers. In the spring many farmworkers would leave the valley, looking for work in the Coachella Valley and San Diego.

The average family earned about $600 a year and was constantly on the move, following the crops. Taylor found that the most common complaint involved tenant farmers and labor contractors failing to pay the wages due to the farmworkers.[32] In April 1928 the Mexicano workers formed a union to challenge the abuses they had been experiencing. As was to be the case in hundreds of other Chicano unions, the original organizational efforts to unionize came from a mutualista, the Sociedad de Benito Juárez led by Filemon B. Gonzales. The new union was called the Imperial Valley Workers Union. Gonzales stated that the idea for the union came originally from the Mexican consul in Calexico, who had been besieged with complaints from Mexican nationals against corrupt labor contractors and tenant farmers.

In May 1928 the union sent out letters to all the growers respectfully asking for wages of 15 cents a crate or 75 cents per hour for picking cantaloupes. They also requested an improvement in working conditions: ice for drinking water, picking sacks, lumber to build outhouses, and compensation to injured workers. A few days later the sheriff arrested thirty-six workers for refusing to leave the fields where they were striking until their demands were met. The arrests provoked community meetings in the Mexican colonias. In one instance, Sheriff Gillette entered a pool hall where laborers were meeting to discuss the strike and Francisca Rodríguez, a farmworker, tried to force him to leave, aided by several others. They were promptly arrested.[33] Although most Mexicanos returned to work at the old rate, the Anglo-Americans began to fear a Communist plot, and rumors circulated about a possible Mexican uprising. The sheriff then began making indiscriminate arrests of Mexicans on the streets and in pool halls, which led to criticism in the Mexican newspapers in Mexicali, an appeal to President Calles for intervention, the dispatch of a state official to investigate the situation, and ultimately to the farmworkers winning most of their demands. More than sixty union activists were jailed for short periods of time, but the union survived for four more harvests.

The final report of the state investigation into what was termed the Cantaloupe Strike was issued as part of Governor C. C. Young's special committee report on Mexican immigration in 1930.[34] That report concluded that, contrary to the sheriff's allegations that "reds" had been responsible for the strike, there was "no tangible evidence to support this view" and that the workers' demands needed to be seriously considered.[35] Among these were the need for better housing, regulation of labor contractors, and better compliance with workmen's compensation insurance laws.

The investigation concluded that "future amicable relations between the growers and their laborers will be assured only by directing attention to the fundamental causes of the strike, rather than by resorting to the easier expedient of hurling time-worn and ineffective accusations of radicalism and red propagandism."[36]

Unfortunately, this advice was not followed in subsequent years. Early in 1930 organizers from the Trade Union Unity League (TUUL), a Communist-led group dedicated to overthrowing the factory agricultural system, entered the Imperial Valley and organized the Agricultural Workers Industrial League. This organization then sought to piggyback on the efforts of Mexicano and Filipino workers who had mounted a spontaneous strike during the lettuce harvest seeking improved wages and working conditions. The Mexicano workers, however, were opposed to Communist involvement and forbade the TUUL representatives from speaking at their meetings. Other individuals and organizations also opposed TUUL intervention into strikes in the valley: the Mexican consul supported repatriating Mexicanos who sided with the TUUL and the Mexican Confederación Regional de Obreros Mexicanos labor union worked to undercut the Communist organizers' influence.[37] Thereafter, however, any strikes that local Mexicano workers sought to organize during the cantaloupe harvest were squashed before they began by the joint efforts of Mexican and American authorities, who feared Communist influence.

The final burst of labor organizing in the fields occurred in 1933–1934 during the worst days of the Depression. A new, militant union emerged, partially influenced by Communist organizers: the Cannery and Agricultural Workers Industrial Union (CAWIU). Their organizers found a receptive farm labor force, even more exploited than ever due to falling wages. The CAWIU was opposed by the Mexican consulate who, fearing Communist influence, organized a rival workers' union, La Asociación Mexicana del Valle Imperial. Ultimately, the growers decided to support the Mexican workers' association in order to destroy the CAWIU.

In October 1933 and June 1934 there were many strikes that resulted in violent retaliation by the police and growers. More than one thousand workers walked off their jobs, only to be convinced to return by the Mexican consul.[38] In 1934 the CAWIU called for a general strike of lettuce and vegetable workers, and the authorities responded with mass arrests and prohibitions against meetings. Scores of individuals were arrested on mere suspicion of supporting the strike. Isolated instances of violence and wholesale violations of civil liberties continued until the federal government sent a special conciliator to the Imperial Valley to try to mediate a resolution. General Pelham D. Glassford sought out Joaquín Terrazas, the Mexican consul in Calexico who had organized La Asociación Mexicana and had personally intervened to prevent strikes in the past. Under Terrazas' guidance the growers agreed to a new wage agreement and a number of other provisions, among them to employ only members of La Asociación Mexicana. For their part the workers agreed to keep Communists out of their union and not to strike.

For the next year the CAWIU and La Asociación Mexicana competed for support. To many observers the Mexican association was nothing more than a company union designed to promote the growers' interests. The growers refused to conduct elections to allow the workers to choose which union they wanted to represent them, and were supported in this stance by California authorities. Ultimately, the CAWIU lost the battle, overwhelmed by the alliance of growers, Mexican authorities, and the California government. The Mexicano agricultural workers of the Imperial Valley would have to wait more than thirty years for another unionization effort, this one led by César Chávez, himself a farmworker.

The Lemon Grove Case

During the period of the labor struggles in the Imperial Valley, the children of Mexican immigrants throughout Southern California were increasingly being segregated into separate schools. The boards of education in scores of towns and cities followed a policy of establishing "Americanization schools," which were separate facilities or classrooms where Mexican students were to be given special instruction in English and American culture. Behind the supposed pedagogical benefits of this policy was a racial agenda of separating Euro-American and Mexican children in order to protect the former from the ostensibly corrupting influence of the latter. The Los Angeles School District, for example, justified segregation by saying that Mexican children "are more interested in action and emotion but grow listless under purely mental effort."[39] Other educators, such as Merton Hill, principal of Chafee Union High School, advocated that in the Americanization schools' curriculum "girls should be trained to be neat and efficient servants . . . boys should be taught to make use of discarded tin cans in the development of useful kitchen utensils."[40] The Americanization program became widespread throughout the Southwest, promoting inferior education for

Mexican-origin children. It lasted until the Supreme Court declared this kind of segregation illegal in the *Mendez v. Westminster* case in 1947.[41]

It is not known how widespread segregated schools were in San Diego. Due to the demographic concentration of Mexicanos in certain towns in the Imperial Valley, it is certain that many elementary schools there were de facto segregated. Taylor compiled a 1927 school census in the valley and found that Mexican schoolchildren comprised more than 50 percent of the school-age population in the towns of Brawley, Calexico, Glamis, Niland, and Heber.[42] In semi-rural regions of San Diego, it is probable that segregation prevailed.

One notable challenge to the Americanization schools came from the Mexican immigrant parents living in Lemon Grove, a rural hamlet near San Diego where the main employers were citrus growers. This event has come to be known as the Lemon Grove Incident, thanks to the research of Robert Alvarez Jr. and the television documentary produced by Paul Espinosa.[43] This was the first successful legal challenge to the segregation of Mexicanos in the public schools in the United States.

The growers of Lemon Grove had attracted hundreds of Mexicano families, mostly from Baja California, to come and work in the citrus fields. Many of the Mexicano residents were related by blood, having come from the same region of Mexico. Their children, born in the United States, began to enter the local school system in the late 1920s. On July 23, 1930, the Lemon Grove School Board began to discuss what to do with the more than seventy-five Mexican students who were attending the Lemon Grove Grammar School (fig 3.2). The board decided to build a separate school for them, but failed to notify the students' parents of this decision.

On January 5, 1931, the principal of the Lemon Grove Grammar School, Jerome T. Greene, stood at the door of the school and directed the incoming Mexican students to go to the new school building, a wooden structure that came to be called "La Caballeriza" (the barn). Instead, the students returned home, and thereafter their parents refused to send their children to the separate school. This became known in the press as the "Mexican student strike," but in reality it was the parents who, with the support of the Mexican consul in San Diego, decided to oppose the segregation of their children. They formed a group called La Comité de Vecinos de Lemon Grove (Lemon Grove Residents Committee) and asked the Mexican consul, Enrique Ferreira, for advice. Ferreira put the parents in touch with Fred C. Noon and A. C. Brinkley, two lawyers who had

FIGURE 3.2. A class photo taken in 1930 of one of the Americanization classes at the Lemon Grove Grammar School, composed entirely of children of Mexican descent. Their parents were involved in fighting and winning the first desegregation lawsuit in California involving Mexicans. (Courtesy of Paul Espinosa)

worked for the consul in the past. The attorneys filed a writ of mandate to prevent the school board from forcing the Mexicano children to attend the segregated school.[44] They chose a student, Roberto Alvarez, to be the plaintiff in the class-action suit.

The Comité de Vecinos sought support from other Mexicano communities by contacting the Spanish-language press in Tijuana and Los Angeles. *La Opinión*, the largest Spanish-language newspaper in California, published an editorial stating, "We are not in agreement with, which is very natural, nor do we consider just, the separation of our children, without any reason, to send them to another establishment that distinguishes Mexican children from children of other nationalities."[45] Soon donations began arriving from Mexicanos throughout California to help with the litigation costs.

The battle lines were being drawn. The president of the Lemon Grove School Board responded to *La Opinión* by claiming that the strike was being orchestrated by "an intense Mexican national organization." The San Diego district attorney decided to defend the school board in the impending case. Simultaneously, Assemblyman George R. Bliss introduced a bill to legalize the segregation of Mexican children, and other legislators announced that if the Lemon Grove School Board lost the case, they would see to it that other bills would go to the legislature. Eventually the Bliss bill was defeated, as were all other segregationist measures.

The court case proceeded to trial. The writ of mandate that went before the Superior Court called for reinstatement of the Mexican children and argued that the board had "no legal right or power to exclude [the Mexican children] from receiving instruction on an equal basis."[46]

The San Diego district attorney argued that the new school was appropriate because it was in the Mexican neighborhood and was large enough for all the students; because most of the students were below grade level in their knowledge of English; and because they would receive better instruction in this Americanization school. Incidentally, they suggested that Euro-American students would benefit from not having contact with the Mexican students.

On February 24, 1931, Judge Claude Chambers began hearing the case. Fred Noon, the Mexican parents' attorney, called ten witnesses to the stand to challenge the school board's contention that the Mexican children were educationally backward. Most of the students had been born in the United States and spoke English fluently. At least one student spoke no Spanish at all. In the interrogatory, Judge Chambers dramatically revealed the injustice of the differential treatment of Mexican students:

> JUDGE CHAMBERS: When there are American children who are behind, what do you do with them?
>
> ANSWER: They are kept in a lower grade.
>
> JUDGE: You don't segregate them? Why not do the same with the other children? Wouldn't the association of American and Mexican children be favorable to the learning of English for these children?
>
> ANSWER: (silence)

In the final arguments, the judge was convinced that there was no reason to segregate the Mexican children and that the separation would probably hinder their learning of the English language and American customs. He ruled against the Lemon Grove School District and ordered them to reinstate the children in the regular school. Although this case was a victory for Mexicano students, the judge held that their segregation violated a state law that allowed for the segregation of African and Indian children. Thus, the verdict did not challenge racial segregation per se, and it would remain for later court cases to outlaw that injustice for all students of color.

The Lemon Grove case was the first legal victory by Mexicanos challenging their children's separation in the school system. Unfortunately, the case did not set a precedent for other districts, and segregation continued outside of Lemon Grove. Nevertheless, Espinosa's dramatization of the incident in the television documentary "The Lemon Grove Incident" served to educate later generations about the struggles of their forbearers to achieve justice.

The Neighborhood House

During the period following the Mexican Revolution and World War I, Anglo-American liberals and social reformers sought to "uplift" Mexican and European immigrants who were streaming into the nation's urban areas. One of the efforts to reach the impoverished immigrants was the settlement house movement. The settlement houses provided basic services to the working poor and introduced the concept of kindergarten schools in the United States. The settlement houses, located in the poorest sections of cities, became centers for immigrant education and social activities, as well as places where immigrants could celebrate their native language and culture. While many settlement houses had as their goal the Americanization of immigrants through the teaching of English and American customs, sometimes they became centers of cultural pluralism and opposition to assimilation.

In San Diego the settlement movement began as a charitable outreach program of the College Women's Club in 1914 and later was incorporated as the Neighborhood House of San Diego in 1923, with its main building located at 1809 National Avenue.[47] The Neighborhood House had been preceded by the San Diego Industrial School, an evening and weekend school staffed by volunteers who taught Mexican immigrants industrial and domestic arts. The Industrial School had had little social or cultural outreach to the growing Mexican barrio. The Neighborhood House directors and staff were part of a nationwide philanthropic movement that sought to ameliorate the evil effects of industrialization

FIGURE 3.3. A youth dance at the Neighborhood House. Pictured are Eddie López and Joe Márquez with their friends. The Neighborhood House continued to be a social center for Mexican American youth well into the 1950s. (Courtesy of Salvador Torres)

and modernization on the lives of the immigrant and working classes. During the 1910s the settlement house staff had been concerned with issues of abolishing child labor and other labor abuses. But by the time the Neighborhood House of San Diego was organized in the 1920s, the settlement house movement had shifted its concern away from reform issues and now concentrated almost exclusively on public health, education, and cultural and social activities (fig. 3.3).

The Neighborhood House official literature from 1920 stated the goals of the settlement house that the Woman's Club had constructed in Logan Heights as follows:

To understand its Mexican Neighbors.
To interpret the needs of the community.
To perform the intimate and friendly service of a good neighbor.
To direct needed educational and recreational work.[48]

To many Anglo-Americans, especially those who contributed money, the most important role of the Neighborhood House was the Americanization of Mexican immigrants. One reporter for the *San Diego Union* called the Neighborhood House an "Americanization Factory."[49] And it was true that the directors sought to justify the budget of the Neighborhood House in terms of Americanization. But not all of the clients served were Mexican, perhaps 20 percent were African Americans and European immigrants. The funding for the Neighborhood House initially came from the Community Chest and later from the city government. The range of activities sponsored by this barrio settlement house included classes in drama, English, and math; summer school for children; and lectures, dances, and community sings for the entire family. The Neighborhood House also received some city funding during the 1920s to sponsor a nurse, a prenatal and well-baby clinic, and Red Cross classes.[50] The clinic was immensely popular because many of the Mexican immigrants were reluctant to use the county hospital for illnesses. During the 1920s the Neighborhood House sponsored a milk station for mothers, who received free baby formula and milk for their families. There was also a small library of donated books which the barrio residents could check out. Annually the Neighborhood House sponsored a traditional production of La Pastorela, a Mexican folk play about the shepherds and the Christ child.

One of the major obstacles to the Neighborhood House's outreach was the reluctance of Mexican men to allow their women to attend social and educational activities by themselves. In the 1920s and into the 1930s, the barrio women succeeded in establishing a mother's club where they could gather to discuss issues of common concern and to participate in social and cultural activities. By the 1930s the Neighborhood House had become a center for immigrant education, offering classes in English, math, and health, as well as a kindergarten.[51] Except for some community-wide events, most of the Neighborhood House programs were segregated by race and gender, with separate workshops and classes being given for African Americans, Mexicans, and Anglos, as well as for girls and boys (fig. 3.4).

In the 1930s programs expanded to include the construction of a community oven for use by people who could not afford their own and a class in how to be a hotel maid for young girls. In 1933 the Neighborhood House built a new adobe building to house the baby and mother's clinic. Later, in the 1940s, the Neighborhood House further expanded its facilities and programs to include a dental clinic and nursery.

FIGURE 3.4. Mexican American children at a local school in Barrio Logan about 1929. In the background is the Neighborhood House. (Courtesy of Robert Rodríguez)

The Neighborhood House was administered by Anglo-Americans whose charitable desire to help the poor was laudable. Spanish-speaking nurses and program aides were hired in an attempt to reach the Mexican population, and many of the programs that they offered were sorely needed. One of the well-known directors of the Neighborhood House in the 1930s was Anita Jones, who had worked at Hull House in Chicago, a noted progressive institution. She had been director of the Mexican Immigrants Protective League there and had a degree from the University of Chicago. As director of the San Diego settlement house, she continued to administer to the Mexican immigrant community, as by now more than 90 percent of the clientele were Mexican-born, with the balance being Greek, Portuguese, Japanese, and Italian.[52] Old-timers, including Laura Rodríguez, who was later an administrator of the Chicano Free Clinic, remembered the Neighborhood House staff as kindly, well-intentioned individuals who sought to learn the language and culture of their Mexican clients.

Whereas the Neighborhood House served many of the estimated five thousand Mexican immigrants in San Diego during the 1930s, the city and county agencies almost completely ignored the economic and public health problems of Mexican immigrants. In fact, in this period the government was trying to deport and repatriate Mexican immigrants and so was openly hostile toward their economic and social plight. The Neighborhood House consequently became a well-known and well-respected community resource regarded by many Mexican Americans as a barrio institution—despite the sometimes heavy-handed efforts at Americanization and the administrators' failure to promote and encourage Mexican culture.

This all changed during the 1960s, when the Neighborhood House administration came under attack by Chicano activists who wanted a different kind of locally controlled service agency. The origins of the takeover of the Neighborhood House facility on National Avenue and the new Chicano-oriented program will be the subject of a later chapter. For now, it is important to note that during the Depression years the Neighborhood House was the only public agency devoted to improving the lives of Mexican and Chicano residents in Logan Heights.

The Mexicano Community during the Depression

Estimates of the numbers of Mexicans and Mexican Americans who lived in urban San Diego during the 1920s vary. Local officials estimated that there were approximately 20,000 Mexicans in San Diego by 1928, but the U.S. census in 1930 counted only 9,266 Mexican-born. The discrepancy may be due to the notorious undercounting of Mexicans by the U.S. Census Bureau, as well as to migratory patterns of employment and residence.[53] The 1930 census also did not count the American-born children of Mexican parents, a group that probably tripled the reported figures. Whatever their actual numbers in the 1920s, during the 1930s the Mexican-born population of San Diego declined because of the repatriation drive and the difficulties in finding employment during the Depression.

What was it like to be a Mexicano in San Diego in this period? Constantine Panunzio, an Italian-immigrant sociologist who was director of the Neighborhood House in 1930, studied the community. He wrote one of the few social-scientific surveys of the Mexicano community of this era, published by the University of California as *How Mexicans Earn and Live: A Study of the Incomes and Expenditures of One Hundred Mexican Families in San Diego, California*. This depression-era study was done to determine the degree of "national adjustment" undergone by Mexican immigrants and their offspring who were living in San Diego. Panunzio studied the consumption patterns of one hundred "Mexicans" and found "habits of living of a group not yet wholly adjusted to the American standard."[54] He described the Logan Heights barrio in 1930:

> Mexicans live in San Diego under conditions that are, possibly, more than usually favorable. Most of them are in the southwestern portion of the city along the

waterfront close to the factories and canneries. The streets are wide; sanitation is moderately good. Mexican stores, churches, pool halls, and the Neighborhood House are part of the district. Living conditions are reasonably good. There is little or no serious congestion. The cottage type of house prevails. There are no slum tenements.[55]

This upbeat description is at odds with that of the Community Welfare Council, which reported in 1928 that there were "a multitude of undesirable conditions" in the barrio; that housing was substandard; and that the residents suffered from malnutrition, unemployment, lack of education, communicable diseases, and a high infant mortality rate.[56] The Welfare Council lamented that the Mexicans were responsible for creating "un-American conditions" that led to disease and poverty. This indictment of Mexicans as being responsible for their own misery would emerge again and again in the popular mind.

What were the true conditions in the barrio? No doubt better than what many had left in Mexico but at the same time probably shocking to middle-class officials. Panunzio preferred to accentuate the positive in his report; others, such as the Americanizers in city and county government, saw the Mexican section of town as alien and un-American. As to who was to blame for the substandard conditions, it would be forty years until the Chicano Movement would indict the real culprits: racist officials, apathetic bureaucrats, exploitative employers, and slumlords.

Another impression of barrio life in the '20s and '30s comes from those who actually lived there. In the 1930s Luis Alvarez was a little boy living in Logan Heights. His father was a painter and his mother worked in a local fish cannery. He was sent to a parochial school, where he remembered being in class with Anglo kids. When he attended public school, he recalled that it "was more or less segregated on a voluntary basis, the people seemed to stay in tune with their race of their own will. In those days they used to kind of look down on the Italians, they were known as 'Diegos' and the Mexican people were known as 'greasers' and the colored were known as 'niggers.'" Alvarez remembered Logan Heights as a neighborhood where he felt safe. "People were very united, very friendly; you could leave your home without having to bolt it down or lock it down and feel pretty safe that no one would bother you. There was more respect between people especially the younger people towards their seniors."[57]

Logan Heights during the 1920s and 1930s was in transition, becoming a community of Mexican immigrants and African Americans. One of the indications of that change was the beginnings of mural art. The first Mexican-inspired murals in San Diego were done in 1934 by José Moya del Pino, who was commissioned by the Aztec Brewery in Logan Heights to illustrate the interior of the building with scenes from Mexico. Moya was a Spanish immigrant who lived in San Francisco and had been commissioned to paint murals there. During the '30s he was an instructor at the California School of Fine Arts. The Aztec Brewery was owned by Edward Baker and Herbert Jaffee, who had moved the brewery equipment from their original plant in Mexicali into the building that formerly housed the Savage Tire Company. The images Moya painted inside the brewery in Logan Heights included a large Aztec calendar, scenes from the daily lives of the Mayans and Aztecs, and the flora and fauna of Mexico. In addition to these murals, the brewery had a good deal of woodwork with hand-painted pre-Columbian motifs and framed art pieces depicting aspects of Aztec culture.[58] This building with its art remained hidden in the barrio until 1989, when the city gave permission for it to be destroyed to make way for new construction. Prior to the building's demolition some samples of the murals and artwork were stored in Chuey's Restaurant nearby, where people could view them. Today, no one knows where the murals are. The Moya murals were the precursors of later murals that would adorn the concrete pillars of the Coronado Bridge, the expressions of Chicano art that would be part of Chicano Park.[59]

Repatriation

During the Depression, conditions for Mexicans in San Diego became worse as unemployment increased and it became harder to find and keep a job. Adding to the oppressive situation was a political campaign to force Mexicans to go back to Mexico, with little regard to whether they were citizens or legal residents of the United States. This nationwide repatriation movement broke up families, disrupted the lives of hundreds of thousands of individuals, and violated the civil rights of many U.S.–born Mexican Americans. In the early 1930s more than a million Mexicanos were forced to leave the United States.

The pressures to "get rid of the Mexicans" intensified in the economic hard times of the Depression. Local municipalities were encouraged by the Immigration and Naturalization Service and the American Federation of Labor to deport undocumented Mexican residents and to mount campaigns of harassment to frighten others into returning to their homeland. In the early 1930s, numerous roundups or raids were conducted within Mexican colonias throughout the United States. The Mexican consuls general in most of the major cities where the raids took place complained about the beatings and terror but were not able to stop the campaign.

In the popular imagination, then as now, it was assumed that the Mexican population was taking welfare services and jobs from U.S. citizens. In reality, Mexican nationals nationwide were among the least likely to rely on county welfare or charitable services, and the vast majority of them were already unemployed. Local governments passed laws making it illegal to hire noncitizens. Groups such as the San Diego–based National Club of America for Americans, Inc., drafted anti-alien ordinances for local governments.

Meanwhile, thousands of older, American-born children of immigrants, who were citizens of the United States, were forced to decide whether to go to live in a country they had never seen or to stay behind without their family. Women without husbands and children in orphanages were forcibly repatriated, as were people who were mentally ill. Many employed, healthy citizens were coerced into leaving through threats of physical violence and loss of their jobs.

Once the deportees arrived in Mexico, the Mexican government tried its best to resettle them on agricultural lands, but the planning and resources for such an effort were inadequate. Most of the *repatriados* had a hard time adjusting to their new country. They encountered some discrimination against them from native Mexicans and found the government's promises of economic assistance unfulfilled. Most of the new colonies were economic failures.[60]

In San Diego charitable organizations worked with the Mexican consulate to arrange the transportation of immigrants back to Mexico. Many began asking the consulate for financial help to make the move. Consul Enrique Ferreira reported in 1931 that most of those asking for help had been unemployed for months and were desperate for jobs. Ferreira managed to waive the entry fees for those who wanted to return and helped get relocation funds for others. In August 1931 the County Welfare Commission, working with other local agencies, told Ferreira that a train would be available to transport indigent Mexicans, and soon thirty-five families departed. In 1932 the Mexican government decided to use the Mexican warship ironically named *Progreso* to transport repatriados from San Diego and Los Angeles to Mexico. The plan was to land in the port of Topolobambo, Sinaloa, and from there to distribute the repatriados to various land grants in the surrounding states. Far fewer than the envisioned eight hundred people took advantage of this "cruise." The consul estimated that only about 250 departed. One passenger, Jimeno Hernández, a fourteen-year-old, wrote about his experiences on the ship.

He recounted how the Mexican officials at Manzanillo extorted money from the passengers by claiming that their baggage exceeded the limit.[61]

Camille Guerin-Gonzales, who has done the only study of repatriation from San Diego, found that the typical repatriado was a family of more than three people headed by a man of about forty years old. Half of the repatriados were children. Very few extended family members traveled back to Mexico. About half of the San Diego repatriados ended up settling in the border states.[62] Colonia Libertad in Tijuana, for example, was settled by repatriates from San Diego. For the next sixty years, this colonia adjacent to the international boundary fence would be the jumping-off point for generations of immigrants heading north.

Conclusions

During the 1920–1930 period, Mexicano immigrants in San Diego and Imperial counties contributed the sweat of their brow, their blood, and their life spirit to building the economic infrastructure of a modern society. The construction of the San Diego and Arizona Railroad, the agricultural concerns and irrigation canals in the Imperial Valley, the trolley car system, new housing developments in eastern San Diego, and the growth of the fish canning industry all were accomplished with Mexicano and Chicano laborers. The new immigrants' first challenge was to survive economically, given the low wages and hard living conditions. Segregated in Mexican colonias and barrios, they relied on their families, compadres, and neighbors for day-to-day survival. They experienced racism, discrimination, and hostility from teachers, employers, and local officials. Sometimes they benefited from the charitable efforts of sympathetic groups like those working with the Neighborhood House. But ultimately, they were expected to give up their language and customs and become Americanized in order to receive the basic rights to which they were entitled. Mexicanos not only endured but also organized to improve their children's lives, as exemplified during the labor strikes in the Imperial Valley and in the Lemon Grove struggle. These actions were the beginnings of Chicano activism in San Diego and the Imperial Valley. Later generations would draw from these traditions in their community and labor organizing. The Depression of the 1930s increased the hardships they had to endure and resulted in a campaign to repatriate Mexican immigrants and their children back to Mexico. The Mexicano community declined in these years, but those that remained or returned during World War II continued to struggle for justice and equality. Unfortunately, it would take the cataclysm of World War II to truly begin to change these conditions.

4

WORLD WAR II
AND THE EMERGING CIVIL RIGHTS STRUGGLE

José Rodolfo Jacobo
and Richard Griswold del Castillo

During the 1940s and 1950s the Mexicanos and Mexican Americans of the San Diego and Imperial Valley border regions underwent profound changes due to the cataclysmic events of World War II, a trauma that affected everyone's lives. Thousands of young Mexican American men joined the military and went off to fight in the war; many of them died heroes' deaths, others returned with a new commitment to rebuild their lives and their communities. Young Mexican-origin women contributed to the war effort by working in the many war industries that were created in San Diego. They developed a new sense of independence and self-confidence that provided the basis for the later Chicana Movement. Those who lived through these years were part of the later struggle to achieve the full civil rights that they had been promised during the war. As a result of the changes during the war years, Chicanos and Mexicanos in San Diego gained valuable experience they used to continue their struggle against discrimination and segregation. The barriers they encountered in these years included segregation and socioeconomic exclusion, yet they collectively never accepted these limitations, instead joining with others to eliminate them and establish a strong sense of community.

Although World War II was a war against injustice and totalitarianism abroad, there were also struggles on the home front, as racial discrimination in employment, in public services, in schools, and by public officials continued. Beginning in 1942 Mexican laborers (braceros) were brought under contract to the United States, and they influenced the development of the barrios and colonias. A new labor activism was born through the efforts of Luisa Moreno, an organizer who lived and worked in San Diego, fighting for labor rights and against the discrimination toward Mexican youth identified as pachucos. Racism continued to plague San Diego, and the Ku Klux Klan staged ongoing anti-Mexican operations. In 1953 the federal government sponsored Operation Wetback, which resulted in the repatriation of thousands of immigrants, creating a period of fear and intimidation. All of this ferment prepared the ground for a resurgence of community organizing and the civil rights activism of the 1960s.

Luisa Moreno: Labor Activism and the Zoot-Suit Riots

One prominent San Diego Latina who remained a leader in the struggle for civil rights during the war was Luisa Moreno (fig. 4.1).[1] She was a Guatemalan-born labor leader who was active in organizing for the United Cannery, Agricultural, and Packing Workers Association (UCAPAWA) during the 1930s. In July 1940, Luisa Moreno moved to San Diego to work on a labor union newspaper and to continue her organizing activities among the women cannery workers. She and her friend Robert Galván helped organize the United Fish Cannery Workers Union, UCAPAWA Local 64, and they soon organized hundreds of fish and cannery workers in the largest San Diego canneries: California Packing Corporation, Marine Products Company, the Old Mission Packing Corporation, Van Camp Sea Food Company, and Westgate Sea Products.[2]

While Luisa Moreno was organizing the cannery workers, the United States entered into World War II on December 7, 1942. Within a short time, Southern California, and especially San Diego, was transformed into a military-industrial center for the war effort. As a result San Diego became even more conservative, politically and culturally. Local Japanese Americans were sent to internment camps, officially called War Relocation Authority Camps, while a disproportionate number of Mexican Americans were drafted because they lacked jobs that carried draft-deferral status. Lured by jobs in agriculture and other sectors, thousands of Mexicans poured across the border. Forbidden to work in the petroleum industry, shipyards, and other vital industries, they took the least skilled, lowest-paying jobs.[3] These immigrants were soon joined by bracero workers who were contracted beginning in 1943 to come to the United States to work in selected industries, mostly in agriculture and railroads.

As a union consultant for the cannery workers in San Diego, Moreno gave speeches arguing that legal and illegal Mexican immigrants used fewer government resources than native-born citizens. She pointed out that they contributed

FIGURE 4.1. Luisa Moreno in 1940. (Courtesy of the California Ethnic and Multicultural Archives, Special Collections, Donald C. Davidson Library, University of California at Santa Barbara)

FIGURE 4.2. During World War II Benjamin Torres was a driver for Arden Milk Company, located on Eleventh Street in San Diego. Illustrative of the many Mexican immigrants and Mexican Americans in San Diego, he delivered milk to restaurants and the U.S. Navy in five-gallon containers. (Courtesy of Cynthia Torres)

more to the public coffers in taxes than they took from the region (fig. 4.2).
She was angered and annoyed when conservatives, including remnants of the Ku
Klux Klan, publicly disparaged Mexican immigrants.[4]

Moreno was also active in protesting the mistreatment of Mexican American
youth arising from the infamous Sleepy Lagoon case and Zoot-Suit Riots in Los
Angeles. Both these events had important implications for the civil rights of all
Mexicanos and Mexican Americans in Southern California and beyond.

On August 2, 1942, José Díaz was found dead near a gravel pit in East Los
Angeles, a tragedy that would have far-reaching consequences. In Los Angeles
following the murder, the police ordered a dragnet and arrested three hundred
young Chicanos. Following days of sensational newspaper articles labeling all
Mexican American youths as gangsters and pachucos, twenty-three young men
were indicted for murder. On January 13, 1943, twelve young Chicanos were
convicted of murder and five of assault in "the largest mass-murder trial ever
conducted in Los Angeles. The trial took place in an atmosphere of intense prejudice, before a biased judge, and with a stubborn and courageous but inadequate
defense."[5] Newspaper, public, and judicial bias as well as police prejudice and
blatant mistreatment molded the juries' verdicts.

During 1943, Luisa Moreno, Bert Corona of the Warehouseman's Union,
and others joined the Sleepy Lagoon Defense Committee chaired by Carey
McWilliams, attorney and director of the California Division of Immigration
and Housing, seeking to overturn the defendants' convictions. Moreno stressed
that the grand jury testimony, based on racially biased assumptions about the
Chicano juveniles, created unavoidable conflicts. As she explained, "The Sleepy
Lagoon Case is a reflection of the general reactionary drive against organized
labor and minority problems. This case now sows all sorts of division among the
various racial, national, and religious groups among the workers."[6] In 1944 the
California Appeals Court overturned the Sleepy Lagoon defendants' convictions
for lack of evidence, but without acknowledging any racial bias in the case.

Moreno sensed the uneasiness generated by the war in Southern California,
particularly in San Diego. Housing was in short supply. Rationing became a nui-
sance. Transportation was a problem. Racial conflicts in the U.S. Navy and in
San Diego became intense. People searched for scapegoats.[7] The war triggered
anxiety, ambiguity, and frustration. Wild stories abounded that U.S. ships had
been shelled and torpedoed along the Southern California coast. Most people in
1943 felt the United States was losing the war.

The racial tension Moreno feared erupted into full-scale violence in Los Angeles in June 1943. Youths known as pachucos—mostly Chicanos, but also Negroes, Filipinos, and some whites, who wore distinctive zoot suits with long peg-bottom pants and thigh-length coats with padded shoulders—were prime targets. In Los Angeles, Chicanos were the majority of zoot-suiters. Their dark skin, accent, and distinctive mannerisms—not to mention the stereotype that pachucos were gangsters—were enough to set them apart from the average Angeleño. "Basically bilingual, they spoke both Spanish and English with an accent that could be mimicked by either or both groups," wrote McWilliams. "The *Pachuco* also had a uniform, the zoot-suit, which served to make him conspicuous."[8]

In early June 1943, a rumor circulated that some sailors had been attacked for insulting a Mexican American woman. About two hundred sailors took the law into their own hands. Heading out from the Navy Armory in Chávez Ravine into the center of downtown Los Angeles, they formed a brigade of twenty taxicabs. Several young Chicano zoot-suiters were spotted. They were badly beaten and left bleeding on the pavement. Later one of the sailors who led the expedition made a bland statement: "We're out to do what the police have failed to do. . . . [W]e're going to clean up this situation."[9]

Sensational articles flourished for several days on the front pages of newspapers. "The worst came from the Hearst Press, which in Los Angeles was represented by the *L.A. Herald* and the *L.A. Examiner*." As Luisa Moreno pointed out, "These papers assaulted Mexican *pachucos* and zoot-suiters. They insinuated that Mexicans were the cause of all the crime and delinquency in California."[10] Mobs grew larger. "Squads of servicemen, arms linked, paraded through downtown Los Angeles four abreast, stopped anyone wearing zoot-suits and made them suffer the consequences." They were encouraged by police indifference. "Aside from a few half-hearted admonitions, the police made no effort whatever to interfere with these hordes of disorder."[11] The highly publicized Sleepy Lagoon case of the previous year had, of course, created an atmosphere of racial tension.[12]

One evening, zoot-suiters were dragged out of downtown motion picture theaters. Their fancy suits were torn from their bodies. They were beaten and chased through the streets. Yet it was the pachucos, not the sailors, who were arrested. An emergency meeting of several hundred citizens was called. Moreno, Corona, and other Mexican American community leaders sprang into action. "They mobilized a defense committee on behalf of the youngsters who were being arrested and detained even though they were the victims" of racist, paranoid servicemen.[13]

Intense emotions gripped Angeleños. Military authorities declared downtown Los Angeles off-limits to servicemen. The city's police department was indifferent to the brutality. The *Los Angeles Times* meanwhile went berserk printing inflammatory headlines, such as this one on November 2, 1942: "Ten Seized in Drive on Zoot-Suit Gangsters." Then on February 23, 1943, another headline read, "One Slain and Another Knifed in Zoot Fracas."[14] According to Alice McGraff, one of the women working on the Sleepy Lagoon Defense Committee, sailors from San Diego were among the instigators of the violence in Los Angeles. McGraff stated that busloads of servicemen from San Diego convoyed up to Los Angeles to participate in the riots.

In San Diego stories spread that blacks, Chicanos, and unpatriotic whites were abusing military personal. In retaliation, several taverns and other favorite Mexican American gathering spots were vandalized. As one report stated, "Damage done on the Fifth Street Landing in the way of malicious mischief possibly by enlisted men of *USS Kilty*."[15] Rumors spread about night spots, mostly located on Mission Boulevard, such as the Beach Club Cafe and the Casino Club, that catered to Mexican Americans and people of color. La Reine Cafe at 2003 Logan Street, owned by "a large hard Negress" was described as "a low class business frequented by civilians and service men of mixed races and by a large number of common unescorted women." The "general air of drunkenness" created fights over attractive prostitutes.[16] The San Diego County Council, consisting of veterans of foreign wars, concluded in its investigation of civilian violence "that service men in the uniform of our navy, were being beaten, robbed, drugged, and subjected to other such acts, common to places of low repute."[17]

On June 10, 1943, the *San Diego Union* reported that groups of servicemen, ranging in size from a dozen to several hundred, had roamed San Diego's downtown streets south of Broadway, searching for "zoot-suited hoodlums reported to be infiltrating into San Diego from Los Angeles." About one hundred sailors and marines stormed downtown San Diego on G Street below First Avenue to chase several youths wearing "the outlandish zoot-suit garb. The youths made their getaway in the darkness." About three hundred other servicemen gathered at Third Avenue and East Street. They were quickly dispersed by city and military police before any zoot-suiters were discovered. San Diego police, the article continued, were ordered to search suspicious individuals who "appeared to be members of a

Pachuco gang. Those found to be carrying the usual Pachuco weapons—knives, chains and clubs—will be booked in the city jail on charges of carrying deadly weapons, police reported."[18]

Charles C. Dail, a San Diego city councilman, was concerned about the violence and informed Rear Admiral David Bagley, commandant of the Eleventh Naval District in San Diego, that the harassment by the sailors and marines against the so-called zoot-suiters was actually aimed at civilians in general. "There has been numerous instances in San Diego where members of the military forces have insulted and vilified civilians on public streets."[19] Admiral Bagley at first ignored Dail's complaint; he then tried to discredit him. Later, he denied the charges leveled by Dail, who was supported by W. J. Decker, secretary of the San Diego Industrial Union Council. The navy kept a lid on the San Diego disturbances. Luisa Moreno invited Bagley to meet with San Diego community labor and political figures. As she explained, "arrogance, pretense, and pride have no place in a commitment to serve the public. I wanted to have every avenue open to avoid blood and tears. In negotiations, you will never get everything you want. That is why you need to be flexible. You will need manipulative ways to get out of conflicts."[20]

Meanwhile ugly racial incidents continued. There were military reports from El Centro that sailors were "maliciously assaulted by Mexican police." The Teddy Orias Cafe, at 522 Sixth Avenue in San Diego, refused to serve blacks, and tensions escalated.[21] A frustrated Moreno wanted an investigation of racial issues that marred San Diego and the naval base. As she explained, "Without a stable political and social environment, nothing can be done. Political power belongs to those who can sustain growth and deliver prosperity. Then they can inspire loyalty and cooperation from the people."[22]

Finally, on November 30, 1950, because of her involvement with Mexican American civil rights issues, the Sleepy Lagoon Case, and the protests against the Zoot-Suit Riots, Luisa Moreno was deported to Mexico. Representative Jack Tenney, who headed a committee hunting for communists, branded Luisa Moreno a "dangerous alien."[23] Desperate for peace and rest, she and her husband went into Mexico through Ciudad Juárez.[24] The terms of her exit visa were listed as "voluntary departure under warrant of deportation" on the grounds that she had once been a member of the Communist Party.[25] She never again stepped onto U.S. soil. In fact, were she to have done so without permission, she would have been guilty of a felony, fined, and imprisoned.[26] For a time she and her husband lived in Tijuana, where they operated a furniture store. There she maintained contacts with friends and associates in San Diego. In her final years, she lived in her native Guatemala, where she died in 1992.

Mexican and Mexican American GIs

More than 2,500,000 persons of Mexican descent lived in the U.S. Southwest when the Japanese bombed Pearl Harbor on December 7, 1941. Of that number more than half were native-born U.S. citizens, and probably about one-third, or just fewer than one million, were men of draft age. While there are no reliable statistics, impressionistic accounts indicate that large numbers of Mexican Americans either volunteered or were drafted into the armed services during World War II. It is estimated that about 500,000 Mexican American men joined the armed services during the war.[27] Their experience served as a platform for later activism when they sought to redeem the promises of a more democratic society that were made during the war.

Mexican Americans volunteered for a variety of reasons: some sought escape from poverty and discrimination at home; others wanted adventure or enlisted out of pride and a sense of manhood. Some joined because their families expected them to contribute, some out of patriotic motives, and some because their friends or relatives had enlisted. Raúl Morín, a veteran whose book *Among the Valiant* is a personal account of Mexican Americans during World War II, put it this way:

> We felt that this was an opportunity to show the rest of the nation that we too were also ready, willing, and able to fight for our nation. It did not matter whether we were looked upon as Mexicans, Mexican-Americans, or belonging to a minority group; the war soon made us all genuine Americans, eligible and available immediately to fight and to defend our country, the United States of America.[28]

In addition to the U.S.–born Mexican Americans, hundreds of thousands of Mexican citizens who were resident in the United States were eligible for the draft. After June 1942, when Mexico declared war on the Axis powers, Mexican nationals living along the border crossed into the United States to join up as well.

There are hundreds of stories of the bravery and sacrifices of the Mexican American GIs during the war.[29] As many historians have noted, as a group, Mexican

Americans earned seventeen Congressional Medals of Honor, the nation's high-est award for bravery and valor, more than any other racial/ethnic group. In addi-tion to the accounts of unimaginable bravery and hardship are descriptions of the strength of friendships and Mexicanidad. The family back home learned of the experiences of their menfolk only after the war, due to strict censorship of the mail in wartime. Even after the war many veterans preferred to keep silent about their experiences. Oscar Romero and Alfredo Sepulveda, the former a Chicano and the latter a Mexicano, are two examples of men who distinguished themselves as heroes during the war and later became community leaders in San Diego, part of the generation that led the civil rights movement after the war.

Oscar Romero was a Chicano who was drafted into the army in 1942. He was sent to basic training in Little Rock, Arkansas, where many volunteers from Mexico were stationed. The 76th Infantry Division, in particular, had many Chicanos from Southern California. Oscar remembers going through basic training with Maracario García, who was from Guanajuato, Mexico, and later received the Congressional Medal of Honor, and also recalls serving with many other Mexicanos and Chicanos who gave their lives for the United States during World War II. Romero was in the D-Day landing at Normandy and fought to liberate France. Later, when crossing the Rhine River, he received the Bronze Star for taking command of his platoon after the lieutenant and sergeant were killed. In 1955 Oscar was one of the founders of the all-Chicano VFW Don Diego Post in Logan Heights, formed because the local VFW did not want any Mexican or Chicano members. Today, Oscar is still active in the post along with his wife, Ruth, who was a founder of the women's auxiliary organizations for the post.

Alfredo Sepulveda was born in 1920 in La Paz, Mexico, and moved to Los Angeles with his family when he was six. His family was related to the Sepulveda family who had owned a California rancho in the 1840s. He became a profes-sional boxer and got married before volunteering to join the armed services when the war broke out. He remembers being rejected from flight school because he was a Mexican national. He joined the paratroopers, fought at Normandy and in the Battle of the Bulge, and was wounded three times. Alfredo won the Silver Star and two Bronze Stars, one with clusters, for valiant action in the war. After the war he worked as a truck driver and later moved to San Diego, where he and his wife also became leaders in the Don Diego Post of the VFW.[30]

Rosita the Riveter

Women too were mobilized during World War II and their experience was crucial for the later struggle for civil rights. The lives of hundreds of thousands of Mexican American women were drastically changed by the national emergency of war, as they went to work in jobs that had previously been reserved for men, in aircraft factories or other war industries. While a great diversity of experiences arose out of these years, one generalization seems to summarize the importance of this period: the war created new awareness of women's abilities outside the domestic sphere. In Richard Santillán's words, the war developed among Mexican American women a "political awareness, social independence, grass-roots leadership, and economic self reliance—personal strengths which greatly enhanced the post-war civil rights movement."[31]

For Mexican American women, entering the workforce meant overcoming strong cultural pressures. Lorinda Flores, a Mexican immigrant to San Diego in the 1930s remembered her experience: "I really enjoyed working. . . . I wanted to grow up and be a buyer and work in a store, but I married a typical Mexican male who said you're not going to work, you're going to have kids and stay home. So that was my *jale*, I was a housewife."[32] Additionally, married women usually had small children and growing families to care for, making it very difficult to hold down a full-time job. Countering these cultural and situational limits on Mexican American women's working for wages was a long tradition of their working in part time and occasional jobs to support the family. This was especially true for migrant farmworker families, where the entire family worked to make ends meet. The experience of Hortencia Carrasco, a farmworker in San Diego during the 1930s was typical: "When I started working I was about 14 or 15 years. I started working at Van Camp in 1943. I went to work to help the family. I had no choice, I had to help my mother, my parents, and the younger kids."[33] Many Mexican American women were already working when the war began, and the war enabled them to get better-paying jobs. The traditional expectations of putting family first and of a woman being primarily a mother and wife did not necessarily change because of their wartime experience, though. Before the war, working to supplement the male wage earner's income had been seen as an extension of women's family responsibility. Their work during the war was seen in much the same light, as necessary to help win the war and to fill in for the men while they were in the armed forces.

FIGURE 4.3. Jesús Ortiz and
Alejandra Semiental on their
wedding day, ca. 1922, in
Mexico. Jesús came the United
States alone during World War
II and later lived in San Diego.
(Courtesy of Rose M. Conde)

Yet the majority of Mexican American women during World War II were
not Rosita the Riveters. They contributed to the war effort in other ways, by
raising families and taking care of others. Their prosaic stories have not yet been
told—of the difficulties of making ends meet with rationing and scarcity, of the
continued discrimination in public services and in education, of the grief over
the loss of brothers, uncles, fathers, and husbands, of the heroic sacrifices made to
keep families together and support the morale of loved ones. All these dimensions
of life have yet to be the subject of social historians studying Mexican American
women during the war, but they were the dominant experiences for most adult
Mexican American women. San Diego native Marcy Gastelum remembered, "A
lot of women preferred to be housewives. But many did work because a lot of
them had to. A lot of my friends quit school during my high school years to get
married, most of them. The first thing on their mind was leaving school, getting
married, raising a family and let the man go to work" (fig. 4.3).[34]

Some of the oral histories gathered from Mexican American women in San
Diego illustrate the many themes of their experience. Emma López was a native

San Diegan whose parents owned a small barrio restaurant. During the war she quit high school to get good-paying jobs, first in the tuna canneries and then at Convair, an aircraft assembly plant. After the swing shift, there were big band dances; Emma and her friends had enough energy to go almost every week: "I'd go around picking everybody up. We didn't want dates, we wanted to dance with the guys from Texas or New York, New Jersey, New Mexico." She recalled lots of late-night parties, grunion running, and all-night movies. All this had the blessing of her parents, who saw it as part of the war effort.[35] During the war many women reported more independence in their social lives despite very restrictive attitudes of their parents. Indeed Americanization, whether in dress, speech, expectations, or culture progressed faster during the war than before. And pressures for Americanization would continue after the war as well.

One factor that dramatically increased young women's freedom and sense of independence was the money they had to spend on activities that had been considered frivolous during the Depression of the 1930s. Now they had the ability to indulge themselves. Hortencia Carrasco, another San Diego native with Mexican immigrant parents recalled deciding to quit high school because she "had no clothes to wear." She started working at the tuna canneries rather than at the aircraft factories because she could earn more money through piece rates—up to one hundred dollars a week. To get the job she lied about her age, saying she was eighteen. "A couple of times we worked the whole month without a day off," she recalls. After working so hard she felt she had earned the right to have fun without the strict supervision of her parents.[36]

Another theme that links the diverse remembrances of Mexican American women during World War II is Americanization. In general, the war had the effect of stimulating patriotism through the common bond of suffering and sacrifice. Beyond that, Mexican Americans along with African Americans felt more justified in asserting their rights as U.S. citizens who had fought and worked for the victory over totalitarianism and fascism. Scores of historians have dated the origins of the Civil Rights Movement to 1945 and the return of servicemen of color. This demand for equal treatment gained force because of the common affirmation of loyalty to flag and country.

For Mexican American women this meant voting for the first time during the war. It meant buying war bonds and volunteering for the USO and Red Cross. It meant gaining a new awareness of the injustice of unequal treatment. As one woman told Richard Santillán,

During the war, there was a lessening of discrimination by some public places only because they needed our money, with so many Anglos in the service. After the war, some restaurants, stores, and taverns again refused to serve us on an equal basis with whites. We knew this was totally unfair because we had worked hard to win the war. My generation realized then that we had to do something to change this condition, not only for ourselves but for the next generation.[37]

Mexican American women encountered the color barrier in employment. In many aircraft assembly plants, whites refused to work with African American women, so the employers assigned Mexican American women to work with them. The result was an education in how racism affected everyone and the formation of cross-ethnic and interracial friendships. Many Mexican American women reported forming friendships for the first time with non-Mexicanos and with other women.

Elvira Esparza was born and raised in San Diego of Mexican immigrant parents. During the war she worked at Solar, making B24s, the first Mexican American woman hired there. She got men's wages because of the quality of her work. She remembered men saying that they liked her but couldn't date her because she was Mexican. "They didn't understand that this person because she had brown skin she had a head just like anyone else, she could do the work, sometimes better."[38]

There were other internal battles to be fought. Then, as now, Mexican American women had to confront negative stereotypes about who they were. During the 1930s pachuquismo emerged as a cultural expression and added new negative views that young women had to combat. Even though Mexican American women working in the war industries generally had neither time nor inclination to affect the pachuca style, they were often lumped with this subculture in the popular mind. Pachuquismo was a style of dress, talk, and behavior that openly flouted conventional Mexican as well as Anglo-American society. In the late 1930s, influenced by African Americana and big band culture, the pachucos created a distinctive youth subculture among younger Mexican Americans who were rebelling against their parents' conventional values. They adopted their own music, language, and dress. For men, the style was to wear a zoot suit. For the women, the style was to wear short skirts, tight sweaters, and jackets with padded shoulders. They wore their hair in high style and used lots of makeup. They called themselves "pachucos" or "pachucas," a word of uncertain origin but generally referring to U.S.–born Mexican American youth who dressed in the style and spoke Calo, a highly inventive slang that mixed English and Spanish.[39]

Many Mexican parents were shocked and outraged by the pachuco style, and especially by the pachucas, who were considered to represent sexual immorality and violence. Needless to say the Anglo-American press also portrayed the pachuca as the newest incarnation of the Mexican spitfire stereotype. For older Mexican Americans as well as Anglos, the pachuca represented a threat to the traditional roles of women.

In San Diego, Marcy Gastelum, who worked as a riveter at Convair thought that the threat of the pachucos was much exaggerated: "The pachucos used to stand in front of the Cornet Theater, but they were harmless: they never hurt anybody, they just wanted to be the little tough guy, show off their clothing and the way they did their hair do. . . . No one was afraid of them. . . . We never heard of any incidents where there was violence or killings."[40] During the aftermath of the infamous Zoot-Suit Riots, pachucas became scapegoats in the Mexican and mainstream press, which accused them of being pot-smoking prostitutes and cultural traitors.

Los Braceros

One consequence of the war was to formalize the legal immigration of hundreds of thousands of Mexicano workers through the Bracero Program. This program had two consequences for the struggle for civil rights. First, it increased the numbers of Mexicanos who came to live in San Diego and elsewhere because many braceros did not go back to Mexico and many more crossed into the United States without documents because of the unmet demand for farm laborers. Second, the Bracero Program heightened the awareness of labor union activists and others concerned with labor rights about the injustices and exploitation experienced by Mexican-origin workers, which generally increased under the program. The campaign to eliminate the Bracero Program began with Mexican American activists in the 1950s, who saw in it a corporate-controlled effort to keep wages low for all Mexican workers.

The program began during World War II when the U.S. government signed an agreement with the Mexican government to allow for the temporary migration of contract workers. Although initiated as an emergency wartime measure, the Bracero Program was renewed after the war and continued until 1964, providing a huge stimulus for Mexican immigration to the United States. During the Bracero Program almost five million Mexican workers came to the United States. Some scholars suggest that the program established the contours of modern Mexican immigration flows and gave rise to the social, political, and cultural issues that dominate the current debates over immigration.[41]

California's powerful agribusiness sector was involved early in the recruitment of Mexican labor. A newspaper article in September 1942 read, "The first contingent of Mexican field workers assigned to alleviate U.S. farm labor shortages will be en route to California beet and cotton fields."[42] Locally, San Diego County farmers filed a request for the importation of three hundred Mexican agricultural workers on January 29, 1943. In Oceanside, Harold E. Person, chairman of the Agricultural Corporation's board and one of the county's largest strawberry growers, asked for fifty workers. Some experts estimated that the local agricultural industry needed as many as 1,500 workers early in 1943.

Under the law, the braceros were to be paid a specified minimum wage, receive basic amenities, and work only at agricultural jobs. But bracero workers complained of violations of wage agreements, substandard living quarters, exorbitant charges for food and clothing, and racial discrimination. Growers, on the other hand, liked the Bracero Program and constantly lobbied for its continuance. Growers could use braceros to break strikes and to keep wages low, and they could easily terminate their employment when their labor was no longer needed.[43]

The bracero camps became a special kind of Mexican community in many rural areas of the Southwest. As a camp they were segregated from whites and even from the Mexican American sections of town. Braceros lived in extreme poverty and worked in dangerous conditions. When they ventured outside the camps on weekends, they frequently were victims of racially motivated beatings and robberies. They were paid very low wages, even lower than those paid to Mexican American workers; hence, there was animosity when braceros were used in place of local workers or when they were illegally used to break strikes.

The braceros were not entirely complacent in their role. In May 1944, for example, a group of braceros in Idaho went on strike demanding better wages, and talk of a bracero strike spread throughout the Pacific Northwest.[44] After the war the Bracero Program continued to be a thorn in the side of organized labor and an example for many Mexican Americans of how their labor as farmworkers was devalued. Criticism of the program based on humanitarian and economic grounds led by Ernesto Garlarza during the 1950s eventually helped end it.

While official data and reports abound on the Bracero Program, almost nothing has been written about the perspectives of the braceros themselves. How did they experience World War II in the United States? Amazingly, there has not yet been a published collection of bracero stories. The following account tells how one bracero, known only as Don Jesús, remembered his recruitment in Mexico and his experience in the United States.

A Bracero Remembers: Don Jesús

When we heard that they were contracting workers to go to the United States, we all wanted to go. I, however, could not go because I was a soldier in the Mexican army. I was the chauffeur of a general by the name of Anacleto López. But I really needed to go because I had a son that was ill, and I needed the money for his surgery. So I asked the general for permission to allow me to go. Laughing, he said, "sure go try your luck," and so I came. The year was 1942. My compadre, José Manuel Sandoval, and I went to the stadium in Mexico where we were to gather.

There, in the middle of a crowd, we found ourselves being sprayed with hoses in order to stop a lice infestation. Boy, they gave us quite a shower! The next morning the man in charge of the contracts, his name was Guillermo, came by and I explained my situation. I told him I needed to go to the United States because of the illness in my family. He told me to go ahead and go to the United States, and that once I was there to write him and he would send my son to Mexico [City] so that he could receive medical attention.

So that happened, and we soon found ourselves on our way to the United States. When we crossed the border at Ciudad Juárez, our hearts pounded wildly. We were afraid because we were in a totally strange country, and I had never really done any other kind of work but mine. They took José Manuel and me to Riverside, near Colton. It was a long way from Ciudad Juárez to California. During the trip we entertained ourselves by counting the wagons on the trains that were going by with military equipment and personnel on their way to Europe. Sometimes the soldiers would wave at us and we waved back. The trains passed really close to each other and sometimes the American soldiers would even give us a cigarette.

Colton was the location for the base of a military squadron, but the squadron was not there. The men had been shipped out to Europe to fight in the Second World War, and we were housed there. It was nice and clean there, and we even had a Catholic priest. He saw that most of us were Catholic, and he started to build a small shrine so that we could attend Mass on Sundays. However, not everyone attended Mass. On Sundays, five buses would also arrive to take us to town to the movies or to drink wine. There was a lot of drinking, and sometimes, even, fancy women would come to take the money from the braceros and things would get very wild.

Buses arrived early in the day to take us to work. There were about twenty of us per bus. They would take us to some groves to pick oranges. There, we had to put one ladder on top of the other to reach one or two oranges that were way on top of the trees. Sometimes, however, they would take us to Japanese groves, and there the trees were really short but falling over full of oranges. We were given cutters to cut the oranges; but some, in order to go faster, would just pull the fruit from the tree. I did everything as I was told, and it helped me get along with my boss, and thus I soon became a driver. That was a lot easier, and I even had a helper.

The end of our contract came in 1944, and Rogelio tried to convince me to go to Canada. Work was good there, he said. But I had completed my contract and my son had already received the surgery he needed, so I decided to go back to Mexico. If I had wanted to stay, I could have stayed in the United States. The bosses there wanted me to stay because I was also a mechanic. Nevertheless, I had made my decision. I was worried about my son and wanted to go home. Boy, I remember how the trip to the border seemed endless. The train did not seem to go as fast as when they brought us into the United States. That's the way it always seems when one is coming home. We had some hard times, but we had to better ourselves. What could we do? But I had no desire to go back. That was my luck.[45]

Don Jesús did not return to work in the United States after the war, but he did return in 1997 to live with his daughter in San Diego, where he died in January 2001. A large number of braceros "skipped out on" their contracts and remained in the United States after World War II. Here, they married and had families, and their children, Mexican Americans and Chicanos, became part of the expanding Mexican-origin population in the United States.

A New Identity

World War II changed the Mexican American people's perception of themselves. George Sánchez, author of *Becoming Mexican American*, believes that the war resulted in a shift of leadership, that there was a "transition from a Mexico-centered leadership to one focused on political and social advancement in American society."[46] Throughout the 1930s, the children of Mexican immigrants matured and came of age. They were citizens of the United States, and the 1940 U.S. census showed that native-born Mexican Americans outnumbered

FIGURE 4.4. Los Gallos was a youth club that provided many of the later leaders of the Chicano Movement in San Diego, including Roberto Martínez and Salvador Torres. This photo, taken in the late 1950s, was a fundraiser for the young men's community activities. (Courtesy of Salvador Torres)

Mexican immigrants. They proved themselves in World War II where, on both the home front and in battle, Mexican Americans demonstrated their patriotism and broke with their immigrant identity. Increasingly, they thought of themselves as Americans not Mexicans, at least in a political sense. During and after the war, these Mexican Americans and their children continued to be targets of discrimination and racism, a situation that provoked among their new leadership a renewed commitment to work for civil rights (fig. 4.4). Ultimately, the war changed the larger society too, making the American public more sensitive to the evils of racism. This enabled positive gains in terms of social justice. The next chapter illustrates how the rural communities of farmworkers coped with the segregation and poverty that persisted after World War II. Drawing on the strengths of their culture, family, and community they were able to survive and even flourish as a people.

5

EL CAMPO: MEMORIES OF A CITRUS LABOR CAMP

María de la Luz Ibarra

The previous chapter showed how World War II brought new populations and economies to San Diego and began to change the urban life that surrounded many Mexicanas/os. One important historical border has been that between the urban and the rural. Many Mexicans came to the United States during the 1950s and '60s as braceros or immigrants to work in the fields. Their lives and struggles have largely been ignored by historians. In this reminiscence, María de la Luz Ibarra gives us a personal history of what it was like to grow up in an agricultural labor camp in San Diego. This chapter shows how Chicanas/os overcame the urban-rural border in search of a better life and an escape from the prejudices and poverty by which they were surrounded. Ibarra's story is only one of thousands of examples of how Mexicans transcended the commodification of their lives, succeeded in creating communities that overcame the racialized borders, and established a cultural space that valued social justice.

Agriculture has historically formed a central part of Southern California's economy, and especially, the citrus industry. This industry, in turn, has been characterized by a reliance on foreign migrant workers, and in the last eighty years on Mexican laborers in particular.[1] While the ethno-racial background of workers has remained fairly constant during this time, the organization of labor—the ways in which growers recruit, retain, and discipline workers—has taken different forms. In this chapter, I address one of these forms of labor organization: the use of private farm labor camps. I focus on one labor camp in Escondido, California—in San Diego's north county—from 1967 through 1978, a period when I, then a young girl, lived there with my family. After a brief discussion of agriculture and the citrus industry in Southern California, I describe the physical and historical contours of the Citrus Growers Labor Camp, and then address the social organization of work and leisure in the place known as "El Campo" by Mexican workers. These descriptions of everyday life serve as reminders that while profound structural inequality is a fundamental part of working-class Mexican lives, it is not the only defining feature. Working people's lives also have meaning and purpose beyond that defined through relationships with dominant groups.[2] The everyday practices of Mexican workers reveal aspirations and desires for security and cultural continuity; these practices in turn are, over time, the building blocks of identity and community formation. Thus, the everyday practices of workers serve to create "Mexican" spaces that become anchors for future chains of migration. In this way Escondido is like other contemporary Southern California communities—a thriving center of new Mexican settlement with a long history of past settlement.[3]

Agriculture, Citrus, and Labor Camps in California

After the Mexican War of 1846–48, the transition from a pastoral economy to a capitalist-dominated agricultural economy occurred rapidly in California. Within a period of thirty years, the labor force in Southern California was fully proletarianized and its agricultural production well on the road toward intensive, large-scale farming of vegetables, fruits, and orchard crops. By the early twentieth century, agriculture had become central to the Southern California regional economy, and citrus its most profitable crop, producing wealth even throughout the Great Depression.[4] Not too surprisingly, acreage in citrus grew steadily throughout the region, and farms themselves became larger through the first half of the century.[5]

An array of factors contributed to the successful expansion of the citrus industry. First, the temperate regional microclimates of Southern California are particularly conducive to the growth of various types of citrus, including two types of oranges—the sweet-eating navels and juice-producing Valencias—as well as grapefruits and lemons. Second, powerful grower associations cooperatively influenced consumer demand through a range of collective advertising strategies that made citrus—and in particular oranges—symbols of health, sunshine, and affluence. Finally, the availability of a reliable, cheap, and racialized labor force in Southern California allowed for the profitability of the citrus industry.[6]

This labor force was especially necessary after World War I, when citrus farms grew to an average of fifty acres and labor needs could no longer be met with a mix of family and hired help. Thus, in the early part of the twentieth century, growers increased their recruitment of foreign migrant workers as white workers, who by virtue of their race did not have to stay in a segmented labor market, steadily moved into better-paying urban jobs.[7] While the citrus labor force would continue to include some white workers, as well as Chinese, Japanese, Sikh, and Filipino workers, increasingly the dominant group was Mexican.

As Mexicans became the dominant labor force after World War I, wages steadily declined in relation to wages in industrial jobs. Declining wages were a result of both the ready availability of immigrant Mexican labor, made up of vulnerable families fleeing the ravages and consequences of the Mexican Revolution, and the tight organization of powerful grower associations. Grower associations were affiliated with specific packinghouses, which in turn, served as the "nerve centers" of the citrus industry, often controlling all aspects of production—from establishing hiring policies and recruiting workers to establishing picking quotas and wages for the area.[8] In terms of the last, workers were rarely paid by the hour, but rather by boxes picked or by a combination of a box rate with an hourly rate. Wages, likewise, were determined through complicated wage scales based on varying picking standards. Thus, through a range of policies, grower/packer associations were able to keep wages low and variable.

A tight organization on the part of grower associations and packers was perhaps, from the point of view of employers, particularly necessary in this industry where workers, at least hypothetically, had a good possibility of unionizing. Unlike many other agricultural employees who were seasonal migrants in search of crops, many citrus workers were able to maintain year-round jobs in the region due to the different growing and picking cycles of the various citrus crops. Navel oranges, for example, are grown from October to May and Valencia oranges from April to September.[9] In fact, the Industrial Workers of the World (IWW) took advantage of this relative stability and successfully organized citrus workers early in the century. To the chagrin of growers, the IWW won wage increases through strike actions.[10] Growers subsequently responded quickly and often ruthlessly to any kind of unionization effort.

Among the tactics growers used to deter unionization was to hire vigilante groups who rounded up and physically removed labor organizers. Likewise, some growers carried out tactics of intimidation through their membership in the Klu Klux Klan. "Klan actions served to psychologically intimidate workers and included public parades, drive-by threats, night riding, and cross burning."[11]

Even when workers simply wanted relatively modest wage increases or improvements in working conditions, growers acted. At the Limoneira Camp in Ventura County, employers went so far as to hire a whole new workforce, until the old workforce agreed to withdraw their demands.[12]

Growers did not control workers only through intimidation, but also by providing them with housing.[13] For growers housing projects or labor camps had distinct advantages. They allowed for full supervision of the labor force and ensured that it would be readily available. Housing projects were of a broad range and used distinct types of materials: adobe, wood frame, hollow tile, poured concrete, and ready cut or hollow construction. Houses themselves differed widely—as did their cost.[14] Some growers provided housing for a fee, along with potable water and gas, while others did not directly charge workers.

After World War II, at the inception of the Bracero Program, labor camps became a necessity. Enjoying a limited moment of power in a bilateral labor agreement, the Mexican government demanded, among other things, that temporary guest workers—braceros—be provided with housing.[15] In this context, new camps were built from scratch while older, existing camps were given face-lifts to fulfill the need for worker housing. Some of these camps would continue functioning long after the end of the Bracero Program in 1964, as Mexicans continued to be the dominant labor force in the citrus industry.

Historical and Physical Context: El Campo

The Escondido labor camp occupied about five acres on what was at the time of its construction the outskirts of the west side of town. This location was no coincidence, as it was typical of segregated housing projects favored by local citrus growers throughout Southern California. These private housing projects not only favored greater control of workers but also reinforced the existing racial and class-based stratification in the city and guaranteed white residents limited contact with Mexican workers and their families. While not a completely self-contained universe, the camp nonetheless functioned as a fairly insulated community through the end of the Bracero Program.[16]

The camp was originally built to house the contracted, temporary Mexican agricultural workers under the Bracero Program between 1942 and 1964. The homes were built of wood, painted yellow, and covered with green tarpaper roofs. The site was surrounded by a ring of eucalyptus trees, bordered by railroad tracks, and physically divided into four principal areas: family living quarters, single men's barracks, warehouses, and a dining commons/main office complex. After the Bracero Program came to an end in 1964, the camp would continue to house primarily men but also some women and children until 1988. During this post-bracero period, the camp became a less insulated community, as the west side had continued to expand with increasing Mexican migrant settlement, as well as Mexican-oriented businesses, including restaurants and grocery stores. In written recollections begun in 1997, I describe the camp in the following way:

> 201 North Quince, Escondido, California. That's where I lived from the time I was four years old until I was fourteen. My father even made my sister and me little badges imprinted with this address—just in case we ever got lost and someone found us, they would know where we belonged. Twenty-one years after I moved out of that place, the memory—like a recent burn scar—hurts as I stretch it into focus: a yellow wooden house; a big yard with apricot, walnut, and peach trees; a trellis with grapevines and flowers. My mom planted carnations and roses and my father, marigolds and jasmine all along the sides of the house and, in greater profusion, near the front porch. Thinking about it, it didn't really get bad until after they built a street in what had been the backyard. Then, all of a sudden, we were exposed for the whole world to see. "El Campo"—the labor camp, with small, square barracks and green roofs. El Campo, with the gates that had to be put up and signs that said "no trespassing"—as if anyone who could read English might want to come inside the gates. But, I'm getting ahead of myself, because what I really wanted to write about were the good times—before the gates were shut, before the street was built, before the signs came up.

My memories are thus characterized by increasing conflict as I grew older and the parameters of the camp began to change as the city grew. Going back to my earliest recollections, however, a landscape of flowering backyards predominates, as well as a more peaceful climate.

Family housing consisted of six small square buildings lined up like train cars behind a bigger house where the manager lived. The resemblance to train cars was accentuated by the railroad tracks that ran parallel to the backyards and eventually disappeared somewhere behind the eucalyptus trees that clustered on the western boundary of the camp. These buildings housed nuclear and extended family groups who were settled long term in the city. These individuals invested in visible symbols of "home" and, among other things, planted the flowers that I so vividly remember. In both the front yards and backyards could be found calla lilies, ferns, hierbabuena, and geraniums.

The population of single men who lived in the barracks, or *barracas*, across the way from family housing was—in contrast—less stable. Some men would come to pick for a season never to return again, while others regularly returned to pick fruit for part of the year. This shift in the makeup of the single male population was reflected in the tidy but barren, dusty landscape around buildings. No obvious signs of continuity remained. At the peak of picking season the camp housed up to 150 individuals.

While distinct in terms of their settlement patterns, many of the families and single men were similar in that they had migrated north in search of better opportunity. Most of these families and individuals derived from rural areas in "traditional" sending states in central-western and northern Mexico, where the federal government had "through its manipulation of credit markets, irrigation projects and control of agricultural innovation and diffusion, encouraged the exploitation of the richest and most productive agricultural areas of the country by large firms."[17] This policy favored large growers and increasingly disenfranchised small communal shareholders, or *ejidatarios*. Moreover "the proportion of families that were landless rose from 58 percent in 1940 to 77 percent in 1970."[18] The concrete consequence for individuals in rural areas was that while they might want and choose to maintain a home and family there, an economic infusion from the outside was necessary. Typically, this meant that a male head of household would migrate to a large Mexican urban center, find a job, and send home remittances. Later this migration would also include women who might labor as domestics for the booming urban middle class. Alternatively—especially in the bracero and post-bracero periods—men would migrate to the United States in search of seasonal work. Not surprisingly, in the post-1964 period many of the men at the labor camp—whether single or married—had at one time or another worked as braceros or had family members who had done so. Likewise, many of the people in the camp were transnational residents, living in Mexico for part of the year and working in the United States for another part. Many of the single men had left their family members behind, sending home remittances that might barely be enough to help them, since the amounts were so small. Others were more successful at earning a higher wage and investing it to improve, retain, or expand family property, hoping eventually to retire from picking fruit in the United States and return to Mexico to live a more comfortable life. Yet others, over time, made the United States their principal home, although they retained ties to family and dreams in Mexico.

Organization of Daily Life: Work and Leisure

The daily work routine began at 6:30 a.m., when trucks belonging to the different packers organized under the Citrus Growers corporation arrived at the camp and began transporting men, women, and teenagers to the fields. These trucks were open-air vehicles painted in a distinctive green color and equipped with a few wooden planks for seats. Some people were able to sit, but most stood as the truck made its trip to the local groves surrounding Escondido and Valley Center. Family members took their home-cooked breakfasts and lunches with them—things like *burritos de frijol* or *chorizo y huevo*—along with bottles of water. Meanwhile, single men had gotten up to eat breakfast in the dining hall between 5:00 and 6:00 a.m., and had then prepared themselves lunches of burritos and tacos from food put out for this purpose. All workers, whether men or women, were dressed in similar clothes—long-sleeved shirts and pants, hats, bandanas, and heavy work boots—clothes that would protect them from the sun and sharp branches. For women, these clothes also undoubtedly served as a type of armor, a protection perhaps from unwanted sexual advances.[19] Like clockwork, the trucks would lumber away with their cargo of human labor—unless it rained or the picking season was over.

While the "pickers" were away, the camp was left with a skeleton crew to keep it functioning. The manager, my father, Artemio Ibarra, was a migrant from Monterrey, Nuevo León, a man who in his early thirties had decided that he did not want his father's fate: a lifetime of working at the steel plant Fundidora de Monterrey. Instead, he migrated to California with the hope of finding adventure and a better-paying job. His journey took him to a 1,500-person bracero camp in Anaheim, where he labored as a janitor and office worker for seven years. He was subsequently transferred to Escondido to work as an assistant manager, until he was promoted to manager in 1968. My father's job was to make sure that the infrastructure of the camp remained in good condition—he participated in and oversaw the maintenance of the buildings, plumbing, electricity, and landscaping. Likewise, he made sure that the necessary food had been ordered and was available for the cook, and that all of the residents had paid their rents. He could often be found in his office, typing up reports of meals consumed so that these could be deducted from individual workers' paychecks.

The assistant manager, Mr. López, was a migrant from the state of Jalisco who had come to the United States to labor as a farmworker early in his life. He had been able to obtain legal residency documents and thus never had to labor as a bracero. At the time he was employed at the camp, he was married and led a transnational life: his wife and children lived in Tijuana for most of the year and he commuted back and forth across the border on weekends. During the summer and winter, his wife and family might also stay at the camp for short periods of time. During the week Mr. López was in charge of helping with the physical maintenance of the camp. He could often be seen raking eucalyptus leaves, putting up a new roof, or fixing the plumbing alongside my father. For two weeks during the winter, when my family made our yearly trek to Monterrey, Mr. López became camp manager.

The cook, Mr. Santos, was a migrant from Nayarit who had come to the United States as a bracero. He, like my father, had labored at the Fullerton camp, initially as a fruit picker and later, building on his love of the kitchen, as an assistant cook. When he was transferred to Escondido, he was promoted to cook. In matters of the heart, however, he was less lucky. He also led a transnational life, having a wife and child who lived in Tijuana. His long absences, however, took their toll and his first wife left him. He eventually remarried, and this time made sure that his new bride, Doña Monica—as well as her daughter from a previous relationship and his own son from his first marriage—lived with him at the camp. Mr. Santos worked long days—he was undoubtedly the first one up every day, making sure the breakfast was ready and later that the dishes and pans were washed and put away. Later, he would repeat the routine to make sure that dinner was ready by the time the men returned from the fields.

A few of the wives of this camp crew also were at the camp most of the day. My mother and Doña Monica led lives that largely revolved around cooking, washing, ironing, cleaning, taking care of children, gardening, sewing, and mending. Some of my most vibrant memories revolve around the gendered household tasks assigned to each day of the week. During the summer, for example, Monday was wash day, and for many years, this meant using the electric washer with the hand-cranked wringer that sat alongside the house. Once the clothes were washed and wrung out, we would haul the laundry to the clotheslines in the backyard and hang it up. Occasionally, we would also pull out the large washbasin to wash and scrub very large wool blankets that had been handmade by my mother's mother in Zuazua, Nuevo León, many years before. Washing was interspersed with cooking, and it literally took the whole day. Not surprisingly, my mother recruited my sister and me to help as soon as we were physically able.

If Monday was wash day, then that meant Tuesday was ironing day. This, likewise, was an all-morning task. Everything that had been washed—from the cotton sheets to the cotton underwear—was neatly ironed. My mother would often reminisce about her childhood in Zuazua as we were doing these tasks and would tell us how things were done before "labor-saving" devices were introduced. We thought we had it hard, but in Zuazua, said my mother, women would take their laundry to the river and then haul it back up to where the clotheslines were. All the while, she said, they had to make sure that their arms and faces were protected from the sun, so that they could retain fair complexions.

After 4:00 p.m. the camp began to hum again as the workers returned in separate groups from long days of picking. For the single men, this meant time for a shower and perhaps some socializing in the area of the front office before dinner, which was served between 5:00 and 6:00 p.m. Two long benches sat alongside the office, and they were always full about this time. Light conversation, smoking, joking, and watching the street for the occasional salesperson who would try to come onto the property to sell religious icons, pans, or books were all worthwhile diversions. Likewise, it was often during this time that men in search of work or local ranch managers in search of day workers might come by, peppering the afternoon with a little novelty. Especially exciting was when one of the men seeking work hailed from a resident's hometown. Just as in the rest of Southern California, in Escondido social networks were important to the continued recruitment of workers. Late afternoon before the dinner bell rang was also the time when people could pick up their mail and, once every two weeks, their paychecks. Occasionally, this easygoing camaraderie would be temporarily broken up by some schoolkid shouting "beaner" or "wetback" as he went by in a car or bus. Then, just as quickly, someone might say "cabrones" or some word to that effect. Such words were never directed at the kids but they allowed the men to put the incident aside without actually having to talk about it.

Another important daily hub was the dining hall, where men could catch up on the day's activities at and away from the camp while they ate familiar Mexican dishes like *puerco en salsa verde, mole, picadillo,* or *barbacoa.* Dinnertime provided an opportunity to read and share letters received; reminisce about loved ones at home; and talk about dreams cherished and sought, and, more prosaically, about the daily grind. The dining hall also contained an altar for religious worship. It held an image of Christ and the Virgin Mary as well as candles and flowers. The dining hall, being the place where all the men congregated, also served as the place to discuss disagreeable conditions and even to take action. One such protest occurred when, in an effort to cut costs, Citrus Growers reduced the quality and quantity of food provided. In the dining hall, men made plans to stage a small protest in front of the dining hall, which they did. They were ultimately successful in pressuring the manager to speak up on their behalf with the company and getting the food they liked reinstated.

After dinner, the men left the dining hall and walked over to the area of the barracks. Here they might socialize in the eucalyptus field alongside the camp or go to their sleeping quarters—three men to a bunk—and seek to replenish themselves before the day of picking began anew.

For families, and in particular women, the working day would be a little longer than that of the single men. After they got home from a day of picking fruit, women would still need to prepare the family's dinner and clean up. Meals were therefore often simple: beans, some fried meat, salsa, maybe some eggs, and always tortillas. Occasionally, there were special dishes such as *nopales* in a chile sauce, or even more special, *chiles rellenos*. While three or four people sat around a small dining table in the tiny kitchen, the wife would heat tortillas for her husband and kids. Depending on the size of the family, she might have to do this in two shifts. While one "shift" was eating, others would be in other rooms, which were equally small.

Unlike the manager's home—which had two full bedrooms in addition to a kitchen, formal dining room, and living room—the rest of the family housing was small. The houses consisted of a kitchen, a bathroom with running water, a "living room," a bedroom, and a closet. Living rooms and closets doubled as bedrooms for families whose members ranged from a low of three to a high of six. Pancho Salinas, for example, who had migrated with his family from Michoacán, had three children and a wife. He and his wife slept in a double bed in the living room, which had a gas heater, while his youngest son and daughter shared the bedroom and his teenage daughter had a bed in the closet. Because there was so little space in the house, most people did their socializing out of doors in the backyards. Not that there was much time for socializing during the week. In my reminiscences I wrote,

> The smells of cooking, Zest soap, and earth are so intimately entangled that I can't think of one without the others, and certainly can't think of these smells without remembering how much we loved the adults being home. Too soon, however, it was time to end our socialization as the evening's activity had progressed from lying on top of the bed and planning futures to talking about sleep. Too soon it was time to start another day of picking oranges.

By 9:00 or 10:00 p.m. the lights in the camp would have gone out as most people were in bed.

Backyards

For families, Saturday and Sunday afternoons allowed some opportunity for relaxation, after the laundry had been done and the groceries for the week had been purchased. Relaxation took various forms: for those who had a television, sitting in front of it and watching sports and movies was a favorite diversion. For others, it meant going out for long drives, listening to music, or simply lying in bed and reading the ever-popular *fotonovelas* and comic books. Yet others spent time in their backyards. The backyards were places of both function and beauty that allowed for production, socialization, and play.

The backyard area consisted of approximately five hundred square feet per house. The area immediately adjacent to the houses consisted of hard-packed dirt that women would wet down with hoses or buckets in order to keep the dust down. Here one could find swings attached to awnings and maybe a few chairs. All of the backyards had clotheslines, which were constantly weighed down by wet laundry that had been washed by hand in a large tub, in an old-fashioned washing machine for those families lucky enough to have one under the awning, or by a coin-operated machine that families had to walk or drive to south of the camp. Many families used backyards to grow food and raise animals, and in so doing re-created Mexican rural landscapes. Pancho Sánchez, for example, planted a *milpa* replete with corn, squash, and beans. Immediately next door to Mr. Sánchez's house, "La Güera" kept a few chickens and rabbits that her husband would butcher for eating. Farther down the row of houses, Doña Monica likewise kept chickens under a magnificent large pepper tree. Doña Monica, who did not work in the fields, took great pride in her backyard, filling it with many kinds of flowers, herbs, and vegetables. My mom and dad, on the other hand, maintained a variety of fruit and nut trees as well as grapevines. In the summertime and through the fall we gathered peaches, apricots, plums, and walnuts.

It was in these backyards as well that families celebrated birthdays and anniversaries or simply got together with friends. In my recollections, I describe one of these birthday parties (figs. 5.1, 5.2):

The day of my sister's seventh birthday was one of those glorious Southern California days, with warm Santa Ana winds. On that day, both my sister and I were estrenando, wearing brand-new dresses for the special occasion and eagerly

FIGURE 5.1. A birthday party in El Campo, Escondido, 1970. (Courtesy of María de la Luz Ibarra)

awaiting the arrival of my cousins from Mexicali as well as cousins who lived in Escondido. Meanwhile preparations were taking place: tables and chairs were set outside, Mr. Salinas set up the rope and piñata on one of the many trees, my dad started playing some music—undoubtedly Eydie Gorme and Los Panchos—and my mom was in the kitchen marinating the meat for the carne asada, as well as getting together the ingredients for the rice, beans, and guacamole. Once our family and other guests arrived, the division of labor and space was immediate: the women would work in the kitchen, and the men would take care of the barbecue while drinking Coors beer out of a can sprinkled with lemon and salt. The kids would head toward the swing set or the area in front of the house, where we would play games we had learned in school as well as games that our Mexican cousins taught us. The kids were rarely in the company of the adults for very long, but we could hear from our own space how happy they were: singing was common, along with excited storytelling and reminiscing about childhoods and about relatives in Mexico. Too soon, however, the piñata had been broken, dinner and cake served, and our friends and relatives were heading back home. For a short amount of time, however, the backyard had been transformed into a place where Mexico and the United States fused; where the present and the past intermingled; and where, slowly, the idea that Escondido was home took root.

FIGURE 5.2. Hitting a piñata at the birthday party in El Campo, Escondido, 1970. (Courtesy of María de la Luz Ibarra)

Backyards were also places where children played on a regular basis, once the chores had been done. Sometimes we would play "cooties" on our bikes, spraying boys with a "stinky water" concoction we had made up to get them off our backs. Later in the day we might play "statues," hide-and-go-seek, or "grocery-store," or simply hang out at our "clubhouse." This was a derelict structure we had constructed on top of the train tracks that ran behind our homes. One game that has strong political undertones and that clearly stands out as a testament to how early in life children learned about Mexicans' precarious position in the community was "la migra":

> To play "la migra," one of us was chosen to be the notorious border patrolman. That child was instructed to park his or her bike next to a post that held up one of the awnings, stand at attention, and wait for civilians (the remainder of the kids) to come up and state their nationality. Imitating our parents' car border crossings, we remained on our bikes, came up to la migra, and then at will declared whether we had papers or no papers. If we declared no papers, we would make a dashing getaway, pumping away at the pedals as fast as we could, while the migra scrambled to get on her or his bike and chase after us. If the migra was able to tag us before we got to a previously designated "safe zone," then we

became the migra. If we were able to get away, however, we became "legals" and scored a point for ourselves. There would be many variations on this routine. We might declare ourselves to be legal, but surreptitiously carry a small cat under our shirts, or smuggle fruit or other forbidden products. Then, if la migra did not undertake a search and mistakenly let us go, we would yell something like "fooled you!" and the chase would begin anew. This routine would go on until someone—invariably la migra—got tired or one of us civilians could not think of more vexing, funny, or insulting things to declare.

The real-life game was not so funny, of course, and maybe that is why children re-created the scenes—as a way to get even with the uniformed men who suspended our sense of safety on the border and, frequently, in our backyards.

Conclusion: Migration and Mexican Places

Today, many older Mexicanos in Escondido remember the labor camp located on Quince and Valley Parkway as a place of beginnings in this once-thriving citrus community. It was here that families and single men worked long, hard days to make a living and support themselves in the United States. It was also here, however, that people re-created and created practices that produced a sense of belonging. Backyards, in particular, were important social spaces in which rural Mexican landscapes were reproduced and where recreation and play created a sense of Mexicanness, in both oppositional and non-oppositional contexts. As people outgrew their lives at the camp, many would settle in the surrounding industrial area known as the west side or would venture into other working-class neighborhoods. Over time, these settlers served as social networks for friends and relatives. By 1980, the Latino population had grown to represent 14 percent of the population (9,360 persons); in 1990, to 23 percent of the population (24,984 persons); and by the 2000 census, Mexicans accounted for fully 38 percent of the population (38,000 people). The labor camp is now a ghost landscape—no trace other than the eucalyptus trees is left of its existence: it was torn down in 1988 to make room for the North County Transit Center in a rapidly expanding city. Without excavating into memory and finding echoes of lives that create experience, it is impossible to understand the present reality that defines not only Escondido but also much of Southern California.

6

"¡SÍ, SE PUEDE!":
CHICANA/O ACTIVISM IN SAN DIEGO AT CENTURY'S END

Isidro D. Ortiz

During the last decades of the twentieth century in California, the Chicana/o and Latina/o population was often characterized as "a sleeping giant."[1] Stated in its most basic form, the thesis of the sleeping giant holds that Chicanas/os are a large group that have been politically inactive but could become far more influential. The thesis represents cultural deficiency thinking applied to the question of the political inequality of Chicanas/os in California.[2] This line of thinking locates the inequality in an alleged deficit in Chicana/o culture, specifically the absence of a culture of civic participation.

Careful consideration reveals that this thesis is problematic for several reasons. First, it treats Chicanas/os as if they were an isolated group, unaffected by societal institutions. Second, it denies Chicanas/os agency, albeit that scholars have documented otherwise.[3] Third, it denies the existence of oppression as a factor in the experience and standing of Chicanas/os in the state. Unfortunately, the applicability of the thesis to Chicanos in the concluding decades of the twentieth century has not been systematically assessed. Thus, the thesis has persisted as an accepted, valid description and explanation of Chicano political inequality.

That the thesis of the sleeping giant extended to Chicanas/os in San Diego was implied in at least one journalistic account, which portrayed them as passive observers in the border city.[4] Yet it is not accurate to characterize Chicanas/os in San Diego as politically apathetic during the last three and a half decades of the twentieth century, for during this period they forged a record of consistent, multidimensional activism. Over the twilight years of the twentieth century, individually and collectively, Chicanas/os engaged in direct and indirect forms of political action, in venues ranging from the streets, universities, and parks to electoral booths and courtrooms. Their activism was catalytic and conceptually seminal, as they exerted intellectual leadership throughout the decades. It produced concrete achievements and achieved visibility and influence beyond the boundaries of San Diego. Moreover, it reflected different forms of identity and consciousness. And it remained undaunted by oppression. Indeed, in addition to demonstrating the inapplicability of the thesis, their activism challenges the implied absence of oppression in the Chicana/o experience in California in the last century, for much of the activism in San Diego was a response to oppression. In San Diego, "America's Finest City," the oppression which the activists challenged was multidimensional. It included exploitation, the form of oppression recognized in one influential historical interpretation developed in the early 1980s, as well as other faces of oppression identified by scholars such as Iris Young; namely, cultural imperialism, marginalization, violence, and powerlessness.[5]

Chicana/o Activism: 1965–1975

On September 16, 1965, in Delano, California, Mexican farmworkers in the San Joaquin Valley under the leadership of César Chávez voted to join Filipino farmworkers in a *huelga* (strike) against the grape growers of California. Their action catalyzed the first phase of Chicano Movement activism in San Diego. That activism became part of a movement of students throughout California, many of whom were coming of age socially and politically but whose growing consciousness lacked a specific focus and outlet. As scholar Gustavo Segade observed, the huelga "offered an identification based on race and culture in a movement against social injustice. It was the place to go. Many students immediately went to Delano; others began the Huelga committees on the campuses. The Chicano Student Movement had begun."[6] As they mobilized throughout San Diego, the student activists echoed and implemented César Chávez's slogan "¡Sí Se Puede!" (it can be done). The mantra reflected a new sense of efficacy and faith in the power of organized collective action and a commitment to struggle for social change and social justice. Its adoption also reflected, as Segade observed, that the "Chicano road was to be a political power road, not love, peace, see you later baby!"[7]

In 1967 many of the new student activists attended a conference in Los Angeles and returned home speaking of the "Chicano" and "Chicanismo," reflecting their embrace of a new cultural identity. With a new identity in hand, these students challenged the oppression of cultural imperialism, calling for programs in Chicano studies. These programs, according to Segade, served two important functions for the students. First, "they exacted recognition from the hostile larger culture of a separate and legitimate cultural identity. Second, they provided the money and the access to resources needed to shape and explore that identity."[8] In San Diego, the initial target of these demands was San Diego State University, one of the oldest campuses in the California State University system.

In 1968 students—including Gus Chávez, Enriqueta Valenzuela, Felicitas Núñez, María Sánchez, Vivian Zermenio, Arturo Casarez, Arturo Ayala, Frank Cervantes, Matías Rico, Diana López, Irene Mercado, María Pedroza, Jorge Gonzales, Alurista, Eduardo Díaz, Rudy Sánchez, Tony Rivas, Jesús Méndez, Ernie Barrios, Sylvia Romero, Bert Rivas, and Bob Rodríguez—joined together under the banner of the Mexican American Youth Association (MAYA) to press for the creation of a department that would have as its mission instruction about the history, experiences, contributions, and roles of Chicanas/os in the United States. Gustavo Segade, one of a handful of Spanish-surnamed faculty on the campus, supported the students. To achieve their goals, the activists engaged in confrontation and disruption. The combined actions resulted in the creation of the first department of its kind in the United States, the Mexican American Studies Department. As created, the department's curriculum encompassed forty-one courses on Chicano history, the political and economic roots of the oppression of Chicanas/os, the educational experiences of Chicanas/os, barrio studies, the role of Chicanas/os in the American and Californian political systems, and American history from a Chicano perspective.[9] Through such courses, Chicanas/os would be able to develop and promote a counter-hegemonic self-interpretation, promote the decolonization of Chicano minds, develop leadership, and mobilize the resources of the university on behalf of the community. In spite of opposition to the department in circles across the campus, Segade recruited José Villarino, who in turn began to recruit additional faculty for the department. Ultimately, the faculty came to include Roberto Serros, Juan Gómez-Quiñones, Carlos Vélez-Ibáñez, Rene Núñez, Rita Sánchez, Gracia Molina de Pick, Mario García, Ricardo García, Irma Castro, Mateo Camarillo, Alurista, and Ricardo Griswold del Castillo. Moreover, the department provided a new paradigm of shared governance with extensive student participation.[10]

Across town in late spring 1968 Chicana/o students formed a chapter of MAYA at the fledgling University of California, San Diego (UCSD), campus. The students soon disrupted the UCSD administration's plan for a new college. In conjunction with black students, they formulated a program that called for the creation of Lumumba-Zapata College, an institution which, in the students' vision, could provide them and their peers with knowledge and training supportive of their struggle for liberation. As they struggled to formulate and realize their vision, the students mirrored the ideological diversity characteristic of the Chicano Movement. According to George Mariscal, "throughout the Lumumba-Zapata episode, the Chicana/o campus community was divided along sectarian, nationalist, internationalist, and socialist lines. Differences were often put aside in order to present a united front against the administration, but ideological divisions typical of Movement organizations of the period were real."[11]

In March 1969 more than fifty San Diego Chicana and Chicano activists took another step against cultural imperialism when they traveled to Denver to attend the first Chicano Youth Liberation Conference, sponsored by the Crusade for Justice. At the conference, Olivia Puentes-Reynolds voiced the internalized oppression under which many had labored, the new spirit of resistance to coercive assimilation, and the cultural nationalist consciousness that many of her generation had developed by 1969. The first Chicana to formally speak at the conference, she rose and read a poem that reflects these attitudes:

> I've heard Black is beautiful . . . but
> I WANT BROWN IS BEAUTIFUL
>
> NO MORE, WHITE MAN, NO MORE
> GAVACHO, GAVACHA
>
> I'm brown, I'm beautiful
> I'm a Chicana
>
> y sabes que, white man pig educator
> ¡no chinges conmigo más![12]

The most significant intellectual contribution at the conference was made by her fellow San Diegan, Alurista. He distinguished himself as the intellectual architect of the concept of Aztlán, the Chicano nation, thereby providing a conceptual basis for commonality among the hundreds of activists in attendance. As Segade noted, "For some time, there had been talk of acquiring lands and establishing separate Chicano communities. Not everyone could have land. But, everyone could share a mythic past, and the knowledge that their forebears were buried in lands now lost to strangers."[13]

Alurista penned "El Plan Espiritual de Aztlán," the conference's visionary document. He wrote,

> Brotherhood unites us, love for our brothers makes us a people whose time has come and who struggles against the foreigner "gabacho" who exploits our riches and destroys our culture. With our heart in our hand, our hands in the soil, we declare the independence of our mestizo nation. We are bronze people with a bronze culture. Before the world, before all of North America, before all of our brothers in the Bronze Continent, we are a Nation. We are a union of free pueblos. We are Aztlán.[14]

Aztlán became "the most enduring concept" and legacy of this Chicano movement event."[15] As activists did elsewhere in Aztlán, the new activists in San Diego also strove to overcome the oppression of powerlessness. Building upon the concept that organization and unity were the keys to power, activists such as Mateo Camarillo, David Rico, Rachel Ortiz, and Roger Cazares formed a plethora of community-based organizations, ranging from the Brown Berets to the Chicano Federation (an advocacy social service organization) to a chapter of the La Raza Unida Party, and the Barrio Station, a youth advocacy and service project.

The Chicana/o activists also contributed to organizations beyond the boundaries of San Diego. For example, Rene Núñez joined with other activists in Southern California to create the Chicano Coordinating Committee on Higher Education. Its purpose was "to develop a statewide network of community and campus activists who could put effective pressure on [university and college] campus administrators to expand equal educational opportunity programs to give proper attention to the needs of Mexican-American youth," a group which Núñez and others felt had been ignored in the antidiscrimination initiatives and equal-opportunity programs established during this era.[16] Subsequently, Núñez conceived a statewide conference where issues of student recruitment and retention and faculty hiring would be addressed. He also served on the steering committee for the event.

Núñez's initiative concluded in a conference in Santa Barbara, California, in April 1969. At the three-day gathering Núñez and other attendees crafted a master plan for Chicano higher education, "El Plan de Santa Bárbara." Moreover, student attendees created a new organization which encompassed the new identity and mythic concept of Aztlán, the Movimiento Estudiantil

Chicano de Aztlán (MEChA). "The new name reflected the students' vision of themselves as activists committed to militant struggle against the U.S. institutions that had historically been responsible for the oppression of Mexican Americans."[17]

Chicanas also continued to make contributions, the impact of which was felt beyond San Diego. Perhaps one of the most significant was the creation in October 1970 of Comisión Femenil Mexicana Nacional (CFMN), the first Chicana feminist organization. CFMN was cofounded by Gracia Molina de Pick, a longtime activist and one of the founding faculty members in Mexican American studies at San Diego State University.[18] CFMN and other organizations provided spaces where Chicanas/os could develop political resources, such as leadership, vital to competing within the political arena and addressing the needs of the diverse segments of the Chicano population.

Throughout Aztlán, Chicana/o activism was guided by the principle of self-determination. El Plan de Aztlán envisioned a Chicano nation, an entity seemingly to be achieved via separatism. Separatism was not a feasible course of action, however. Instead, protest—the strategy of the powerless—and community control became the operative daily strategies in the community. In the spring of 1970 such strategies led to the "taking" of land that ultimately became the site for a new park—Chicano Park (fig. 6.1). Through this action, "the myth of Aztlán metamorphosed to reality" on a piece of land in San Diego's oldest barrio, Barrio Logan.[19] On April 22, 1970, shortly after discovering bulldozers on the property, which was to be converted into a parking lot and headquarters for the California Highway Patrol, the residents of the barrio, as Kevin Delgado has noted, "gathered at the site to challenge the construction crew. . . . At nearby high schools and colleges, students left class to join demonstrations. . . . In order to coordinate the occupation of the land and to negotiate with state officials, community leaders formed the Chicano Park Steering Committee. The community remained united and refused to give up the land under the bridge."[20]

In 1970 Chicana/o cultural artists also employed the strategy of community control to create one of the first community-based and -focused Chicano cultural centers, El Centro Cultural de la Raza. Salvador Torres, an artist, joined with Alurista, Guillermo Aranda, Herminia Enrique, Victor Ochoa, and Mario Torero Acevedo to found the center in San Diego's Balboa Park. Initially created as an artists' collective, Toltecas en Aztlán, the center became the center of indigenous artistic contacts and exchanges, and provided space for cultural

FIGURE 6.1. Chicano students in what became Chicano Park in August 1970. The idea of painting murals on the pillars emerged spontaneously within a few weeks. (Courtesy of Salvador Torres)

exhibits and performances. It also institutionalized a forum for the expression of a counter-hegemonic cultural expression centered around the slogan "One continent, one culture."[21]

Throughout 1970 Chicanas and Chicanos in San Diego also protested the war in Vietnam, an action rooted in part in knowledge that Chicanas/os were dying at disproportionate rates in Vietnam while continuing to experience oppression at home. One, Ricardo Romo, became the gubernatorial candidate for the Peace and Freedom Party and promoted its antiwar platform.[22] Others, in addition to participating in local protests in San Diego, participated in organizing and attending the largest Chicano protest against the war, the Chicano Moratorium held on August 29, 1970, in East Los Angeles. Planned as a nonviolent event, the protest was disrupted by violence by law enforcement authorities. The experience proved to be traumatic, memorable, and painful, as Herman Baca, one of the many attendees, later recalled:

> As the police advanced, I witnessed scenes that I will never forget. Before my eyes, hundreds of our people—children, women, young and old persons—were beaten, tear-gassed, maimed and arrested.

The police and the sheriff's deputies appeared to be totally out of control and crazed with a desire to hurt, maim and kill Chicana/os.

Many of us remembered the zoot-suit riots, and it was 1940 all over again.

The experience also was instructive and became a turning point in Chicano activism, as Baca noted: "Things were never the same for Chicano movement activists. Many individuals fearful of police violence and government surveillance left the movement and never returned. A large number simply buckled down and started to 'work within the system,' while others . . . became angrier, lost their fear, and had their political resolve strengthened, and continued the struggle."[23]

Baca was among those who continued the struggle. In the succeeding months, the fruits of activism emerged. An educator, Peter Chacon, became the first Chicano from San Diego elected to the California State Assembly. Upon taking office he introduced and carried the legislation that implemented bilingual education in California public schools, an achievement that led to his designation as "the father of bilingual education" in the state.[24] The achievement also marked another victory against cultural imperialism.

Yet the need for activism became even more urgent as the early 1970s witnessed a significant increase in immigration from third world countries, especially Mexico, into California. This wave of immigration, primarily illegal and from Mexico and other Spanish-speaking countries, aroused a "new nativism" that triggered harsh new restrictions, policies, and practices.[25] The Immigration and Naturalization Service (INS) and the Border Patrol stepped up apprehensions and deportations. Across Southern California, the INS conducted raids in industrial, commercial, and residential areas, placing both citizens and noncitizens at risk for violation of their rights and deportation.

In the San Diego region, these official actions were accompanied by rallies and patrols by local chapters of the Ku Klux Klan. These actions were allegedly aimed at apprehending immigrants illegally crossing the U.S.–Mexico border, especially at San Ysidro. By the early 1970s, San Ysidro had become the busiest crossing point on the border.

In response to these developments, in 1971 Herman Baca created the Ad Hoc Committee on Chicano Rights (CCR) to protect the rights of Chicanas/os (fig. 6.2). Shortly after its formation, the group challenged the white supremacist mobilizations and the practices of local law enforcement authorities. For example, they protested a memorandum written by the San Diego County sheriff instructing taxicab drivers who suspected their passengers of being "illegal aliens"

FIGURE 6.2. A Committee on Chicano Rights press conference; pictured in center, left to right: Corky Gonzales, Herman Baca, and Bert Corona. (Courtesy of the Herman Baca Papers, Mandeville Special Collections Library, University of California, San Diego)

to call in a secret code to alert law enforcement authorities. The latter would then proceed to stop the cab and ask the passengers for immigration documents. As a result of the memorandum, as Baca noted, "Many Chicanos were being harassed and intimidated and, in most cases, simply refused cab service. This was a gross violation of our people's Fourth and Fourteenth Amendment rights to be free of search and seizure, the right to travel, as well as the right of equal protection under the law. We were just questioning, 'why just Chicana/os?'"[26] To achieve the rescindment of the memorandum, the CCR conducted a successful six-month campaign involving demonstrations, picketing, and letter writing.

Immediately thereafter, the organization waged a similar campaign against the police chief of San Diego, after he issued a similar memorandum and claimed that San Diego police had the right to search people. The CCR demanded that the chief be fired for illegal and unconstitutional acts against Chicanas/os. Its campaign lasted until the chief's termination in 1975, an outcome that encouraged Baca and the CCR to continue their activism.[27]

Chicana/o Activism in the Era of the New Nativism, Neoliberalism, and Neoconservatism

While Baca and the CCR challenged violent oppression, other Chicana/o activists addressed the oppression of powerlessness. In the mid-1970s, this face of oppression manifested itself in the absence of Chicana/o representation on the San Diego City Council, the governing board of the San Diego Unified School District, and the Board of Supervisors of San Diego County, the major public policymaking bodies in the city and county.

In 1975 representation on the San Diego City Council was achieved when an incumbent, Jim Bates, won election to the U.S. House of Representatives. Jess Haro, chairman of the Chicano Federation, accepted appointment to the city council to fill the remainder of Bates' term. He was inspired to run for a full term when the city council redrew Bates' former district into two predominantly minority and Democratic districts, Districts 4 and 8—enhancing the prospects for the election of Chicanas/os to the city council. Mobilizing Chicano and other support, Haro was elected from District 8 in 1976.[28]

The achievement of representation on the city council enabled the articulation of a Chicano perspective on municipal affairs in San Diego. A critical student voice on border-related issues and supportive of Chicano activism remained conspicuous by its absence. In 1975 the voice emerged and proceeded to become institutionalized when students at the University of California at San Diego created the *Voz Fronteriza* newspaper. Immediately after its creation, the newspaper rallied support for Herman Baca and the CCR as the federal government expanded its border control measures.[29]

In August 1977 President Jimmy Carter proposed increasing patrols of the U.S.–Mexico border through the addition of more than two thousand officers. Baca characterized the proposal as a "dangerous" idea that would lead to violation of civil rights. After the Ku Klux Klan announced that it planned to patrol the border, Baca and the CCR mobilized the support of a wide array of organizations and announced that any attempts by unofficial organizations to apprehend undocumented immigrants would be met with resistance. At a press conference Baca declared,

> These extremist, racist vigilante groups have declared their intent to roam the border areas, armed, with the stated purpose of apprehending Mexican-looking individuals.

We are here to state today that Chicano communities from the United States will not tolerate or meekly submit to terrorist harassment, intimidations, or interruption of our daily lives.[30]

In conjunction with other organizations, Baca and the CCR in early 1978 also wrote a report documenting sexual assaults against women by Border Patrol agents, beatings in Border Patrol detention centers, and "Gestapo-type" neighborhood sweeps in cities across the Southwest. Upon its completion, they presented the report to selected federal officials, including Senator Ted Kennedy, chairman of the Senate Judiciary Committee, a member of the Senate Select Commission on Immigration, and a candidate for the Democratic presidential nomination. After Kennedy did not respond to a request by Baca to meet with him and other Chicano activists to discuss violence along the border, Baca accused Kennedy of "stonewalling" on immigration and border issues. Baca also drew attention to the resumption of large-scale deportations and pointed out that undocumented immigration was being used to reduce or eliminate political gains made by Chicanos, such as bilingual education and bilingual ballots, a device that opponents alleged was enabling undocumented immigrants to vote in elections. Lastly, Baca condemned racism and the repression and scapegoating of undocumented workers.[31]

Several months later, Baca accused interim U.S. Attorney M. James Lorenz of failing to protect the civil rights of Mexican-origin individuals and of covering up abuses by Border Patrol agents. Subsequently, in January 1981, Baca and the CCR denounced a Supreme Court ruling that broadened the Border Patrol's authority to stop vehicles for investigation. They called the decision a "carte blanche" that would "in practice have the effect of targeting every person of Latino ancestry in the United States to the whims, impulses, and feelings of the INS, Border Patrol, or any law enforcement official."[32] The ruling made Latinas/os "sacrificial lambs" in the federal effort to control illegal immigration. Baca declared, "What the government has decided is that it's okay to take away our constitutional rights as long as they're trying to catch undocumented aliens." Baca also noted that the ruling was "disturbing" because it marked a growing pattern of anti-Chicano decisions. These included a 1976 Supreme Court ruling reinstituting on-land immigration checkpoints and an order by U.S. Attorney General Benjamin Civiletti lifting a ban on Border Patrol raids on workplaces suspected of employing undocumented immigrants. He also predicted, "Whatever might be said in defense of these actions, it's not the blue-eyed, blond-haired person that will be stopped. It's the

Mexican, the so-called foreign-looking individual."[33] In order to draw attention to and raise awareness of such actions, Baca also spoke to groups on immigration and granted interviews to the media.

In April 1981 President Ronald Reagan appointed Attorney General William French Smith to chair a panel charged with formulating a new immigration policy proposal. Immediately after the proposal was released, Chicano and Latino groups across the United States denounced it and coalesced to block its passage. In late 1981 Baca spoke in Washington on behalf of more than two hundred groups and called for a campaign of national resistance against the proposal. Subsequently, he criticized the plan point by point, comparing it to the slavery issues of the eighteenth century and describing it as "a colossal attempt by the Reagan Administration to subsidize the interests of big business which will be the only group benefiting from it." As part of his campaign against the proposal, Baca also offered solutions to the immigration problem. Specifically, he called for the abolishment of the INS as a step toward the creation of an equitable system of immigration. To his fellow Chicanas/os he declared, "As Chicanos, we must find the solution in our community. We can't expect the government to do it for us. There is a great need to organize, educate, and politicize."[34] Baca's analysis was embraced by several young nationalist Chicanos. In 1981 Ernesto Bustillos, Jeffrey Garcilazo, David Rico, and other activists, organized La Unión del Barrio with the purpose of raising the consciousness of Chicanas/os and advocating for the rights of Chicanas/os as part of a militant struggle for "Chicano liberation."[35] Shortly after its formation, the organization launched a series of protests against the Border Patrol, denouncing the agency's brutality against Chicanas/os as part of a larger pattern of governmental oppression against Chicanas/os.

La Unión also joined with other Chicano Movement organizations to create Chicanos in Solidarity with the People of Central America (CHISPA) Coalition. The coalition waged a campaign to close down the INS Service Centers that were being used to house political refugees from Central America who were facing deportation. The activists strove to connect the issue of American intervention in Central America with the Chicanas/os struggle against governmental oppression. La Unión also expanded the boycott of the Adolph Coors Brewing Company for alleged discrimination against Chicanos in hiring practices and conducted educational activities aimed at raising public consciousness and understanding on issues ranging from counterinsurgency in Central America to Chicano studies to the role of multinational corporations in the oppression of la raza and other nationalities. It also promoted unity forums among the activists.[36] Unfortunately, the initial unity was not in the context envisioned by the activists.

Unity in grief was achieved in July 1984, when an unemployed welder, James Oliver Huberty, convinced that immigrants were to blame for his employment problems, walked into a fast-food restaurant in the San Diego community of San Ysidro armed with an array of weapons. He proceeded to murder twenty people and injure fifteen others, the majority of whom were of Mexican descent. Known as the San Ysidro Massacre, the event dramatically and poignantly illuminated the increasing anti-immigrant sentiment in the border region and achieved notoriety as "the largest mass murder in American history" to that date.[37]

Activists and non-activists across San Diego responded to the tragedy in a number of ways; some challenged the claim of public officials that the tragedy was unrelated to the new nativism.[38] For example, Pepe Villarino and Oscar Galván commemorated the tragedy in a *corrido* (ballad) that voiced and validated the community-based counter-perspective that the violence had nativist and racist roots:

> When they were on the floor
> He fired and assassinated the people
> The bodies of the innocent victims
> Lay scattered everywhere . . .
>
> The town of San Ysidro
> Already knew of his emotions
> That he hated Mexicans
> And that his plan was preconceived.
>
> So you see, my brothers and sisters
> With his actions well planned,
> His dislike for "La Raza"
> And this is what resulted.[39]

As the campaign to reduce border crossings and erect barriers at the border gained momentum across the United States, David Avalos, an artist based at the Centro Cultural de la Raza, defied the trend in June 1984, by spearheading a new cross-border and interethnic alliance. In conjunction with Sara-Jo Berman, Isaac Artenstein, Guillermo Gómez-Peña, Michael Schnorr, Jude Eberhardt, and fellow Centro artist Victor Ochoa, Avalos founded the Border Arts Workshop/

Taller de Arte Fronterizo arts collective (BAW/TAF), which initiated pioneering discussions and activities that made strategic use of art to critique border politics and imagine a utopian, borderless future. Shortly after its creation, the BAW/TAF addressed these goals through a series of "extraordinary" artworks ranging from installations to site-specific performance art.[40] The actions were timely, as public concern over immigration and border issues gained momentum, much to the chagrin and dismay of activists such as Avalos and Baca.

In late 1986 Congress passed, and President Reagan signed, the Immigration Reform and Control Act of 1986 (IRCA). Baca and other Chicano activists immediately criticized the legislation as legalizing "exploitation, racial discrimination and false promises" through its authorization of guest workers, employer sanctions, and amnesty provisions, and as reflecting "a massive capitulation" of labor and liberals to the "tremendous pressures" of the "anti-Mexican hysteria" across the United States. Baca also alleged that Hispanic congressional representatives and advocacy organizations, which had endorsed the legislation, had "sold out."[41]

IRCA served as a first step toward regularizing the status of approximately 2.5 million immigrants living in the United States; however, it left many others more vulnerable than before to abuse and exploitation. In response, the American Friends Service Committee Border Program initiated the Immigration Law Enforcement Monitoring Project (ILEMP). The project was designed to protect the human rights of those fleeing across the U.S.–Mexico border and address the societal response to their search for security and respect. To achieve these goals, the project emphasized investigation and documentation. In San Diego, Roberto Martínez assumed responsibility for these activities. (See chapter 9 for Martínez's personal account of his experiences.)

As Martínez assumed his new role, other Chicano activists addressed the oppression of powerlessness. In the 1970s, California Governor Edmund "Jerry" Brown had "tilted" the state government toward Mexican Americans, appointing Mexican Americans to various positions in the executive branch.[42] The new appointees included Celia Ballesteros, a San Diego attorney who was appointed to the California State University Board of Trustees, making her the first Chicana to serve on this policymaking body in the history of California. Besides making history, the appointment enabled Ballesteros to begin to develop the credentials for holding elected office in a community where the absence of representation by Chicanas/os in government had been explained by some observers as a function of the lack of individuals with appropriate qualifications.

In 1983 she declared her candidacy for the District 8 seat, placing her in opposition to Uvaldo Martínez. Martínez had chosen to seek election to the seat after being appointed to serve the remainder of Haro's term when Haro resigned after pleading guilty to a misdemeanor stemming from personal business dealings. The Chicano voters in District 8, a predominantly Democratic district, supported Ballesteros, a Democrat, in the primary. However, Martínez, a Republican was elected by voters citywide in the general election, much to the dismay of Chicano activists, who desired strong advocacy and promotion of Chicano interests.

In 1986, Ballesteros became a member of the city council when Martínez was removed after being convicted of misusing his city-issued credit card. Ballesteros' appointment was on the condition that she not run for re-election, however, making the maintenance of representation for Chicanas/os problematic. And, in November 1987, Chicana/o representation ended when Robert Filner defeated Michael Aguirre, the candidate supported by the Chicano Federation, in the District 8 runoff election.[43]

Aguirre's defeat again highlighted the barrier for Chicano candidates posed by the city's at-large election system (where the primaries are conducted by ward but the general election is citywide). As Ballesteros had learned earlier, the election system, among other things, imposed the financial burden of running a citywide political campaign, which few Chicano candidates could bear. Aguirre's defeat underscored that "playing by the rules" was unlikely to translate into actual representation. Therefore, Chicanas/os decided to focus their efforts on leveling the playing field. One of the major legacies of the Chicano Movement, the Chicano Federation, spearheaded this challenge to the rules. First, it joined with several organizations to form Neighborhoods for District Elections (NDE) and began waging a campaign to establish a by-district election system. Next, it sought to capitalize on a historic development six years earlier, the passage of the 1982 Voting Rights Act.

Historically, the federal government had refrained from intervening to protect the voting rights of Chicanas/os. For example, the Voting Rights Act of 1965 protected the voting rights of African Americans but did not address Mexican Americans. Consequently, Chicanas/os continued to be denied their full voting rights by local and state governmental authorities. In 1975 Congress departed from its noninterventionist stance by passing the Voting Rights Act (VRA) of 1975, which did offer protections of Mexican American voting rights. Electoral discrimination continued to plague Chicanas/os, however. In 1982 Congress reauthorized and extended the VRA after extensive lobbying by Chicanas/os. The VRA of 1982, in conjunction with subsequent court decisions, provided mechanisms for combating electoral discrimination. In enacting the VRA of 1982 the federal government, particularly Congress, signaled a willingness to encourage the full enfranchisement of Mexican Americans in communities such as San Diego where they had confronted perceived electoral discrimination since the latter part of the nineteenth century. The federal actions also provided a new opportunity for Chicanas/os to achieve representation on local governmental bodies.

On January 25, 1988, the Chicano Federation filed a class-action lawsuit, *Chicano Federation and Mirna Pérez v. City of San Diego*, alleging that the city's at-large election system and the division of city council districts had disenfranchised Latino voters, excluding them from meaningful participation in the political process. According to the suit, the city's electoral practices violated the Voting Rights Acts of 1975 and 1982 by "diluting" the impact of the Chicano vote to the point where it had no effect. The Federation also claimed that San Diego city officials had engaged in intentional discrimination against Latino voters by "fracturing" their communities through the districting process.[44]

While the Chicano Federation pursued its litigation, Roberto Martínez and other activists sustained their campaign to stop violence against undocumented workers. As the 1990s began, such actions became more urgent as the violence continued and, in the view of Martínez and other activists, escalated across the border region.

Thus, in early 1991, the American Friends Service Committee U.S.–Mexico Border Program, under Martínez's leadership, joined with other organizations on both sides of the border to organize a protest at the border fence after the shooting of a young boy by a U.S. Border Patrol agent. More than 150 demonstrators from the United States met with a slightly larger group from Mexico and linked fingers in a show of "binational unity." They decried the Border Patrol's "record of violence with impunity" and called for civilian oversight of the agency.[45]

Subsequently, Roberto Martínez and the Border Program sponsored a three-day investigation of border violence by the Border Violence Delegation Project, a coalition led by the Mexican American Legal Defense and Education Fund with other immigrant and civil rights organizations. The investigation included hearings, which served as another forum to call for the creation of a civilian review board to oversee complaints of Border Patrol abuse.[46]

Approximately one month later, Martínez and the Border Violence Delegation Project again alleged widespread abuse by Border Patrol agents. Rejecting the "border is out of control" narrative of immigration opponents, he charged, "It's not the border that is out of control; it's the Border Patrol that is out of control." Martínez and the project claimed chronic harassment and unprovoked arrests by San Diego police, who were allegedly systematically questioning the residents of two neighborhoods regarding their citizenship status. They then convened a press conference to report data showing that 149 victims in the city of San Diego claimed to have suffered a total of 405 abuses at the hands of law officers—primarily Board Patrol agents—during the preceding two years. After reporting the data, Martínez and the project again called for a civilian review board.[47]

In October Martínez and the U.S.–Mexico Border Program, in conjunction with other Latino organizations, criticized a pro–law enforcement organization, the Stamp Out Crime Council (SOCC), for its sponsorship of a conference on illegal immigration. Described as an attempt to examine the relationship between undocumented immigration and crime, the environment, quality of life, public schools, and American institutions, the conference was criticized as divisive and improper by Martínez and the other activists.[48] Subsequently, in 1992 Martínez and the project joined activists from La Raza Rights Coalition and other Chicano and non-Chicano organizations in a counter-protest against a protest at the border organized by American Spring, a white supremacist organization calling for the military to seal the U.S.–Mexico border. In response to shouts of "white power," Martínez and the other activists denounced the American Spring protest and issued a call for an end to "immigrant bashing and hate mongering."[49] Several weeks later Martínez and other activists expressed concerns about the Border Patrol's policy regarding pursuits of vehicles suspected of transporting undocumented immigrants, when a pursuit concluded in a collision at a busy intersection in the suburban community of Chula Vista. They also criticized a plan developed by the California Highway Patrol to remove undocumented immigrants from the shoulders and medians of freeways as a way of reducing the frequency of pedestrian deaths and other accidents. According to the Highway Patrol, the exclusive goal of the project was to clear the freeways of pedestrians rather than to arrest undocumented immigrants. Martínez disagreed, characterizing the effort as a "veiled attempt" to hand migrants over to the Border Patrol.[50]

In an effort to enhance the accountability of the Border Patrol, Martínez and the program joined with other organizations, including the California Rural Legal Assistance and the Federal Defender of San Diego, to form the San Diego

Coalition for Border Patrol Accountability. In late August the coalition "warned that a widely praised federal plan to add agents to the Border Patrol was flawed unless it included an independent board to investigate alleged abuses." The board was "needed at time when the country's strong anti-immigration mood appeared to be shielding the Border Patrol from criticism and closer scrutiny." They urged passage of a bill introduced in May in the U.S. House of Representatives that would create a seven-member commission to investigate complaints of human rights violations committed by the INS and the U.S. Customs Service.[51]

After an undocumented worker was fatally shot near the U.S.–Mexico border as he attempted to scale a wall in a private yard to reach Interstate 5 in San Ysidro, Martínez blamed anti-immigrant feelings for the incident. Shortly thereafter, the coalition's Pro-Derechos de La Raza/Raza Rights Coalition called a press conference to demand that the shooting be prosecuted as a hate crime. Classifying the shooting as a hate crime would add five years to the shooter's sentence if he were convicted. Speaking for the coalition, Paul Aceves portrayed the incident as "another example of violence based on bigotry," attributable to the adoption of a "vigilante mentality" rooted in a "brown scare hype being pushed on people by the government and law enforcement."[52]

The coalition also organized the Public Tribunal on Police and Border Patrol Violence. At the forum on May 29 Aceves, Martínez, and others speaking on behalf of the Raza Rights Coalition and the Border Violence Project declared that the San Diego Police Department and the Border Patrol were "persecuting Latinos and blacks indiscriminately" and that abuses by both agencies were increasing in San Diego. Héctor Ríos noted, "We're under a siege of terror." He reiterated the call for the resignation of Gustavo de la Vina, head of the Border Patrol's San Diego Sector who, he said, was "being used by the system to carry out a campaign of terror against his own people."[53]

La Unión del Barrio also endorsed a labor strike called by drywallers in Southern California. By the early 1990s, foreign-born workers, especially from Mexico and Central America, had become the core workforce of this segment of the construction industry in the region. Such workers were ignored by most labor unions because of their presumed unorganizability due to their vulnerability to deportation, limits on their rights, and alleged lack of interest in unionization. So the workers mobilized themselves to resist exploitation. In so doing, they challenged the claim that they were impossible to unionize.[54] By June 1992 they had experienced successes in halting some residential construction from San Diego to Los Angeles. Workers in San Diego, however, were meeting with vigorous resistance from employers and local authorities and lacked logistical support. Ríos and other members of La Unión provided logistical support throughout 1992.[55] The workers also garnered the support of Roberto Martínez and other Chicano activists.

In February 1993 Roberto Martínez joined with other leaders of Latino community organizations from throughout California to devise a statewide strategy against "immigrant bashing." They founded a new statewide organization, the Latino Civil Rights Action Network, intended to assist immigrant-rights advocates in developing "a stronger and more consistent effort throughout the state," and "set the groundwork" for a "massive campaign" against the initiatives that anti-immigrant forces were seeking to place on the ballot.[56]

Martínez and other activists also continued to question the allegedly high costs for public services associated with undocumented immigrants in California. In May, after Governor Wilson filed a lawsuit against the federal government in order to secure reimbursement for the cost of services provided to undocumented immigrants, Martínez denounced the action, called for new leadership, and exhorted fellow Latinas/os to lobby against an anti-immigrant initiative— Proposition 187, which would bar illegal immigrants from receiving state health care, education, and welfare benefits—that Governor Wilson was championing in his re-election campaign.[57]

Martínez's activism was complemented by an act of creative defiance. Joaquín McWhinney, the founder and lead singer of the local reggae band Big Mountain, wrote and began to perform a song entitled "Border Town." In the song McWhinney challenged the tourist industry–promoted image of San Diego as paradise, the demonization of immigrants, and the increasing attempts to draw distinctions among the Mexican-origin population on the basis of citizenship. The song also illuminated everyday violence in the border town of San Diego, established solidarity with undocumented workers, recalled overlooked history, and challenged the hypocrisy of immigrant scapegoating, with these lyrics:

> Living in a border town
> You see good men get pushed around
> It's not hard to see that they are my brothers
> If it weren't for fate
> We might be each other

Living in a border town
You see women and children get hunted down
Silly fools in their big green vans
Officiously attempting to keep our people from their fatherlands

How can we call these people aliens when
We here are standing on stolen ground
Oh and them wanna keep a mystery
The biggest scam in all of history[58]

In July 1994, the Chicano Federation and other groups that shared a liberal ideological orientation formed San Diegans Against 187 (SDAG 187) and initiated a campaign to defeat the proposition. In its campaign, SDAG 187 appealed to reason and to Chicanos' and other Latinos' self-interest by emphasizing the initiative's threat to their civil rights. SDAG 187 also contested the argument that Proposition 187 was not anti-immigrant and race related, as some of the initiative's supporters claimed.[59]

During July and August, members of SDAG 187 sent representatives to forums on 187 and meetings of organizations such as the Anti-Defamation League; developed information summaries on developments related to 187 and mailed them to Latinas/os in San Diego County; sponsored briefings on 187 by organizations such as the Mexican American Legal Defense and Education Fund; and launched voter registration drives. In early September the organization held a rally in downtown San Diego.[60] Opposition to Proposition 187 by SDAG 187 and other organizations was fueled by the launching on October 1 of a new initiative by the INS under the leadership of the U.S. attorney general for the border region, Alan Bersin. Dubbed Operation Gatekeeper, the initiative was designed to stem illegal entry south of San Diego through flooding the westernmost section of the border with Border Patrol agents.[61] SDAG 187 and other Chicano immigrant advocates declared that the initiative was actually aimed at reducing the visibility of border crossings in the San Diego area and would merely shift the movement of undocumented immigrants eastward into the deserts, where the harsh environment would exact a fatal cost on the immigrants.

SDAG 187 also attempted to influence and channel the responses of high school and college students who were angered by the proposition. In late October and November, the students publicly articulated their anger in a series of walkouts and marches in opposition to the ballot measure. On November 7, for example, hundreds of students walked out of Gompers Secondary School and Memorial Junior High School in San Diego and marched to Chicano Park, where they held a rally against Proposition 187.[62]

As they marched, many students waved Mexican flags to demonstrate their pride in a heritage that they perceived to be under attack. Like their counterparts, these students waged their protests in the face of discouragement from SDAG 187 and repeated efforts by administrators to channel their anger in ways that kept them on the campuses. A student leader of the protests declared

> Who cares if people didn't like us marching down the street? We wanted to show people we weren't scared of making noise and that the next generation was growing up and becoming aware of what is going wrong in the United States of America.
>
> If I have 150 people coming to me asking me "Come on, let's do something," and I'm pretty much the leader, I'm not going to tell them to go back inside. If I can't suppress my feelings towards something I feel is racist, how can I expect them to not feel the same?[63]

Still other students joined chapters of MEChA or formed new chapters of the organization, in anticipation of the advent of additional anti-immigrant and anti-Latino developments in the future. As a result extant chapters of MEChA were invigorated and ten new chapters of the organization emerged on secondary campuses.[64]

The youths' resistance was endorsed and welcomed by La Unión del Barrio and the Raza Rights Coalition, because the student protests were consistent with their effort to raise consciousness and promote mobilization as part of a campaign to build a liberation movement. Once it became clear that the initiative would be on the ballot, the organizations attempted "to expose 187 as part of a major campaign against Mexicans and other oppressed people." In contrast to analyses that treated the proposition as the result solely of demagoguery on the part of Governor Wilson and the handiwork of a few nativists, La Unión, under the leadership of Ernesto Bustillos, linked the proposition to recent global political developments, in particular the rise of neoliberalism. La Unión declared that Proposition 187 was "part of the New World Order to keep Mexicans colonized."[65] This analysis carried the potential to move political thinking beyond the city, region, and state and enhance understanding of the consequences of globalization and the rise of neoliberalism.

As predicted by the findings of voter surveys, voters approved Proposition 187 in late November. Shortly thereafter the proposition's constitutionality was successfully challenged. Buoyed by the action, SDAG 187 began to disseminate information about the status of the proposition, the rights of undocumented immigrants, and possible actions of law enforcement authorities. They also continued to encourage students to become involved in electoral politics and encouraged Mexicans to become naturalized.[66] The latter effort evoked a responsive chord among many Mexican immigrants, for whom the advent and passage of the proposition became a political turning point. Immediately after the passage of the proposition, many eligible immigrants began the process to achieve naturalization and subsequently registered to vote.[67] In a rebuke of the Republican Party and Governor Pete Wilson, who had ridden the initiative to re-election, many of the subsequent new citizens embraced the portrayal of Wilson and the Republican Party as foes and registered as Democrats. Their alienation from the Republican Party was affirmed shortly thereafter by a new development.

In early 1995 the anti-immigrant sentiment across the United States expressed itself in the introduction of legislation in the U.S. House of Representatives that would deny automatic citizenship to children born in the United States to illegal immigrants. Republican Congressman Brian Bilbray, who represented the district encompassing the San Diego suburb of Imperial Beach, introduced the legislation. Chicanas/os in San Diego immediately criticized Bilbray's proposal.[68]

In January 1996 the Clinton administration announced that it was increasing the number of U.S. Army personnel stationed along the California and Arizona border as part of a new multi-agency effort to curb immigration. The initiative was aimed at preventing the anticipated seasonal increase in illegal border crossings after the new year, as workers who had gone home for the Christmas holidays returned to work in the United States. Roberto Martínez criticized the initiative as "low intensity warfare."[69]

In early April Riverside County sheriff's deputies were videotaped beating two undocumented immigrants, an incident that attracted international attention to the issue of abuse of undocumented immigrants. One week after the incident, Martínez and other Latino activists used it to draw attention to abuse of undocumented workers in San Diego County, alleging that excessive force was frequently used against undocumented workers in San Diego County.

Several weeks later, on May 21, a coalition of Chicano organizations—including the Chicano Federation, the Latina/Latino Unity Coalition, California

Rural Legal Assistance, La Raza Lawyers Association, and other organizations—held a press conference at the San Diego airport to protest the actions of a vigilante-style organization, the U.S. Citizens Patrol. In April this "posse" had been scouring the airport in search of undocumented immigrants, stopping and questioning "suspected illegal aliens."[70]

With the "neutralization" of the Citizens Patrol accomplished, the Federation, under the leadership of David Valladolid, spearheaded the organization of a National Unity Summit during the Republican Convention, which was to be held in San Diego. The mission of the summit was "to exhort American voters to reject the increasingly hateful and dishonest campaign being waged against Latinas/os." As conceived by the Federation, the summit would bring together leaders of national, state, and local Latino organizations to discuss strategy, hold a national press conference, promote citizenship, and exhort the Latino community to vote in the November elections. The coalition also joined with the American Civil Liberties Union and other organizations in successful litigation against the city of San Diego and the Republican National Committee after city authorities relocated the site for demonstrations during the Republican Party National Convention. The suit claimed that the new site infringed on the constitutional right of protesters to be seen and heard during the convention.

On August 13 the Chicano Federation held its planned Latino summit. More than three hundred participants attended the conference, including representatives of the National Council of La Raza, the Southwest Voter Registration and Education Project, the United Farm Workers, the Mexican American Legal Defense and Education Fund, the American GI Forum, the National Association of Latino Elected Officials, the League of United Latin American Citizens, MEChA, and the U.S. Hispanic Chamber of Commerce. Together they denounced the "politics of fear and scapegoating" against Latinas/os by the Republican and Democratic parties, and resolved to work together to strengthen Latino political power.[71]

La Unión del Barrio, under the auspices of the National Chicano Movement Committee (NCMC), also protested at the Republican National Convention. The NCMC organized the two-day National Raza Unity Conference and on August 12 conducted the National Raza March against the Republican National Convention. Unlike the National Latino Summit, these activities were designed to advance the movement toward self-determination for the Chicano/Mexican people.[72]

The intensity of the anti-immigrant hostility made activism on the issue of immigration imperative. However, it did not preclude activism on other issues. Like elsewhere in the Southwest, education and youth attracted the energy and efforts of Chicanas and Chicanos in the face of intense and growing campaigns against the programmatic gains of the late 1960s and early 1970s.

In the late 1990s in San Diego, collective activism on educational issues built upon work begun in 1987 when the Reverend Vahac Maradorsian, retired pastor and activist, and Dr. Alberto Ochoa, professor of education at San Diego State, invited parents to discuss the social conditions, the school system, and the low educational achievement of their children at Sherman Elementary School. Chicano students comprised 99 percent of the student body. The school ranked at the bottom of the 109 elementary schools of the San Diego Unified School District. The initial dialogue evolved into eight weeks of two-hour weekly sessions with more than ninety parents from the school. In the subsequent eight-week discussion with parents, fifty-four areas of concern were documented and the parents issued a mandate to expand the discussions to other schools in the district. The mandate provided the impetus for the creation of the Parent Institute for Quality Education (PIQE). As envisioned by the parents and educators, the mission of PIQE was to "bring schools, parents and community together as equal partners in the education of every child." The objectives of PIQE were to encourage and support low-income, ethnically diverse parents of elementary- and middle-school children in taking a participatory role in assisting their children "by increasing the parents' knowledge and skills." PIQE was to develop and implement a model for increasing parent involvement in K–12 schools, where parental participation had been difficult to achieve in the past. The tools were to be "informal education techniques that have been promoted by Paulo Freire and others dedicated to promoting social change, such as using dialogue to build community and social capital, situating educational activity in the lived experiences of participants and raising participants' consciousness about their situations and their own power to take informed action."[73]

In 1990 the first Latino Educational Summit was held. Convened by the Chicano Federation, the meeting brought together more than one hundred parents, educators, and students. They identified and discussed points of concern regarding the low academic achievement of Latino students in the public schools and colleges in the county. Two years later, some student attendees of the summit took a step toward "turning around the grim statistics concerning Latino student achievement," by founding Izcalli, a year-round free Saturday school for young Chicanas/os. To combat cultural imperialism, the sessions provided information on indigenous Mexican/Chicano cultural heritage and utilized it as a foundation for improving the youths' economic and social circumstances.[74]

Izcalli's founder, Victor Chávez Jr., sought the assistance of active or former members of the San Diego State University chapter of MEChA, because Izcalli represented the extension of MEChA's emphasis on education in a community context and "giving back to the community." As they had done since the creation of MEChA at the historic Santa Barbara conference, MEChistas at SDSU, such as Tomás Carrasco, Lalo Alcaraz, Joe Lara, Carmen Chávez, Carlos Razo, Carmen Moffet, Cynthia Torres, and Eddie Torres, organized annual high school conferences to promote interest in enrollment in higher education among high-school students.[75] The Association of Chicana Activists (AChA), which began to hold conferences specifically addressing the issue of access for young Chicanas, followed this lead. Like the MEChistas, Achistas such as founders Guadalupe Corona and Silvia Bustamente also countered the Eurocentric curriculum, promoted cultural resilience, and celebrated a spirit of resistance and independence by celebrating the Cinco de Mayo and Mexican Independence Day holidays.

In addition, with MEChA, Achistas successfully mobilized to capture elected and appointed positions in the Associated Student Government at SDSU. Once in office, students such as Celinda Vásquez, César Padilla, Memo Mayer, and José Preciado used their positions to articulate and advocate for admission and retention practices and policies that would enhance access to and continuation in the university by Chicano and other Latino students.[76] Moreover, they mobilized against the violence against undocumented workers, joining the marches, rallies, and demonstrations organized by Roberto Martínez, La Unión del Barrio, the Raza Rights Coalition, and SDAG 187. In their protests, they literally and symbolically questioned the legitimacy of anti-immigrant advocates and implicitly reasserted the indigenous roots of Chicanas/os and Mexican undocumented workers, carrying signs that posed the question: "Who's the Illegal Alien, Pilgrim?"

In 1996 the MEChistas joined organizations throughout San Diego ranging from the Chicano Federation to the American Civil Liberties Union in opposition to Proposition 209, the California Civil Rights Initiative, which would eliminate most affirmative action programs for women and minorities operated by state and local governments in California. As part of its education campaign, the activists conducted teach-ins, marches, and rallies. The goals of the campaign included dispelling myths about affirmative action, informing the public about the benefits of and continuing need for affirmative action, and increasing the number of students registered to vote in the forthcoming election.[77]

MEChistas also renewed and extended the celebration of Chicanos' indigenous roots by participating in Sundance Ceremonies, Azteca dance troupes, and the Latino/Indigenous Peoples' Unity Coalition organized by elders such as Olivia Puentes-Reynolds, Mario Aguilar, and Luis Natividad, as well as by supporting the Zapatista movement in Mexico. They attempted to keep the concept of Aztlán and the memory of struggle and victory alive by contributing to the annual Chicano Park Day celebration. They also supported the continuing efforts by the United Farm Workers to sustain the legacy of César Chávez, inviting leaders of the organization to speak on campus and conducting education campaigns to raise consciousness among their peers regarding "La Causa," the farmworkers' cause. After Chávez's death, MEChistas such as Pedro Anaya called for the designation of César Chávez's birthday as a state holiday. Across town at the University of California, San Diego, MEChistas and other Chicana/o activists pursued similar actions.

As the student activists struggled on campus, the San Diego County Latino Coalition in Education mobilized to address the educational achievement gap in the San Diego Unified School District. Created in 1997, after the second Latino Summit on Education, the coalition consisted of Chicano/Latino organizations from throughout the county, including the Chicano Federation, the Mexican/American Business and Professional Association, and MANA: a national Latina organization. Under the leadership of Dr. Alberto Ochoa and Olivia Puentes-Reynolds the coalition focused on the "English for the children" initiative, which would mandate English-only instruction in California public schools. Adopting James Crawford's analysis that for Ron Unz, the initiative's sponsor, "the assault on bilingual education served a broader neo-conservative agenda" and reflected his goal of dismantling the social programs and civil rights reforms of the 1960s, the coalition informed parents and educators about the initiative and urged them to reject it.[78]

Likewise, at San Diego State University, MEChA recognized that the gains of earlier decades were at risk of being lost. Thus, when it hosted the annual statewide MEChA conference in March 1998, the chapter adopted the theme "Protegiendo nuestro pasado para asegurar nuestro futuro" (Protecting our past to secure our future) and focused on educating other MEChistas about the urgency of preserving bilingual education and other programs and about the continuing need for collective action. Speaking on behalf of the Steering Committee for the conference, Carlos Razo and Arturo Cervantes declared, "The struggle for quality education into the next century continues."[79]

Coinciding with the last day of the conference, the Board of Education of the San Diego Unified School District offered Alan Bersin the post of superintendent of the San Diego Unified School District. At the time Bersin continued to serve as the "border czar" under whose leadership Operation Gatekeeper and the militarization of the border had become institutionalized.

Bersin's appointment provoked opposition from members of the Latino Coalition. They denounced Bersin as "anti-Latino" and an unacceptable choice for the position. However, when they were unable to sway the board, they grudgingly accepted Bersin's appointment and began to monitor his actions. In contrast, La Unión del Barrio mounted an extensive campaign against Bersin's appointment, the "Fuera Bersin!" campaign. With the objective of raising consciousness about the attacks on the educational gains of Chicanos, the campaign included protests and community outreach activities. La Unión also engaged in muckraking through its newspaper, *La Verdad*. The organization criticized the selection process as undemocratic, analyzed how it had come about, denounced the limited response of self-described Latino advocates, and assessed the results of its campaign to draw lessons for future activism. Then it turned its attention to analyzing Proposition 227, an English-only ballot initiative.[80]

After the passage of Proposition 227 in June 1998, activists increasingly turned their attention to the threats posed to youth by the advent of a new proposition, Proposition 21, the Juvenile Crime Initiative, which would toughen punishments for juveniles and expand the prosecution of juveniles in adult courts. Scheduled to appear on the March 2000 ballot, the initiative was promoted as a deterrent to juvenile crime by its sponsors, who included Governor Pete Wilson. Its appearance evoked differential strategic assessments and prescriptions from the Chicano activists. As *Voz Fronteriza* declared

> The reality is that only by organizing our community to defend our human and civil rights will our people be able to feel justice. Proposition 21 is a step to stop our people's ability to organize and wage a struggle for freedom and dignity. Proposition 21 is specifically designed to attack the future generations of our people by targeting youth. To the gringos and rich capitalist ruling class, this is

a key component in maintaining their power over our gente, because by incarcerating our young people they defuse the revolutionary potential of an entire population.[81]

La Verdad and other opponents of the initiative faced an uphill battle, but they were not deterred by the odds against them. The last two decades of the twentieth century had witnessed the emergence of a demonization campaign against youth of color by neoconservatives.[82] The advocates of Proposition 21 built upon the foundation of fear constructed by this campaign.

The Latino Coalition, likewise, was not daunted by the institutionalization of the Bersin administration in the San Diego Unified School District. Its members investigated the effects of the implementation of a curricular reform, the Blueprint for Success, and administrative and logistical changes initiated as part of it. During the summer of 1999 they questioned the reports of improvements in test scores among students in the school district, especially among students of color, and analyses offered by district officials which attributed the alleged gains to the reforms implemented during Bersin's first year in office. Moreover, they disputed the claim that the scores vindicated the new English-only instruction policy institutionalized by the passage of Proposition 227 in June 1998.

Toward a New Millennium: Continuing Activism against Oppression

Roberto Martínez and other human rights advocates continued to challenge official claims about undocumented immigration. Throughout the latter part of 1999, in addition to continuing to make the situation of undocumented workers visible on both sides of the border, they contested and rejected claims regarding the effectiveness of Operation Gatekeeper and documented its human cost in the fifth year of its existence. Among other actions, Martínez wrote U.S. Attorney General Janet Reno informing her that Operation Gatekeeper was "causing one of the worst human rights tragedies in border history" and was "totally ineffective in stopping the flow of people across the border."[83] In various forums, he called for suspension of the operation and reevaluation of the circumstances in the region. In a similar vein Claudia Smith of the California Rural Legal Assistance Foundation declared that the operation had "been a political success" but ineffective in deterring undocumented immigration.[84] In collaboration with Martínez, she documented and reported the death toll associated with the federal operation. By the date of its fifth anniversary, the reported deaths among undocumented workers in that section had climbed to a total of 408.

As the twentieth century concluded, Chicano artists and activists historically associated with the Centro Cultural de la Raza found themselves confronting, challenging, and coping with a new role as outsiders. Artists such as Victor Ochoa and Victor Payan protested the administration and programming changes undertaken by a new administrative and leadership team. The changes, in their view, in effect "purged" artists and denied them and the working-class community a role in determining the future of the iconic institution of Chicano activism.

La Unión del Barrio protested the invited appearance of the San Diego police chief at the center. In addition to criticizing the actions of the new management and leadership, La Unión allied itself with the artists against the effort to take control of El Centro Cultural de la Raza away from artists and the community. Victor Payan wrote, "We are not here to be left in the cold and dark. We are here because it is our Centro. We are here because we want a Centro that is open and where all members of our community are welcome and respected. We do not want a Centro in which the Chief of Police is welcome and peaceful protests are not. Is this where the Chicano struggle ended up at the end of the Century? The answer is a strong and resounding no."[85] The artists and activists also formed a new organization, the Save Our Centro Coalition, and called on members of the larger community to join the struggle: "We must stand tall against oppression. We must all work together to save this hard-won space for all members to feel safe, respected, and valued and above all, to be free. Join us in the struggle. We are many. We are strong. We shall overcome. The Centro Cultural de la Raza will not fall."[86]

Since the mid-1960s such faith coupled with a willingness to engage in protest had enabled the Chicana/o activists to achieve unprecedented gains. As the twentieth century drew to a close, that faith was once again being tested. The years of the new millennium would reveal whether the faith in "Sí, Se Puede" was merited in San Diego. Through their activism, however, they were renewing and extending a tradition that illuminated the inapplicability of the sleeping giant thesis and underscored the need for a shift to a new paradigm that would capture the historical realities of the Chicana/o experience.

7

CHICANAS IN THE ARTS, 1970–1995: WITH PERSONAL REFLECTIONS

Rita Sánchez

The Chicano arts in San Diego have an impressive history, and Chicanas have been crucial in their development. These artistic expressions emerged from the Civil Rights Movement of the 1960s, which provided the impetus for all people to seek justice and equality in American life. Mexican Americans organized around the liberating term *Chicano*. Early on, Chicanas became important activist leaders. In California Dolores Huerta worked with César Chávez in the United Farm Workers' struggle; in New Mexico, Elizabeth Martínez's activism gave strength to Reies López Tijerina's fight to regain the land rights promised Mexican Americans in the Treaty of Guadalupe Hidalgo. In Colorado, Enriqueta Vasquez actively supported the Crusade for Justice, organized by her good friend Rodolfo "Corky" Gonzales. In Texas, Virginia Múzquiz succeeded José Ángel Gutiérrez as the head of the Raza Unida Party in 1972; and in San Diego, women such as Gracia Molina de Pick supported the student movement, which pressed for Chicano studies departments at colleges and universities.

Hundreds of women like these worked for change, and their efforts found expression in the arts. They demanded cultural history, identity, and economic and social justice. The Mexican American people's call for fair treatment in the courts, the workplace, and the schools became highly visible as art on walls; as spoken poetry on theater stages; and as actos in colleges, in communities, and on farmlands all over the Southwest. The Chicano Movement asserted an Indo-Hispano identity while demanding full rights under the U.S. constitution. It became vivid and exciting as it found voice in the arts and especially as women contributed to it.[1] Through the arts and the creation of cultural space, Chicana voices resounded for social justice and women's rights. Chicana artists redefined political and cultural borders as they challenged patriarchal and racial limits. Art and activism in San Diego memory can be evoked by looking at cultural centers and community spaces all over San Diego, that attest to the liveliness of the arts: Chicano Park, the Centro Cultural de la Raza, the Centro de Salud, the Barrio Station, and the Senior Citizens Center, for example.

In 1995 I was given the opportunity to look back in time when I was invited to participate as one of the masters of ceremonies at the twenty-fifth anniversary celebration for Chicano Park. Chicano Park has become one of the most note-worthy expressions of public art in California, and so is a good starting point for my reflection. Chicano Park Day, April 22, has been a significant day in San Diego since 1970. The twenty-fifth anniversary celebration, organized by a Chicana, Tomasa "Tommie" Camarillo, was a fitting reminder of women's participation in the arts and activism since the Civil Rights Movement. This essay, while it focuses on key events and persons in San Diego, shows the movement as part of a national consciousness. It is also a personal reflection, moving beyond San Diego to demonstrate the extent of the Chicano Movement and the presence of women in culture and the arts. My reflection begins and ends with Chicano Park.

Many others have written about Chicanos in the arts; and art critics and journal articles have discussed Chicana artists. This chapter attempts to show the extent of Chicana art in San Diego. In it I have chosen to explore women's work by focusing on key exhibits from 1970 to 1995 through research and personal experience. I also try to include as many contributors as possible, women I either read about or met during the crucial years of Chicana activism.

I found scattered throughout the many resources on the arts in San Diego bits and pieces of information that attest to the extent of Chicana involvement. Many individuals may have their own versions of Chicana history, some written, some not. I recognize that no one person can possibly write the complete story and that each woman has her own version. As a researcher, I went beyond memoir, piecing together the jigsaw puzzle to sort out how women have been involved.[2] I have divided the essay into five sections, corresponding to my research and per-sonal experiences. The first two address Chicanas in the San Diego arts from 1970 to 1974, before I arrived, followed by Chicana activism in other parts of California and my own coming to consciousness in the same period. The third section covers 1974–1984, when I was Chicana studies professor at San Diego State University. During 1984–1990, covered in the next section, I was a gallery co-owner and sup-porter of the arts; and in the last section, 1990–1995, I cover the ongoing Chicana presence in the arts during my first five years at San Diego's Mesa College.

Chicanas and the Arts in San Diego, 1970–1974

Chicanas have long been exploring their particular strengths in poetry, music, *teatro*, dance, and visual arts. At first they did so in private, in the home; then publicly, to assert pride in their culture and to demand justice for the people in keeping with the Chicano Movement's call for unity in the 1960s. During that initial period Chicanos came together for this common cause, but the words "unity and brotherhood" were also a reminder that patriarchy had not yet been addressed. Nevertheless, Chicanas answered the call for unity, even as they began to form their own perspectives.

The first National Chicano Youth Liberation Conference at Denver in 1969 showed how activism informed the arts. San Diego artists were in the forefront. They heard poetry, including the epic *I Am Joaquín/Yo soy Joaquín*, written in 1967 by Rodolfo "Corky" Gonzales, who organized the conference. "El Plan Espiritual de Aztlán" was drafted by San Diego poet Alurista at Denver, and meanwhile visual artist Salvador Roberto Torres was calling for a cultural center in San Diego.[3] San Diego Chicanas became active participants in the movement. SDSU students like Enriqueta Chávez, Teresa Pascual, and Olivia Puentes-Reynolds attended the Denver Conference, with the encouragement and mentoring of Professor Gracia Molina de Pick.

Poet and musician Olivia Puentes-Reynolds was the first Chicana to read at the conference. She received a standing ovation following the presentation of her passionate poem, appropriately entitled "No me chingas más!" expressing outrage at racism and sexism while at the same time asserting pride in her culture: "I hear Black is beautiful; I want Brown is beautiful!" Years later, these three young Chicana students made history when they appeared in the documentary video series *Chicano!* Activism informed the arts; the two could not be separated.

At SDSU in 1969, Chicanas participated in the first courses taught by Chicano studies professors like Rene Núñez, Sonia López, Enriqueta Chávez, Francisca Rascón, and Clarissa Torres Rojas. José Villarino taught music and Alurista taught poetry, while Professor Ruth Robinson taught the first members of Teatro Mestizo, the newly formed teatro that addressed Chicana concerns. Cast members Josie and Dale Montoy wrote a play about the power struggles inherent in male-female relationships. In one act, Olivia Puentes-Reynolds played the role of a woman who is cast aside by her man, but finds harmony with indigenous forces by acknowledging her Indian ancestry. Olivia recalls the teatro's goals as being to seek gender balance and to become aware of male-female struggle. When Teatro Mascarones came to San Diego, they invited the San Diegans to Mexico City and Cuernavaca to perform. Olivia brought back to San Diego the liberating lyrics given to her by Gabriela Wesco Morán, who sang with the Mascarones "Somos de Piedra/We Are Rock." Teatro Mestizo included many Chicanas who taught others about the political issues of the day. Between 1971 and 1974 some of the actos performed were *No saco nada de la escuela*, *Soldado Razo*, *Los agachados*, and the militant *La Reconquista*. They performed on university campuses, in community centers, on flatbed trucks in the Coachella Valley, and anywhere else they could.

Chicana teatro endured because of people like Felicitas Núñez and Delia Ravelo, who formed Teatro de las Chicanas and kept it alive for many years through different names: Teatro de las Chicanas, Teatro Laboral, Teatro Raíces. Teatro de las Chicanas performed plays critical of *machismo* within the Chicano Movement. Chicana participants offered different degrees of commitment but their contributions are a testimony to the teatro's longevity.[4]

The United Farm Workers movement, organized by César Chávez and Dolores Huerta, relied on actos, or agitprop (short skits), to gather supporters to their cause. In 1966, students Linda and Carlos LeGerrette represented the United Farm Workers of America (UFW). They reached San Diego audiences through the documentary film *Yo Soy Chicano*, which told the story of their involvement with the UFW. Linda LeGerrette was one of the early Chicana activist leaders to bring a consciousness of the UFW to San Diego. As newlyweds and college students, Linda and Carlos helped establish the first San Diego chapter of MAYA (Mexican American Youth Association—now MEChA). Gracia Molina de Pick, their advisor, also encouraged them to attend a meeting of the local Delano grape strike support group. That grape strike became a perfect foundation for raising consciousness and building MAYA at SDSU. In 1966, the two volunteered their summer to help the farmworkers. That summer was to last twelve years: Linda LeGerrette had "an almost immediate 'calling' to become part of the farmworker struggle." This fervor built as she and Carlos stayed on to organize official UFW boycott activities, spreading an activist fervor to others. Linda LeGerrette is described in the UFW archives as "competitive, hard-driving, and well-studied," qualities Chicanas need to persevere in the many struggles they address in their communities.[5]

Women's voices became crucial in the Chicano Movement. Chicanas challenged, "the relationship of women to domination" and "relocated women to a central emancipated position," says Amalia Mesa-Bains, artist and art critic, in her writing.[6] Diana López Blanks, speaking in 2005 after the passing of her friend Viviana Zermeño, captured those early days at SDSU. She recalled the meetings on campus where "females were not equal participants with males." She said they used to go to the home of Gracia Molina de Pick to talk about issues. Diana recalls, "We listened to Chavela Vargas and Gracia de Pick's analysis as she cooked us dinner. We saw *teatro* performed and heard songs like *La Adelita*, *Gabino Barerra*, and *Yo Soy Chicano*, where through song we learned the value of honor, justice, truth, equity, and integrity." Diana López and Viviana Zermeño soon became co-chairs of the SDSU High School Student Conference. "Could two Chicanas handle it?" was the pervading question. Apparently they could, because they did.[7]

Diana López Blanks also acknowledges Gracia de Pick as a mentor who created a dialogue among Chicanas, first as an activist herself and later as one who was educated about and conscious of the Chicana struggle. Gracia Molina de Pick, a powerful activist for women's rights in Mexico, brought her consciousness to San Diego. She was one of four women and twenty-nine men on the steering committee at the formation of El Plan de Santa Bárbara, a manifesto for the implementation of Chicano studies programs throughout California universities.[8] Soon after El Plan was adopted in April 1969 at UCSB, Professor Molina de Pick founded the Mesa College Chicano Studies Program, the first to be initiated. She also was a leader in the Chicano Moratorium to end the war in Vietnam and a founding faculty member of UCSD's Third College.

Her aunt was a friend of Frida Kahlo in Mexico. "Two of my most intimate people that were close to me suffered from an injustice that society brought upon them," says Molina de Pick. She knew her aunt to be a lesbian, and seeing the struggles that went with that identity gave her an empathy that still motivates her today. As a young girl she spent time with her aunt and Kahlo. "I learned from them that great people defend not only themselves but those who cannot defend themselves." Molina de Pick believes that she has seen discrimination in every form possible. Because this is in large part what drives her activism, she says, "My last breath will be fighting for those human rights."[9]

Soon after the Denver Youth Conference, Chicanas began to identify inconsistencies they observed in the movement and to talk about what it felt like to be in a male-dominated movement where women were not recognized as equals. Women spoke, women wrote, and women created, yet their voices were not published nor acknowledged until they articulated these concerns on their own by creating a forum to address their specific needs related to gender inequality. "It was their direct participation in the movement that made them aware of the Chicanas' double oppression," wrote Sonia López in *Essays on La Mujer*. "Chicanas became more politically aware," she continued, "when they had begun to question assigned gender roles" (28).

Men in the movement immediately reacted to women gathering separately with charges that these women were dividing the Chicano cause. Unity could come only with equality was the response from the Chicanas, thus sparking the formation of a Chicana feminist consciousness in the Chicano Movement.[10]

Art was one way Chicanas could express their identity; they used it to celebrate and affirm their mestiza ancestry, as a political statement that challenged injustice, and as an aesthetic response to particular conditions related to gender inequalities. Today art critics talk about how Chicanas captured those times and conditions in their art. Amalia Mesa-Bains sees the need for people "to understand the conditions and concerns that shape the work of Chicana artists" and their "gender expressiveness."[11] Shifra Goldman and Tomás Ybarra-Frausto, noted art historians, point out that in place of art picturing men as heroic figures and women as passive, "Chicana artists exhibited the heroines of the Mexican Revolution . . . labor leaders, women associated with alternative schools and clinics, women workers, women in protest . . . active women who shaped their lives and environments."[12]

Chicana activism grew as artists in San Diego formed the collective called Toltecas en Aztlán and began to practice at the Ford building, the space occupied by Salvador Roberto Torres, then later at the Centro Cultural de la Raza. Among the founding members of Toltecas en Aztlán were Viviana Zermeño and Delia Moreno. Although women worked on some murals created in this period, visual artists at the Centro Cultural and Chicano Park were mostly men.[13]

This male camaraderie, a tenor of the times, dominated. Today it invites a contemporary analysis. Chicanos were responding in kind to the years of injustices the Mexican people had faced in San Diego following the takeover of the land and its citizens after the Mexican War. But now it was the 1970s, the beginning of the Chicana women's rights movement. Women were beginning to address their oppression within their own culture. Chicana activists were also fighting vigorously for their civil rights, for a cultural center, a health clinic, and a park. Women's resistance was not something fully articulated at first, but it has been called "a historical moment that responded to social realities."[14]

Women participated fully in the struggle for a park and a cultural center, not just for themselves, but also to ensure a definitive space for future generations. Before the tumultuous park takeover, activist artists had been fighting for a cultural center. Visual artist Salvador Roberto Torres, having just returned from meeting with other artists in the Bay Area, became aware of the need for a Chicano community center in San Diego. He was given permission to use the abandoned Ford building, now the Aerospace Museum, for his art, and began to share the space with other artists, including women like Viviana Zermeño, Delia Moreno, Leticia de Baca, Olivia Puentes-Reynolds, and Herminia Enrique. Señora Enrique, a mother, organizer, and community activist, had been teaching at Casa de Salud in National City before joining the other artists at the Ford building in 1969 and forming the Ballet Folklórico en Aztlán.

In 1970, a growing community consciousness led to the takeover of land that became Chicano Park. For three years, neighbors in Logan Heights had been negotiating for a park on the site. Then Mario Solis, a student, discovered that the city of San Diego was moving to build a highway patrol station there. The people, having no recourse, responded to this betrayal by forming a human chain in front of the bulldozers prepared to clear the land. Laura Rodríguez, a longtime San Diego resident, remembered how she, a mother, became involved in the Chicano Mural Arts movement and the takeover of Chicano Park (fig. 7.1). She happened to walk by the park and see a group of people gathered there. "I was going to the grocery store. I saw young people in a circle [and] joined in. . . . I never went back home from the store. I went every day after that." Laura Rodríguez is one of the best examples of how the arts and activism were wedded during those days of political activism. "All we wanted was a park," she added. "It soon became apparent that after three years of meetings that we were not going to get it . . . We just stood there and let them roll over us if they wanted," Rodríguez said proudly.[15]

Out of this initial struggle and victory for a people's park, Laura Rodríguez and others moved on to address the most pressing need of the people—health. The people began to use the Neighborhood House for a health clinic. Fearing that the building would be taken from them, she just stayed overnight. "I slept outside on the porch to guard the place to see that nobody took it away from

FIGURE 7.1. Laura Rodríguez, a longtime community activist and supporter of Chicano Park. (Courtesy of Robert Rodríguez)

us." Thus, the Centro de Salud—eventually named after Rodríguez—was born. Today, on the Laura Rodríguez Health Clinic in Logan Heights, a giant mural celebrates this victory of the people.

What was occurring at Chicano Park, the Centro Cultural, and the colleges, especially SDSU, became a kind of cultural revolution. Chicanas were becoming politically aware. They were very conscious of poverty, struggles in the fields, discrimination against their culture, and sexism in the colleges, which became the bases for making statements in the arts. They were also seeking the space necessary to establish an identity, to create and produce their art. The work of San Diego artist Yolanda López reveals the Chicana artists' search for space in a community very important to them. As artist-critic Amalia Mesa-Bains points out, "The need to circumscribe space in the community is a driving force in the lives of women artists."[16]

Yolanda López, born in San Diego's Logan Heights neighborhood, was one of those artists. Her mother worked as a seamstress at the Naval Training Center. Yolanda graduated from SDSU with a BA in drawing and painting and got her master's degree in the visual arts from UCSD. Her works have appeared in exhibitions since the 1970s. In 1974, she exhibited in "Las Tres Mujeres," the first Chicana show at the Centro Cultural de la Raza's Gallery Poxteca, which featured works by Yolanda López, Gloria Amalia Flores, and Victoria del Castello.[17] In 1975, she exhibited in "Exposición Chicanarte" at the Los Angeles Municipal Art Gallery and at UCLA.

Yolanda López, a strong community advocate, supported the takeover of Chicano Park, yet "had never been invited by the men to paint with them." She believed that the men were uncomfortable with her, not being used to relating to a confident, trained, verbal artist at a time when women were expected to fulfill traditional roles as supports to men.[18] Yet she continued to paint.

Her greatest motivation was the young women who came to her with their mural idea for Chicano Park. They had already asked to work with the male artists but had been turned down, so they turned to López for guidance. Contributors Julietta A. García-Torres, Cecilia de la Torre, Rosa de la Torre, and Eva Craig designed the mural "Preserve Our Heritage," calling themselves Mujeres Muralistas. López saw her role as that of advisor to these young women, the artists who primarily painted it. In the mural they pictured themselves growing out of maize, representing the earth. Through her role as facilitator of this project, López represents the Chicana artist, the activist woman, always doing her art. She was one of the first women to challenge the male voices through sheer action.[19]

In 1970 the Toltecas en Aztlán who were using the abandoned Ford building saw the need for a permanent Chicano community and cultural center. They lobbied at city council meetings, actively trying to acquire the building for that purpose. In the end, the community was awarded an abandoned water tank in Balboa Park for the Centro Cultural de la Raza, a space that became the pride of the Chicano community. In 1971, a year after the Chicano Park victory, the Centro Cultural was dedicated as an arts and culture center. Veronica Enrique, Herminia's daughter, remembers being deeply affected by the ritual celebration, even though she was only eleven years old at the time. "We had a blessing all the way around the building. I was given the honor of being the one to release the dove into the air," representing the spirit of the people set free.[20]

In 1974 Antonia Pérez was the only woman in a nine-artist mural-painting project on the outside walls of the Centro Cultural. She was responsible for a grand-scale image, 18 by 25 feet. This indigenous graphic with contemporary design and color entitled "El Sol" (The Sun) complemented Antonio Pazo's "Mujer de Luna" (Mother Moon). On a consciousness level, Sol and Luna represent separate male and female entities, each part of a whole. One cannot exist without the other.[21] This concept is poetically expressed by the *curandera* in Rudolfo Anaya's novel *Bless Me, Última*: "Without the waters of the moon to replenish the heavens there would be no oceans. And the same salt waters of the oceans are drawn by the sun to the heavens, and in turn again become the waters of the moon. The waters are one."[22] Pérez's mural has given us one part of this unified whole and an awareness of the need that Chicanos and Chicanas have for each other. Pérez also contributed other work to the center, including silk screen posters for "Summer Workshops 1977," representing the early work of Chicanas in the arts.

These Chicana artists had one thing in common, a desire to do something for future generations. One of those women was Delia Moreno. Moreno and her daughters, María and Delia ("Chica"), formed Trio Moreno, one of the earliest Chicana groups to perform socially conscious music. They performed at many community events, rallies, workshops, and UFW gatherings, including at the dedication of the Centro Cultural de la Raza. The Morenos gave guitar lessons, played guitar accompaniments at poetry readings, and performed their own compositions as well as traditional songs like "Llegaron los Toltecas" and "Mañanitas de Aztlan." They took their activism "very seriously," Moreno remembers, and "it meant giving up lots of things. We were doing it for a cause . . . to perpetuate and promote the arts for the younger generation."[23]

Other artists, dancers, musicians, and actors like Socorro Gamboa, Carolina Flores, Carlota Hernández, and Velma Losoya all promoted issues of concern to the audiences of San Diego through their art. They addressed farm labor injustices exposed by César Chávez and urban and community concerns in their plays, songs, and poetry. Lin Romero wrote one of the first published works of poetry in San Diego, *Happy Songs and Bleeding Hearts.* She traveled with others to read her poetry and published a newsletter called "La Mazorca." Gloria Amalia Flores wrote an early poetic statement of a woman's perspective entitled "And Her Children Lived." In short, Chicana activism in the arts thrived, with one thought in mind—their future.

A Broader Perspective on Chicana Activism, 1970–1974

Chicana activism was becoming a nationwide phenomenon during the period from 1970 to 1974. Hijas de Cuauhtémoc formed in Long Beach, and other parts of California saw the founding of community-based groups like La Comisión Femenil Mexicana Nacional, the National Chicana Political Caucus, and MARA at the California Institute for Women. Chicana conferences took place in Houston, Whittier, Sacramento, and Los Angeles. Chicana consciousness was forming in other parts of the nation, at Stanford University in Palo Alto, where I was a student, and at San Francisco State, San Jose State, Sacramento State, UCLA, and UC Berkeley. Chicana activists in Texas and New Mexico were also writing and speaking out. In the San Francisco Bay Area the Mujeres Muralistas formed a collective to paint murals.[24]

My political awareness began in Southern California and developed in the Bay Area. I grew up in San Bernardino's west side as the seventh of eleven children born to parents whose ancestors had survived the U.S. takeover of Santa Fe, New Mexico, in 1846, and who themselves had survived the Great Depression and World War II. An artist from childhood, I decided instead to follow in my sister Mary's footsteps and major in journalism at San Jose State. She and my older sisters, Josephine and Theresa, countered my parents' objections to my going away to school and advocated for me to attend college. I left behind four younger sisters and brothers: Angelica, Emily, Joseph, and Severo.[25]

After one year, however, at age twenty in 1958, I got married and worked at putting a husband through law school and raising two daughters, Lisa and Lauri. My daughters had the best of both worlds, we told them, Mexican ancestry on one side, and Anglo, German, and Scots-Irish on the other. The American dream. It was not to last. When my marriage ended in 1968, I became a reentry student at Foothill Community College and then at Stanford University from 1970 to 1974.

To survive, my children and I first joined together in the simple songs of our faith that my mother had taught us. "Of This Day I Give to You, O Lord," resounded in Stanford's Memorial Church and Saint Anne's Catholic Community, which had become our home. In the church we also listened to songs of struggle and revolution and joined together on the picket lines. My daughters made art and banners of their own as they heard me call on the manager of Safeway to stop selling non-union grapes and support the struggle of the UFW. They wrote notes at the bottom of my letters to my sister Mary, who was living and working with the UFW community at La Paz, near Bakersfield, California, in support of the workers and the poor.[26] Thus, my children, the daughters of change, were also included in the cause.

In 1973, I did not realize we were all part of making history until I met Antonia Castañeda, an author and graduate student of history. Castañeda, the daughter of farmworkers, taught the first course on Chicanas at the University of Washington. She was also coeditor with Tomás Ybarra Frausto and Joseph Sommers of *Literatura Chicana*. To see Antonia's name and photograph on the back of a book may not seem surprising today, but it was a first for us Mexican American women in 1969. As I was soon to begin teaching the first Chicana course in the Stanford Graduate Fellows Program, I asked Antonia what she had used in her Visión de la Mujer de la Raza course at Washington. She handed me what was analogous to a lump of clay to an artist—a big cardboard box filled with photocopied materials, everything she had found of relevance to the topic for students to read.

That is all we had then—newspaper clippings, articles, essays, thoughts, speeches by Dolores Huerta on La Huelga; writings by Enriqueta Vásquez on the "Women of La Raza"; poetry by Sor Juana Inés de la Cruz; stories about La Virgen de Guadalupe, La Malinche, La Llorona. The night before the first class, a group of women helped me photocopy articles and bind them with fasteners in bright red, hard-covered folders, the closest thing we could get to a book. One student remarked that we were women in the process of giving birth. I recall my first day of teaching began with the arts. I reproduced a drawing that I had found in Antonia's materials, an image of a woman looking out from under a shawl, half of her face covered. Art spoke louder than words.

Art and creativity similarly became a vital part of creating a journal of Chicana thought, another first. Dr. Rosaura Sánchez, a professor at UCSD, mentored Chicanas. She edited an anthology with Rosa Martínez Cruz, *Essays on La Mujer* published by UCLA in 1977. One of the first professors in Chicano Studies at SDSU, Sonia López wrote "Chicanas in the Student Movement." Adelaida Del Castillo, now a professor at San Diego State, challenged the myth of La Malinche as the betrayer of Mexico in an article entitled "Malintzin Tenépal." Ana Nieto Gómez, the editor of *Encuentro Femenil*, later became a professor of women's studies at Cal State Northridge. I was a graduate student at Stanford when she was invited to speak at a Chicana conference and stayed with us in our home. I remember how she spoke on the importance of child care. No one agreed more than I, a student and single mother.

Dorinda Moreno, another author and performance artist we met at Stanford, was the author of *La Mujer en Pie de la Lucha*. When she performed at Stanford, her tall, statuesque figure dominated the space. Her performance art spoke loudly and passionately about women's issues, emulating the sounds of our culture. She began softly, cooing the quieting lullabies of our *abuelitas* as they cradled us in their arms, "amaroo, roo roo." Then she echoed the intrusive sounds of kitchen utensils being dragged across jail bars, like the women did in the film *Salt of the Earth*. She enacted the copper miners' wives being jailed for picketing. She became the women in the film, crying out for plumbing, hot water, baby formula, and food: "¡Queremos comida! ¡Queremos formula! ¡Queremos justicia!" Finally, her voice built to a crescendo as she screamed the terrifying cry of La Llorona, "¡Ayeeeeeeee!" Chicanas recognized these sounds. These were the sounds that moved us to action.[27]

Dorinda Moreno also introduced my daughters to Sasheen Little Feather, the actress who had accepted the academy award for Marlon Brando when he protested the treatment of Indians in film. She taught us a native chant (spelled phonetically): "Hinameya, Hinameya, Hinamey Chinchayo." The sounds still ring in my ears. I especially recall them because when we got home, I found the words written along with beautiful Indian designs in my daughter Lisa's journal and found protest poetry in Lauri's theme book. The arts had an impact on the young.

In 1973, Joan Baez, the famous social protest singer, came to Stanford. She stood on stage with the wife of Victor Jara, the musician who had just been part of the genocide of the Chilean coup. Baez sang a song she had just written, the *Ballad of Sacco and Vanzetti*, for men and women she called political prisoners: "My crime is loving the forsaken. And only silence is shame." I remember that day because I attended with a sister Chicana, Teresa Guerrero. We saw teatro enacting the horror of the coup, demonstrating to the audience its injustice. Our Spanish professor, Fernando Alegría, spoke of the events leading to the death of his friend, the poet Pablo Neruda. "He died of a broken heart," Professor Alegría said tearfully. The audience sang the African American theme song of the Civil Rights Movement, "We Shall Overcome," in Spanish—"Nosotros Venceremos"—and I heard my sister and friend shout, "¡Que viva!" In time, Teresa's brother, Zarco Guerrero, painted three women on the wall of Casa Zapata Dorm, depicting Chicana strength through our Mexican Indian ancestry.

My daughters participated in their own ways too, Lauri with her own poetry and Lisa with her drawings. They marched in picket lines. They visited the college classroom where they listened to poetry and dialogue about current issues. They heard about César Chávez, Dolores Huerta, Martin Luther King, and Rosa Parks, voices speaking out for youth, for women, and for change.

Chicana Artists and Activists in San Diego, 1974–1990

I came to San Diego in 1974, hired as a professor of English and Chicano Studies at San Diego State University. I heard about the women who had formed Las Chicanas at SDSU; the women who contributed art, danza, music, teatro, and mural art in Chicano Park and at the Centro Cultural de la Raza. But the first mural I saw was at the Grossmont Shopping Center, a most unlikely place; the artist had painted a massive figure, arms outstretched, representing the beauty of Chicano culture. It took me a while to look away as I felt a longing for my family, my roots, and my Bay Area community. I had no idea that one day I would meet and marry the artist who had painted it.

Thereafter, my life in San Diego was intimately shaped by the Chicano art movement and the men and women who participated in it. What follows are my recollections of the Chicanas I joined with, who took part in shaping an important activist movement in San Diego.

When I arrived in San Diego I wondered what I could contribute to the activism already well begun in San Diego. First, I brought my experiences of teaching the Chicana course at Stanford and of helping to create a journal of Chicana writings there. Although we were at opposite ends of the state—the Bay Area and Southern California—I knew we were all contributing to new Chicana thought, feminist theory, and gender expression in the arts. My *comadres* in the Bay Area used to say, "We are not an isolated movement: we are part of a unified struggle for justice, for education, and Chicana equality." With those words I knew I was not alone in San Diego. I realized I was connected to history—to those who had been with me before and the ones I was yet to meet.

In San Diego in the 1970s my children listened with me to the music of Argentine singer Suni Paz, whose *Songs of Struggle and Revolution: Brotando del Silencio/Breaking Out of Silence* were in keeping with the times.[28] I invited the popular Latina artist to come to SDSU. Her music provided a political voice for Chicanas in San Diego when she came to visit; her album inspired the premier issue of a journal I edited, encouraging Chicanas to write.[29]

Soon after I arrived in San Diego I met another vocal artist, Charlotte, or Carlota, Hernández Terry. She had also painted a mural in Chicano Park, one of the first women to do so. She was commissioned by Tommie Camarillo, one of the original park activists, to paint the Chicano Park logo on one of the pillars. From a design conceived by Rico Bueno, who left San Diego, Carlota calculated

FIGURE 7.2. Chicano Park logo painted by Charlotte
Hernández Terry in Chicano Park. (Courtesy of Chicano
Park Steering Committee)

the dimensions of the logo to fit the pillar. She prepared it in a drafting course
where she was one of only two women in a class of twenty men. She then painted
the historical image in Chicano Park. It stands seven feet tall today, in homage to
the first woman to paint in the park and as tangible evidence of women's contributions to Chicano Park (fig. 7.2). The Chicano Park logo and the words that appear
on it, "La Tierra Mia"—taken from the mouth of Emiliano Zapata, a hero of
the Mexican Revolution who fought for the poor and landless people—connote
resistance to injustice and pride in Mexican culture. In the image, a hand holds a
little piece of land on a map of California, surrounded by Zapata's words.[30]

 Carlota Hernández Terry was the first person to introduce me to the history
of Chicano Park. A single mother like me, she was proud of having contributed
something important to the park in the early days when women were not recognized. And so she told me the park story. More than that, Carlota Hernández was
a talented musician, guitarist, and singer who both performed and composed.
In 1974, I invited her to speak and perform in my Chicano studies classroom

at SDSU. My daughters heard her music, and the students in my classes learned about the history and culture of the Mexican people born on U.S. land. They appreciated her *cuentos*, stories of struggle and change, especially those exhibiting a Chicana consciousness. Our history was not written down, and they wanted to hear more about how women had contributed to civil rights in San Diego. Hernández Terry's songs challenged the students to think about the struggles of the women. "Mama Works Hard Every Day" was a kind of chant, a song of daily and difficult struggle, almost a *grito*. The words "Mama works hard for her weekly pay" became a demand for change and justice, belted out as she strummed rhythms to the beat on her guitar. Most of her works were corridos, ballads of the people, delivered in a broad vocal range, adding to the drama of her passion.

Hernández Terry performed at the Ford Theatre in Washington, DC, to celebrate the U.S. bicentennial. In 1975 she attended the International Women's Conference in Mexico City, where she was invited to perform for Mexican diplomats; and the Women's Folk Art Festival in Lansing, Michigan; and in 1977 she received a National Endowment for the Arts Teacher in the Schools grant.[31]

The Royal Chicano Air Force (RCAF) was an example of an art collective who painted in Chicano Park. They came to San Diego from Sacramento to leave beautiful examples of their work under the Coronado Bridge. When they arrived, the women of RCAF took off on their own to paint in the park. "Tantamount to treason," because the group always traveled together, said José Montoya, one of the leaders of the group who painted "Farmworker Family." Still, their actions presented a powerful role model of a women's art collective in action.

One of the artists, Rosalina Balaciosos, had previously attended the International Women's Conference in Mexico City. Full of enthusiasm, she encouraged the other female members to join her in a mural celebrating women from around the world. So Celia Rodríguez, Tina Lerma Barbosa, Antonia Mendoza, Rosalina Balaciosos, and Barbara Desmangles with community volunteers painted "Female Inteligencia." The mural presents five women in a variety of costumes and positions, holding up the sky, alluding to the work's alternate title, "Women Hold up Half of Heaven." Below the central figure, a powerful female deity, a mother and child are engulfed within a golden halo. The mother's arms embrace the world, which supports the child in front of her, reminding us of women's power and consciousness (fig. 7.3).[32]

By 1976 women were intent on publishing. At San Diego State University, I decided to work with women to edit a Chicana student journal of poetry and

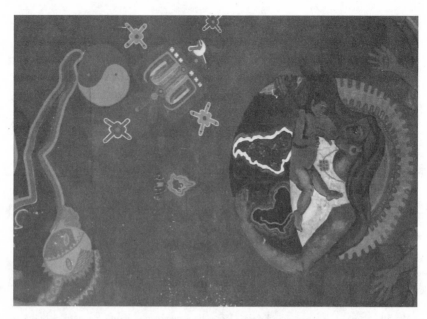

FIGURE 7.3. Detail from "Female Inteligencia," a mural in Chicano Park done by RCAF women Celia Rodríguez, Tina Lerma Barbosa, Antonia Mendoza, Rosalina Balaciosos, Barbara Desmangles, and community volunteers. (Courtesy of the Chicano Park Steering Committee)

art like the one the students and I had produced at Stanford. We called it *Visión de la Mujer de la Raza*, in honor of Antonia Castañeda's Chicana studies course at the University of Washington. The cover pictured a young Chicana with long black hair blending into the *trenzas* of her grandmother, surrounded by symbols representing our Indian ancestors. The third issue, which was produced by SDSU students and staff, included an interview with Olga Talamante by SDSU student María Elena Ávila Félix. Olga Talamante, a Chicana, grew up in Gilroy as the daughter of a farmworker family. After attending the University of California at Santa Cruz, she visited Argentina, where she got caught in the middle of a political coup. While at a party she was mistakenly arrested along with others, tortured, and imprisoned for nearly two years. She was released after much advocacy by several U.S. committees. In an essay, "Notes from an Argentine Prison," Olga described how she was able to bear her circumstances, "I love life enough to struggle for it, and I'm happy to be living this historic moment, even if I'm imprisoned, knowing that in spite of it, my thoughts, and others like you, are free," sentiments she echoed in her poem "Mujer de Fuerza."

Another article, "A Chicana Feminist Perspective," by Ana Nieto Gómez, discussed how men are also victims of sexism when "they are labeled effeminate." Sexism omits the woman question from research or analysis, she continued. "Women fight in the struggles but are rarely depicted as participating." Mary Sánchez, a journalist and UFW volunteer at the César Chávez headquarters at La Paz wrote "On Non-Violence"; Artist Hilda Flores provided the cover art and an interview with her grandmother; while Elizabeth Alvarado and Diane Borrego wrote about how, as counselors wanting to reach Chicanas, "It is necessary to build on our assets, recognizing our elders as deep and intuitive philosophers." As Chicanas proud of our efforts at publishing, we celebrated with a reception at Scripps Cottage on the SDSU campus.[33] The 1977 "Third World Conference" at SDSU also honored women and the arts. Chicana art and activism had contributed to the release of Olga Talamante from an Argentine prison. As a member of the conference committee, I invited her to be the keynote speaker at SDSU. Women wanted to welcome her home, listen to her story, and hear her liberating poetry. SDSU Chicanas, including my daughters, were among the first ones to get to know her upon her return; my daughters listened to us talk with her the night before the conference, and as young women, were gaining consciousness from willing mentors.[34]

In 1977 women's art became part of the Chicano Park "Muralthon" mural painting project (the play on words was the invention of Mario Torero). Socorro Gamboa designed "Sueño Serpentino," completed in 1978. Other Muralthon artists left images of women on the pillars. One of them is an image of Frida Kahlo by San Francisco artist Rupert García, proposed for inclusion in the murals by Mario Torero and painted by Victor Ochoa. The inclusion of the important Mexicana artist La Frida shows innovation, a way of incorporating works by artists from outside San Diego, as it also shows signs of a growing consciousness regarding women in the arts. Yet as Yolanda López describes in the film *Chicano Park*, Chicanas experienced exclusion during this peak period of painting under the bridge. Another artist, Patricia Rodríguez of Mujeres Muralistas in San Francisco, acknowledged the "male exclusivity that required women to form their own collectives" because we were driven by consciousness and duty.[35]

In sorting out slides from the online archives of the Centro Cultural, I identified other women who headed or assisted in the painting of murals and other works in San Diego: (1) 1974, Laurie Manzano with Mario Torero and Mano Lima painted "Colossus"; (2) 1975, Rosa Olga Navarro with Victor Ochoa painted "Los Niños Son el Tesoro del Barrio"; (3) 1976, Denise García, Marisela Domínguez, Rosemary González, and Sophia García with David Avalos painted "Viva La Raza"; (4) 1977, Tonantzin Lizarraga with Victor Ochoa painted "The Bridge"; (5) 1978, Ana Tellez with Michael Schnorr painted "Chicano Park"; (6) 1978, Dolores Serrano-Vélez painted "Chicano Park Horoscope";[36] (7) 1989, Deborah Small, Elizabeth Sisco, and Louis Hock with David Avalos painted the Martin Luther King billboard "Welcome to America's Finest (a) City, (b) Tourist Plantation, (c) Convention Center"; and (8) 1991, Geraldina Rocha and Carlota Hernández Terry painted "Aerosol from Calles Viva Exhibition."[37] In 1977, the journal *Maize* debuted. Xelina came from San Antonio to San Diego to edit the literary quarterly, and women's work began to appear in it. The result of her effort was five volumes of the journal, each with five issues, and a book by Gina Valdez. *Maize* was born about the same time as Xelina and Alurista's first son was born. The cover art for the first issue began as the idea of an artist I met at their home. Mario Torero and I worked on it together to give to the couple—an Indian mother holding her son.[38] That December, Mario and I got married. Present at our wedding were my two children, Lisa and Lauri, and his three children, Natalie, María, and Mayo.

After that, I fully supported the artist's goals. I also contributed ideas to a few of Mario's works; one of them pictured his opposition to the word *minority*. In 1977, after discussing the term, I recalled an image from my childhood: the famous "Uncle Sam Wants You" poster. I pictured a popular icon of conscious-ness, like Che Guevara, the doctor ministering to the poor people's struggles, saying, "You Are Not a Minority." From that idea came the Che image pointing at us from Torero's painting on walls and posters, reminding Chicanos never to accept minority status. The finished product was his work derived from our col-laboration of ideas. I say this as a reminder that women's work, no matter its form, should never be negated. Mario might also articulate an idea that I, as a writer, could put into words. I wrote for a local community magazine thoughts we had both shared on the term *minority*. The finished product, under my byline, came after collaborating with him. Collaboration is good; the results can be effective.

The idea to open SolArt Gallery in Golden Hill in 1978 was entirely Mario's.[39] However, he accepted the help I could provide; he also knew how important it was to me that women be included. I remember the amount of effort that went into building SolArt from scratch. I worked so hard to prepare for opening night that I was too exhausted to attend. I was expecting a baby, our daughter Lucia, when I helped prepare one of San Diego's first Chicano art openings. That exhibit included the works of Barbara Carrasco, Judith Hernández, John Valadez, and Carlos Almaraz, from Los Angeles. They came to SolArt to exhibit in a neighborhood gallery—a first.[40]

Around that time the female icon La Virgen de Guadalupe became a central symbol on one of the pillars in Chicano Park, painted during Muralthon. The painting was based on a photograph Mario took of me holding a rose in my hand when I was expecting our firstborn. The mural represented La Virgen with child, her pink dress covering her unborn baby. We announced my pregnancy at Chicano Park in April 1978. Lucia was born on August 28.

Soon thereafter, I brought home a design I had envisioned, a Chicana being born from a stalk of maize. Mario produced it exquisitely on canvas, her arms outstretched, her long black hair flowing out, becoming part of the cornstalk. That image he called "Nucleus," a consciousness-raising concept, the power of woman exhibited as central to life. First exhibited at the Centro Cultural, the painting years later was chosen for Gary Keller's two-volume work, *Chicana and Chicano Contemporary Art*, and then given as a gift to our daughter Lucia. Another shared idea resulted in a proposal I wrote in 1980 to the Latin Academy Awards, Nosotros. That year Nosotros presented the Life Achievement Award to Rita Hayworth. I proposed that Torero's rendition of the actress, a serigraph, be presented to her. That proposal was accepted; we attended the awards ceremony and sold serigraphs, two of which Ricardo Montalbán purchased! A portion of the proceeds went to Alzheimer's research.

These reflections help document Chicanas' often hidden contributions to the arts. Chicanas have produced—often behind the scenes—writing, teaching, and painting while caring for children and holding families together. Women have made contributions to larger projects that may not have been acknowledged, and so their work has often gone unrecognized. Yet Chicanas have long challenged oppression. I was influenced by role models in films like *Salt of the Earth*, discovering only later that I was related to one of the strikers in the film, and *Lucia*, the 1970s film that gave me the inspiration for my daughter's name. I was also deeply affected by the Frida Kahlo exhibit that traveled to San Diego in April 1978 from Chicago.

That year, Yolanda López, one of the most important, powerful, and challenging voices in women's art, had begun to search for and then paint from her own perspective as a woman. In 1978 she chose as her subject the highest and most sacred icon of the culture, La Virgen de Guadalupe. Yet López generated controversy when she said the Virgen was a passive role model who "could not even walk in the dress she was wearing"; other women in the community challenged her, for to them La Virgen was the spiritual mother. La Virgin did not have to walk when she could fly. Of this painting Yolanda said, "I found a new revolutionary way of looking at myself as a woman."[41] Yolanda López had indeed found her subject in herself.

Exclusion, a known motivator, comes in many forms. In 1980, I was invited to a brainstorming session at the San Diego Museum of Art. The director invited suggestions from the almost all-white audience. When I boldly dared to suggest an exhibit of Chicano art, the audience spontaneously burst into laughter. Their response, a form of exclusion, may have resulted in the first multiethnic exhibit at the San Diego Museum of Art in 1988, "Cultural Currents." Curated by Mary Stofflet, it examined the differences in cultural styles and heritage in the work of various artists of color. A first in San Diego, it included a work by Chicana artist Carmen Lomas Garza, "Lotería Tablas," among works by Gronk and Rupert García. Thus, a Chicana artist was one of the first to break institutional barriers in the arts in San Diego.[42]

Chicano art could also easily be co-opted by outsiders then given back to an unknowing audience in a more palatable form. I saw this insidious process in operation when I attended the opening night of *Murs, Murs* by the French film director Agnes Varda. The film on mural art in Los Angeles was now considered important, as it was the work of a foreigner. Featured at the Museum of Contemporary Art in San Diego, it contained the work of San Diego Chicano artists.[43] The opening night of this film in 1980 was another first for Chicanas and Chicanos in San Diego, as local artists and friends of the arts were invited to attend by Eva Cockcroft, the New York author of a book on muralism and a critic on the subject.[44] An advocate for Chicano art, she wrote an article on the film for the *San Diego Union*. At that time the news media barely dared mention Chicano art; when they did, they often demeaned it, dismissing it as street art, comprehending neither its value nor its purpose. Ironically, the artists present at the opening night gala were the innovators of mural art, the very people represented in the film. Yet they were listening to a French film producer become the expert on mural art, speaking on the subject to the experts in the audience, the Chicanas and Chicanos present. However, the true irony was the La Jollans dressed in furs and jewels who highly lauded the film whereas the artists themselves had never been able to reach them. It took a French filmmaker coming to the United States and screening a film in La Jolla to get them to pay attention to Chicano art. I felt deeply enough about what I observed to write my own piece, which was published in the *San Diego Community News*.[45] I also recognize that similar examples of exclusion that render Chicanas invisible are what have motivated many Chicana intellectuals and artists to express themselves. Another irony.

Chicana artists such as Gloria Robledo Torres give credibility and power to everyday work and accomplishments. Gloria grew up in San Diego, drawing and painting her whole life. The granddaughter of a cattle rancher whose animals went to slaughter, she was provided with an alternative by her mother, who wisely gave the children baby goats to raise. These animals of her childhood became the subject of Torres' paintings.

Gloria's marriage to one of the park's founders, Salvador Roberto Torres, on October 11, 1987, in Chicano Park, formed a union of two distinctive artists. As I danced at their wedding I visualized this marriage as the relationship of Chicano and Chicana. Gloria and Salvador organized campaigns for the upkeep and beautification of the park, becoming known in the community as loving keepers of the park and inspiring others to care for it. Gloria's touch will also be remembered by the large number of young students she and Salvador reached as they opened their gallery and home studio to more than four thousand students as artists/teachers in the "Young at Art" program in the San Diego City Schools.[46]

Gloria's presence and her art also added a new dimension to Chicano Park. Her work was life-giving, telling stories about Chicano life before the intrusion of freeways and shopping centers. Her characteristic subject was the little *chivos*, or baby goats. Her art filled art exhibits and walls, capturing a love of animals and children, a celebration of life, painterly and lush. While the teamwork of Gloria and Salvador made a strong statement about human relationships in the San Diego arts community, Gloria Torres' contribution revealed a strength of its own. Her hard work is now evident on walls all over San Diego. Vibrant colors represent life in "Young Mother Earth," painted in Chicano Park in 1990, and in the Kelco Community mural she helped complete in 1993. It has been called an "evocative historical account of contributions by the people of Logan Heights."

Twenty-five feet high and more than one hundred feet in length, it welcomes all who enter the neighborhood via Harbor Drive.[47]

Gloria's personal works reflect San Diego community life since 1939. In "Loving Mother Earth," painted in 1987, she pictures 38th and Broadway right after the war, when the land was so empty that her family could build bonfires there to warm the goats. Gloria recalls herding goats from Ocean Beach to El Cajon and from San Ysidro to La Mesa. "There were no obstructions then, so my sisters and I created our own paths."[48] She remembers walking through Sweetwater and Spring Valley, right through San Diego's oldest golf course. She also remembers when there were no car dealerships in Mission Valley, only beautiful Japanese gardens. In "Symphony of Love," painted in 1986, she depicts herself as a young girl in 1939, serenading her goats at 70th and El Cajon. A tragic work, neither pastoral nor verdant, recalls the brutal killing of the goats by packs of vicious wild dogs. In this linoleum cut, the dogs, wearing bowties, vertically face the innocent goats. Ready to devour the innocents, they represent the corrupt political forces that have no concern for the poor, for people who seek food or shelter or who try to get ahead, only to be thwarted by the powers of wealth and corruption. In 2006 Gloria Robledo Torres was honored at the Mesa College Gallery with a one-woman exhibition of her works, "Memories from the Rolling Hills of Old San Diego," a retrospective from 1986 to 2006.

Stories, whether told through visual art, music, or dance, became a strong way for Chicana artists to find their place in history during the 1970s. I remember Señora Herminia Enrique inviting me to dance in an epic presentation, *Women in the Mexican Revolution*. She needed a woman who could play the role of a young girl who aged throughout the dramatic episode, and she thought I could do it. I wanted that part, but as a full-time teacher and a full-time mother, I had to say no for lack of time. When I saw her daughter, Veronica Enrique, dance the lead, I felt a tinge of regret; yet I was certain I had made the right decision. Not only did Veronica dance the role exquisitely, her youth and stamina projected the powerful figure and beauty of the women of the Mexican Revolution. Women like Herminia Enrique have not been honored enough, but in 2004, she was inducted into the Women's Hall of Fame by the San Diego Women's History Museum in recognition of her accomplishments.

Teatro was another place where women could voice their desires for power and liberation. A few years after I arrived in San Diego, I remember watching Rosa Arreola intently as she demonstrated to audiences at the Centro Cultural how to move on stage, showing us ways to make large movements that would be effective to an audience seated some distance away. I used her techniques in my communications class at SDSU, teaching what Rosa had taught me about posture and voice projection. Rosa also invited me to join the board of directors at the Centro Cultural, just as Señora Enrique had invited me to be a part of her dance group. Chicanas were expected to take on such extra responsibilities, often falling into the role of Super-Chicanas. Required to do double duty, working full time and keeping a home, we rarely had energy left over for creative efforts. I was a full-time professor of English and Chicano studies and a mother of four, including two small children. I was also a full-time graduate student at UCSD required to complete my PhD before I could be tenured, and I was an advisor to Las Chicanas on campus. But other women worked as hard, or even harder. Like Señora Enrique, they rejected the meaning of the word *can't*, refusing to take no for an answer.

I recall one event that I gave my whole heart to, because it was about the oppression of the New Mexican neighborhood where my ancestors were born. I helped organize an anti-nuclear rally at SDSU and invited Rachel Ortiz, director of the Barrio Station, to speak about toxic wastes in Barrio Logan, while I spoke about the dangers of nuclear waste disposal in New Mexico neighborhoods. During those days there were so many needs and options, the danger was in taking on too much work.

Rosa Arreola was one of those women who did. A dramatist, she developed community outreach to students in local schools, while at the same time she was actively engaged in Teatro Mestizo. This artist-activist was the first woman director of the Centro Cultural in the early 1970s.[49]

In 1979 Josie Talamantez, born and raised in Logan Heights, became director of the Centro Cultural. Her ambitious efforts to build a binational consciousness in art and education led to several notable programs, including exchanges between San Diego and Mexico. To promote cultural preservation, she conceptualized a museum for Chicano, Mexican, and Native American arts and culture. In 1980, the first exhibit she curated at the center included a major showing of prints by José Guadalupe Posada, the renowned Mexican graphic artist. It was followed by an exhibition of photographs by Agustín Casásola, who photographed the Mexican Revolution, turning the Centro Cultural into a true gallery. Since museums and galleries in San Diego were not exhibiting Mexican or Chicano art in this era, this was the first time that San Diegans had the opportunity to view important art from Mexico. A woman expecting a child of her own had accomplished this.

Suddenly in the 1980s, Chicano art became noticed in the broader San Diego arts community beyond the Chicano populace. Expressions once denigrated as street art were being recognized as innovative, representing the spirit of history. City officials at the highest levels, including the mayor, began to pay attention to Chicano art. Chicano artists were also moving in various new directions, as was true in my own family. Mario had closed SolArt. Change was in the air. These events inspired me to think of opening a commercial gallery.

I also had other reasons for making such a career shift. In 1984 my college teaching career was changing, in part because of the birth of my children and also because I still needed to complete my PhD. I remember my last day of class at UCSD. I was unusually tired that night and so asked Mario for a ride to the La Jolla campus. The next day, April 22, 1980, the tenth anniversary of Chicano Park, my son, Pablo, was born. Lucia was eighteen months old. The final straw that made me decide to stop was when the phone rang while I had Pablo in my arms and Lucia tugging at my dress. It was my daughter Lauri, who had recently graduated from high school. She announced she wanted to live on the island of Kauai. Lisa called next. She was about to graduate from the University of California, Santa Barbara, and wanted me to visit her campus. When Pablo was a few weeks old and Lucia not yet two, we visited Lisa to watch her dance the ballet folklórico beautifully and win first prize in a talent contest. My life was overwhelming, with full-time teaching, full-time studies, two daughters in transition, a toddler, and a new baby boy. But it was also rewarding, as I watched my daughters excel while I completed all my coursework, my foreign language requirements, and my preliminary paper, "Utopia Now: Utopian Elements in Chicano Literature," for the PhD program. Still, I decided not to return to UCSD. I hope my story speaks to other Chicanas.

San Diego as an Arts Community, 1984–1990

I knew that eventually I would have to find other work. The arts were erupting in San Diego, and I wanted to be part of it. Ready for the gallery venture, I found myself at the mercy of attitudes toward commercial art. Determined, I read books that convinced me of the need for art and the need to represent artists. I had two things going for me: hard work and perseverance, and in-laws with expertise in the arts.

Galleries, art spaces, and grassroots theater opened up new ideas and opportunities. My family began to gather new ideas for making art and making a living. That's when I met the Singers, the owners of Pendragon's Antiques in Uptown San Diego, more a family neighborhood than downtown was. It drew all kinds of people from all over the city who were interested in art. Not wanting to work downtown, I made a proposal to the owners of the antique store: art above, antiques below, and books alongside. The Singers liked the idea and generously remodeled the space to accommodate the Acevedo Gallery, which opened in 1984.

The gallery could not have happened without the Singers and the gallery expertise of the Acevedo family, Guillermo and Lydia Acevedo, especially my father-in-law, don Guillermo, a supporter of the Chicano arts. His works were lauded by the San Diego Historical Society and by the city of San Diego. (Mayor Maureen O'Connor proclaimed August 12, 1988, Guillermo Acevedo Day.) The gallery prospered from the day it opened, attracting the attention of the art community and art critics. To glimpse the exhibits held at the Acevedo Gallery is to see the making of a commercial gallery during one peak period of the arts in San Diego. "Of the Human Spirit" was the title of the first group show, which was followed by an invitation to exhibit the works on television during a fundraiser for the local Public Broadcasting Service station, KPBS. The gallery sold work for the KPBS fundraiser exhibit and gained tremendous publicity in San Diego.[50]

I designed many exhibits over the next six years, from 1984 to 1990. This effort represents one Chicana's contribution to Chicano art. By discussing these exhibitions, I hope to show the effects of these kinds of grassroots projects and the surprising results they can have. The work that I accomplished during this time was possible because of the Chicano Movement, because of a family steeped in the arts, and because of the many connections Mario made with Chicana artists like Bárbara Carrasco, Diane Gamboa, Judith Hernández, Judith E. Baca, and Sonya Fe, to name a few, whose work we brought to San Diego. I also got to visit the art studios of many prominent artists who exhibited with us. The idea of running a gallery may seem glamorous, but sometimes the day-to-day work is like the domestic labor once called women's work but more creative. I designed the invitations and the framing, organized the openings, and ordered the food; we both invited the artists and traveled to other cities to acquire art; while he hung the exhibits and framed much of the art, I did the bookkeeping, including the taxes, and paid all the expenses. A lonely job, but a labor of love really, and the timing was perfect; 1984 proved to be an explosion in the arts.

The gallery was committed to Chicano art but not exclusive to it. We visited Taos, New Mexico, where art flourished and where we met Navajo artist R. C. Gorman and New Mexico artist Miguel Martínez. That is also where we heard about Corita Kent through one of her admirers who knew her as Sister Mary in the 1960s at Immaculate Heart College. Corita represented movement art, spiritual direction, and the spirit of the 1960s, the spontaneity of the times, the colors of life—De Colores. Corita knew of the work of César Chávez and Dolores Huerta. She had produced hundreds of socially conscious silk screen prints in the 1960s, one dedicated to César Chávez. I told her more about the farmworkers' struggle and the cry of the people, "¡Sí, Se Puede!" Not long after that, a client asked if we could cosponsor a fundraiser and commission Corita to do a work of art for it. Corita agreed. The fundraiser would be at the home of Linda Smith, daughter of the late Joan Kroc, a well-known philanthropist. When I saw the silk screen, my mouth dropped. "Yes, We Can!" (an English translation of Sí, Se Puede) was written in the clouds on a blue backdrop. It was her final work of art. Corita Kent, former nun and artist, died in 1986. We had a closing and sendoff for her by releasing balloons into the air. And our children helped their father paint a mural on the wall near Christ the King Church in southeast San Diego near his images of César Chávez and Martin Luther King.

Among the Chicana artists who contributed to the gallery, one stands out: Sonya Fe. Fe exhibited with us from 1985 to 1990, but I met her long before the gallery opened. She was Sonya Martínez then, her mother's maiden name. We shared mutual concerns. Her story is worth telling as it encompasses a Chicana's journey and development in the arts in San Diego. Sonya had been married to one of the formidable figures in the founding of Chicano Park and the Toltecas de Aztlán, Tomás "Coyote" Castañeda. At the time I met her, she was a single mother with a son. While married, she feared having to forfeit her dreams of becoming an artist. Now she was at a crossroads, faced with uncertainties about her own identity.

One day, exasperated, she threw up her hands, exclaiming that she wasn't sure what she wanted to paint anymore. After all, was she really Chicana, she wondered? Her mother was Mexican; was that enough? "I am a Martínez, but I am also Goldfein, my father's name." I just remember telling her what I had learned as a writer: "Just create from your own experience." Sonya's story reminded me of La Frida's. I first heard of Frida Kahlo from one of the other writers I presented with at a conference in the San Francisco Bay Area.[51] Then I saw Frida's art at UCSD in 1978 at the Mandeville Center, her first solo exhibit on the West Coast. I shared my knowledge about her with Sonja: Frida was Mexican and German and, like Sonya, had been married to a forceful artist, Diego Rivera. Frida also became a compelling artist in her own right, painting her own struggles as a woman, about women, while addressing her mixed ancestry.

Nearly a year later I received a letter from Sonya. "I am painting women and children. I have traveled to Mexico to discover my roots and I am selling my art." Indeed she was. She painted from her own consciousness and her own experience, and the world witnessed her newfound power. I had almost forgotten our conversation some time before. Like me, Sonya had been affected by the work of Frida Kahlo and other Mexican masters. She began signing her name Sonya Martínez Goldfein to acknowledge her mixed ancestry, but that wasn't entirely satisfactory either. "I like my name," she said, "but it is such a long signature. It's exhausting."

One day she phoned and enthusiastically announced her new name: Sonya Fe. Sonya had visited New Mexico, and further influenced by the arts of her ancestors, had found the perfect way to sign her work. The Spanish word for faith, la fe, fit her perfectly. After that she had several exhibits in the Acevedo Gallery. In *Contemporary Chicana and Chicano Art*, Sonya Fe recalls, "My style changed dramatically after my visit to Mexico" (118–19). She also acknowledged being influenced by the work of Frida Kahlo. The critics responded especially to the aspect of her work dealing with women's sexuality and male-female relationships. In one painting, "You Must Make a Choice," the woman is forced to choose between two lovers pictured in the work as *calaveras*, each manipulating her as a puppet on a string. The woman presents a mask of beauty to the world while hiding her true emotions. Her deepest source of femininity, however, is at stake, as one can see exposed through a sheer dress her breasts and her menstrual flow. Sonya's own vulnerability and her outrage show up in this work, as they do in another massive piece, "La Llorona," the wailing woman. Her stature as a mature artist shines through.[52]

The Acevedo Gallery began at a fortuitous moment when San Diego was becoming a city in support of the arts. This era has become known for a great flourishing of art in the Southwest. That was evident in the Indian art showings in commercial galleries; the "Young at Art" artists being hired in the schools; the workshops for families given by the San Diego Museum of Art and the Museum of Contemporary Art; a new Children's Museum; and the Commission of Arts and Culture for the City of San Diego. In 1988, I applied, as did Mario, to be a commissioner of arts and culture. I thought as a Chicana, an educator, and a gallery co-director I might be chosen; I also applied for the position of artist in the schools with the "Young at Art" program, directed by Kay Wagner. I was not accepted as a commissioner; Mario was. We were, however, both hired as artists in the schools. That year Mario Acevedo became one of the notables to observe according to "People to Watch in San Diego in 1988," in *San Diego Magazine*.

As the co-director of an art gallery and a teacher of the arts in city schools, my children and stepchildren became steeped in the arts. Lucia and Pablo both contributed works to the San Diego Museum of Art for its innovative "Young at Art" exhibit. My contribution, designed to be consciousness raising, was the Rain Forest exhibit, with Te Mattel, for which the students designed birds. Huge papier-mâché birds, in exaggerated colors and shapes, hung from the ceiling and stood on displays. Our daughter, Lucia, ten, sculpted a fantasy bird she dressed in a fancy jacket, created separately. Our eight-year-old son, Pablo's, design of Van Gogh became the centerpiece on one of the Young at Art vans. San Diego schoolchildren walked in huge parades carrying the massive papier-mâché heads, figures, and suns we made at school. Others carried art on a grander scale, including walking puppets created with "Young at Art" teachers. Art was everywhere. It was a sight to behold. Between 1984 and 1990, I saw two breakthrough exhibits that affected Chicanas in the arts: the Border Arts Workshop in 1984 and Las Comadres exhibit in 1990, both in San Diego.

The Border Arts Workshop/Taller de Arte Fronterizo

The Border Arts Workshop/Taller de Arte Fronterizo opened in 1984 and was important because it propelled consciousness about the border and the people who cross it to a higher level. However, it did not include Chicanas. The Border Arts Workshop began as a collaboration of two Chicano artists at the Centro Cultural de la Raza with two Mexican artists and their wives, and an Anglo artist from San Diego. The artists examined the Mexican–U.S. international border and its subjects, those who crossed from either side. This artists' collective began with those seven members: five men, David Avalos, Victor Ochoa, Guillermo Gómez-Peña, Isaac Artenstein, and Michael Schnorr; and two women, Jude

Eberhardt and Sara Jo Berman; and later included Chicano artists Richard Lou and Robert Sánchez.[53]

Border consciousness with cross-ethnic collaboration was a first for San Diego, and not everyone was ready to accept it. At first, the fact that no Chicanas had been invited to participate created some stir. Chicanas questioned this situation in part because they had traditionally been excluded by white feminist groups, or if not excluded, had grappled with joining them because they did not deal with racism or poverty, issues of primary concern to Chicanas. As it turned out, the makeup of the group was in keeping with the message these artists wanted to convey—that border crossing was not exclusive to one side. They brought that message home, and Chicanas were expected to digest it.

In the final analysis, however, some Chicanas judged that the double standard was still operating. Chicanas had long been criticized during the Chicano Movement for forming separate groups apart from the men and supposedly disrupting unity within the movement. Yet when Chicanos proceeded to take off on their own, not only did they exclude Chicanas, but they included non-Chicanas, and they did so without benefit of debate. That is, men were still making the rules; so they could break the rules, it appeared.

Nevertheless, the Border Artists, as they came to be known, had begun to cross important boundaries in their art. The press and the public were astounded at the scope of the exhibit and its ability to unearth serious border concerns. Even so, the debut was like a crack that broke open a wall, exposing divisions between artists and between male and female. Opening night of the exhibit provided some drama as artists stood face-to-face while not seeing eye-to-eye. The exhibit did not get full acceptance from women because of the missing element, the Chicana, arguably the group most affected by the border. Some Chicanas expressed discomfort as they watched Anglo females boldly walking in and out of the Centro Cultural offices. No matter how innovative this phase in the arts might be, it represented a temporary unrest.

The BAW/TAF marked a new and productive period in the arts in San Diego, an awakening to border consciousness, which was its intent. In 1985 Chicanas participated in the Border Realities exhibit at the Centro. Various installation pieces in designated rooms were created by women alone or by women in collaboration with men. This time, the exhibit included Chicana and non-Chicana artists: Aída Mancillas, Sara Jo Berman, Emily Hicks with Robert Sánchez, Carmela Castrejón with Victor Ochoa, Berta Jottar with Michael Schnorr, and Deborah

Small with David Avalos.[54] The Border Realities exhibit made a significant contribution to the arts as it brought new life to Chicano Arts and a shift to international concerns. More than that, it motivated Chicanas and others interested in a feminine consciousness to act on their own.

In 1985, Veronica Enrique, the executive director of the Centro Cultural, organized the fifteenth anniversary exhibit, *Made in Aztlán*. It included a history of the Centro in a book by the same title. Twelve Chicanas were represented in the seventy-person exhibit: Judith Baca, Liz Lerma Bowman, Barbara Carrasco, Diane Gamboa, Lorraine García, Yolanda López, Patricia Mercado, Amalia Mesa-Bains, Patricia Rodríguez, Olivia Sánchez Brown, Patssi Valdez, and Linda Vallejo.

Las Comadres

San Diego women of various ethnicities also responded to what they perceived to be the BAW/TAF's inability to address issues of gender and sexuality important to them. Moreover, they wanted to explore the history of women's oppression, so they met to dialogue about their concerns. They tackled problems related to the U.S.–Mexican border, but also issues related to gender and sexuality. They read works by Gloria Anzaldúa, innovator of border consciousness, and other Chicana writers in *Making Face, Making Soul / Haciendo Caras: Creative and Critical Perspectives by Feminists of Color.*[55] Their priorities were to understand the history and struggles of Chicanas in relationship to the border.

In 1988, to form a community of women in solidarity with one another and against racism and sexism, the group called themselves Las Comadres. They chose a name from the Mexican culture that connotes more than sisterhood—an almost blood relationship called *compadrazgo*. Las Comadres consisted of artists, workers, teachers, and college professors Kirsten Aaboe, Yareli Arizmendi, Carmela Castrejón, Frances Charteris, Magali Dama, Kristina Dybbro-Aguirre, María Eraña, Laura Esparza, Madeleine Grynsztejn, Emily Hicks, Berta Jottar, María Eloise de León, Aída Mancillas, Anna O'Cain, Graciela Ovejero, Lynn Susholtz, Ruth Wallen, Marguerite Waller, Rocio Weiss, and Cindy Zimmerman.[56]

Their intellectual debate soon became a physical challenge when some of the women decided to respond to a reactionary element in a vigilante movement that was flooding the border with spotlights. Las Comadres, in response to "Light Up the Border: One Thousand Points of Light," countered with a banner reading

"One Thousand Points of Fear." In order to expose the vigilante group and its inherent fear of Mexicans, as well as to question the actions of people who would go to such extremes to stop Mexican workers from coming to the United States, these women hired a plane to fly their banner over the border. The wall between the United States and Mexico was stronger than ever, held up more by ignorance and fear than by justice and the rule of law.

Some of the women of Las Comadres even went to the border to counter face-to-face the extreme anti-immigrant fervor. However, their hopes for creating a dialogue of understanding were overly optimistic. Their opponents met them with emotional attacks, anger, and refusal to debate, and the women realized that intellectual exchange and education were not what these outraged citizens wanted. Nevertheless, the courage displayed by these women far outweighed the fear in those who wanted to stop what they hated most, the Mexicans coming to the United States.

In 1990, Las Comadres staged a multimedia exhibition, art installation, and teatro performance at the Centro Cultural de la Raza that gained national attention. Grand in scale and passionate in its statement about women's exploitation, "La Vecindad" drew large crowds and lots of press, both locally and nationally, along with invitations to perform in other cities.

The art installation represented the kitchen as a definitive space, not just a site of exploitation, but also one where women gained power. They described it as a crossing from complacency to assertion and challenge. Their strength came from conversation and dialogue. In one theater piece, spoken words that appeared to be gossip to the opposite sex were, in fact, quite serious to the women, a starting point for dialogue where women shared secrets, challenged oppression, made choices about their lives, and decided to act. In other words, within their own oppression women contrived ways to overcome it. Out of subjugation, women became conscious, educated, and active.

The performance I most remember was the "Border Boda," which pointed to the wedding as the most significant moment in a young Mexicana's life. Eloise de León played the young woman preparing for her marriage ceremony, which would unite her to an Anglo. The artist's statement to the audience explained that the piece represented the "dissension and struggle, displaced history of colonization, beneath the backdrop of a joyous event." On the night before her wedding, the bride listens to her grandmother tell stories representing the history and culture she fears her granddaughter is losing. The bride's aunt, Rocio Weiss, cannot speak but communicates through songs of struggle, corridos, representing the people's history now preserved only as oral tradition. She tells her niece the dark secret of her mother's rape and murder by an Anglo land grabber. The bride-to-be comes to realize that she is a product of violation, representing the rape of the Chicanas' homeland by the U.S. takeover of Mexico in the Mexican War of 1848. Her beloved's history is one of aggression against her own people, who were made subjects by virtue of war, a contradiction she must face.

In this performance piece, Las Comadres gave San Diego audiences a new way of looking at the world. Chicanas especially absorbed this message: the continuity of generations in search of their roots, language, and culture, lost to foreign invasion. Despite this harsh reality, though, the play represented borders as something meant to be crossed, not closed; confronted and debated, not silenced. The audience and the actors at this performance were called on to recognize that they were all participants in the crossing. To make this point, the audience was invited on stage to share music and drink. The drama of women talking and cooking in the huge family kitchen represented women's coming to consciousness, an opening of borders through dialogue; the audience recognized the power of women and celebrated with them on stage. Las Comadres of various ethnicities were willing to cross the borders of their differences, daring to discover themselves while addressing this border reality through publicly sharing their personal narratives.

In 1990, about the same time as I witnessed the Las Comadres exhibition, Mario and I decided to close the gallery we had worked at for six years. When as gallery owners and as parents Mario and I went our separate ways, our children were hurt. But I hoped they carried with them the love we had given them and their love of art. Art continued to take center stage in the new home where I moved with my children. People who visited us walked up to it and asked about the artist, their father. I had to find my own world. I had to find the people who cared about me and about my children. I had to find myself. I returned to teaching in the college classroom and, as a way of healing myself and my children, I began mentoring young Chicanas through Niñas de Aztlán, founded by Irma Castro. That same year our daughter, Lucia Acevedo, won first prize in the San Diego–Tijuana History Fair. She was awarded the blue ribbon at the Casa de Prado in Balboa Park for her art board honoring her grandfather, "Guillermo Acevedo: Immigrant Artist/Artista Inmigrante." Another example of healing through art.

The Ongoing Chicana Presence, 1990–1995

The 1990s did not represent the end of my involvement in the arts. I began teaching courses in the English and Chicano Studies departments at Mesa College, including La Chicana, Chicana literature, and Chicano culture. I was also introduced to emerging Chicana writers from all over the United States and to more major art exhibits, particularly the CARA exhibit at UCLA; La Frontera/The Border exhibit at the Centro Cultural and the San Diego Museum of Contemporary Art; and the Sin Fronteras exhibit in San Diego. An important feature of these exhibits is that they included Chicana artists, influencing the state of the arts in San Diego.

When I began at Mesa College in 1990, Chicanas were producing art and literature. If ever there was a Chicana renaissance in the arts, it was in Chicana literature. Professors César González and Mike Ornelas of the Chicano Studies Department had been planning a seminar with Chicana authors when I arrived. As the first full-time Chicana faculty member, I was invited to be the moderator for the three poets invited by Professor González: Alma Luz Villanueva, Lucha Corpi, and Ana Castillo. These women were the first of several Chicana writers to come to San Diego. Others who performed or read their works in San Diego were Sandra Cisneros, author of *Woman Hollering Creek*; Diana García of San Diego, author of *When Living Was a Labor Camp*; and Josefina López, author of *Real Women Have Curves*, who performed in her own play at the Lyceum Theatre and gave other performances at the Centro Cultural. Other Chicana professors published and taught courses in San Diego, highly influencing the arts and literature: Gail Pérez at the University of San Diego; Rosaura Sánchez and Martha Sánchez at UCSD; and later, Elva Salinas and María Figueroa at San Diego City College.

Another woman stands out during this period for her contribution to the theater arts. After acting as administrative assistant for the Chicana and Chicano Studies Department at SDSU for more than ten years, Evelyn Díaz Cruz, a mother herself and wife of musician Saúl Cruz, graduated with an MFA in playwriting and returned to SDSU to teach courses in the department. She then received the national UC Irvine Literary Prize for her play "Glass Cord," performed in New York and San Diego. Now an assistant professor at USD, Evelyn Cruz teaches courses in theater arts.

A new generation of women artist-activists performed with the Taco Shop Poets. Originated by four men, Miguel Ángel Soria, Adrian Arancelina, Adolfo

Guzmán, and Tomás Riley, it soon shifted to an almost all-women group with only two males. Among them were Lin Romero, Adela Carrasco, Elizabeth Barron, María Figueroa, Esmerelda Jiménez, Pat Payne, Kathleen Pendleton-Jiménez, Fran Illich, Jackolean López, Olympia Rodríguez, Nydia Sánchez, and Regina Swain. The group found a place to stage events at Voz Alta in downtown San Diego, which continues today to be a lively performance venue with a strong emphasis on women's work. Voz Alta has become a multi-performance space where women read their poetry and show their art. Among these women was my student María Julia Urías.

The CARA Exhibit, 1990

The Chicano Art: Resistance and Affirmation (CARA) exhibit at the UCLA Wight Gallery in 1990 was a twenty-year retrospective representing the period 1965–1985. In this important major exhibit, women had a highly visible presence. For the first time Chicanas could see the extent of their art over a twenty-year period in the exhibit and in the bound exhibit catalog.[57] San Diego artists were represented in this milestone exhibition.

The first image in the exhibit catalog was a work by San Diego artist Salvador Roberto Torres. But especially notable was the work of Yolanda López, by then living in San Francisco. López's "Virgen de Guadalupe Series" and Torres's "Viva La Raza," a 1969 interpretation of the UFW eagle, were at the forefront. Other San Diego artists were represented as well: David Avalos, Guillermo Gómez Peña, Mario Torero, Salvador Torres, and Victor Ochoa. But the works by the Chicanas, especially Yolanda López, presented a visible milestone.

Yolanda López, one of more than thirty Chicana artists included in the show, had her "Portrait of the Artist as the Virgin of Guadalupe" prominently displayed (fig. 7.4). The essay on Chicana art in the exhibit catalog praised the work, "The potential of feminine images to emancipate women is best realized in the landmark Guadalupe series by Yolanda Lopez." She had come to be known as "one of the most challenging artists in the Chicano movement."[58]

The CARA exhibit catalogue featured an essay on Chicana artists. Amalia Mesa-Bains selected six women out of the thirty in the exhibit to represent Chicana artists of the movement: Yolanda López, Judith Baca, Santa Barraza, Carmen Lomas Garza, Ester Hernández, and Patricia Rodríguez. Mesa-Bains says their "presence as leaders, activists, and artists has been critical to achieving large-scale social change."[59]

FIGURE 7.4. Yolanda López, "Portrait of the Artist as the Virgen de Guadalupe." (Courtesy of the artist; from Griswold del Castillo, McKenna, and Yarbro-Bejarano, *CARA*, 64)

The essay describes Yolanda López's work as picturing the symbolic power of women for young and old women alike. "But her most famous piece is the image of La Virgen throwing up her dress by forcefully taking off in her running shoes" (see fig. 7.4). She added, in "repositioning the traditional," the work becomes "both satire and provocation . . . a critique of the way these icons have been interpreted in male tradition."[60] Feminist author Elizabeth "Betita" Martínez had this to say about López and artists like her in her book, *De Colores Means All of Us*, "We would not be as far along as we are today without the heretical work of Yolanda López . . . Ester Hernández [and] Juana Alicia." Author of the new *500 Years of Chicana Women's History* Elizabeth Martínez calls this art militant transformation, offering "a liberation never before available."[61]

Yolanda López's images from her Guadalupe series are also featured in a fold-out in *Contemporary Chicana and Chicano Art*. The text interprets her special series as re-centering "the sacred and intrinsically spiritual figure to express beauty, dignity, and multiple struggles that living Mexicans possess and negotiate on a daily basis."[62] The book also describes the extent of her accomplishments. López has exhibited at the New York Museum of Contemporary Art, the Museum of Contemporary Hispanic Art, Studio M in Harlem, and the Museum of Modern Art in New York City. In 2002 she exhibited at the Los Angeles County Museum and in the same year was listed in *100 Years of California Women Artists* at the San Jose Museum of Contemporary Art.

Much of Yolanda López's work challenges sexism and subverts traditional constructions of gender. Another piece by López featured in the two-volume *Contemporary Chicana and Chicano Art* is "Who Is the Illegal Alien, Pilgrim?" It "challenges the fallacies of U.S. nativist thought regarding 'illegal immigration'" exposing anti-immigrant attitudes and behavior. López makes a powerful statement as a native San Diegan reaching a national and international audience.[63] San Diego made art history because of her.

I attended the CARA Exhibit opening in 1990 and reveled in the work of Yolanda López and other Chicana artists. Amalia Mesa-Bains had built an altar, dedicated to Dolores del Río, in keeping with themes for Día de los Muertos. Santa Barraza had painted "El Descanso Final," a mixed-media work representing death as an end and a beginning. Barraza came to San Diego with the Latina Leadership Conference, organized by Adela Jacobson with faculty at Mesa College. There, she showed her version of "La Malinche" as a beautiful woman of Indian royalty, betrayed by the patriarchy who courted her, captured her, seduced, and abandoned her.

In 1993, I felt that I had contributed to the early period of Chicana productivity in the arts. Inspired by these artists' works and wishing to sustain the ongoing female energy in the arts, I proposed painting a women's peace mural with Chicana students at Mesa College. In my La Chicana class, we were reading *I, Rigoberta Menchú*, the testimony of a Guatemalan Indian woman who had recently won the Nobel Peace Prize. One student, Bernice Badilla, expressed anger that her San Diego High School art instructor criticized her drawings of Chicano icons. Determined to counter these kinds of judgments, I proposed a mural project. For some expert advice, I called Judith Baca, then a professor at the University of California at Irvine; the creator of "The Great Wall of Los Angeles," considered the world's largest mural; and founder/artistic director of the Social and Public Art Resource Center (SPARC) in Venice. Judy Baca has been described by art critic Shifra Goldman as "one of the earliest (beginning in 1969) and most enduring of Chicana women muralists in California."[64] SPARC was run by women with the purpose of documenting and preserving mural images. Judith Baca invited us to a seminar in her college classroom. She took our field trip of women through an all-day process of mural painting.

From that visit, a design soon evolved. Bernice Badilla garnered ideas from the class. The centerpiece she designed for "The Peace Mural" showed Rigoberta Menchú holding a baby, its face the globe of the earth, representing her choice to commit her life to the world. The mural was approved, the wall of building I-100 prepared for the mural, and a fundraiser set in motion.

Then on Columbus Day, a group of students decided to physically take over our wall at Mesa College in response to the "discovery of America," the Christopher Columbus narrative, using the consciousness-raising slogan of artists Coco Fusco and Guillermo Gómez Peña, "Do Not Discover Me." The city police intervened to stop what they called defacing property, an irony given that the students were protesting the takeover of Indian land. A long period of dialogue followed, with Chicano Studies faculty mentoring the students. My feeling was that the police acted hastily: the wall of I-100 already belonged to us; we had obtained permission to paint the women's mural there, and it had been approved by the Arts Committee and the college president. The students had used our wall to make a political statement. There were bigger battles to fight, I thought.

On the other hand, the students, among them Chicana activist Erica Zamora, wanted to make a strong statement about colonialism. Their courageous act included placing a high ladder on the wall, climbing to the top, and "discovering the wall," to dramatize the meaning of the words. Police rushed in before notifying the administration, and soon helicopters hovered over the campus. The students were detained and suffered consequences that affected their academic standing. But not in vain, many agreed, if their action demonstrated that to discover another culture does not mean the right to take it over. However, the women's mural project was postponed, displaced by other activities.[65]

Mesa College would get its mural, but not in the way we expected. While the campus became preoccupied with how to deal with student unrest, other real struggles were about to be addressed: one was the brutal beating of Rodney King by four policemen. King became a symbol of police brutality when an amateur videographer provided unmistakable evidence thereof: a videotape showing several white Los Angeles police officers using their batons to beat King. When the four policemen charged in the case were acquitted, it set off one of the worst riots in Los Angeles history. Students and faculty came out in droves from different campuses to protest the unjust verdict, unleashing an outpouring of concern about police brutality, racism, and unequal treatment.

At Mesa College students wanted to make a radical statement about the brutality against King, and the verdict of the Los Angeles jury that condoned it. I met with students, along with other faculty and staff. In the end, I proposed painting a mural. I recalled the political statement made at SDSU by students of Nick Nichols, who had, overnight, painted a mural honoring the workers and the poor; it still stands in a classroom in the Adams Humanities Building.

After much debate, the Rodney King mural was painted overnight on the Chicano Studies building, a "temporary" bungalow on the far side of campus where the department had been housed for twenty-five years, another focus of student protests. This historic gesture was painted by Mesa College students, including Erica Zamora, with the help of Mario and me. The nonviolent gesture appeared on the wall the next day.

La Frontera/The Border, 1993

That same year, the Centro Cultural de la Raza and the La Jolla Museum of Contemporary Art collaborated on a thirty-seven artist exhibit called *La Frontera/ The Border: Art About the Mexico/United States Border Experience*. The hand-bound book published in conjunction with this exhibition featured some fifteen women, including Las Comadres. Nearly half the artists were women, as were half the curators and authors, which included noted Chicana writers Gloria Anzaldúa and Sandra Cisneros.

The Sin Fronteras Exhibit, 1994

In 1994, I saw another consciousness-raising exhibit in San Diego. The Sin Fronteras exhibit was important for bringing more Chicana art to San Diego. The exhibit also traveled to Manchester, England, raising international awareness about the U.S.–Mexican border while heightening Chicana consciousness at home. It included works by Chicana artists Amalia Mesa-Bains of San Francisco, Celia Muñoz of El Paso, and Patssi Valdez of Los Angeles. San Diego artists represented were Richard Lou, Robert Sánchez, Guillermo Gómez Peña, and David Avalos exhibiting with Deborah Small.

David Avalos and Deborah Small entitled their installation piece "Miscege-Nation" to emphasize North Americans' repulsion toward *mestizaje*, the very essence of our Mexican identity. The English word *miscegenation* has a history of ethnocentrism whereas the Spanish term *mestizaje* does not. This exhibit necessitated not only the dual authorship of Chicano and non-Chicana but also a marriage bed, to make this point.[66] Meanwhile, Richard Lou and Robert Sánchez countered the official border voice whose anti-Mexican sentiment was evident in Proposition 187, an attempt to curb immigration by preventing the children of Mexican workers who provide the United States with cheap labor from receiving health care or education. Chicana artist Amalia Mesa-Bains made a political statement using the *ofrenda*, or spiritual offering, as metaphor. Dirt filled the drawers of a dresser, representing our deepest desires to hold on to the land, *la tierra*, which belonged to Mexico prior to the U.S. takeover in 1848. Patssi Valdes' rich, colorful rooms represented the grandeur of our mestizaje; indigenous colors mixed with the sacred icons of our Spanish past. The dark Madonna, both Indian and Spanish, showed how we cannot escape our mestizo roots. Celia Muñoz drew from her Tejana roots and the areas where she has felt the most discriminated, "being Chicana, being Catholic, and being Tejana," to make her art.[67] The presenters and art critics called Sin Fronteras bold, challenging, colorful, Mexican, Chicano-Chicana contemporary art, focusing on the border as a metaphor of cultural disparity and a desire to end cultural stereotypes from both sides of the border. In it, Chicana and Chicano artists together examined their relationship with the United States and Mexico.

Other notable Chicanas have contributed to the arts in San Diego, among them Valerie Aranda, Alessandra Moctezuma, and Natasha Bonillo Martínez. In this period Valerie Aranda exhibited and taught in San Diego. Significantly, her art drew deeply from her family roots, representing her Mexican ancestry and family's history in the arts. Her paternal grandfather was a painter and her maternal grandmother "created beautiful *altares* in the home for deceased family members." Valerie's art became well known to San Diegans through various exhibits at area colleges and at the Centro Cultural de la Raza. She has taught art courses at Mesa College, Miracosta College, and Oceanside College in San Diego. Some of her local exhibits include "La Mano y La Historia," UCSD 1996; "Celebrating Women and Art," Women's Center, UCSD, 1997; "Hispanic Portraits," Paladion, San Diego, 1997; "Imagen de San Diego: Tercer Vision" at the Centro Cultural, 1998; and "Independencia," at the Centro Cultural, 1999. She received her MFA from UCSD in 2000. In *Contemporary Chicana and Chicano Art* Gary Keller says her work "develops a vibrant interplay of personal history and cultural reclamation" where culture is reinforced across generations. One work is especially poignant as it is reminiscent of Frida Kahlo's "My Birth." Aranda's "Our Birth," 1995, creates a more "raw and transcendent" contrast, as it is more fully human than the tortured work of the Mexican artist. Aranda's painting shows a grandmother's warm touch extended to the birthing mother and a child's doll at her feet, suggesting the generations of women. Aranda explains this work, which draws on her connection to Frida Kahlo's art, as representing her personal rebirth and the physical birth of her daughter.[68]

Alessandra Moctezuma came to San Diego as director of the Mesa College Gallery and professor of Chicano art following a history of art activism in Los Angeles. She was previously the gallery curator for SPARC, a space designed especially for women, and public arts officer for the Los Angeles County Metropolitan Transit Authority. Moctezuma and Eva Cockcroft worked together on the "Homage to Siqueiros" mural painted at the Self-Help Graphics and Cultural Center on César Chávez Boulevard in Los Angeles.

Natasha Bonillo Martínez, as a student of art history at San Diego State University, worked with Victor Ochoa and Richard Griswold del Castillo on an exhibit showcasing San Diego's Chicano history as part of a grant she obtained. The exhibit later traveled to Chihuahua in an exchange with Mexican museums. Soon thereafter, Natasha was one of several biographers for *Women Artists of the American West*, an online resource featuring the vital contributions women have made to art and history. Her biography of Delilah Montoya describes many of the artist's works, including "A Journey from Mechica to Chicana," which was part of the 1992–94 traveling exhibit *The Chicano Codices: Encountering Art of the Americas*, when it came to San Diego's Centro Cultural de la Raza. Her writing also appeared in *Spirit Capture, Photographs from the National Museum of the American Indian* in Washington DC, where she commented on the sometimes intrusive nature of field photographers into sacred ceremonies. She then became the director of education at the California Center for the Arts in Escondido. She accomplished so much that when she left after ten years, it took two people to replace her.

In 1999 the leadership at the Centro Cultural de la Raza changed hands. Nancy Rodríguez of San Antonio, Texas, took over as director, while Viviana Enrique became artistic director. Soon thereafter, Aída Mancillas became president of the board of directors, vowing in a 2004 *La Prensa* article to work tirelessly "in an atmosphere of inclusiveness and in the spirit of grassroots activism." Aída Mancillas had been consistently active in the arts in San Diego since the

1980s. She was a member of Las Comadres while a professor of languages at UCSD and a member of the Centro's arts advisory committee from 1989 to 1993. She contributed to several exhibitions in San Diego. In 1985 she was one of the first Chicanas to exhibit at the Centro Cultural in "Border Realities." In 1987 she teamed with Robert Sánchez in "En Memoria"; in 1988 she contributed to a history of the events surrounding the Battle of Puebla. Then in 1990 as part of Las Comadres, she participated in the installation and exhibit "La Vecindad."

In the 1990s, Mancillas also crossed borders into other community projects. She received a grant from the National Endowment for the Arts for works on paper, exhibited at the San Diego Museum of Art, and founded an arts advisory group in San Diego. Then, in 1993, she and Lynn Susholtz were hired as artists for the Vermont Street Bridge project, a four hundred–foot pedestrian crossing over Washington Street in Hillcrest. The design won several awards for the contribution it made to the built environment and community planning. In 1995 it won the American Institute of Architects' Orchid Award and the American Planners' Association Award of Excellence and was featured in *Art in America*. In her definitive essay "The Citizen Artist" she describes how she and Susholtz reached the community as fellow activists not adversaries, with their ideas for the bridge.[69] In 1998, Mancillas was one of eleven artists chosen because of their commitment to public art to transform Adams Avenue into a public gallery with 120 banners on lampposts. She also served as commissioner of arts for the city of San Diego. Aída Mancillas will always be known as a breakthrough artist for being among the first Chicanas to bring her art to the Centro Cultural, and by the Hillcrest community for being one of the "Women who changed San Diego and Our Neighborhood."[70]

Now, after thirty years, the extent of women's struggle for self-determination is visible in Chicana art. Spaces like Chicano Park and the Centro Cultural de la Raza stand out as the most notable expressions of Chicano art, and Chicanas have indeed proven to be at the forefront of the movement. As chair of the Chicano Park Steering Committee and a founder of the park, Tommie Camarillo has been lauded for "giving her life to maintain the murals" that represent the struggles of the Chicano people. Her work includes the fight in the 1990s against plans to earthquake-proof the pillars underneath the Coronado Bridge where the art lives, which would have destroyed the art. To her, the murals constitute an "open-air museum," preserved mostly by community volunteers. She observes, however, that the park and the art are about the Chicano people and their history and that "the result from the continuing gentrification of Logan [where the Park is centered] would push the community residents out, bringing more commercial [enterprises] in." As a keynote speaker at the Comité de Mujeres Patricia Marín, Tommie Camarillo spoke about the park. At the *plática*, designed to bring together Chicana and Mexicana activists, she described the urgency and the years of effort it has taken to maintain the park and the art. Yet, as she reminds us, "Chicano Park is a clear example of how through struggle, self-determination is possible."[71]

At the Centro Cultural, Herminia Enrique has been the guiding force in folklórico dance for more than thirty years, as one of the first artists at the Ford building in 1969. She and her extended family, including Isabel Enrique, Veronica Enrique, Viviana Enrique, and Armida Valencia, have given great hope to future generations of Chicanas. They have also given immeasurably to the cultural vitality of the performing arts in the San Diego Community.

Nineteen ninety-six was a momentous year. That year, I became chair of the Chicano Studies Department at Mesa College—at last, a woman had become chair. My youngest daughter Lucia, seventeen, graduated from Our Lady of Peace Academy; my son Pablo, sixteen, received an art scholarship, one of 200 recipients out of 2,000 applicants for summer training at Cal Arts; and I remarried. That year Richard Griswold del Castillo and I became a blended family, with my four and his two children, Charles and Ariel. Together Richard and I have eight grandchildren: Serena, Melissa, and Joey La Rossa; Kidone and Dante Viscarra; and Adrian, Elyssa, and Ryan Gonzales. Since Richard was chairperson of the Chicana and Chicano Studies Department at SDSU and I held the same position at Mesa College, we became a marriage of Chicana/Chicano studies. Our interest in history was not all that we had in common. As he edited the CARA exhibit catalog and I worked feverishly for the arts, we found another mutual interest.

In 1998, Richard was on the site committee with Shifra Goldman for the College Arts Association Conference at the Los Angeles Convention Center, where I presented my research on Frida Kahlo, "Suffering, Rage, and Redemption: Frida Kahlo and the Tradition of Santera Art."[72] In 1998, Richard and I saw "Beyond Frida," at the Oceanside Museum of Art, a joint exhibit with the Centro Cultural de Tijuana. Participating artists were Ana María Herrera, Rosa Robles, Irma Sofía Poeter, Monica Escutia, María Romero, and Tanya Candiani from San Diego and Tijuana. Shifra Goldman gave a talk, "Contra Kahlo: Quest for Women Artists in Twentieth-Century Mexico."

In 2000, at the thirtieth anniversary of Chicano Park, we gave a tour of the park for local television stations covering the event. In 2004, I was invited by Olivia Puentes-Reynolds to present my Frida Kahlo paper at the opening of the "Women Who Dare" exhibit at the Women's History Museum in San Diego,[73] honoring women in the arts and activism. In 2005 Richard and I together presented the arts tour of the Cheech Marin Exhibit at the Museum of Contemporary Art in La Jolla.

This essay represents a Chicana perspective, a bird's-eye view, witnessing, researching, and remembering what occurred during a thirty-year period in the arts in San Diego. I hope this memoir and research is also a reminder of how much Chicanas have persevered in the struggle to accomplish their goals of contributing to the arts at a time when women's participation was not entirely accepted. I also hope that through cherishing the collective memory of those who came before, readers can see the historical evolution of women's struggle for identity and a lasting place in society.

8

THE STRUGGLE AGAINST GENTRIFICATION IN BARRIO LOGAN

Emmanuelle Le Texier

As Rita Sánchez's personal reflections trace the Chicana Movement and the arts in San Diego, this chapter contributes another perspective on the role of women in political activism. In Barrio Logan, the issue of gentrification is an important one, especially in the global context of California's urban renewal policies and the rise in housing prices. Indeed, transformations provoked by the gentrification of this Mexican-Chicano community involve questions not only about the sense of history, space, and place but also about cultural recognition and political participation in the global city. Gentrification is yet another boundary that is being constructed within our community, one that barrio residents are struggling to overcome. The resistance to gentrification, led by barrio women, is a fascinating case study of Chicano politics. The gentrification struggle allows us to understand how the contemporary Chicano/Mexicano experience in one San Diego barrio is both unique and similar to experiences in other American barrios struggling for social justice. In the struggle against gentrification is an attempt to preserve a cultural and social space which is important to the values and heritage of Mexicans in San Diego.

The city of San Diego, billed as "America's finest city," has recently become one of the wealthiest areas in the United States. It is home to approximately 1.2 million people.[1] However, its economic success has not been distributed evenly, and the local Latino population has not benefited from it as much as the population at large has. First, the residential segregation in San Diego has deepened in the last decade, in both the city and the suburbs. In 1990, suburban Latinos lived in census tracts that were 58 percent non-Hispanic white, whereas in 2000, they lived in census tracts that were 45 percent white. Segregation rates are even higher for Latino children than for the adult population. The San Diego inner-city barrio, located southeast of downtown, is composed of three neighborhoods: Barrio Logan, Logan Heights, and Sherman Heights. Together they comprise an enclave that has been ignored politically. A barrio has been defined as an ethnic neighborhood where at least 40 percent of the population is of Latino origin and at least 40 percent of the residents live in poverty.[2] The San Diego barrio fits this definition perfectly. The three neighborhoods of the barrio host approximately 5,000 inhabitants, 68 percent of whom are Latinos (primarily of Mexican origin); 40 percent live below poverty level. Second, the census data for 2000 reveal a set of factors that reinforces political disenfranchisement in the area. Specifically, the heterogeneity of migratory experiences within the barrio population contributes to a kind of political invisibility. Two-thirds of the residents are native-born, whereas one-third are foreign-born. Among the foreign-born population, only 22 percent are naturalized citizens. Political enfranchisement is thus limited to a fraction of the residents. In both local and state elections, voter registration and turnout are indeed extremely low. For instance, turnout for city council District 8 elections (which includes the barrio) ranged from 7 percent to 35 percent of the registered voters between 1983 and 2005. In addition, another large segment of the barrio population does not have legal immigration status. Thus, not only is access to voting limited, but for many residents the cost of visible participation in the community is possible deportation.

Moreover, socioeconomic criteria also negatively influence the political participation of barrio residents. Unemployment rates in this community were more than triple those for the entire city (21.7 percent versus 6.1 percent), and the median household income was 57 percent less than the median income for the city of San Diego ($19,968 versus $45,733), according to the 2000 census. Education levels are also extremely low, which disfavor involvement in politics. Finally, the barrio is not a place that many formal organizations and institutions have invested in. The community organizations inherited from the Chicano Movement that are still operating in the barrio have been incorporated into social service agencies (namely, San Diego County Chicano Federation; Barrio Station; Logan Heights Family Heath Center, formerly known as the Chicano Clinic; and outside of the barrio, the Centro Cultural de la Raza). The Chicano Park Steering Committee, which is not yet incorporated, and other organizations born at the end of the 1980s are either mainly state-funded (Environmental Health Coalition and Metropolitan Area Advisory Committee) or voluntary grassroots organizations (Unión del Barrio, Raza Rights Coalition, Steering Committee).[3]

Community organizations encounter obstacles to activism in the barrio. This situation contrasts with the mobilization of residents during the Chicano Movement era described by Isidro Ortiz in chapter 6. In San Diego, numerous organizations were created by Chicano activists, and among the most symbolic of many political acts was the takeover of land to create a community park. Chicano Park and the murals that covered the Coronado Bridge pillars in the 1970s (and later in the 1980s) are a significant artistic and political heritage of the *movimiento* in Barrio Logan.[4]

References to the barrio in San Diego city official documents and in the main daily newspaper (*San Diego Union-Tribune*) demonstrate that a highly stereotyped vision of the area pervades. They describe the barrio as a dangerous and apathetic space. For instance, the 2002–2004 *Community and Economic Development Strategy Plan* for revitalization of the city of San Diego states that "low-income households are concentrated in the oldest and least expensive parts of the City. A concentration of poverty leads to what sociologists refer to as a 'culture of poverty,' in which social interactions are governed by short term survival, including success in high risk, high-reward, illegal activities, while the values of the broader culture, such as workforce responsibility and success at school are avoided."[5]

The use of "culture of poverty," Oscar Lewis' highly debated concept,[6] does not seem to be a matter of controversy for policymakers dealing with the barrio community in San Diego. Nevertheless, when Lewis elaborated the concept of a culture of poverty, he was describing the pathological expressions of a particular subculture among the poorest of Mexico City. He then applied the definition to Mexican immigrants in U.S. barrios to explain the passivity of the population and the self-reproduction of poverty. As a consequence, this perspective does not account for structural causes of poverty and social and political marginalization. At the same time, the widespread perception of a "culture of dependence" was then a major argument against the welfare and assistance programs in marginalized urban areas. Criticizing this theory, academics shifted their perspective in the 1970s and elaborated the concept of barrios as "internal colonies."[7] They suggested that barrios were the result of a history of class, ethnic, and cultural oppression. They also pointed out barrio residents' structural incapacity to participate in the political process. To sum up, scholars generally outlined the political disenfranchisement of barrio communities and provided a justification for policymakers in search of reasons to limit public investment in these areas.

Reinforcing San Diego policymakers' negative perceptions of the barrio, the *San Diego Union-Tribune* draws a portrait of the barrio as a dangerous place. A review of news articles from 2000 to 2003 reveals that of 230 references to the barrio, 65 percent are short reports relating to violence, crimes, and gang- and drug-related activities. The remaining 35 percent are long articles that describe the multiple risks present in that space, in predominantly negative terms. Different topics addressed include environmental hazards, homelessness, declining educational achievement, and health problems. The barrio is "a crime-ridden area," the city's "poorest neighborhood," "plagued by gang-related activities and drive-by-shootings," in brief a "ghetto." For instance, "Of 42 homicides in the city during the period, 14 were in southeastern San Diego. Violence is just a part of life down here, always has been," stated a newspaper article that seemed to present only one side of the story.[8] The only positive images of the barrio are cultural references, especially to Mexican celebrations and culture (Cinco de Mayo, Virgen de Guadalupe), food traditions, and the Chicano Park murals. But even positive images recall internal problems of the barrio. As an example, one article stressed the role of local artists in the revitalization of the neighborhood but emphasized at the same time that they were fighting a losing battle: "Mario Torero restores a mural that he hopes will symbolize the rebirth of three San Diego inner-city neighborhoods. I thought the mural's poor condition reflected the mood of the community—neglected, old and tarnished."[9] All representations of the barrio and discourses about it are important because the struggle over the meaning and the boundaries of the barrio is also a struggle for power. Barrio Logan is thus similar to other barrios in terms of socio-demographic characteristics: it is a disenfranchised community defined by low income and poor social, economic, and political achievement. It suffers from the consequences of the city of San Diego's public policy choices.

Barrios and Political Participation

The phenomenon of residential segregation raises concerns not only of social justice but also of political incorporation. Residential segregation refers to the degree to which certain types of people live separately from one another. To the extent that segregation constrains social, educational, political, and economic advancement for ethnic groups such as Latinos in the United States, it is a salient public policy issue. Ghettos and barrios are radical figures of the multifaceted urban marginalization of minorities in American metropolises.[10] Barrio residents have been defined as apolitical or politically deficient. Many believe that neighborhood poverty leads to political passivity, and the few existing empirical studies certainly support the lack of participation in these areas.[11] The number of Latinos living in impoverished barrios continues to grow at a rate that is disproportionate to their representation in the overall population. From 1970 to 1990, the number of Latinos in barrios rose from 730,000 to more than 2,000,000. In 1990, when the Mexican-origin population represented 5.4 percent of the total U.S. population, 14.3 percent of them lived in barrios.[12] Barrios are characterized by physical deterioration (vacant lots, housing in disrepair, abandoned housing, and low rates of homeownership); economic depression (low employment and labor force participation, long working hours and low wages, sectored occupation, low household income); and social marginalization (prevalence of single-parent families—especially female-headed families—poor educational attainment, high teenage pregnancy rates). These characteristics are present in the San Diego barrio.

Nevertheless, a shift in perspective may lead us to question the thesis that barrio residents are not politically involved. I argue that previous models are not totally accurate, because literature on political participation has focused on conventional forms of participation (such as electoral behavior; membership in unions, political parties or formal institutions; and campaigning activities) and ignores gender. Instead of asking why barrio residents do not participate and what conditions lead to political incapacity, I propose to widen the definition of political participation to any "activity that has the intent or effect of influencing government action—either directly, by affecting the making or implementation of public policy, or indirectly, by influencing the selection of people who make those policies."[13] This broader definition enables me not only to focus on a diversity of unorthodox forms of participation but also to measure outcomes differently. I ask the following questions: Which unorthodox forms of participation may take place in the barrio? Which resources make the emergence of collective action possible in the barrio? Scholars have rarely addressed poor people's political activities, except in the negative context of urban riots or upheaval. When confronted by the Chicano Movement involving barrio residents in the late 1960s or by the Civil Rights Movement, they opted to analyze collective action as a psychological disruption that served to alleviate grievances.

Some authors have argued that violent protest is the only effective form of political participation available to marginalized populations.[14] I shall develop another approach to the study of poor people's political participation by stressing the role of representations, symbols, and collective identities as determinants for collective action.[15] In addition, I rely on the standard definition of "social capital," that is, networks, norms and social trust that facilitate coordination and cooperation for mutual benefits to formulate new hypotheses regarding participation in the barrio.[16] I use the case of the struggle against gentrification in Barrio Logan in which respondents have expressed resistance to the ongoing urban renewal process there. Interestingly enough, the voices heard are mainly women's. First, I will demonstrate the extent to which gentrification has become a mobilizing agenda for barrio residents, and especially for women. Second, I will emphasize that certain forms of resources, such as social networks based on collective identity, extend the definition and role of social capital in determining participation.

Methodology

Barrio Logan, located in the southeast section of San Diego, California, has not been studied by political scientists except in the late 1960s and early 1970s. From a theoretical perspective, the literature specific to San Diego and to the barrio is extremely scarce and dates back to the War on Poverty program. San Diego has always been portrayed and considered as a place where nothing much happens or where everything is "under the perfect sun."[17] Various hypotheses can explain this lack of interest. First, scholars have studied mainly Chicago, Los Angeles, and larger southwestern cities. Scholars of Mexican American or Latina/o political participation have focused more on electoral participation or pan-ethnic forms of activity. Local research traditionally has favored nonlocal issues such as border policies or binational and transnational politics. Second, the decline in political mobilization after the 1960s Chicano Movement has given the impression that there is no longer any political activity. The community organizations surviving from that time have become part of regular urban politics. They are much less threatening to established power and work mainly within the political system. As a consequence, the context seems less favorable for the study of political mobilization. Third, minorities in San Diego have long been denied access to the electoral sphere. The 1990 redistricting and lawsuits led by the Chicano Federation of San Diego County helped terminate the at-large election system and initiate the rise of Hispanic/Latino electoral representation at both city and state levels. Nevertheless, San Diego's political system is still perceived as "static and boring."

I conducted an ethnographic study in the barrio from August 2002 to December 2003, observing community meetings, cultural events, political demonstrations, and marches. I participated in the daily life of the community at different stages and levels (voluntary work). I designed a photographic database in order to present the diversity and complexity of the barrio. In addition to participant observation, I held ninety-eight semi-structured interviews with community leaders, members of organizations, elected officials, and representatives of government agencies involved in the barrio; and eighteen life-story interviews with non-mobilized residents. More than a hundred informal discussions took place during the fieldwork. In addition, I observed citizenship classes in barrio schools during a period of four months. During the classes, I distributed a questionnaire to a sample of residents who were first-generation Mexican immigrants applying for citizenship. The questions concerned political participation issues, dual nationality, socialization, citizenship practices, and electoral representation. Finally, I examined local newspapers and archives from the San Diego City Redevelopment Agency for a twelve-year period, from 1991 to 2003. I used this triangulation of sources and methods to provide as complex and comprehensive a picture of the barrio as possible.

It is often stated that poverty leads to mistrust and is strongly associated with fatalism. In particular, civic culture theorists have linked this distrust to the development of a passive political culture among Mexican-origin people.[18] Indeed, people in barrios have little confidence in the system or in other people. The *desconfianza* (mistrust) is expressed both horizontally, along class lines, between legal and illegal immigrants, residents and citizens, first and second generations, or renters and owners; and vertically between residents and public authorities, political leaders and local representatives, developers and landlords, and so on. The desconfianza factor hindered my entry into the community. As a local artist warned me, "the Chicano Movement was like a big table, some of the people sat there and were sharing their meal, some others just wanted to be close to the table, to grasp some part of the meal and leave: So, where will you be seated? What do you want from us, and what will you do and give to us?" Multiple outsider factors (nationality, racial background, and gender) delayed the process of my acceptance by residents. Simultaneously, these factors helped differentiate me from both community members and institutional representatives. They provided a source for curiosity and trust, openness and comfort. This fieldwork leads me to argue that the main outcome of barrio residents' resistance to gentrification is indeed the framing of the barrio image and of its territorial and symbolic boundaries.

Gentrification in San Diego

Gentrification is the process "by which poor and working-class neighborhoods in the inner city [neighborhoods that have previously experienced disinvestment and a middle-class exodus] are refurbished via an influx of private capital and middle-class homebuyers and renters."[19] It usually happens in three phases: (1) the deterioration of life and housing conditions; (2) a transitory period characterized by renovation of housing and "beautification" usually by Anglo outsiders; and (3) a final phase where only former homeowners among the original residents remain in a mainly Anglo neighborhood. Indeed, it is not a phenomenon specific to San Diego. Paradoxically, after a period of official neglect of deprived areas, a new form of interventionism is taking place in American cities. These newly adopted policies aim at encouraging private enterprise to make up for government disinvestment through a policy of preferential taxation to favor free enterprise in certain urban areas (enterprise zones) and the promotion of inner-city revitalization with community involvement (empowerment zones).

San Diego local government initiated a process of urban renewal in the late 1980s. The "redevelopment," "revitalization," and "beautification" programs started with large investments in the downtown area, which was transformed into an entertainment and commercial area (with cafés, restaurants, movie theaters, etc.). The construction of the Padres baseball stadium accelerated the gentrification. Meanwhile, the City of Villages plan promoted a "smart growth" approach and focused on redeveloping "historically or culturally distinct communities."[20] Notably, since part of the barrio was turned into a Redevelopment Project Area in 1998, residents have suffered from a sharp increase in rents, eviction, and displacement (fig. 8.1). As a resident stated, "They [elected officials] have to be aware that here, two or three families live in one house in order to afford the rent, that there is no privacy for anyone, that some of them live in garage rooms, and that we need apartments for low-income people."[21] In fact, data show that 80 percent of San Diego inner-city barrio residents are renters. More than one-quarter of the barrio population spends more half of its household income in gross rent; and more than half pays one-third or more.

The complexity of gentrification is reflected in the changing discourses in the media and by public officials about San Diego's "poor inner-city area." The

FIGURE 8.1. Casitas built in the 1920s to house Mexican immigrant families in Logan Heights barrio. Still in use today, they are prime targets of urban redevelopment. (Courtesy of Richard Griswold del Castillo)

metaphors have shifted from the barrio as a "gang-plagued neighborhood" to a "vibrant residential community."[22] An optimistic vision stresses the revitalization of neighborhoods through ethnic mixing and private investments. But a pessimistic approach would instead link beautification projects with a form of urban "cleanup" (also labeled a "strategy of containment") that pushes away certain categories of the population from a historically Mexican-origin space. Because recent urban changes threaten barrio residents both individually by displacement and collectively by the disappearance of their community, gentrification constitutes a mobilizing agenda. It activates social networks to resist displacement.

Gender, Gentrification, and Participation

To demonstrate my argument, I take the example of DURO—Developing Unity through Resident Organizing (in Spanish, Desarrollando Unidad a Través de Residentes Organizados). Barrio residents created DURO, an almost exclusively female grassroots group, in the fall of 2000. A loose voluntary association of first- and second-generation Mexican-origin women and students comprises

DURO. It is dedicated, among other things, to the defense of barrio renters and residents against forced and unlawful evictions. The association also lobbies for low-income and affordable housing units, and promotes community input regarding the development of vacant lots in the barrio. As a flyer states, members "who work or were born and raised in the communities of Logan Heights and Sherman Heights [gathered] to dialogue about signs of gentrification that seemed to have gained momentum with the Ballpark development and the downtown redevelopment efforts." The community meetings were held either in private homes or in the local Sherman Community Center. The organization's first victory happened when a DURO member won an eviction court hearing in May 2001. This resident had lived for twenty-three years in the same property, a two-bedroom apartment she was renting for from $300 up to $400 and $550 a month. Now the same unit, after being rehabilitated, commands double that rent. Nevertheless, the resident finally got displaced. She recalled the forced eviction as follows: "I felt it was unfair, it was unfair the way the owner evicted us, because he said he was going to call la migra [the Border Patrol]. I got sick because of the dust and the stress, yes, because of the dust falling when he started to demolish and renovate the house while we were still living there. We were still in there, because the owner only gave us eight days' notice, and we had nowhere to go. . . . I lived twenty-three years in this house." As another resident noted, "In San Diego, everything is more expensive, homes, rents. Before, we paid $500 for a two-bedroom apartment, now it is almost double that. They renovate houses, they send la migra to people, and then rents skyrocket. I am lucky because I bought my house almost ten years ago. But people cannot afford to live here anymore."[23]

The urban transformations sparked a variety of responses, such as door-to-door contacts, distribution of bilingual flyers on tenants' rights and responsibilities, petitions for rent stabilization, community meetings, and marches. For instance, on June 30, 2001, more than one hundred residents participated in a march to protest displacement.[24] Another march called the Trail of Tears March (Caminata de Lágrimas) took place and banners read: "We are organizing to claim our human right to housing. Our inherent dignity is being violated"; "Make your voices heard"; "Aquí estamos y no nos vamos!"; "En unión hay fuerza"; "Únase a nuestro esfuerzo comunitario!"[25] The association attempted to raise consciousness about the housing problem during city council meetings but it got only limited media coverage, mostly in local Spanish-language television channels and newspapers (*La Prensa San Diego*). In 2002 the organization tried to build coalitions and networks with other groups, but the mobilization began to decrease. From 2003 onwards, DURO started to meet on a more regular basis, addressing the specific issues of the use of vacant lots in the barrio and low-income/affordable housing projects.

But DURO's most important aspect is that it is constituted mainly by women. Gender difference in participation has been overlooked in the literature, especially because theoretical analyses have focused on certain forms of conventional participation (turnout in elections, election to government positions, financial contributions). Certainly, three main determinants affect the degree of women's participation in such traditional avenues: differential access to resources, in particular to education; lower integration in the workforce and other social networks, which decreases their chances of being recruited into political activities; and finally, difference in political orientations: less access to information, interest in politics, and feeling of political efficacy than men have. Classic literature would focus on women's political deficiencies, in particular among low-income Mexican or Mexican-origin women.[26] Margarita Melville labeled them "twice a minority."[27] But barrio women are more likely to be four times a minority: as women, as Latinas in a Latino-dominated environment, as Mexican-origin individuals in a racialized society, and as low-income barrio residents. It is thus even more striking that barrio women led the resistance to gentrification. Why do women mobilize against gentrification? How is gentrification a gendered agenda that channels participation?

Public and Private Spheres

I suggest that barrio women's participation is essentially linked to the gentrification issue for two main reasons: the barrio space is highly invested with social meanings for the community; and domestic and community space are intertwined in women's representations and actions. By questioning the traditional dichotomy between private and public spheres, we can understand how women's civic involvement in grassroots associations might provide more benefits to them than would entry into conventional politics.

First, DURO members and residents' narratives constantly illustrate two conflicting visions of space. Elected officials, promoters, institutional representatives, and media discourses present the barrio as a materialized space, a product of costs and benefits. The terms *revitalization, beautification, revival, cleanup,* and *redevelopment* are metaphors of the reification of the barrio territory. A district official expressed her perception of gentrification in these terms: "In terms of issues, I think housing is what my constituents are worried about, the first issue they are concerned about, to beautify the areas, such as Barrio Logan and Sherman Heights." Redevelopment projects are conceived as a privatization of the space, carried out through a rhetoric of progress and security, the stigmatization of the homeless population, and an agenda of ethnic and economic diversity. In contrast, members of DURO and barrio residents recall that the neighborhood space is a product of common history shared among generations. They have a collective desire to preserve the cultural specificity of their community. One activist stated: "The rent is increasing a lot. Then there are no homes anymore for low-income people. . . . It is not fair. This is a very old community, a Latino community, for the Latinos, and it is not good that the Americans come here. Because every community has its own thing, right?"[28] DURO members feel attachment to this territory, because—simply stated—living in a Mexican barrio is something important to them.[29] Thus, in these opposite representations, some individuals seek to maximize the exchange value of the space whereas others privilege its intrinsic value. That's why the struggle against gentrification is a struggle not only for the defense of a physical space but also for the definition of symbolic boundaries and collective identities.

Second, resistance to gentrification is indeed a defense of private homes against eviction and rent increase, but it is also a defense of the overall community. Barrio women see gentrification as a threat because it implies a dramatic disappearance of domestic and community space. Not only are homes being destroyed and renters evicted, but also vacant lots, public parks, community centers, and the character of streets are being redefined by gentrification (fig. 8.2). Studies show that women's common preoccupations with basic common rights, such as education, health, and housing, are essential for collective participation and politicization. In this respect, how increasing housing costs affect housing and living conditions is a key issue. As a DURO member stated, "One of the main problems is to have affordable housing, because there is very little affordable housing here. I think that for a kid to do well at school, his family has to be in a good situation, because when a kid goes to school without food or without a home to sleep in, how do you think he is going to do at school?"[30] As a consequence, barrio women link the private and the public spheres, reinventing forms of participation, dialogue, and political activism that extend beyond the family space. As Pardo noticed in her study of Mexican American women activists in Los

FIGURE 8.2. National Avenue near the heart of Barrio Logan, showing the ongoing redevelopment of the downtown area. (Courtesy of Richard Griswold del Castillo)

Angeles, "The quality of life in a community reflects unrecorded social and political processes, often originating in grassroots activism. Different from electoral politics, grassroots activism happens at the juncture between larger institutional politics and people's daily experiences. Women play a central role in the often unrecorded politics at this level."[31]

If gentrification threatens the public space, it also overlaps into the domestic sphere, and vice versa. One DURO participant remembers the struggle to get a public meeting room: "We struggled for a long time because we did not have any fixed place to meet, the majority of people missed the meetings, because we were always changing from one house to another."[32] An example of this overlap is manifested in the lack of public resources that transforms private homes into meeting places for the association.

The mobilization against gentrification shows that collective action happens in the barrio and is gendered, in particular because of the issue at stake. It is then important to ask what kind of nonmaterial resources barrio women use to enact this participation. I suggest that ethnic and territorial identity forms one of the essential symbolic resources present in the barrio.

Collective Identity and Participation

Collective identities are socially constructed processes difficult to label because they are both reasons for and results of collective action that is intimately imposed, voluntarily chosen, and internalized. They have a complex situational, contextual, and political genesis, but they might favor the emergence of collective action. In the San Diego barrio case, chosen or imposed Latino-origin, Mexican-origin, or barrio-origin identities are all situational. Ethnic identities are used as both reactive and proactive means to define and preserve barrio community boundaries. Scholars have largely focused on ethnic identity as a resource for the elaboration of specific claims and as a means for collective action.[33] Group identity constitutes a resource in the struggle against identified outsiders or gentrifiers. I argue that DURO members use both ethnic and territorial identities. The fact that barrio residents share a set of symbols and representations of their community space helps them build a sense of self-affirmation. Residential segregation is experienced as social and political exclusion and becomes, paradoxically, a source for claiming a right to "live together in difference." Communities are constructed symbolically over time.[34] Barrio residents have built a community, that is to say, a unit of belonging whose members perceive that they share moral, aesthetic/expressive, or cognitive meanings, thereby gaining a sense of personal as well as group identity.

First, narratives show that DURO members and women activists are limited in their choice of resources to build common frames of action and have to use ethnic identity as one resource. In fact, the construction of cultural similarities is not necessarily rational, instrumental, or conscious. It is not always a matter of choice but more often of imposition. At the same time, politically involved individuals have a tendency to use the frames elaborated by the Other. In-group/out-group thinking is constantly present in narratives that identify "the enemy" as "white," or more frequently, as foreign—"they" or "them"—or as a pejorative other: "they" are "not Mexican," or "not Latino." Any whites, be they public authorities, property owners, developers, or journalists, are identified as gentrifiers or developers. The struggle against gentrification is often phrased as a denial of the "whitening" of the area, which contrasts sharply with the metaphors of "cleaning up" used by the gentrifiers. A comment by a community activist expresses this dichotomy: "We are saving this neighborhood, with anger, determination, but we will save it from that; it has already been under attack, in particular with the urban City Planning Department, who is our greatest enemy. This is the issue of the last Mexican American community on the southeast of California."

The barrio's community identity is preserved through the protection of its Mexican history or Mexican American roots. But the reality is more complex than ethnicity, since identified outsiders may share the same ethnic background or, in some cases, may live in the barrio. In these cases, the narratives appear to be more territorial and stigmatize the outsiders as people who "are not from here," "were not born here," "do not live here," "do not belong here," or "do not even come here." During one meeting, a woman declared her anger against outsiders in the following way, "We formed ourselves because there was no organization in the barrio, and those organizations that exist are created by outsiders. The other day we had a community meeting. People came from all over the place, they said: we need this here! They don't even live here!" Such discourses do not fix the limits of who is part of the barrio and who is not based on racial or ethnic categorization, but rather show the complexity and debates on the determination of community boundaries.

The second marker of collective ethnic identity for mobilization is the use of the Spanish language. The inability to speak English and the linguistic isolation of barrio residents are indeed strong obstacles to their participation. Speaking only Spanish or having limited English, as much of the first-generation immigrant population in the barrio does, can be analyzed as a basis for discrimination and political powerlessness.[35] Fluency in the dominant language also conditions access to the workforce, educational success, and integration into the broader society. In the barrio, data from the 2000 census show that almost 38 percent of the population is linguistically isolated and an additional one-third reports difficulties in speaking English.[36] At the same time, a more instrumental perspective on language is interesting to consider: that the capacity to speak Spanish might be used as an instrument for internal solidarity and community empowerment. Language can be seen as an oppositional resource that links Spanish-speaking people together. A Mexican-origin DURO member expresses her desire to link non-English speakers with bilingual ones: "My mom is Mexican, no habla inglés; they don't want to challenge because they've been oppressed for so long. . . . People were scared because they don't know, pero sí pueden hablar." Language use is a vehicle for intragroup protection and reciprocal support. Second, bilingual activists might choose to use Spanish to mark politically and symbolically their relationship to the outsiders. The contextual shifts from one language to another are striking. Speaking Spanish during a meeting may force the outsiders to respect the use of the group language. It forms an attempt both to show systemic oppression by the dominant group and to claim recognition of cultural rights. In part, the use of Spanish might compensate for the lack of traditional resources (money, members, material capital) for political participation. For instance, complaints about translations during public meetings are frequent. One resident had to summarize a meeting with city and district representatives. The first thing he recalled was "The translation was terrible, he was distorting all of what people said. . . . We have to track the entire process, because this is supposed to be an open process." The presence or absence of translation, its quality and accurateness, and its objectivity or distortion, is a matter of conflict. As a matter of fact, symbolically and politically, the debate over language use represents a discussion of cultural and ethnic-specific rights that gives existence, voice, and visibility to the group.

The notion of belonging to a specific territory forms the third component of collective identity. Deeply intertwined with ethnic identities, the representations of the barrio as a common cultural place constitute a powerful tool for the construction of a common identity. El barrio is presented as a social space defined by its territorial boundaries, which have to be preserved (streets, parks, shops, etc.). These physical boundaries delimit who is part of the community and who is not. Direct, personal contacts among residents are extremely important because they allow organizers and potential participants to align frames and transmit cultural messages about the particularities of the space. Collective action against gentrification is rooted in a reaction to interventions by challengers: "I want to live here because this is my barrio. If I buy a home, I will buy it here."[37] In addition, the barrio is defined positively as our community (*nuestra comunidad*), a place of identification, which can become a place for self-determination. Affective ties to the space play an important role in strengthening horizontal networks. An evicted barrio resident, an active member of DURO, talks of her desire to come back to the barrio: "my wishes now . . . are to go back there. . . . I feel a strong identification because everyone is Hispano there. . . . Over there, there is the bazaar, the farmers market, I feel more identified over there."[38] Social ties are thus grounded in the emotional bonds among barrio members. They favor trust and civic and moral commitment thanks to identification with a common shared space.

The feeling of belonging to a group and a specific territory turns into group consciousness, group identity, and eventually into a feeling of political efficacy and capacity. As a consequence, even though they may not be political in origin or intent, affective ties may help recruit people and develop a commitment to the group or the community. In that sense, the feelings of injustice in the face of evictions, rent increases, and worsening of living conditions and the feeling of efficacy to make a change are rather a product of than a reason for the emergence of collective action. In the barrio, the "cognitive liberation" process is fomented through the activity of DURO members and residents, who frame their action as a defense of a cultural and ethnic space. In the following section, I argue that women use barrio social networks and gendered social capital to develop collective action.

Gendered Social Capital and Participation

Gender solidarity in the San Diego barrio establishes bonding forms of social capital that overcome the distrust present within the barrio population. People who are intimately associated tend to build the same views of the world and of the situation they are embedded in. These social ties increase the likelihood of having common ideas, values, interests, and identities, which are the basis for collective action. As a consequence, informal social networks build relations of trust and reciprocity. Putnam's previously cited definition of social capital as "networks, norms and social trust that facilitate coordination and cooperation for mutual benefits" is useful for understanding how political participation emerges in the barrio. It suggests that mobilization can be based on qualitative resources specific to the barrio. In fact, social capital encompasses strengths arising from relationships of mutual trust and collaboration.[39] In an impoverished area, however, social networks are often truncated, not only because distrust runs deep, but also because contacts with external social networks are almost nonexistent. Starting with the question, What kind of benefits do women get from membership in DURO? I have come to distinguish three groups of women who have interests in linking together. Their promotion of reciprocal help generates trust, lowers the costs of participation in the barrio, and transforms social networks into political ones.

First, single mothers participate in collective action against gentrification because it provides them with resources they otherwise would not have access to. Census data from 2000 for family type by presence and age of related children show that in the barrio, female-headed families represent more than 27 percent of all families, and 70 percent of those families have children under eighteen, with an average of 4.5 children per family. Single mothers share meals or information about jobs, prices, and schooling; and exchange clothes, advice, or tips during meetings, potlucks, or fundraising events. A single mother affirms, "The other women always tell me, 'Go and study English at an evening class. You can do it!' they tell me. After work, sometimes some of them take me to school. It is difficult, by myself with my kid. But they say, 'you can do it!' And I go."[40] As a consequence of such networks, single mothers gain material and nonmaterial advantages that help them cope with deprived living conditions.

The second group of women who establish horizontal solidarity networks in the barrio are undocumented women. The fear of deportation and the risks of being arrested by la migra in a border city such as San Diego are high, as post–9/11 Border Patrol cruises in the barrio, on the trolley, and even in front of the Mexican consulate have previously shown. For instance, a barrio activist recalled the dramatic consequences of this policy: "There are still a lot of people without documents here. One day, la migra came at the school entrance, outside of the school, and they arrested a father who was there waiting for his kids. The mother was supplicating to la migra. They took him away; they arrested him, in front of his children." But despite the risk of gaining visibility in the community, undocumented women evaluate the costs of collective action in comparison to the symbolic benefits of action. Undocumented women give value to action as the only way of surviving available to them. Being part of a semi-formal group gives them social status, recognition, and embodiment. They perceive involvement as part of a re-humanization of an invisible minority. As another resident said: "For lots of people without documents, they think they have no rights, but as human beings they have rights!" Access to collective action provides acknowledgment of the contribution undocumented families make to the community.

Finally, ties across generations—both between first- and second-generation Mexican-origin women (immigrants and U.S.-born), and between younger and older women—are essential for two reasons. On one side, the transmission of knowledge, experiences, and stories constitutes a fundamental aspect of the political socialization of young activists: "What I like here is the presence of professional and community women. . . . I can spend three hours in a meeting and not get bored, because I can listen to them and their different points of view, and that's the way I learn about the situation."[41] Meetings in private homes are particular moments to share experiences, cultural practices, and memories of past history and collective identities. On the other hand, collective events are key moments to transmit the action repertoires inherited from past struggles or mobilization.[42] For instance, repeated references to the birth of Chicano Park by a community takeover of public land during the Chicano Movement connect women with a successful instance of community activism. As a participant stated during a discussion, grassroots mobilization has yielded victories in the past: "The reality is that we have to get people active in the process, like when they took over Chicano Park land, right? The community took it over!" Even if idealized, romanticized, or reconstructed, the collective memory is passed from generation to generation, thanks to the social networks established among the different segments of women. In summary, women build up community-based activities and solidarity networks that develop their sense of belonging and civic duty. This form of gendered social capital enhances individuals' capacity to join together in collective action to resolve common problems. It leads to political engagement.[43]

Conclusion

DURO members and barrio residents' resistance to gentrification causes us to reflect, first, on the meaning and value of active citizenship and political participation; and second, on the different avenues available for exercising a political voice in a disenfranchised community. Barrio residents are not politically passive or deficient. Barrios are political spaces where mobilization happens without intervention from outside. Women's community involvement against gentrification demonstrates the importance of preexisting relationships of trust and mutuality among friends and neighbors. Shared concerns about housing and displacement, about community boundaries and collective identity, serve to mobilize residents. They reinforce the politicization of barrio residents and reduce the costs of participation. In turn, they can catalyze more formal political activities as skills and feelings of political efficacy grow. The barrio benefits from this gendered social capital because social ties are transformed into bonding social capital and political networks.

In other words, qualitative research and study of narratives not only make barrio residents visible in politics, but they transform the concept of political participation. In this particular context, social capital is mobilized as a political resource to strengthen civic involvement. Nevertheless, barrio women encounter obstacles in their fight against gentrification. In fact, however much barrio women struggle, obstacles limit their capacity to effect change. First, they need to establish bridging social capital—that is, forms of vertical networks with other organizations—to accomplish their goals. Second, they need to explore different ways to frame the public agenda. As a participant in a DURO meeting pointed out, "Imagine how powerful we can be if we unite with residents and unions and connect with workers, en unirse todos [unite everyone]." But this second step still seems difficult to achieve in the San Diego barrio case. The local environment, quite hostile to immigrants and immigrants' claims for cultural or political recognition, does not offer many opportunities for such a movement. In fact, barrio residents' struggles have rarely been publicized in the local media and barely heard by the local authorities, and have obtained few concrete results. The gentrification process is underway, and public policies have not dramatically changed since the beginning of barrio residents' organization. Nevertheless, pressure exercised during city council meetings and by more formal organizations has succeeded in putting the low-income housing issue on the agenda. It might indicate an opening of the political structure that might allow barrio residents to be heard.

9

THE BORDER AND HUMAN RIGHTS: A TESTIMONY

Roberto L. Martínez

This chapter focuses on the recent historical record involving human and civil rights issues confronting Chicanos/Mexicanos in San Diego. It seeks to tell the truth about the human cost of Mexican immigration and to take a critical look back at the historical and political realities in Southern California in the last part of the twentieth century. The story is told through the *testimonio*, or life story, of Roberto Martínez, a lifelong advocate of civil rights for Mexican Americans and Mexicans. Roberto's testimonio joins those of other activists, such as Reies López Tijerina, José Ángel Gutiérrez, and Bert Corona, who have written their personal stories, seeking to tell of their actions and thoughts during their struggle for human rights.[1] In Roberto's testimonio we have a firsthand account of the struggle to overcome the racism and prejudices generated by the existence of the international border. The creation of a cultural and social space with a sense of social justice is key to Roberto's life work. The transcending of political boundaries to create a community of Mexicans without borders has increasingly been important for Chicana/o and Latina/o activists like Roberto. The struggle for immigrant rights is also one for Chicana/o rights, as Roberto makes clear.

I was born and raised in San Diego, and my adult life has been spent as an activist-organizer working alongside leaders within the Mexican/Chicano communities in a struggle for the human rights of our immigrant brothers and sisters. During the 1990s, I was fortunate to be the director of the American Friends Service Committee's U.S.–Mexico Border Program in San Diego. My work there was to organize investigations into instances of violence and abuse involving Mexican immigrants and Chicanos.

This work that I have been engaged in is not new. During the 1930s there was a massive roundup and deportation of thousands of Chicanos/Mexicanos in California and other parts of the Southwest.[2] Historians have referred to the 1930s as a "decade of betrayal" because of these actions. The same could be said about the decades of the 1940s and 1950s, during which massive roundups of Mexicans continued with major police participation. Scapegoating, racism, and mean-spirited immigration laws all combined to cause Chicanos/Mexicanos to live in constant fear. This set in motion the politics of fear and blame that would dominate the national political agenda for decades to come.

As we have seen in previous chapters, during World War II news media and police officials provoked violence against Mexicans in Southern California by blaming them for the social and economic problems in the country. Chicanos were increasingly depicted as "the enemy within."[3] They were also blamed for attacks on servicemen on leave in Los Angeles. This sparked the so-called Zoot-Suit Riots in June 1943, when servicemen, backed by police, attacked and beat Chicanos. This event would force Chicanos to see themselves not only as a people caught between two cultures but also as people of divided loyalties. To prove their loyalty to the United States, many went to fight in World War II. Others worked for the defense industries or joined organizations supporting the war effort. Chicanos became some of the most decorated servicemen in the war, yet those who returned in coffins were not allowed to be buried in white cemeteries.

In the early 1950s, the Immigration and Naturalization Service (INS) launched Operation Wetback. This was a continuation of the infamous "repatriations" begun in the 1930s, when more than 100,000 Mexicans, U.S. citizens, and legal residents, as well as suspected undocumented immigrants, were rounded up and deported by the U.S. Border Patrol with the help of the U.S. Army and local police. It is estimated that by the time Operation Wetback ended in 1955, more than 1 million Mexicans and Mexican-origin U.S. citizens had been deported to Mexico. But Operation Wetback also affected all Mexican Americans. I was a student attending San Diego High School in the early 1950s. Frequently, the police would stop me as I was coming home from school, and sometimes they would put in me in jail and then turn me over to the Border Patrol for deportation. This happened about two or three times a month. The fact that I was a fifth-generation U.S. citizen didn't seem to matter. My family had lived in the relative tranquility of a farm community in east county, but in 1945 we moved to downtown San Diego after my father was discharged from the service. It was an enormous cultural shock for me. However, nothing could have prepared me for the terror and psychological trauma of being arrested or threatened with deportation by police and Border Patrol officers. Looking back, I realize now how Mexicanos in Los Angeles must have felt during the massive roundups in the previous decades. What made this problem worse was that there was no one to turn to for help. There were no civil rights or immigrant rights organizations.[4]

The Chicano Civil Rights Movement

As Chicanas/os began attending college in record numbers in the 1960s, they began challenging the barriers that had historically blocked their access to equal rights and equal justice. Local, state, and national Chicano rights organizations were being created all over the country. Although the Chicano civil rights movement closely paralleled the black civil rights movement, because of their geographical proximity to the border, Chicanos/Mexicanos had and still have the unique distinction of being subjected to abuses by immigration authorities as well as by police. As a conquered people, Chicanas/os had to fight for every inch of the gains they made in education, housing, employment, and civil rights. This is why the term *Chicano* became popular. The view was "We are Mexican by birth. We are American by an accident of war, and we are Chicano by choice." Chicanos were not afforded the same rights as Anglo-Americans.

The Chicano Movement was about "Chicano power." It was also about self-determination, resistance, and claiming what was rightfully ours. One of the ways to accomplish this was to see more Chicanos in positions of power, not only in government but also locally in community-based organizations. This would not be possible without effective leadership, fundraising, and organizing. Successful models emerged around the country, such as the National Council of La Raza (NCLR), the Mexican-American Legal Defense and Educational Fund (MALDEF), the Southwest Voter Registration and Education Project, and the League of United Latin American Citizens (LULAC). LULAC was founded in 1929 in Corpus Christi, Texas. The GI Forum was another effective organization, organized following World War II to protect Latino veterans and advocate on their behalf because of the widespread discrimination against them across the country.

Influenced by these and other organizations, and by the Chicano Movement, the Chicano Federation was founded in San Diego in 1968 by a group of local Chicano leaders to fight for access to more public services and advocate for the rights and dignity of the Chicano/ Mexicano community.[5] Its primary funding came from the County of San Diego. In addition to offices in the city of San Diego, the federation also had an office in Carlsbad in north San Diego County, which was later closed.

As Chicanos/Mexicanos began to move out of the barrio and into all-white neighborhoods around the county, we were to learn not only the extent of racial intolerance but also the importance of unity in confronting racism and law enforcement abuses. White neighbors weren't the only ones yelling at Chicanos to go back to Mexico; so were law enforcement agencies, such as sheriff's departments.

After I graduated from high school I got married, and in 1965 my family was one of the first Chicano families to move into Santee, in a community called Carleton Hills. The day before we moved in, I went to check on the house to see if it was ready. To my surprise, workers were removing the wall paneling from the living room and throwing it in the front yard. When I asked them why, they said that the house had been vandalized the night before. When I looked at the panels, the words "get out of town wetbacks" were carved into the panels. There were also swastikas scattered throughout the paneling. Although I had experienced racism before, this was the first display of overt racism directed at me and my family. This would be my introduction to the kind of racism and violence I would encounter in my work at the border and with farmworkers in the north and east county.[6]

A month after we moved in, a cross was burned in front of the home of a prominent black doctor and his family who had also just moved in. Vandals also sprayed swastikas on their walls and broke their windows. Within a week the family moved out.

By the early 1970s several more Mexican families had moved into Santee. Some of the children, including mine, had begun attending Santana High School.[7] At this time the Youth Klan Corp was actively recruiting members at Santana High School. The school administrators allowed this recruiting to occur on campus year-round. No one had ever challenged them on this racist policy.[8] By 1973, I began emerging as a leader in the community, primarily in the Mexicano community. We, along with other Mexicanos, felt isolated socially, culturally, and politically in east San Diego County. A few years later, I began receiving complaints that the white kids at Santana High were attacking the Mexican kids after school. Following one particularly vicious attack on the Mexican kids by white youths, including Youth Klan Corps members who wore T-shirts that read

"White Power" on one side and "Youth Klan Corps" on the other, I received a visit that would change my life forever.

In June 1979, three Mexican women called me at home and asked if they could bring over their three teenaged children who had been attacked at Santana High School the day before. That very afternoon the three women brought their three children, two boys and one girl, to my home. The two boys were badly beaten about the face. The girl had bruises on her face and neck where she had been choked by a sheriff's deputy. The three claimed that a group of white boys, including members of the Youth Klan Corps, were waiting for the Mexican kids after school with boards and bats. As usual, the Mexican kids were outnumbered. Shortly after the melee began, sheriff's deputies arrived to break up the fight. However, instead of arresting the white boys who had initiated the fight, the deputies not only arrested just the Mexican kids but also badly beat them in the process. As the kids were relating their horrifying experience to me, all of my own experiences with the police and Border Patrol came rushing forward, and I could feel the anger building inside of me. I knew then that I could not remain silent.[9]

That same afternoon, after the women and children left, I phoned both the school and the sheriff's substation in Santee and demanded a meeting for the next day at the school between the Mexican community, school administrators, and representatives from the Sheriff's Department. Both the school officials and the Sheriff's Department refused to meet, saying that everything had already been resolved. Frustrated but determined to get all three groups together, I called each of them back and warned them that if they didn't meet the next morning at the school, we would hold protests in front of the school and sheriff's substation, as well as a press conference to denounce publicly how the school and the Sheriff's Department were creating a racist and violent atmosphere for Chicano students. Both called back within half an hour and agreed to meet the next day.

At the meeting the next day, we got the school not only to stop allowing the Youth Klan Corps to recruit openly on campus, but also to stop discriminating against the Mexican kids. The Sheriff's Department agreed to discipline and relocate the deputies who were abusing the Mexican kids. This was not my first experience at organizing, but it was my first experience at publicly challenging law enforcement in brutality cases. I also learned that public officials are afraid of the media. As word got around the east county about my confrontation with the Sheriff's Department, I began getting calls from Lemon Grove and Spring Valley about deputies assaulting Mexican families in their homes and at baptisms, parties, and weddings. After meeting with several people in those areas, I decided to form the East County Sheriff's/Community Relations Task Force, which began meeting almost immediately with representatives from the Sheriff's Department in east county.

During this period I began working with attorneys to file lawsuits against the Sheriff's Department. This was also the time when I first made contact with the Chicano Federation, to ask for their support. They sent a representative to attend the task force meetings. Although the Sheriff's Department representatives attended only three or four meetings because Sheriff John Duffy pulled them out, claiming he never authorized the use of the Sheriff's Department's name on the task force, the group continued to meet for another year. Because of the publicity generated by the lawsuits and the task force, which had several high-profile elected officials and members, abuses by the Sheriff's Department in east county were substantially reduced.[10]

In the late 1960s and early 1970s a new, more militant Chicano Movement began to emerge in Los Angeles and San Diego, sparked by the Vietnam War and particularly by the unprovoked violence by the Los Angeles Police Department during the Chicano Moratorium march in East Los Angeles on August 29, 1970, a march held to protest the disproportionate number of Chicano deaths during the Vietnam War. During the march, three Chicanos were shot to death and dozens of people were seriously injured from beatings by police. One of the most tragic consequences of the march was the shooting death of renowned Chicano reporter Rubén Salazar by an LAPD officer. Salazar has been memorialized by the renaming of the park where the march began as Rubén Salazar Park.

Back in San Diego, Chicano leader Herman Baca started the Committee on Chicano Rights (CCR) in 1970 as the Ad Hoc Committee on Chicano Rights. The committee was formed around the shooting death of a young Puerto Rican man, Luis Tacho Rivera, by a National City police officer. There was such a community outcry over the shooting that many people called Baca wanting to join the committee. Membership in the CCR was limited to organizations that were not government funded, the rationale being that organizations should not be constrained by government funding. The CCR was finally incorporated in 1976.[11] It became a powerful voice for Chicano rights in the 1970s and 1980s, addressing police abuse in the South Bay as well as the growing debate on immigration reform laws, such as the Simpson-Mazzoli bill.[12] As the debate heated up, so did the growing anti-immigrant rhetoric and publicity. Today, Herman Baca continues to speak out in defense of Chicano rights.

In 1970, Chicano Park was created after the Chicano community in Logan Heights organized a protest over land the city was giving to the California Highway Patrol to build an office under the Coronado Bridge. More than three hundred Mexican families were displaced to make room for the bridge pillars. An additional two thousand Mexican families had already been displaced to clear a path for construction of the I-5 freeway. The community planted trees and guarded the property twenty-four hours a day until the city finally gave in and turned the land into a park for the community; it was quickly named Chicano Park. Thus, the Chicano Park Steering Committee was born. Every year on April 22 the committee holds a celebration at Chicano Park to mark this important victory.

Nevertheless, the backlash against Mexicans continued. In 1975 INS Commissioner General Leonard Chapman reported a "vast and silent invasion of illegal aliens."[13] Commissioner Chapman, a former commandant in the Marine Corps, publicly announced that twelve million "illegal aliens" were in this country, and that at least eight million of them were Mexicans. Some of the headlines at that time were reminiscent of the yellow journalism of past decades. One of them read "Invisible Invasion." Another read "Illegal Aliens Flooding the United States." Chapman also called for the hiring of 200,000 more Border Patrol agents. The effects of this kind of anti-immigrant rhetoric would be felt for decades to come.

In 1982 I began documenting hate crimes against farmworkers in north San Diego County, some dating back to the 1970s. Most of these hate crimes were occurring in the Carlsbad, Oceanside, Escondido, and Del Mar areas. The Ku Klux Klan, later known as the White Aryan Resistance (WAR), was very active in that area. Later, in the 1980s, organized gangs of white youths would begin beating and shooting migrants and day laborers with BBs, paintballs, and even bullets. They would also go into the fields and migrant camps to beat workers. Farmworkers were being found shot to death along roadsides from Del Mar to Fallbrook to Valley Center. Marines from Camp Pendleton were also arrested for conducting what they called "beaner raids" on migrant camps adjacent to Camp Pendleton on two separate occasions.

Radical anti-immigrant groups began sprouting up around Southern California in the 1980s, such as Americans for Immigration Reform and Voices of

FIGURE 9.1. In May 1990 a group called Light Up the Border opposed to illegal immigration was confronted by counter-protesters holding signs and mirrors. The mirrors reflected back the protestors' car headlights, which were being aimed at Mexico in a symbolic gesture. (From Bartletti, *Between Two Worlds*, p. 52; used courtesy of Don Bartletti)

Citizens Together, both based in the Orange County area. The anti-immigrant group Light Up the Border was driving their vehicles to the border and shining their headlights toward the border as a sign of protest against the crossing of undocumented immigrants. Counter-demonstrators would line up in front of the vehicles, holding up mirrors and tinfoil in order to reflect the light back on the demonstrators (fig. 9.1). Counter-demonstrations were heavily guarded by police and Border Patrol officers, who attempted to keep both sides apart. In the mid-1980s, skinheads and neo-Nazi types were also coming to the border to protest illegal immigration. However, they had a more violent agenda. The neo-Nazis, who didn't care whether their actions were observed by law enforcement, would throw rocks at migrants waiting to cross. The Border Patrol would take their time arresting them, which would, in turn, provoke the neo-Nazis into verbally attacking us counter-demonstrators. The demonstrations ended when one of their members drove a truck into a group of students, injuring two of them. Police arrested the driver and dispersed the rest of the demonstrators.

Although dozens of migrant farmworkers have been killed and beaten by anti-immigrant gangs of white youths over the last twenty-five to thirty years in north and east San Diego County, it's hard to find a hate crime more vicious and senseless than the one committed by eight white teenaged boys from Rancho Penasquitos. They attacked and viciously beat five elderly farmworkers on Black Mountain Road in Del Mar on July 5, 2000. Like the Marines, the eight boys admitted that had they set out to hunt "beaners." The five migrant workers were not only shot at close range with BB guns but also beaten about their heads and bodies with rebar and rocks. One of the farmworkers later said that they were "left for dead." Under Proposition 21, passed only a year before the incident, the eight boys were charged as adults and faced anywhere from twelve to fifteen years in prison. However, they all received light sentences because of their ages.

A Policy of Impunity

In the mid-1970s the San Diego Police Department (SDPD) began a special border crime-fighting unit called the Border Area Robbery Task Force, to begin targeting bandits from both sides of the border who were preying on migrants. The unit was finally disbanded in 1978 because of the controversy it was creating on both sides of the border. In 1983 the unit was reinstated as the Border Crime Prevention Unit (BCPU), which was made up of half SDPD officers and half Border Patrol agents. Small squads of officers from the two agencies would go out patrolling the hills and canyons along the border in San Ysidro and Otay Mesa at night and in the early morning hours dressed as decoys in order to trap the bandits. However, the migrants would mistake them for bandits, would pick up weapons to defend themselves, and would be shot by members of the BCPU (fig. 9.2).

During this period there was economic and political upheaval in Mexico, and much of Central America was embroiled in civil wars. The poor, disenfranchised working-class people were caught in the middle of the wars between government forces and guerrillas and were being massacred by the thousands by death squads, which were allegedly receiving military aid from the United States. The devaluation of the peso and rising unemployment in Mexico launched an exodus of Mexican labor to the United States that is still being felt today. By 1980, tens of thousands of Mexican immigrants and Central American refugees began crossing

FIGURE 9.2. Antonio Campo erected a cross where his friend Miguel Ángel Casino Ríos was shot to death while trying to stop a robbery along the fence. (From Bartletti, *Between Two Worlds*, p. 23; used courtesy of Don Bartletti)

into the United States through California, Arizona, and Texas. As the U.S. Border Patrol began building up its forces at the border to meet this phenomenal flow of immigrants and refugees, unprecedented human rights violations began erupting all along the two thousand–mile U.S.–Mexican border. Border rights and human rights organizations began forming on both sides of the border to protest, as well as monitor and document, these abuses by border agents.

Police violence was rampant around the county, from Oceanside to Escondido and from Encinitas to National City, with the SDPD leading the pack. Responding to Latinas/os' need for protection, the Centro de Asuntos Migratorios (Center for Migration Issues) was created in the late 1970s as the only nonprofit, nongovernmental organization to provide immigration services for low-income Latinos. Later, they played a key role in registering undocumented immigrants and farmworkers for amnesty under the Immigration Reform and Control Act of 1986 (IRCA). In 1982 a group of Chicano activists formed the Coalition for a Just Immigration Policy to monitor enforcement of the Simpson-

Mazzoli bill. In November 1983, I was hired by the American Friends Service Committee (AFSC) to monitor border abuses. I created the U.S.–Mexico Border Program out of an existing AFSC project in San Diego.[14] I had had lots of experience in fighting for civil and human rights. Earlier that year, a friend and I had formed the Coalition for Law and Justice, to address the rising number of complaints about both police and Border Patrol abuses.

There was a great need for advocacy and someone to speak out about what was happening along the U.S.–Mexican border. Between 1984 and 1989, while the BCPU was operating on the San Diego border, twenty-three migrants were killed and dozens more were injured by gunfire, including about a dozen children between the ages of twelve and seventeen. One of them was shot and killed by a gang of white vigilantes. In 1986, the Coalition for Law and Justice organized the March for Justice and Equality at the border to protest inhumane immigration policies and human rights abuses at the border. Almost two thousand people from around the Southwest participated in the march. That march, as well as dozens of press conferences, lawsuits, and complaints, finally forced the Border Patrol and SDPD to disband the BCPU. They claimed that they didn't like the perception that they were "trigger happy."

There were other police interventions into border policy. In 1986 the chief of the SDPD announced publicly that he was contemplating forming a joint foot patrol with the U.S. Border Patrol, because Border Patrol Chief Gus de la Vina had convinced him that such a patrol had worked in El Paso and it could work in Southern California. The Coalition for a Just Immigration Policy called a meeting with Chief Kolender and convinced him the joint patrol was a bad idea. We presented complaints we had received in the AFSC office claiming that when San Diego police officers responded to a call, the first thing they would do if the caller was Mexican was to ask him or her for immigration papers. We told the chief that we didn't want our people to be afraid to call the police and that if they saw the police walking with the Border Patrol, it would destroy whatever trust they had left in the police. Chief Kolender not only agreed to scrap the whole foot patrol idea, but we convinced him to adopt a new policy regarding the circumstances under which SDPD officers could hold a person for the Border Patrol, a policy which exists to this day.[15]

The IRCA of 1986 provided amnesty for undocumented immigrants who could meet specific conditions. The law covered about 2.5 million undocumented immigrants in the United States, approximately half of them in California. An estimated 75,000 to 100,000 undocumented immigrants were living in San Diego County at the time, and perhaps 15,000 to 20,000 were farmworkers scattered all over north county and parts of east county. A few hundred worked on farms on Otay Mesa near the border. In 1985 I opened an AFSC outreach office in Oceanside at Mission San Luis Rey in order to reach and register as many farmworkers for the amnesty as possible.

My office was located in a small outbuilding located on the mission grounds. It was an ideal place because it was accessible from the dozens of farms surrounding the mission. The farmworkers began descending on my office almost immediately. I finally had to ask permission to use some of the classrooms in the mission school. I also had to call the Centro de Asuntos Migratorios for help. Using up to six classrooms at a time, we were able to interview and register hundreds of farmworkers. We finally had to ask the growers if we could process the farmworkers directly on their farms in order to expedite the process, and they agreed.

As quickly as we would register the farmworkers, however, the Border Patrol agents there in north county would arrest and deport the migrants and take away their paperwork, including their receipts, which they needed to prove they had been in the United States during the ninety days required to qualify for the amnesty. These orders came directly from Harold Ezell, who was INS western regional director during the amnesty period of IRCA. We finally began publicizing the harassment to the media. Slowly, the Border Patrol began backing off. Around this time, hate crimes against migrant workers began increasing at an alarming rate, particularly in the Carlsbad, Del Mar, and Escondido areas of north county. In one case a group of white men riding in the back of a pickup truck drove down Black Mountain Road in Del Mar and cut down four farmworkers with an AK-47 automatic rifle. All four of the farmworkers died. The white men were found and arrested. They are all serving twenty-five years to life.

As the immigration debate raged on in Washington, DC, during the 1980s, the AFSC workload, both locally and nationally, began to intensify. As my work began gaining more and more media attention, I also began attracting attention from hate groups in the form of death threats. At first, the threats came out of north San Diego County because of my public criticism of the police, sheriffs, and Border Patrol officers assaulting migrant farmworkers there. Since most of the media attention at the time was focused around the border and the human rights abuses by border agents there, however, the death threats soon began coming from more organized hate groups like WAR and the Militia. I finally had to move my office and my family out of the Victorian house we were living in near downtown San Diego because of the heavy surveillance we were under by the police, INS, Border Patrol, and hate groups.

Perhaps the most terrifying death threat I received was sent to me by WAR in September 1990. The letter that contained the threats was filled with obscenities and vile attacks on Mexican culture. A suspect was arrested and charged with sending me the letter. I was subpoenaed to testify by the U.S. attorney's office, which was representing me in the criminal trial. On September 15, members of WAR threw a pipe bomb into the front of the federal court building where my case was being heard, causing heavy damage to the door and X-ray machines. Fortunately, it was thrown at night, so no one was injured. No one was ever arrested for the crime. Morris Dees, executive director of the Southern Poverty Law Center in Atlanta, Georgia, who is famous for suing the Ku Klux Klan, also was subpoenaed to testify against WAR. He had also received death threats when he sued WAR for killing an Ethiopian man in Portland, Oregon, a year earlier. He later successfully sued and bankrupted WAR over the Portland killing. Mark Somes, a member of WAR, was convicted of sending the letters to Morris Dees and me. He received thirty-seven months in a federal prison.[16]

These were very terrifying times not only for me but also for my wife and children, who didn't understand why there was no one we could turn to for help. To make the situation worse, my wife was being followed and harassed by the Border Patrol whenever she left the house. Other times the Border Patrol would videotape us leaving our house using unmarked vans with tinted windows. This was one of the main reasons we moved to another location. This harassment and government surveillance would continue for at least another ten years.[17]

The involvement of local police in immigration enforcement continued. In January 1990, the BCPU was reinstituted as the Border Crime Intervention Unit. This time, the unit would consist only of San Diego police. The unit would also patrol in uniform, rather than operating as decoys along the border as they had done before. This was welcome news for the AFSC, even though human rights abuses continued all along the border. Also in 1990, the Immigration Law Enforcement Monitoring Project (ILEMP) of the AFSC, a national project based in Houston, Texas, issued its first human rights report based on complaints gathered from border offices in Harlingen and El Paso, Texas; Tucson, Arizona; and San Diego, California. Copies of the report were sent to the Justice Department in Washington, DC, the INS, the U.S. Border Patrol, and the local

U.S. attorney's office. Through the ILEMP, we established a binational network of human rights programs and contacts along the length of the U.S.–Mexican border in all the major border cities, such as San Diego–Tijuana, Tucson-Nogales, El Paso–Juárez, and Harlingen-Reynosa. Binational networking has been key to successfully monitoring and documenting human rights abuses on both sides of the border.

Over the next ten years the reports began to attract national attention, particularly from international human rights organizations such as Human Rights Watch and Amnesty International, who issued their own human rights reports based on interviews with our clients. In 1991 I was invited to testify at a congressional hearing in support of legislation to create a national federal oversight commission to monitor human rights abuses by federal agents at the U.S.–Mexican border. An attorney from San Diego who handled AFSC federal lawsuits against Border Patrol agents, two Border Patrol agents, and I all testified before a congressional panel. The bill, 2119, was rejected, however, because the Justice Department claimed there was already enough oversight by the Federal Bureau of Investigation, the Office of the Inspector General (OIG) Internal Audit, and the Civil Rights Division of the Justice Department. Over the next five years I testified at two more congressional hearings and at two U.S. Commission on Civil Rights hearings, one in San Diego and one in El Paso.[18] Although the hearings didn't lead to any change at the time, they did serve to expose the human rights issue, both nationally and internationally. This translated into more media attention for human rights groups across the entire border.

In December 1992, I received the prestigious Human Rights Watch Monitoring Award from Human Rights Watch, an international organization based in New York. I was one of eleven recipients from around the world to be selected for the award and the first U.S. citizen to receive the award in the history of the organization. The other ten recipients were all from third world countries and had been targets for assassination, torture, or long periods of solitary confinement. One of the recipients, María Elena Moyano, a Peruvian environmental and human rights activist, was assassinated only one month before she was to meet with us in Los Angeles, by the Sendero Luminoso, or Shining Path, a violent Maoist/Marxist organization in Peru.

The message that our organization and other immigrant rights groups were trying to send Congress during this twenty-year period was that "impunity breeds abuse." Without a more humane immigration policy, effective oversight over federal agents, and effective leadership in Washington from representatives such as the Hispanic Caucus, nothing will ever change.

Safety versus Security

On September 11, 2001, the world stood still and watched in stunned silence as three jets slammed into the World Trade Center twin towers in New York and into the Pentagon. A fourth airliner crashed in a Pennsylvania field when passengers overpowered terrorists who were targeting Washington. Almost 3,000 people would die that day. The world was not the only thing that stood still that day—all legislation concerning immigrants and refugees came to a grinding halt, including discussions between Mexico and the United States regarding legalization for the millions of undocumented immigrants presently in the United States. Also at a standstill were debates over legislation that would undo all the damage done by the Illegal Immigration Reform and Immigrant Responsibility Act of 1996 (IIRIRA),[19] which is causing irreparable harm to legal permanent residents and their families all across the country. IIRIRA was made retroactive and targeted legal permanent residents who might have committed minor crimes, or even unknowingly been accessories to crimes, up to twenty years earlier.

On September 22, thousands of immigrant rights activists and supporters had planned to converge on Washington, DC, to lobby representatives and senators on important legislation, as well as to protest increasing militarization of the border, including the alarming increase in deaths along the U.S.–Mexican border caused by deadly Border Patrol strategies, such as Operation Gatekeeper and three similar operations in Arizona and Texas,[20] which have forced immigrants into remote desert and mountain areas to die of dehydration or exposure (fig. 9.3). More than a hundred of us from San Diego, Los Angeles, and San Francisco were planning to attend.

The debates in Washington, DC, however, shifted from protecting immigrants to removing them. Security now took priority over safety. All the gains we had won for immigrants over the previous twenty years were in danger of being lost because of the terrorist attacks. The Patriot Act, passed shortly after September 11, eliminated all due process rights for immigrants and anyone suspected of being a terrorist. Racial profiling was now expanded to include anyone who looked Arab or Muslim. Hate crimes against anyone who looked Middle Eastern were also on the rise.

Civil liberties groups all over the country began sending out alerts warning

FIGURE 9.3. Before 9/11, immigrants would congregate in an area known as "the Soccer Field," across from San Ysidro, California, prior to beginning their perilous journey into the United States. In this photo, Padre Florenzo Rigoni (left) and Father John Jensen bless the immigrants before they leave. (From Bartletti, *Between Two Worlds*, p. 25; used courtesy of Don Bartletti)

of discrimination against Middle Eastern–looking people. However, what really put civil liberties groups and immigrant rights groups alike on major alert was the passing of the Patriot Act. IIRIRA was bad enough, but under the Patriot Act, legal residents can be held indefinitely with no charges. In December 1999 my office formed a support group for the hundreds of families in San Diego affected by this repressive law. The pain and suffering inflicted on these families by this law is unimaginable.

What U.S. policy and law have done is to reduce human migration—a natural, human phenomenon—to a humiliating, dehumanizing experience. It has also turned a fundamental human right into a crime in the eyes of this country. The International Declaration of Human Rights states that every human being has the right to go anywhere in the world in search of a better life. Most of us in immigrant rights work agree that none of the security measures being implemented are going to make the border any more secure.

Un Pueblo Sin Fronteras

Today, Tijuana and San Diego have a combined population of three million people. Not only are we linked economically and culturally, but we also share a common border and a common humanity struggling to survive on both sides of the border. Even more important, there is a common concern over the growing number of deaths on the California–Baja California border. Mexican and Central American immigrants are dying in the deserts, rivers, canals, and mountains due to U.S. Border Patrol attempts to control the flow of humanity seeking a better life for themselves and their families. The human toll has been staggering.

Since the AFSC began keeping count in 1995, almost four thousand men, women, and children are known to have died crossing the California border.[21] The majority are dying in the deserts of Arizona and the Imperial Valley. Hundreds more drown attempting to swim across the All American Canal. No fewer than two people a day die crossing the border. There have also been countless tragic cases of large groups of men, women, and children who are found dead or dying in the mountains after a winter snowstorm, or are found abandoned in the deserts of California and Arizona. As I write this in 2005, this has so far been the deadliest year on record for border crossers. Twenty migrants were found dead in the Sonoran Desert of Arizona in a one-week period. In 2004 fourteen people in one group were found dead in one day in the same desert. In July 2005, however, 116 migrants perished attempting to cross the Sonoran Desert in Arizona and the Imperial Desert in California, making July the deadliest month on record.

The government continues to deny any responsibility for the deaths, blaming smugglers and the weather rather than the four Border Patrol operations along the border. This is the hypocrisy of our immigration laws: the United States needs immigrants to fill low-paying jobs in order to keep wages competitive and prices low. At the same time, however, they blame and often punish employers for hiring undocumented immigrants, and put pressure on the INS to better control the border. These policies lead citizens to believe that the only purpose of the Border Patrol is to control labor, not the border.

Where is the outrage at the deaths of so many people in one geographical area of the United States? Why is it taking the government so long to realize what we've known from the beginning—that these operations are not only ineffective but do not even begin to address the root causes of immigration? For decades the AFSC has been challenging public indifference toward the enormous economic, social, and cultural contributions immigrants make to this country every year. A recently federally mandated study concluded that immigrants are a net boost to the U.S. economy, adding up to $10 billion each year while providing a crucial workforce and lowering consumer prices.[22] One billion dollars of that money boosts California's economy alone. Reports like this continue to dispel the myth that immigrants take jobs away from Americans and are a drain on our social services.

San Diego has been and continues to be a testing ground for every kind of Border Patrol policy and operation at the border, as well as for INS experimental polices in schools, service industries, and local law enforcement. This is a sad commentary on San Diego's relationship with Mexico, our neighbor to the south, especially since Mexicans spend nearly $4 billion a year in San Diego. Also, San Diego benefits from the $1.5 billion that agribusiness in north San Diego County brings in per year.[23] Mexican labor has not only contributed to California's agribusiness, which generates $30 billion a year, but also has helped make California the fifth largest economy in the world. As immigration continues to contribute to California's distinction of being the country's most populous state, new challenges on old issues confront human rights activists. Add to that the fact that nine million—or one-third—of all new immigrants entering the United States through 2025 will settle in California, and the challenge rises to the level of urgency in terms of immigration and human rights.

New Challenges for the New Millennium

By the year 2020 the Chicano/Mexicano population is expected to represent fully one-third of the projected 3.8 million total population of San Diego. According to the 2000 census, there are presently about 750,000 Latinos living in San Diego County, including 310,000 in the city of San Diego.[24] The economic, political, and cultural implications of these demographic changes are enormous. Chicanas/os have the opportunity not only to flex their collective political muscle in terms of voting on critical issues but also to unite in increasing our political representation on the local, state, and national levels. These challenges are already being met at the national level by immigrant rights groups across the country. National immigrant rights organizations like the Border Project of the American Friends Service Committee or the National Network for Immigrant and Refugee Rights, and state organizations like the Interfaith Coalition for Immigrant Rights, find themselves in a holding pattern on some issues following 9/11, but are regrouping on others. National organizations are reframing immigration within the context of globalization and international human rights accords. Why? Because after twenty years of protesting, testifying at congressional hearings, marching, and conducting endless letter-writing campaigns, little has changed.

As protagonists of the new millennium, the challenges for Chicanos/Mexicanos are clear: immigration is changing the face of America forever. This is why the AFSC has launched a nationwide project to build a national immigrant-led organization called Voices.[25] Voices is also a call to action to immigrant rights groups across the country to develop a leadership strategy for immigrants in order to give them a greater voice on issues that affect them and to bring them directly into the policy debate. The project would also serve as a center for national mobilization and a common ground for diverse communities to work together on issues of diversity and multiculturalism. Some of the objectives include influencing national policy, promoting and strengthening grassroots organizing, developing collective immigrant leadership, and supporting national mobilization on crucial issues.

The U.S.–Mexico Border Program of the AFSC in San Diego has implemented many of these objectives almost from its inception twenty years ago, especially those of influencing national policy, promoting grassroots organizing, and supporting national mobilization. The San Diego program will play a major role in the Voices project, as well as continuing to monitor and document human and civil rights abuses in this section of the border. Over the last ten years, police shootings and beatings of Chicanas/os, immigrants, and homeless people in San Diego has provoked an angry response from the Chicano, African American, and homeless communities.

Although police violence is nothing new in San Diego, or in Southern California for that matter, it has recently become a national scandal. Again, at the root of the problem is the issue of accountability and oversight. It can also be attributed to the lack of local government leadership and their support for the ineffective Citizens' Review Board in San Diego. There will never be an effective system of accountability and oversight in San Diego as long as the SDPD has the only authority to investigate citizen complaints and as long as the Review Board and the district attorney "rubber stamp" everything the police send them. The National City Police Department and the Chula Vista Police Department run close seconds in terms of police violence and lack of oversight.

Since the police and the district attorney are all part of the same criminal justice system, it's not surprising that the criminal justice system in San Diego discriminates against the poor and immigrant populations in the community. This discrimination is evidenced by the disproportionate number of Chicanos and blacks in California prisons today. The system begins to break down at the juvenile offender level. A national study released in July 2002 disclosed that Chicanos detained in the juvenile justice system were twice as likely to be incarcerated as their white peers. This raises serious concerns for Chicanos in California—home to more than eleven million Latinos—where 48 percent of those in California Youth Authority lockups are Latino, according to state and federal figures. The report states that not only do Latinos receive harsher sentences than whites for the same crimes but the average stay in prison is longer for Latinos—34.3 months, compared to 30 months for whites.[26]

As a Chicano who was born and raised in Barrio Logan and Sherman Heights, and as one who has monitored and documented abuses there by both police and Border Patrol agents, I have never had any question in my mind that the police have gotten away with abuses there that they would not get away with in a white community. The same has been true in all areas of San Diego where there are large concentrations of Chicanos and immigrants.

The root of the problem lies in the lack of understanding and involvement within the community. Police and Border Patrol agents rarely live in communities of color; therefore, they do not have a vested interest in what happens there, much less in whether or not the residents suffer abuses by these two agencies. In the 1960s and 1970s Chicanos and African Americans began protesting the lack of Latino and black officers on the force, under the rationale that perhaps if there were more Latino and black officers, there would be fewer abuses by police. However, when the AFSC began tracking complaints against the police in 1982, we were disappointed to find that abuses by Latino police officers were beginning to rise at an alarming rate. The situation was even worse in the Border Patrol, where almost half of the complaints were against Latino agents. That statistic has not changed. As it turns out, there is a logical explanation for the Border Patrol statistic. Almost 50 percent of the two thousand Border Patrol agents in the San Diego sector are Latino. Nationwide, Latinos make up 40 percent of the eleven thousand Border Patrol agents, so the number of complaints is simply proportional to their representation in the Border Patrol.[27]

There has never been any question that racism is another root cause of police and Border Patrol violence. Racism is part of the historical culture of these two agencies. In fact, the two agencies not only work together very closely in Chicano communities but actually operate on the same radio frequencies in order that the police can radio the Border Patrol when they detain suspected undocumented immigrants. It is not coincidental that as the immigration debate began to heat up in the early 1980s, so too did the question of whether police should be authorized to enforce immigration law.

If there is one common denominator throughout California history and the lives of Chicanos/Mexicanos, it is the fear factor. As immigrant rights activists, we can file complaints and we can help remove bad cops and bad Border Patrol agents from the community, but we cannot remove the fear. Of the many aspects of my work, this is the one factor that causes me the most anguish: to see the fear and terror in people's faces after a raid on their home by police or Border Patrol officers, or the fear caused by anticipation of a raid on their home. The anguish is worse when it involves women and children. An immigrant rights leader here in San Diego once related to me that at a forum for immigrants, he asked the people what his organization could do to help. One gentleman stood up and said, "remove the fear."[28]

A key element in this fear is the fact that the vast majority of police officers are white males. As the National Minority Advisory Council on Criminal Justice stated,

> Throughout the history of the United States the white majority has felt compelled to use economic and political power, and particularly the criminal justice system, to maintain control and authority over the racial minorities in American society. The oppression of minorities in America is supported by a system of racial beliefs and ideologies that has pervaded the nation's major political and cultural institutions, especially the criminal justice system.[29]

This report substantiates and underscores what Chicano history, even before the Treaty of Guadalupe Hidalgo, has taught us: that all of our issues, even today, can be traced directly to the historical negation of equal access and participation in the economic, political, and cultural development in the United States.

Chicano and Mexicano History and Leadership in San Diego

As has been pointed out in previous chapters, there have been many efforts to fight for equal access, whether in the lawsuit against educational segregation in Lemon Grove in 1930, in the establishment of cannery unions in Barrio Logan, or in political organizations like MAPA and the Southwest Voter Registration Project. Because of San Diego's proximity to the U.S.–Mexican border, the struggle has had an added dimension. Beginning in the 1970s the Movimiento Estudiantil Chicano en Aztlán (MEChA), the statewide student organization, has led the way in student activism. They have not only provided support on major issues but, along with students in Chicano studies classes, have also provided interns and volunteers to immigrant rights organizations like the AFSC. Student newspapers—like *Voz Fronteriza* at UCSD, which has had decades of experience of struggle, militancy, and exposing critical issues in our community—have also led the way in providing Chicanas/os with an alternative media forum.

Providing much of the stimulus for the student movement and on other issues involving self-determination of the Mexicano/Chicano community has been the Raza Rights Coalition.[30] Founded as a spin-off of the Unión del Barrio in 1989, the coalition has successfully taken on many of the most unpopular issues confronting San Diego today. They are also well known for holding press conferences and demonstrations in front of the police department, the Mexican consulate, and the homes of politicians. The Raza Rights Coalition has served as an umbrella group for many Chicano, African American, and Asian organizations in San Diego County.

The Raza Rights Coalition's methods have often been criticized, but the increase in police and Border Patrol violence in San Diego has required a strong response. The coalition has always provided immediate, strong responses when needed. Throughout California over the past forty years, marches and protests have always been successful in calling attention to the issues at hand. One of the most remarkable developments over the years is that marches and protests now no longer involve just one ethnic group. In marches and protests today one is likely to find a mixture of Chicanos, whites, African Americans, and Asians, even when the issue is primarily of concern to Chicanos. This is largely as a result of including labor unions, church groups, peace activist groups, and student groups in these issues. Coalition building is not only on the increase but is a necessity in confronting some of the major national issues affecting the Chicana/o community today.

In developing Chicana/o leadership today it is important to recognize that not only are we labeling ourselves as Chicana/o, Hispanic, Latina/o, Mexican American, or in rare cases white, but we also find ourselves running the full range of the political spectrum from Republican to Democrat to Libertarian to Green Party. In some parts of the Southwest, Chicanas/os belong to such parties as the Raza Unida Party, Socialist Worker Party, and Revolutionary Communist Party (RCP). The RCP uses La Resistencia as a front for recruiting Chicanos and other ethnic groups around the Southwest, including in San Diego.

As a fifth-generation U.S. citizen and a Chicano, I have learned to appreciate the importance of Chicano history in defining who we are and in tracing the roots of many of the problems we are facing today. Some of the border and human rights problems, for example, are directly attributable to the creation of the U.S.–Mexican border, westward expansion, and Manifest Destiny. I believe that Chicano history also teaches our children to have pride in who they are. I believe that if more young Chicanos/Mexicanos had more pride in their culture, they would be a lot less involved in gangs and drugs, because gangs and drugs are not part of Chicano culture and history. These are American phenomena. They are also problems that are being exported to other parts of Latin America, including Mexico and Central America. Grinding poverty and chronic unemployment breed crime—whether in the United States or Latin America.

Every day we witness history being made on the U.S.–Mexican border, at the international level, the national level, or the policy level. Every day a migrant dies crossing the border a new chapter in Chicano history is being written, because the United States is ignoring its moral and Christian responsibility to "welcome the stranger." The United States is also in violation of international human rights laws stating that all human beings have the right to leave their homelands in search of a better life. Every time a migrant dies crossing the border, we are all diminished as human beings. Regardless of one's religious beliefs, undocumented immigrants are our brothers and sisters in distress. They are the migrant face of God in search of the Promised Land.[31]

The border endures as a wound that never heals as hundreds of migrants die or nearly die each year along the border. On October 1, 2005, as we marked the eleventh anniversary of Operation Gatekeeper, a deadly milestone was reached: the death toll on the U.S.–Mexico border has reached almost four thousand since that operation was launched. Immigrant rights activists along the length of the border used the anniversary to demand again that the government abolish these deadly policies.

San Diego's struggle is not local, but rather national and even international. National church groups are beginning to voice strong opposition to inhumane immigration policies, immigrant deaths, and the deadly Border Patrol policies that cause them. Ecumenical groups, such as the Washington, DC–based Border Working Group coordinated by the Religious Task Force on Central America and Mexico, have issued reports and sponsored fact-finding border tours. The National Conference of Catholic Bishops has held hearings and conferences in order to gather live testimonies of the incredible suffering migrants must endure on their way north to the United States, as well as the mistreatment they suffer at the hands of Border Patrol agents.

In the fall of 2003, interfaith groups from across the country held a pilgrimage along the length of the U.S.–Mexican border to call attention to the deaths on the border and, they hoped, spark a national debate on the subject. The pilgrimage terminated in El Paso with workshops, speeches, music, and an interfaith religious service at the border fence on the Day of the Dead, All Souls Day. During this event we also called for a greater voice for immigrants in the United States, as well as for changes in national immigration policies in order to protect immigrants from persecution by the INS, such as the recent INS raids on airports in the name of "national security." A border delegation traveled to Washington, DC, to lobby for an end to the border deaths and the policies that cause them.

I can summarize the meaning of my struggle for human rights by saying, "Chicano power translates into Chicano pride. Chicano pride translates into Chicano history, which we continue to write every day. Every time a young Chicana/o graduates from college and becomes a teacher, lawyer, or elected official, Chicano power, pride, and history are being made. ¡Sí, Se Puede!"

10

LEARNING FROM THE PAST: SOME CONCLUDING COMMENTS

This book has attempted to shape a new vision of a place and a people by giving visibility to the Indian, Spanish, Mexican, and Chicana/o men and women in the San Diego–Tijuana border region. In our vision of the past, Chicanas and Chicanos emerge as more than an immigrant group defined by a political border. They are a people who have been engaged in the creation of a border culture, "a third space" shaped by accommodation, rejection, and acceptance. The U.S. Mexicans in San Diego have been more than just commodity labor. They remain a people who have been creating a homeland, a cultural space, while struggling for social justice alongside their counterparts across the border. In this historical process they have become Mexicans without borders.

In this concluding chapter we come together as collaborative students, scholars, and activists to offer our own multifaceted ideas about the meaning of our work while reflecting on the underlying theme of shaping a border culture. We invite you as readers to join in this discussion as well by sharing and publishing your criticisms, views, impressions, and histories. Collectively, we can add to what has been offered here and expand on themes and ideas that have been introduced, as well as offer new interpretations of the past and present.

Richard Griswold del Castillo

San Diego's early history was greatly influenced by the indigenous peoples who first came here more than 13,000 years ago. They vastly outnumbered the Spanish-speaking settlers who arrived in 1769 and made possible the growth of Spanish settlements in the missions, presidios, ranchos, and pueblos. The first mestizo settlers were influenced by these indigenous people's culture, foods, medicines, and worldviews. Early Mexicanos were dependent on the Indian people for labor, food, and their daily survival. The struggle for social justice fell to the Indians who rebelled against their forced enslavement by the Mexicans, but it also involved Mexicans who sought to protect and empower them. The Mexican War created a new boundary between Mexico and the United States immediately south of San Diego, which set in motion struggles for social justice against the economic and social discrimination that came with the American takeover. San Diego's Spanish-speaking community was historically tied to developments in Mexico, through the Mexican Revolution and Mexican immigration. The struggles for cultural space and social justice focused on the old and new barrios of Old Town and Logan Heights. With the growth of Tijuana and Mexicali in the twentieth century, the Chicano communities in San Diego and the Imperial Valley have grown through migration and immigration from these cities and towns. The binational alliance of Mexican families, friends, and acquaintances on both sides of the border is largely invisible, but is a tangible and important aspect of the construction of social space for Chicanas and Chicanos.

José Rodolfo Jacobo

It is said that in Mexico there is a pervasive awareness of the past, that the past intrudes on the national psyche, that it suffuses art, philosophy, and literature. The same holds true of San Diego and its community of Mexican descent. The region is a museum of Mexican and Chicano history. The indigenous, Spanish, Mexican, and Euro-American cultures that have shaped and defined our existence are ever-present. The language, architecture, food, and art all remind us not just of our past but also of who we are. Just like in Mexico, however, ethnocentrism has often discounted the value of this history, giving it little importance other than marking historical sites for tourist attractions. Part of our mission here is to change that perception, so that the historical sites and events can be seen not just as part of San Diego's history but as the patrimony of the Mexican American community here.

San Diego's history, like that of other communities in the Southwest, has been shaped by historical factors such as the evolution of indigenous culture, Spanish exploration, the Mexican period, and American control. The region as a whole experienced the social, political, and economic integration that came with the change of political authority in the mid-nineteenth century. It also witnessed the structuring of a new social order and its sometimes less than democratic institutions, as well as the long road to justice and equality for the Mexican American people. In all corners of the Southwest there exists a common interest in recovering the past. This search for our roots, which led to an explosion of literature in the 1960s and 1970s, has not subsided.

Historically, the San Diego–Tijuana region has both enjoyed and suffered from a complex socioeconomic relationship. It is here that, according to the poet Mario Martín Flores, "the land goes on living at the edge of the longest gash in the world." Our border is a monument to war and to the inhumanity of humanity. On any given Sunday one can witness family picnics in the shadow of the fence that divides Mexico and the United States. The fence divides the family as well. La *abuela* is on the south side with the *buñuelos* and *cacahuates,* while on the north side of the fence there are *jamón* sandwiches that Mom and the children have brought. But just as we witness such calamities, we can also bear witness to the people's spirit. Our pueblo has an ability to turn tragedy into celebration. We are resilient. We have learned resilience from our parents and their parents, from our ancestors. There are smiles on the children's faces as they share pictures with their abuelita, and on the Mexican side, a person is selling corn to those of us on the north side of the tortilla fence. Here, there is no NAFTA, no migra, just a family enjoying a family day. *Es verdad, que por mi raza hablará el espíritu.* This is the gift of the Kumeyaay, *los braceros,* and the old Chicano *veteranos.* It is vital that we maintain this way of life as we continue on the path toward globalization.

Roberto Martínez

Since I began working on the border more than twenty-five years ago, addressing human and civil rights abuses, we have always referred to ourselves as "un pueblo sin fronteras," a people without borders. This slogan became a reality when we formed a binational, borderwide network to address social, economic, and environmental justice issues.

We share a common border and a common humanity struggling for equal justice. When it comes to oppression, Chicanos/Mexicanos share the same space in society. Current immigration and border enforcement laws don't always distinguish between the two. For instance, laws authorizing local police to enforce immigration laws turn all Chicanos and Mexicanos into suspects.

Our proximity to the border means that Chicanos and Mexicanos must always be alert to the ever-changing immigration and civil rights laws that are constantly challenging our civil liberties. This is why I say in my chapter that we are still writing Chicano history, because we have not yet reached full equality in

U.S. society. There are three things that make Chicano/Mexicano history in San Diego different from the histories of other Chicano/Mexicano communities in the United States. First, apart from the San Diego port of entry being the busiest land border crossing in the world, the economic interdependence between San Diego and Tijuana is increasing, estimated at more than $4 billion a year. Second, this border area has the unfortunate distinction of having one of the most oppressive Border Patrol and police policies against Chicanos/Mexicanos on the U.S.–Mexico border. Last, San Diego County, including the border region, has a nearly one hundred–year history of hate violence against Native Americans, Mexicans, (particularly farmworkers), and Mexican Americans by Ku Klux Klan–type organizations, law enforcement officials, and youth white power groups. The significance of this history is that San Diego and Tijuana have become *one region—economically, environmentally, and politically* because of the pressing immigration/migration issues confronting the United States.

The history of this region is similar to that of other areas of the Southwest in terms of the rapidly changing demographics caused by both immigration and the historical struggle by Chicanos/Mexicanos for political representation at the local, state, and national levels. The importance of the historical presence of the Indian, Chicana/o, and Mexicana/o in the San Diego–Tijuana region for the future is that they serve as a reminder that this region is, has been, and always will be deeply rooted in indigenous and Chicano/Mexicano history. However, they are also reminders of the inequality that continues to exist in many aspects of our society, such as the criminal justice system, civil rights, labor rights, immigration, and farmworker rights.

Emmanuelle Le Texier

The representations of the barrio as a common cultural place deeply intertwined with a Mexican cultural identity constitute a powerful tool for the construction of a common identity. El barrio is presented as a social space defined by territorial boundaries that have to be preserved. These physical boundaries delimit who is part of the community and who is not. In addition, the barrio is defined positively as "our community" (*nuestra comunidad*), a place of identification which can become a place for self-determination. The feeling of belonging to a group and a specific territory turns into group consciousness and, eventually, into a feeling of political efficacy and capacity. In San Diego, Chicanas/os have been confronted by different forms of oppression, but the reference to a common space and place have allowed them to mount multiple responses. In that sense, the contemporary Chicano/Mexicano experience in the San Diego barrio is both unique and similar to that in other American barrios. It is similar in terms of socio-demographic characteristics: Barrio Logan is a disenfranchised community defined by low-income residents with poor social, economic, and political achievement. Barrio Logan suffers from marginalization and from the consequences of the public policy of the city of San Diego, especially the current redevelopment and revitalization programs. Gentrification is affecting Barrio Logan as well as other barrios in Los Angeles, El Paso, and San Jose. But San Diego's experience is distinct from those of other communities for three main reasons. First, San Diego is a border city, and its proximity to *la frontera* affects the politics of identity and empowerment. Second, San Diego is an extremely conservative city, closed to minority political expression and participation. Third, Barrio Logan has a history of political mobilization rooted in the 1970s birth of Chicano Park and its murals, as well as community organizations that have left a symbolic legacy of struggle in the heart of the barrio.

As a consequence, Barrio Logan deserves specific attention. There has been barely any study of the barrio among social scientists. The literature mostly dates from the 1970s, and there is a lot to be done in terms of both micro- and macro-level research: on the one hand, we need studies of political coalitions, the impact of community organizations in the areas of health and the environment, educational attainment by barrio students, and equal opportunity in employment. On the other hand, we need research on electoral participation, campaigning, housing and redevelopment projects, and longitudinal historical studies.

Rita Sánchez

The history of the Chicano arts movement in San Diego gives us insight into the ways in which the region differs from other areas of Aztlán. For one, the U.S.–Mexican border has exerted a strong influence on the consciousness of Chicana and Chicano artists in San Diego. Some of the most dynamic and creative artistic expressions have dealt with themes arising from our marginalization with respect to U.S. society and from San Diego being a border community. For many of us, the border is an artificial line that we choose to cross every day in our consciousness as well as with our bodies.

While the border gives us our distinctive identity as Chicanas and Chicanos from San Diego, it also unites us with our brothers and sisters in Mexico and in the rest of Aztlán. Increasingly, artists are the ones who push the boundaries and borders beyond their everyday limits. Chicana artists, whether from San Diego or elsewhere, have a common struggle in this endeavor. First, we seek to gain the recognition, space, and resources we need to fully express our identity and our realities. Second, we share with our sisters everywhere a common goal of working for world peace and spreading our spiritual gifts and insights, which we have nurtured from antiquity. Chicana and Chicano artists in San Diego together represent the future as well as the past of the Chicano Movement.

San Diego's history is Chicano history. Yet it is not entirely unique. We are connected *los unos a los otros* (one to another), as the Aztec poet says. It is amazing to discover that the civil rights work done by Chicanos in San Francisco streets has the same goal as the work being done by *hermanas y hermanos* in the cotton fields of Texas. Because we do not recognize arbitrary borders, we are fully connected to the undocumented workers who join us in the cause when they come to the United States to work and face injustices here. Until we all are free, none of us is truly free.

The doors to our future are open. Every day we discover the great amounts of work we have yet to do. Each one of us has a different task. Mine is writing. If our stories do not reach the next generation, our job is not complete. The greatest gift we can give to the future is our connection to one another. That sense of unity has always been the byword of our community. It is what makes us strong. That we are Hispana, Mexicana, Indígena can never be denied. Without this great understanding, we are lost. With it, we can go forward ready to build the future.

María de la Luz Ibarra

In an article addressing the varied meanings of *Aztlán*, Rafael Pérez Torres argues that it can be understood as an "empty signifier." By this he means that the word highlights not that which is, but that which is missing—namely, unity, liberty, nation. In this sense Aztlán reveals the social imaginary of Chicanas/os who find themselves in a borderlands of contradictions, in Gloria Anzaldúa's terms, a "crossfire of camps," where identity as well as terrain are contested. The immigrants who are central to my chapter worked and lived at the *campo*, and had no conception of the term *Aztlán*; nonetheless, as part of a people that form a diaspora, they yearned for something that was missing, something that did not exist until they made it; something they came to call "home."

The creation of home for these Mexicanas/os involved in great part actively

re-creating familiar landscapes and, as far as possible, reproducing other important cultural practices—preparing specific foods and listening to particular
types of music, for example. In these ways, Mexicanas/os at that time and in that
particular place "transcended" cultural borders, since specifically working-class
Mexican cultural practices were not a normalized part of the society. And in fact,
the dominant white society actively worked to isolate and segregate Mexicanas/
os from public spaces and life.

Over time, however, as the demographics of the community changed due
both to labor demand and to the maturation of social networks, cultural practices that had once transcended borders have become an integral part of the
city. Over the last thirty-five years, many communities throughout Southern
California—and indeed other parts of the United States—have been described
as "little Mexicos" because of the predominance of Mexican-origin people and
Mexican-specific cultural practices. In this sense, Mexicanas/os have not just
transcended borders, but have transformed the American landscape. Mexicanas
and Mexicanos have thus used their social imaginary to create real and palpable
communities that tie together distinctive places and historical moments.

Isidro D. Ortiz

In the early 1980s, in an article entitled "Chicanos in the U.S.: A History of
Exploitation and Resistance," Leobardo Estrada and three colleagues set forth the
thesis that the history of Chicanos has been a history of exploitation and resistance. The history of Chicanas/os in San Diego, as documented in this anthology, informs us that the history of Chicanas/os is characterized by a complexity
richer than the thesis suggests.

In San Diego, Chicanas/os have been subjected to the oppression of exploitation and have engaged in resistance to it. However, their history may also be
described as a history of multiple oppressions and multiple responses. In addition
to exploitation, a form of oppression, Chicanos have also experienced the other
faces of oppression identified by the political theorist Iris Young: powerlessness,
violence, marginalization, and cultural imperialism. Moreover, while some in our
community have resisted, others have responded with conformity, status seeking,
assimilation, withdrawal, and innovation.

The complexity of our history, in terms of forms of oppression experienced
and responses manifested, calls for a paradigm shift. For lack of a better term,
the paradigm may be described for now as the history of multiple oppressions

and multiple responses model. The applicability of this model to other regions remains to be determined through scholarly investigations, although I would hypothesize that the model would be broadly applicable. Scholarly investigations have documented that Chicanas/os have experienced oppression elsewhere. In the past, the range of oppression has not been fully documented. A reliance on the categories developed by Iris Young may facilitate such efforts. Likewise, responses that parallel those occurring in San Diego have been documented. To what extent Chicana/o responses are parallel throughout the borderlands must await investigation.

The record of activism in San Diego during the 1970s and 1980s also challenges the depiction of these decades as years of apathy and "me-ism." As documented in the chapters by Martínez and Ortiz, Chicanas and Chicanos during these years engaged in sustained activism. Their activism was often focused on the most oppressed segments of the Mexican-origin population in San Diego: undocumented workers from Mexico. And the impact of this activism was felt beyond the city limits.

The Chicano/Mexican history of San Diego also offers important lessons regarding the resilience and tenacity of the Chicanos, their capacity for agency, the impermanency of political gains, and the capacity of the state to contain nationalism and insurgency. The history reveals that Chicanos/Mexicanos are a highly resilient and tenacious population that has repeatedly overcome oppression and its consequences. But Chicanas and Chicanos do not simply survive or accept oppression. They are capable of acting to transform their condition. Through such struggles, Chicanas/os have made important gains; however, the gains are not permanent. They have been under constant attack and indeed many have been lost. Others appear to be eroding. The experiences of Chicanas/os in San Diego again underscore that constant struggle is necessary to preserve the gains our community has made. At the same time, the capacity of the state to contain nationalistic insurgency is profound. It has many tools at its disposal and will employ them.

Nationalism can be seen as a response to repeated hostility and rejection of Chicanos by the political majority. Certainly, Chicanos and Mexicanos have been subjected to hostile treatment. Nevertheless, many Chicanas/os in San Diego continue to pursue the goal of structural assimilation. This pursuit challenges recent catastrophic assessments of the effects of Mexicanization on California and of Latinization on the United States offered by scholars such as

Victor Hansen and Samuel Huntington. It suggests that, even when they become a majority in the not too distant future, Mexican and Latino populations will continue to affirm rather than pose a threat to the society or cultural integrity of the United States, as they have done historically.

notes

Introduction

1. San Diego Association of Governments (SANDAG). "Mapping the Census: Race and Ethnicity in the San Diego Region." *SANDAG Info* 1 (April 2002), www.sandag.org/uploads/publicationid/publicationid_722_1120.pdf.

2. San Diego Regional Economic Development Corporation, www.sandiegobusiness.org/article_template.asp?articleID=51 (accessed 4/10/2007).

3. SANDAG, *San Diego Demographic Profile*, 2000, http://ssdc.ucsd.edu/ssdc/cen2k.html (accessed 4/10/2007).

4. The contributors to this anthology have used a variety of terms to refer to the people of the San Diego region who came here originally from Mexico, whether in the 1700s or in 2006. The variety of terminology arose in different historical, cultural, and socioeconomic contexts. In general in this work *Latino* is used synonymously with the term *Hispanic*, to refer to all persons of Latin American origin in the United States. The term *Chicana/o*, refers more specifically to people of Mexican origin, but with the connotation that they have retained an awareness of and pride in their mestizo and indigenous roots. *Mexican American* is used to refer to the bilingual, bicultural people of Mexican origin who are naturalized or native-born citizens of the United States. It is important to stress that terminology varies with usage, geographic locale, and even political context. Appropriately, there is no universal agreement among "Latinos" about the "correct term" to use for self-identification. Rather, there is an understanding that the variation in terminology reflects the inherent diversity of these people's origins.

5. Davis, Mayhew, and Miller, *Under the Perfect Sun*.

6. The concept of the third space has gained wide acceptance among scholars who theorize about the creation of hybrid cultural and historical spaces, especially those created by the U.S.–Mexican border (see Gutiérrez, "Migration, Emergent Ethnicity, and the Third Space," 481–83).

7. Vélez-Ibáñez, *Border Visions*, 8.

8. See Mario García, "Californios of San Diego and the Politics of Accommodation"; also his "Merchants and Dons." Another important early contribution was that of Charles Hughes in "Decline of the Californios."

9. Norris, "Logan Heights."

10. Alvarez, "Lemon Grove Incident." Also see the video documentary *The Lemon Grove Incident*, produced and written by Paul Espinosa, directed and edited by Frank Christopher (KPBS-TV, 1985).

11. Ortiz, "Latinos against City Hall"; G. González, "Company Unions"; and Griswold del Castillo, "San Ysidro Massacre."

Chapter 1

1. M. Wilson, "Legends of the Diegueño Indians," 24–64.

2. Shipek, *Myth and Reality*. Shipek argues that many other myths of the Kumeyaay or Diegueño Indians reflect ancient geological events, such as the earlier creation of the Salton Sea (in 700 ACE) by the diversion of the Colorado River. Other myths tell of the primordial unity of the Kumeyaay with peoples from the Mexican mainland.

3. R. Carrico, *Strangers in a Stolen Land*, 5–9.

4. Cook, "Aboriginal Population of Upper California," 71. Cook calculates California's total aboriginal population in 1769 as between 250,000 and 300,000 (see p. 72). Note variations in the spelling of *Kumeyaay*. In Mexico the name is spelled *Kumia*.

5. M. Wilson, "Legends of the Diegueño Indians," 69; see also Dubois, *Religion of the Luiseño and Diegueño Indians*, 75.

6. For stories about the missions passed down through the generations, see Costo and Costo, *Missions of California*. There appear to be only two personal accounts of the post-conquest period written by natives from San Diego region who learned Spanish. These are found in Shipek, *Delfina Cuero*, 21–66, and Hewes and Hewes, *Indian Life and Customs at Mission San Luis Rey*.

7. J. Smith, "Healing Practices of Southern California Indians in San Diego County," 26.

8. As Kroeber noted, "Being essentially an emphasizing of individual experience obtained in a certain way, dreaming engulfed shamanism as a separate activity; prevented associations or organizations; forbade the adoption of ritual apparatus or even curtailed such as existed" (Kroeber, "History of Native Culture in California," 125).

9. Shipek, *Delfina Cuero*, 51–52, 84–98; Toffelmeir and Loumala, "Dreams and Dream Interpretations of the Diegueño Indians."

10. Shipek, "Kuuchamaa."

11. Heizer and Whipple, *California Indians*, 8–9. Today, women and children as well as individuals of non-Indian backgrounds are allowed to participate.

12. Ibid., 120.

13. Gifford, "California Balanophagy," 303.

14. Shipek, "Example of Intensive Plant Husbandry."

15. Ibid., 162.

16. Shipek, "Native American Adaptation to Drought," 297.

17. This apparent statement of simple fact is really an educated guess. Bancroft discusses the many problems in establishing with certainty that San Miguel, rather than San Mateo, was indeed the name given San Diego Bay (Bancroft, *History of California*, 1:70–71).

18. Bancroft believes that it was "not impossible, though not probable" that the Indians had heard of members of a Spanish expedition on the gulf led by Díaz, Alarcón, and Ulloa (Bancroft, *History of California*, 1:71); see also Paez de Castro, Moriarty, and Keistman, "Cabrillo's Log," 6–7.

19. Paez de Castro, Moriarty, and Keistman, "Cabrillo's Log," 98.

20. Ibid., 137.

21. Bancroft, *History of California*, 1:128. The tent camp was probably located near the present-day downtown area. The names of the dead were recorded but later destroyed during an Indian attack on the mission a few years later.

22. At that time the San Diego River curved south and emptied into the bay. It would be channeled to its present course in the twentieth century.

23. The official name of the settlement was now San Diego de Alcalá. St. Diego, or Didacus in Latin and English, originally was a Spanish Franciscan priest who had worked as a infirmarian (hospital attendant) in the university town of Alcalá in the early fifteenth century. He attained sainthood in 1588 after his incorrupt body miraculously cured the king's son of a fatal illness (Eagen, "San Diego de Alcalá"). The other priests at the official founding mass were Fr. Juan Vizcaino, Fr. Fernando Parron, and Fr. Francisco Gómez.

24. In October 1770, Sergeant José Francisco de Ortega listed these people as being at San Diego (from Mason, "Garrisons of San Diego Presidio," 400):

Captain Don Fernando de Rivera y Moncada, married
Corporal Guillermo Carrillo
Soldiers:

Juan José Robles	José Ignacio Olivera
Bernardo Rubio, married, sick with scurvy	Mariano de la Luz Verdugo
Mateo Ignacio de Soto	Alejo Antonio Gonzáles
Juan María Miranda, married	Juan de Osuna, married, sick with fever
Francisco de Ávila	Sebastián Alvitre
Rafael Hernández	Andrés Cota, married
Marcelo Bravo	José Joaquín Espinoza, married
Nicolás Antonio Sambrano	Agustín Castelo

25. Ibid.

26. Engstrand, "Occupation of the Port of San Diego de Alcalá," 96.

27. Geiger, *Letter of Luis Jayme*, 39–44. When Fr. Jayme heard about how ethical the Indians were and how the soldiers violated their morality, he noted, "I burst into tears to see how these gentiles were setting an example for us Christians" (42).

28. Bancroft, *History of California* 1:250–54.

29. Ibid., 1:589.

30. The best single source presenting traditional and revisionist positions on the California missions is Costo and Costo, *Missions of California*. The appendixes to this book present the traditional defense of Serra and the missionaries. For more defenses of the missions, see works by Francis F. Guest, director of the Santa Barbara Museum Archive-Library. A scholarly compendium studying the impact of disease and food shortages on the California Indians in general is Cook, *Conflict between the California Indian and White Civilization*.

31. Monroy, *Thrown among Strangers*, 79.

32. Ubelaker, "North American Indian Population Size," 292.

33. Surrounding the mission were a number of rancherías: Cosoy, Soledad, San Antonio or Las Coyas, Santa Cruz or Coapan in San Luis Valley, Purísima or Apuoquele, San Miguel or Janat, San Jocome de la Marca or Jamocha, San Juan Capistrano or Matamo, and San Jorge or Meti (see Bancroft, *History of California*, 2:656).

34. Cook, *Conflict between the California Indian and White Civilization*, 346.

35. Ibid., 37; the average was computed for the period 1783–1834. San Diego was not the worst in this regard. Mission San Antonio Indians ate an average of 715 calories per day, and those at Mission San Miguel, 865. The poor diet may be explained by the mission

fathers assuming that the natives would supplement their diet with their traditional foods. In addition, some have questioned Cook's methodology in computing food intake. It may have been that he miscalculated the Spanish unit of grain measure, the *fanega*, as being smaller than it actually was.

36. Benjamin Hayes, "San Diego, Index of Archives," Bancroft Library, manuscript C-E 69, vol. 42, p. 6. Hayes gave the 1811 presidio population as 57 men, 59 women, 57 boys, and 64 girls for a total of 237. The mission population was 583 men, 572 women, 248 boys, and 234 girls for a total of 1,637.

37. Bancroft, *History of California* 1:53; Castañeda, "Presidarias y pobladores." Chapter 2 of Castañeda's dissertation discusses rape as a mode of conquest and subjugation in California. For a list of the military men and their families, see Provincial State Papers, Benicia, Military, Bancroft Library, pp. xvii, 14–16.

38. Bancroft, *History of California*, 2:651.

39. Pío Pico remembered that in 1813 his father and some Spanish troops brought back a number of neophytes who had been captured after their participation in a rebellion at Mission San Gabriel. "Nearly all of the prisoners were whipped and those that lived, remained in prison at San Diego until their deaths" (Cole and Wallace, *Pío Pico's Historical Narrative*, 23–24).

40. Bancroft, *History of California*, 2:198. Mariano Vallejo, "Historia de California," Bancroft Library ms. vol. 1, 108–16, discusses the seditious literature sent to California during the revolt. See also Langum, "Caring Colony," 308. A personal account of this incident is in Cole and Wallace, *Pío Pico's Historical Narrative*, 22.

41. The earliest house in what is today Old Town was built by Henry Delano Fitch in 1821. It was followed by small adobes built by Francisco María Ruiz, María Reyes Ybáñez, Pío Pico, and Rafaela Serrano. See Ray Brandes, "Report on the Historical Research—Old Town, San Diego, California—the period 1821–1874," unpublished ms., p. 2.

42. Bancroft, *History of California*, 2:334.

43. Hayes, "San Diego, Index of Archives," p. 14 (p. 195 of index).

44. "Pronunciamiento de San Diego contra el jefe político y comandante general de California, Don Manuel Victoria, en 29 Noviembre y 1 de Diciembre de 1831." A translation appears in Bancroft, *History of California*, 2:202–3.

45. Bancroft, *History of California*, 2:210.

46. Ibid., 2:331–32.

47. The Indian pueblo of Las Flores, sometimes called San Pedro, had been organized in 1823 by Christianized natives who did not return to their villages but lived near Mission San Luis Rey with the permission of the mission padres (see Brandes, "Times Gone by in California," 219).

48. Brackett, *History of the Ranchos*, 20–77.

49. Lothrop, "Rancheras and the Land," 68.

50. Bancroft, *History of California*, 2:548.

51. Killea, "Political History of a Mexican Pueblo," 24–29.

52. Ibid., 29–30; Brandes, "Times Gone by in California," 220–28.

53. The story of "El Plan de San Diego" and the complicated maneuvering in 1837–38 is well told by Lucy Killea in "Political History of a Mexican Pueblo," 22–27. Her story has been much simplified for our purposes.

54. During the 1831 revolt against Victoria, for example, the San Diego military

contingent consisted of fourteen armed soldiers and five hundred Indians armed with spears and bows and arrows (Cole and Wallace, *Pío Pico's Historical Narrative*, 56).

55. Bancroft, *History of California*, 3:70.

56. This thesis is well developed by Hughes, "Decline of the Californios."

57. The romantic story has been told in almost every history of San Diego and California (see, for example, Bancroft, *History of California*, 3:125). To get the story from Josefa's point of view see "Dictation of Mrs. Capt. Henry D. Fitch/Narración de la Sra. Viuda del Capitán Enrique D. Fitch (Josefa Carrillo)," Bancroft Library ms. CE 67. Pío Pico also tells the story in his *Historical Narrative*, since he was the person who helped them elope.

Chapter 2

1. Grugal, "Military Movements into San Diego," 3–6.

2. S. Jones, "Battle of San Pascual," 72. Various estimates of troop sizes are discussed in Jones' work. A partial list of the Californio soldiers commanded by Andrés Pico at San Pascual are as follows (from Grugal, "Military Movements into San Diego," 114):

Andrés Pico, commander	Cristóbal López
Leonardo Cota, officer	Jesús Machado
Tomás Sánchez, officer	Juan Manríquez
José Aguilar	Juan Bautista Moreno
Dionisio Alipas	Isidoro Olivares
José Alipas	Leandro Osuna
José María Alvarado	Ramón Osuna
Juan Alvarado	Felipe or Rafael Peralta
Pablo Apis	Pedro Pérez
Felipe or Salvador Canedo	Gregorio Santiago
Ramón Carrillo	Casimiro Rubio
José Duarte	José Antonio Serrano
Gabriel García	Joaquín Valenzuela
Francisco Higuera	Pablo Vejar
José María Ibarra	Miguel or Pedro Verdugo
Francisco Dorio Lara	Domingo Yorba
Juan Lobo Mariano	José Antonio Yorba III
Santiago Lobo	Romualdo Young

3. S. Jones, "Battle of San Pascual," 139.

4. Ibid., 83–93. See also Benjamin Hayes, "Notes on California Affairs," undated ms. in Bancroft Library.

5. S. Jones, "Battle of San Pascual," 164–66.

6. Ibid., 173.

7. Ibid., 130–31.

8. Ibid., 140; *Nile's National Register*, November 7, 1846, p. 146, in Tays, "Pío Pico's Correspondence with the Mexican Government," 132.

9. Brackett, *History of the Ranchos*, 59.

10. See Teisher, "Rise of Na'at."

11. According to Alberto Camarillo's analysis of the 1860 census of San Diego, there

were 731 non-Indians and 3,067 Indians in the region, but this census did not count the "wild" Indian populations living in the many villages in the backcountry (Camarillo, *Chicanos in a Changing Society*, 116).

12. Evans, "Garra Uprising," 342.

13. References to duels and accusations of Californio treachery can be found in the *San Diego Herald*, November 27, 1851, December 11, 1851, December 25, 1851, January 1, 1852, January 5, 1852, and January 10, 1852.

14. Phillips, "Indian Resistance and Cooperation," 182.

15. Ibid., 282–83.

16. *San Diego Herald*, January 10, 1852.

17. Pitt, *Decline of the Californios*, 296.

18. Hughes, "Decline of the Californios," 14.

19. Mario García, "Merchants and Dons," 69–85.

20. Hughes, "Decline of the Californios?: The Case of San Diego, 1846–1856." Master's thesis, History, SDSU, 1974, pp. 33–35.

21. Ibid., 54–65.

22. Mario García, "Californios of San Diego and the Politics of Accommodation," 80.

23. Mario García, "Merchants and Dons," 56, 70.

24. See Griswold del Castillo, *Los Angeles Barrio*, 150–64.

25. Ibid., 68.

26. Mario García, "Californios of San Diego and the Politics of Accommodation," 73.

27. Ibid., 65, 73, 77.

28. Ibid., 73.

29. Hughes, "Decline of the Californios?" Master's thesis, History, SDSU, 1974, pp. 71–72.

30. Ibid., 75–79.

31. Ibid., 80–81.

32. Alexandra Luberski, "The Community of Old Town San Diego, 1850 to 1870, as Revealed through the United States Federal Census," unpublished ms. in Griswold del Castillo's possession, p. 7.

33. Griswold del Castillo, *Familia*, 69.

34. Ibid., 32.

35. *San Diego Union*, July 1873, quoted in Engstrand and Brandes, "Brief History of Old Town," 11.

36. Ibid., 10.

37. The following commentary on Old Town's celebrations is based on the research of María Elena Mendoza, "Mexican and Spanish Celebrations in Old Town," unpublished paper, 1996, Griswold del Castillo Collection, Chicano Studies Research Center, UCLA.

38. Arcadia Bandini Brennan (Scott), "Arcadian Memories of California," Bancroft Library, ms. C-D 5206, typescript.

39. Ibid., 42–43.

40. Ibid., 32, 34, 38.

41. Oden, "Maid of Monterey." *Who Would Have Thought It?* was published by J. B. Lippincott and Co., Philadelphia, 1872, and *The Squatter and the Don* by S. Carson and Co., San Francisco, 1885.

42. María Ruiz de Burton to M. G. Vallejo, November 23, 1851, in Maria A. R. Burton,

Collection of Eighty-one Letters to General Mariano Guadalupe Vallejo, 1858–1890, in the H. E. Huntington Library. A translation by Oden appears in "Maid of Monterey," 18.

43. Ruiz de Burton to Vallejo, August 26, 1867, February 15, 1869. Reprinted in Oden, "Maid of Monterey," 74, 77.

44. Ibid., 159.

45. S. Carrico, "Urban Indians in San Diego," 28–29.

46. Shipek, *Delfina Cuero*, 55, 60.

47. Ibid., 59.

48. Ibid., 90.

49. Ibid., 72.

50. An example of this is María Eugenia Silvas, whose offspring married into the native families of Canedo, Cota, Lugo, and Rosas (María Elena Mendoza, "Silvas Family Presentation," unpublished paper, May 15, 1996, Exhibit D, Griswold del Castillo Collection, UCLA).

51. *Mexicans in California*, 46. The committee counted 1,461 Mexicans in Imperial County, 2,224 in San Diego County, and 1,222 in the city of San Diego.

52. 1910 manuscript census returns, taken April 1910. See U.S. Bureau of the Census, Thirteenth Census, 1910, microform (Washington, DC: National Archives and Records Service, 1980).

Chapter 3

1. Mario García, *Desert Immigrants*.

2. R. García, *Rise of the Mexican American Middle Class*; R. Romo, *East Los Angeles*.

3. Proffitt, *Tijuana*, 101.

4. The origin of the name Tijuana is shrouded in mystery and legend. A few believe that it derives from the personage of Tía Juana (Aunt Jane), a colorful woman who worked for the Argüellos in the ranching camps around the turn of the last century. In the early 1900s the few settlements on the Mexican side of the border were known alternatively as San Ysidro or Tía Juana. Protests over the government's changing the town's name to Zaragoza in 1925 led to its being renamed Tijuana in 1929 (see Price, *Tijuana*, 45). Some have explored a possible derivation for Tijuana from the Kumeyaay languages, but no definitive link with an indigenous tongue has been made.

5. Price, *Tijuana '68*, 4.

6. P. Martínez, *History of Lower California*, 459–60.

7. K. Smith, "Reclamation of the Imperial Valley," 81.

8. Taylor, *Mexican Labor in the United States*, 29.

9. Ibid., 40.

10. Griswold del Castillo, "Discredited Revolution," 259–60.

11. Oral interview with Joe Montijo, 1996, video archive, Old Town History Project, SDSU, Griswold del Castillo Collection, UCLA.

12. Ibid., 268.

13. Owen, "Indians and Revolution," 377–79.

14. This is Owen's conclusion in ibid., 389.

15. Héctor Ríos, "Mexicans in San Diego between 1910 and 1920," unpublished ms. on file at SDSU Love Library, Chicano Collection; M. Lewis, "Ethnic and Racial Violence in San Diego," 3.

16. Taylor, *Mexican Labor in the United States*, 11.

17. Camarillo, *Chicanos in California*, 5.

18. Ríos, "Mexicans in San Diego between 1910 and 1920," 6.

19. Ibid., 7–8.

20. Cited in ibid., 9.

21. Ibid.

22. Ibid., 12.

23. *San Diego Union*, March 23, 1914.

24. The "Mexican Files" are on microfilm in Love Library at SDSU. A partial index of these files has been constructed by students in Chicano history classes.

25. Proffitt, *Tijuana*, 188.

26. Griswold del Castillo, "Brief Synopsis of San Ysidro's History." This article and several others written and researched by Professor Griswold del Castillo's students in the early 1980s were published in mimeograph as "The San Ysidro Community History Project," edited by Richard Griswold del Castillo, professor of Mexican American Studies, San Diego State University. A copy of this booklet is in the San Ysidro Public Library.

27. Lawrence Lee, "The Little Landers Colony of San Ysidro," 26–51.

28. Interview with Ermanie G. Celicio, San Ysidro, November 15, 1982, SDSU Oral History Collection.

29. This and subsequent quotations are from interviews conducted by Rosalinda M. González at San Ysidro Senior Center in 1994. Interviews were carried out by Professor González and research assistants Yolanda James and Maribel Castaneda with the following San Ysidro residents as part of a California Council of the Humanities Grant, "Searching for San Diego II," under the direction of Ralph Lewin: Lydia Armenia Beltrán, Edward M. Cuen, Klaudia Gómez, Paloma Gómez, Steven Andrew Gómez, Joyce Hettich, Margaret Lashlee, Nicolás López, Francisco Salazar, Alicia Serrano Valadez, and Andrea Skorepa.

30. Taylor, *Mexican Labor in the United States*, 18.

31. Ibid., 29.

32. Taylor found that about 90 percent of the complaints by Mexican workers filed before the California State Labor Commission in 1926 were for unpaid wages. The next most prevalent category of abuses were violations of the eight-hour law for women and the child labor regulations (see Paul Taylor Collection, Bancroft Library, Z-R, Box 1, "Report of Complaints Filed by Mexican Laborers . . ." January 1, 1926–December 31, 1926).

33. *Imperial Valley Press*, May 10, 1928.

34. *Mexicans in California*.

35. Ibid., 146.

36. Ibid., 147.

37. G. González, "Company Unions," 5–6.

38. Ibid., 8–10.

39. Quoted in R. Romo, *East Los Angeles*, 139.

40. Griswold del Castillo, "Mexican Problem," 257–58.

41. See G. González, *Chicano Education in the Era of Segregation*, for a detailed discussion of this case and of the Americanization schools.

42. Taylor, *Mexican Labor in the United States*, 25.

43. Alvarez, "Lemon Grove Incident"; see also his *Familia*; *The Lemon Grove Incident*

documentary was produced and written by Paul Espinosa, directed and edited by Frank Christopher, a production of KPBS-TV San Diego, 1985.

44. Alvarez, "Lemon Grove Incident," 118–19.

45. Ibid., 119.

46. Ibid., 123.

47. Dittmyer, "Historical Study of the Neighborhood House Association," 5.

48. Ibid., 38.

49. Shelton, "Neighborhood House of San Diego," 53.

50. Ibid., 39.

51. Ibid., 46.

52. Ibid., 48.

53. Ibid., 62–63.

54. Panunzio, *How Mexicans Earn and Live*, vii.

55. Ibid., 4.

56. Shelton, "Neighborhood House of San Diego," 66–72, summarizes the various county and city reports on conditions in the Mexican barrio.

57. Interview with Luis L. Alvarez, April 25, 1978, SDSU Oral History Collection, Love Library, Special Collections, pp. 4, 7.

58. City of San Diego, Planning Department, "Environmental Impact Report, Aztec Brewery," Nov. 7, 1988.

59. Another artist who was born and raised in San Diego in the 1920s was Pablo O'Higgins. Pablo, or Paul, was an Irish American who attended San Diego High School and was influenced by Mexican and Spanish artistic traditions. In 1923 he went to Mexico, where he became a well-known Mexican muralist, an associate and disciple of Diego Rivera, Siqueiros, and Orozco. He was an art teacher at the Misiones Culturales de Zacatecas y Durango and published the first monograph on the work of José Guadalupe Posada. He was cofounder with Leopoldo Méndez and Luis Arenal of the Taller de Gráfica Popular in 1937. His murals are scattered about Mexico in Durango, Michoacán, Veracruz, and the Federal District, as well as in the United States. His best-known work was the mural in the patio of the old Colegio de Indios de San Gregorio. He was part of LEAR (Liga de Escritores y Artistas Revolucionarios), who helped paint murals for the Museo Nacional de Antropología. Today, his image is part of the historical mural along Logan Avenue in Chicano Park (see *Exposición Homenaje Pablo O'Higgins*).

60. The most complete discussion of repatriation is Balderrama and Rodríguez, *Decade of Betrayal.*

61. Guerin-Gonzales, *Mexican Workers and American Dreams*, 36, 39.

62. Ibid., 41.

Chapter 4

1. The following is taken from a more detailed discussion in Larralde and Griswold del Castillo, "Luisa Moreno."

2. Carlos Larralde interview with Luisa Moreno, April 17, 1971. California's port cities have had a long tradition of cannery industries. While in San Francisco, D. M. Bennett wrote, "We visited one of the large canning establishments where California fruits are put up in immense quantities, and where hundreds of hands are employed in the business" (Bennett, *Truth Seeker around the World*, 458).

3. Letter of S. Dewberry to C. Larralde, November 22, 1995. Petroleum Administration for War Records, National Archives Records Center, Pacific Southwest Region, Laguna Niguel, California (hereafter cited as National Archives Records Center).

4. Ironically, the same conclusion was reported by Bornemeier, "Study Paints Positive Picture of Immigration."

5. McWilliams, *Education of Carey McWilliams*, 109.

6. Carlos Larralde interview with Luisa Moreno, June 2, 1971; see also Carey McWilliams, *The New Republic*, January 18, 1943.

7. See Celardo, "Shifting Seas."

8. McWilliams, *North from Mexico*, 242.

9. Ibid., 245, 246 (quotation on 246).

10. Carlos Larralde interview with Moreno, April 20, 1971.

11. McWilliams, *North from Mexico*, 246.

12. McWilliams, *Education of Carey McWilliams*, 113.

13. Mario García, *Memories of Chicano History*, 143. For more information about the Zoot-Suit Riots, see Mauricio Mazón, *Zoot-Suit Riots.*

14. See also the *Los Angeles Times*, May 25, June 16, and June 18, 1943.

15. Port Director Routing Slip, October 23, 1942, Records of Shore Establishments and Naval Districts: Eleventh Naval District, Records of the Commandant's Office, General Correspondence, 1924–1955, National Archives Records Center, Box No. 296, File No. P 8-5, 1942 [2/2].

16. Statement of Provost Marshal John E. Hudson regarding La Reine Cafe, August 10, 1942, National Archives Records Center, Box No. 296, File No. P 8-5, 1942 [1/2].

17. Dan Buckly, Adjutant, San Diego County Council, to Commander 11th Naval District, June 29, 1942, National Archives Records Center, Box No. 295, File No. P 8-5, 1942 [1/2].

18. "Zoot-Suiters Hunted in S.D.," *San Diego Union*, June 10, 1943, 1; Carlos Larralde interview with Luisa Moreno, April 28, 1971.

19. Councilman Charles C. Dail to Admiral David W. Bagley, June 10, 1943, National Archives Records Center, Box No. 296, File No. P 8-5 [Zoot Suit Gang] 1943, 296.

20. Carlos Larralde interview with Luisa Moreno, April 20, 1971.

21. Routing slip, January 27, 1994; T. M. Leovy, district patrol officer, to chief of staff, May 1, 1944, National Archives Record Center, Box No. 297, File No. P 8-5 [Zoot Suit Gang] 1944 [1/2].

22. Carlos Larrlade interview with Moreno, April 20, 1971.

23. Ibid.

24. Luisa Moreno to Robert Morris, December 1, 1950, Folder 56, Robert Kenny Collection. Moreno and her husband, Gray Bemis, first went to Chihuahua, Mexico, then slowly drove in their Studebaker down to the interior of the country. Later they went to Guatemala to see her family (see the correspondence of Moreno to Kenny, also in Folder 56).

25. W. F. Kelly, assistant commissioner, Immigration and Naturalization Service, to Robert Kenny, November 1, 1950; Luisa Moreno, "Application for Voluntary Departure," November 1, 1950, both in Folder 55, Robert Kenny Collection.

26. H. R. Landon, district director, Los Angeles, Immigration and Naturalization Service, Folder 54, Robert Kenny Collection.

27. Acuña, *Occupied America*, 264.

28. Morin, *Among the Valiant*, 24.

29. Every community has its aging veterans, but those of World War II are dying off quickly. It is very important that historians collect their stories and histories so that later generations can understand the sacrifices they made. Professor Maggie Rivas-Rodríguez at the University of Texas School of Journalism has organized a project to collect the oral histories of the Latinos and Latinas who lived through World War II. Many of these stories are available online at http://utopia.utexas.edu/explore/latino. At this site you can also read their *Narratives* publication, which contains stories of Mexican American GIs during the war. In June 2000 the school sponsored the first ever national conference to bring together veterans and scholars to begin assembling the national story of Mexican Americans during World War II. For recent scholarship on aspects of the war experience, see Rivas-Rodríguez, *Mexican Americans and World War II*.

30. Oral interviews by Richard Griswold del Castillo, February 23, 1993.

31. Santillán, "Rosita the Riveter," 138.

32. Solis interviews, 55.

33. Solis interviews, 70.

34. Ibid., 61.

35. Ibid.

36. Solis interviews.

37. Santillán, "Rosita the Riveter," 137.

38. Solis interviews, 98.

39. The classic critique of Pachuquismo appears in Octavio Paz, *Labyrinth of Solitude*, chap. 1; For contemporary interpretations of this phenomenon, see Griffith, *American Me*, 15–28; G. Sánchez, "Pachucos in the Making"; Tuck, *Not with the Fist*; Turner and Surace, "Zoot-Suiters and Mexicans."

40. Solis interviews, 64.

41. D. Gutiérrez, *Between Two Worlds*, i.

42. "Mexican Labor Due Soon in California," *San Diego Union-Tribune*, September 18, 1942, 10.

43. "Farmers to Ask for 300 Mexicans," *San Diego Union-Tribune*, January 29, 1943, 10; Takaki, *Double Victory*, 96.

44. Takaki, *Double Victory*, 96.

45. Don Jesús, oral interview by José Rodolfo Jacobo, September 6, 2002, SDSU.

46. G. Sánchez, *Becoming Mexican American*, 274.

Chapter 5

1. Barrera, *Race and Class in the Southwest*; Juan Vicente Palerm, "The Formation and Expansion of Chicano/Mexican Enclaves in Rural California," unpublished manuscript, Department of Anthropology, University of California, Santa Barbara, 1989.

2. Ortner, *Fate of "Culture,"* 18.

3. Chávez, *Shadowed Lives*.

4. Almaguer, *Racial Fault Lines*.

5. Matt García, *World of Its Own*, 23.

6. Ibid.; Bays, "Women of the Valley of the Sun."

7. Guerin-Gonzales, *Mexican Workers and American Dreams*.

8. Matt García, *World of Its Own*, 36; Bays, "Women of the Valley of the Sun."

9. Bays, "Women of the Valley of the Sun," 23.

10. Matt García, *World of Its Own*, 38.

11. Ibid., 76.

12. Almaguer, *Racial Fault Lines*.

13. Guerin-Gonzales, *Mexican Workers and American Dreams*, 63.

14. Ibid., 61–63.

15. García y Griego, "Importation of Mexican Contract Laborers."

16. Ibid., 52.

17. Massey and Durand, *Return to Aztlan*, 43.

18. Ibid.

19. Zavella, "Engendering Transnationalism in Food Processing."

Chapter 6

1. R. González, "Myth of the Chicano Sleeping Giant," 46–47.

2. The origins, evolution, and influence of cultural deficiency thinking are discussed in Valencia, *Evolution of Cultural Deficiency Thinking*.

3. Estrada et al., "Chicanos in the United States." This essay treats Chicana/o agency up to 1975. It implies but does not demonstrate that agency was universal. Moreover, it acknowledges only one form of oppression in the Chicana/o experience, namely, exploitation.

4. Montemayor, "Border Divides the Best of Both Worlds."

5. Estrada et al., "Chicanos in the United States," 103; Young, "Five Faces of Oppression." This discussion of Chicana/o activism in San Diego does not pretend to be exhaustive or comprehensive. Rather it is an overview that seeks to illuminate the contours of the activism.

6. Segade, "Identity and Power," 87.

7. Quoted in Starr, *San Diego State University*, 81.

8. Segade, "Identity and Power," 88.

9. Starr, *San Diego State University*, 81.

10. "Mexican American Studies Department Self-Assessment, 1980," on file at SDSU.

11. Mariscal, *Brown-Eyed Children of the Sun*, 223.

12. Poem in author's files.

13. Segade, "Identity and Power," 90.

14. "El Plan Espiritual de Aztlán," Crusade for Justice Youth Conference, Denver, Colorado, March 31, 1969. Reprinted in *Documents of the Chicano Struggle*.

15. Rosales, *Chicano!* 81.

16. Muñoz, *Youth, Identity and Power*, 134.

17. Ibid., 87–88.

18. Mark Gabrish Conlan. "Queer Demos Honor Gracia Molina de Pick." November 16, 2003. San Diego Independent Media Center newswire. http://sandiego.indymedia .org/en/2003/11/101947.shtml; Mirta Vidal, "Women: New Voice of La Raza," Documents from the Women's Liberation Movement, An On-line Archival Collection http://clnet .sscnet.ucla.edu/research/docs/chunas/women.htm.

19. Anguiano, "Battle of Chicano Park."

20. Delgado, "Turning Point," paras. 8, 15.

21. Brookman and Gómez Peña, *Made in Aztlán.*

22. Peters, "Peace and Freedom Party."

23. Baca, "The Day the Police Rioted!"

24. California Latino Legislative Caucus, "History and Purpose," http://democrats
.assembly.ca.gov/latinocaucus/history.htm.

25. Cornelius, "America in the Era of Limits."

26. David Avalos, Roberto Robledo, and Enrique Torres, "National City Recall:
An Interview with the Chairman of the Ad Hoc Committee on Chicano Rights," *Voz
Fronteriza*, February 2, 1976, included in Herman Baca information packet, Committee
on Chicano Rights, 1980.

27. Ibid.

28. Rene Kaprielian, "Local Hispanics Plot Drive for More Power," *Newsline*, April
1987, 2.

29. "25 años de lucha en defensa del pueblo mexicano," *Voz Fronteriza*, 2006, http://
razapressassociation.org/vozfronteriza.

30. Paul Von Nostrand, "Klan Receives Chicano Warning," *San Diego Union-Tribune*,
October 21, 1977, A-1, included in Herman Baca information packet, Committee on
Chicano Rights, 1980.

31. Robert Montemayor, "Baca Accuses Kennedy of Evading Border Concerns," *Los
Angeles Times*, November 30, 1979, II-5; "The Border," *Nuestro*, September 1979, included
in Herman Baca information packet, Committee on Chicano Rights, 1980.

32. *San Diego Union-Tribune*, "Baca Says U.S. Fails to Guard Civil Rights," August 8,
1980, B-18.

33. Ricardo Chavira, "Baca Protests Car Check Decision," *San Diego Union-Tribune*,
January 30, 1981, B-7; Steve Quinliran, "Baca Criticizes Immigration Proposal," *San Diego
Union-Tribune*, April 3, 1981, B-1; Joe Applegate, "Some People in This Town Don't Like
Herman Baca and He Doesn't Care," *Reader*, June 21, 1979, 1–3.

34. Quoted in Robert Quinlivan, "CRC's Herman Baca on the Issue," *Caminos*,
January 1982.

35. "La Unión del Barrio History," *La Verdad*, January–May 1977.

36. Ibid.

37. Griswold del Castillo, "San Ysidro Massacre," 65.

38. Ibid.

39. Reproduced as appendix A in Griswold del Castillo, "The San Ysidro Massacre,"
78–79.

40. David Avalos, oral history interview conducted by Margarita Nieto at the Southern
California Research Center in San Diego, CA, June 16 and July 5, 1988, for the Archives
of American Art, Smithsonian Institution, July 5, 1988, www.aaa.si.edu/collections/
oralhistories/transcripts/avalos88.htm (accessed March 8, 2006); Antonio Prieto, "Border
Art as a Political Strategy," Information Services Latin America (ISLA), feature coverage,
1999, http://isla.igc.org/Features/Border/mex6.html (accessed March 23, 2007).

41. "Congreso pasa ley anti-mexicana: millones los afectados: Baca denounces proposed law; calls it racist–anti-Mexican," *El Grito Sureño*, October 1986, 6.

42. Lorenz, *Jerry Brown.*

43. Kaprielian, "Local Hispanics Plot," 3.

44. Ortiz, "Latinos against City Hall."

45. Ernesto Portillo Jr., "Call Issued for Border Review Panel," *San Diego Union-Tribune*, February 7, 1991, B-2.

46. Dwight C. Daniels, "Chicanos Protest Border Patrol's Record of Violence," *San Diego Union-Tribune*, February 3, 1991, B-1.

47. Ernesto Portillo Jr., "Abuse by Agents Is Widespread along Border, Group Alleges," *San Diego Union-Tribune*, March 6, 1991, B–1; Chet Barfield, "Border Patrol Abuse Stirs Call by Rights Group for Civilian Review Boards," *San Diego Union-Tribune*, June 8, 1991, B-1; Jeff Ristine, "Critics Assail Efforts to Limit Aliens' Crime," *San Diego Union-Tribune*, November 8, 1991, B-1.

48. Ernesto Portillo Jr., "Conference on Alien Problems Rouses Protest," *San Diego Union-Tribune*, November 13, 1991, B-2.

49. Graciela Sevilla, "Crowds Clash at Border Protest," *San Diego Union-Tribune*, June 8, 1992, B-1.

50. Jim O'Donnell, "CHP Struggles to Get Migrants Off Highly Dangerous Freeways," *San Diego Union-Tribune*, July 2, 1992, B-6.

51. Ernesto Portillo Jr., "Selections for Migrant Panel Stir Dispute," *San Diego Union-Tribune*, December 9, 1992, B-2.

52. Graciela Sevilla, "Latinos Demand Killing Be Tried as Hate Crime," *San Diego Union-Tribune*, May 3, 1993, B-1.

53. Fernando Romero, "Activists Claim Police, Border Patrol Abuses on Rise," *San Diego Union-Tribune*, May 30, 1993, B-1.

54. Milkman and Wong, "Organizing Immigrant Workers."

55. "La Unión del Barrio History," *La Verdad,* January–May 1977.

56. Ed Mandel, "New State Latino Group Flays Immigrant-Bashing," *San Diego Union-Tribune*, February 23, 1994, A-17.

57. Roberto Martínez, "Fueling the Flames of Anti-immigrant Hysteria," *El Sol de San Diego*, May 12, 1994, 4.

58. Big Mountain, "Border Town," *Unity*, compact disk, B000002L27, ℗ and © 1994 by Giant Records.

59. SDAG 187, "News from the Political Battleground over Immigration," newsletter in the author's files.

60. Ibid.

61. Nevins, *Operation Gatekeeper.*

62. Leonel Sánchez, "600 Students Protest Prop. 187," *San Diego Union-Tribune*, October 29, 1994, A-1; L. Erik Bratt, "Anti-187 March Turns Dangerous: Flag Burns," *San Diego Union-Tribune*, November 11, 1994, B-1; "Abajo con 187! Los estudiantes toman las calles en protesta de la Proposición 187," *Pueblo Unido*, September–November 1994, 1–3.

63. Quoted in Leonel Sánchez, "Proposition 187 Led Young Chicanos to Action," *San Diego Union-Tribune*, January 3, 1995, A-1.

64. Ibid.

65. "The Raza Rights Coalition Continues the Struggles against Racist Attacks on Our People," *La Verdad*, October–December 1994; "What Proposition 187 Represents, What the Vendidos Are Doing and What We Must Do," *La Verdad*, October–December 1994, 6–7.

66. SDAG 187, "Information on Proposition 187," February 19, 1995.

67. "Prop. 187 Approved in California," *Migration News*, http://migration.ucdavis.edu/mn/comments.php?id=492_0_2_0.

68. Eric Bilbray, "Bilbray Proposes Law Curbing Citizenship as U.S. Birthright," *San Diego Union-Tribune*, April 1, 1995, B-1.

69. Marcus Stein, "Army Gets Bigger Role in Border: Military Reinforcements to Include East County," *San Diego Union-Tribune*, January 12, 1996, A-1.

70. Leonel Sánchez, "Latinos Call Excessive Force Frequent Here," *San Diego Union-Tribune*, April 10, 1996, B-2.

71. Julie Rocha, "National Latino Leaders Outline Strategies to Boost Political Clout," *El Sol de San Diego*, August 22, 1996, 1.

72. "Raza from throughout Aztlán Come to San Diego to Create National Moratorium and to Protest the Racist Republican Party Convention," *La Verdad*, April–August 1996.

73. Parent Institute for Quality Education, "The History of PIQE," http://piqe.org/Assets/Home/History.htm.

74. David E. Graham, "Classes Celebrate Culture and Pride: Chicano Kids Learn History at Izcalli," *San Diego Union-Tribune*, August 22, 2000; see also "History of Izcalli," www.izcalli.org.

75. Alma Osorio, "Chicano Aztecs Reach out to High Schoolers," *Daily Aztec*, November 22, 1999, 5. (The *Daily Aztec* is the SDSU student newspaper. Articles from 1996 on are available online at www.thedailyaztec.com/home/archives.)

76. Paulette Cannon, "'And the Winner Is . . .' Mayer, Roberts, Razo, and Torres Emerge Victorious," *Daily Aztec*, March 22, 1996; Kate Nelson, "Student Leaders Discuss Future of SDSU," *Daily Aztec*, April 4, 1997; Dana Bushbee, "Voter Turnout Low, but Vasquez Prevails," *Daily Aztec*, April 14, 1998.

77. Coco Baker, "Campus Rally against CCRI," *Daily Aztec*, May 2, 1996; Leonie Porcher, "Prop 209's Passage Spurs Protest," *Daily Aztec*, November 7, 1996; Shana Starkand and Melissa Caudillo, "Students Rally to Support Diversity," *Daily Aztec*, October 17, 1997.

78. Crawford, "Campaign against 227," 12.

79. "Juntos Estamos Unidos," Statewide MEChA Conference Program, Spring 1998, p. 4.

80. "San Diego Millionaire Elites Unite around Educational Fraud and to Consolidate Their Anti-Mexicano Grip on San Diego through Border Czar Alan Bersin," *La Verdad*, May–June 1998; "Proposition 227 and What It Represents: Another Attack on the Dignity, Culture, and History of the Mexicano People," *La Verdad*, November–December 1997, 6.

81. "The Time for Voting Is Over! The Time to Organize Is Now!" *Voz Fronteriza*, March 2000, 4.

82. Lipsitz, "We Know What Time It Is."

83. "U.S. Border Patrol in S. California Developing Deadly but Ineffective Operation Gatekeeper: Interview with Roberto Martinez," *In Motion Magazine*, December 12, 1999, www.inmotionmagazine.com/rm99.html; California Endowment, Conditions at the Border Seminar Series proceedings, July 1999.

84. California Endowment, Conditions at the Border Seminar Series proceedings.

85. Letter to Arts Advisory Board, December 1999, "What the Artists Say," CENTROWATCH, www.calacapress.com/centrowatch.html.

86. Save Our Centro Coalition, "Why We Struggle," CENTROWATCH, HELPING SAVE OUR CENTRO; www.saveourcentro.org/centrowatch/index2.html.

Chapter 7

1. *Chicano! History of the Mexican American Civil Rights Movement.* Four-part video. NLCC Educational Media, 1996.

2. See R. Sanchez, "Chicana Writer"; also Sánchez and Martínez Cruz, *Essays on La Mujer.*

3. Alurista, "Plan Espiritual de Aztlán," *Documents of the Chicano Struggle.*

4. Courtesy of Laura García, one the writers with Teatro Mestizo, 1971–1975. Some seventeen women, mainly from San Diego State University, have written a book on their experience with Teatro de las Chicanas/Laboral/Raíces, edited by Laura García, Felicitas Núñez, and Sandra Gutiérrez, to be published by the University of Texas Press.

5. United Farm Workers of America Web site, Essays by Author, 1970s, "Carlos and Linda LeGerrette, 1966–1978" www.farmworkermovement.org/essays/essays/038%20 LeGerrette_Carlos%20and%20Linda.pdf.

6. Mesa-Bains, "Mundo Femenino," 132.

7. Diana López Blanks, "Eulogy to Viviana Zermeño," San Diego, April 23, 2005, unpublished manuscript.

8. "El Plan de Santa Bárbara" written by the Coordinating Council on Higher Education and adopted in 1969 at UCSB. Women on the Steering Committee were Gracia Molina de Pick, San Diego; Ana Nieto Gómez, UMAS, Marymount; María Díaz, Cal State LA; and Rosalina Méndez, UMAS, UC Irvine (see www.chavez.ucla.edu).

9. "Friend of Pride: Gracia Molina de Pick—Radical Politics May Be Genetic," *Gay and Lesbian Times*, February 2, 2006. Molina de Pick is the regional vice-chair of the Veteran Feminists of America; credited as a founder of the "second wave of feminism," she serves on the board of the Women's History Museum and Education Center downtown. She is on the Central Committee of the San Diego County Democratic Club and the advisory board of the Latino/Latina Unity Coalition, is a founder of the Chicano and Chicana Studies Department at Mesa College, and is a lecturer at the University of California, San Diego. In 2001, California State Assembly member Christine Kehoe named Molina de Pick "Woman of the Year." In 2002, she was inducted into the San Diego Women's Hall of Fame. In 2006, Molina de Pick received the prestigious Jesse de la Cruz award from the California Rural and Legal Assistance organization.

10. See A. García, *Chicana Feminist Thought*; S. López, "The Role of the Chicana in the Student Movement"; Mesa-Bains, "Mundo Femenino."

11. Mesa-Bains, "Mundo Femenino," 131, 90.

12. Goldman and Ybarra-Frausto, "Political and Social Contexts of Chicano Art," 90.

13. Toltecas in 1969 included Alurista, Jorge González, Viviana Zermeño, Ricardo Mendoza, Delia Moreno, Tupac, Aztleca, Guillermo Rosete, and Juan Felipe Herrera. Visual artists included Salvador Torres, Guillermo Aranda, Victor Ochoa, Mario Torero, Tomás Castaneda, José Gómez, Abran Quevedo, Salvador Barajas, Arturo Roman, Rubén de Anda, and José Cervantes (see Brookman and Gómez Peña, *Made in Aztlán*, 58).

14. Rosaldo, "Changing Chicano Narrative."

15. Mesa-Bains, "Mundo Femenino," 136.

16. Ibid., 135.

17. Brookman and Gómez Peña, *Made in Aztlán*, 40.

18. Y. López, "Chicana's Look at the International Women's Conference," 18. This was written after her bus trip with 42 women and one man, arranged by the Chicano Federation.

19. Pamela Jane Ferree, "Chicano Park Murals," master's thesis, SDSU, 1994.

20. Brookman and Gómez Peña, *Made in Aztlán*, 24.

21. California Ethnic and Multicultural Archives (CEMA) at the University of Santa Barbara, http://cemaweb.library.ucsb.edu (accessed April 2006).

22. Anaya, *Bless Me, Última*, 126.

23. Brookman and Gómez Peña, *Made in Aztlán*, 34–36.

24. T. Romo, "Collective History."

25. My two older sisters and three older brothers were no longer living at home: Josephine, Theresa, Leo, Chris, and Emiliano.

26. See "Mary Sánchez, 1974–1975" under Essays by Author, 1970s, on the United Farm Workers of America Web site www.farmworkermovement.org/essays/essays/Mary%20Sanchez%20Essay.pdf.

27. Charles Coleman, my mother's cousin, was in the film *Salt of the Earth* and was one of the strikers. Susana Montoya, Coleman's wife, marched with the women in the picket lines during this strike (see Sánchez, *Cochise Remembers: Our Great-Grandfather*).

28. Suni Paz, "Songs of Struggle and Revolution," *Breaking Out of the Silence*, Paredon Records PAR01016, 1973.

29. R. Sánchez, "Breaking out of Silence," *Visión de la Mujer de la Raza* (San Diego: SDSU, 1976).

30. Today an original painting of this logo from which the mural was painted, donated by Charlotte Hernández Terry, is located in the Chicano Collection at San Diego State University's Love Library.

31. Charlotte Marie Hernández was born April 13, 1937, and died June 16, 2006. She is survived by six daughters: Teresa Hernández, Deborah Riegel, Rebecca Rose, Charlotte M. Terry, Christine Clausner, and Leslie Aguirre (see Jack Williams, "Charlotte Hernández Terry—Musical Talent," *San Diego Union-Tribune*, June 24, 2006).

32. Ferree, "Chicano Park Murals," 25.

33. A portion of the printing costs were donated to Las Chicanas by Diego and Son Printers of San Diego.

34. The "Third World Conference" was organized by Professors Prescott "Nick" Nichols and Jacqueline Tunberg in 1977 at SDSU.

35. Mesa-Bains, "Mundo Femenino," 138.

36. Ferree, "Chicano Park Murals," 89.

37. CEMA, http://cemaweb.library.ucsb.edu (accessed April 2006).

38. *Maize* 1, no. 1 (fall 1977).

39. Mario opened SolArt in Golden Hill in 1978. He learned the gallery business from his father, Guillermo Acevedo, who opened the galleries in the Bazaar del Mundo in Old Town and in downtown San Diego.

40. Keller, *Contemporary Chicana and Chicano Art*. Soon thereafter, Carlos Almaraz

exhibited at the Museum of Contemporary Art in La Jolla in a one-person show—a first.

41. In Mario Barrera and Marilyn Mulford, producers, *Chicano Park* (video), Cinema Guild, 1988.

42. Special thanks to Nancy Emerson, research librarian at the San Diego Museum of Art, for this information.

43. Known as the "Grandmother of the French New Wave," Varda began making films in the 1950s and has since compiled a unique, far-ranging body of work celebrating the independence of women. In 1980 she came to San Diego for the opening of her film *Murs, Murs*. In 2001, Varda's *The Gleaners and I* was named best documentary by the New York Film Critics Circle and the Los Angeles Film Critics Association.

44. Eva Cockcroft, "The Story of Chicano Park," *Aztlán* 15 (Spring 1984).

45. Rita Sánchez, "La Jollans View Mural Art in San Diego," *San Diego Community News*, 1980.

46. Funded by a private donation to the city schools from the Muriel Gluck Foundation.

47. From the CEMA archives, http://cemaweb.library.ucsb.edu/torres.html.

48. From a public interview of Gloria Torres by Alessandra Moctezuma, gallery director, at Torres' 2006 Retrospective Exhibit, "Memories from the Rolling Hills of Old San Diego" at Mesa College.

49. Brookman and Gómez Peña, *Made in Aztlán*, 34.

50. See *Los Angeles Times*, May 8, 1987, B-18, for a survey of the gallery activities.

51. My paper was Rita Sánchez, "Chicana Writer: Breaking Out of Silence," presented at the Women's International Writers Conference, San Jose State University, 1976, published in *La Cosecha*, UCLA, 1977. I was invited by noted author Tillie Olsen to present parts of my essay with her at the keynote luncheon address at this conference. The Kahlo exhibit at UCSD was curated by Gerry McAllister in April 1978.

52. Keller, *Contemporary Chicana and Chicano Art*.

53. Berelowitz, "Comadres."

54. CEMA, "Installation Art," op. cit.

55. Ed. Gloria Anzaldúa. From a written statement by Las Comadres, Centro Cultural de la Raza, San Diego, unpublished manuscript, 1990.

56. See Berelowitz, "Comadres," for a unique and rich interpretation of this breakthrough exhibition.

57. Griswold del Castillo, McKenna, and Yarbro-Bejarano, *CARA*, 33.

58. Ibid.

59. Mesa-Bains, "Mundo Femenino," 131.

60. Ibid.

61. Martínez, *De Colores Means All of Us*, 169, 163.

62. Keller, *Contemporary Chicana and Chicano Art*, 90.

63. Ibid., 2:90–91, 2:80–85.

64. Goldman, *Dimensions of the Americas*, 212.

65. Inspired by the art of Guillermo Gómez Peña, who wrote "Do not discover me" on his body. His protest art became so recognized in San Diego that it was taken as performance art to New York, where Coco Fusco was one of the performers. Voices were raised

against the border mythology idealizing Columbus and his "discovery" of America, which displaced the indigenous people from the land.

66. From a multimedia video by San Diego artist Richard Lou which included excerpts from the PBS documentary "Sin Fronteras" as broadcast on the BBC, 1994, a copy of which is stored at the Mesa College Audio-Visual Center.

67. Ibid.

68. All quotations from Keller, *Contemporary Chicana and Chicano Art*, 1:48–49.

69. This essay appeared in Burnham and Durland, *The Citizen Artist*, an anthology of essays from *High Performance Magazine*.

70. www.hillquest.com/index.htm (accessed May 2, 2007).

71. www.uniondelbarrio.org.

72. I wrote this paper while on sabbatical from Mesa College in 1997, for a Latin American studies course (LAS 580) I completed with Dr. Janet Esser at SDSU.

73. Olivia Puentes-Reynolds with the WIM, formerly the Women's History Reclamation Project, is one of the founders of California Women's Agenda (CAWA), an action network of six hundred organizations in the state formed after the Fourth World Conference on Women in Beijing in 1995. See www.sandiegohistory.org (accessed April 2006).

Chapter 8

1. *Forbes Magazine*, May 21, 2002.

2. Logan, Alba, and Wenqan, "Immigrant Enclaves and Ethnic Communities."

3. Unión del Barrio is composed of the Comité de Mujeres Patricia Marin, Somos Raza, La Verdad Publications, and the Chicano-Mexicano Prison Project (see http://uniondelbarrio.org). For La Raza Rights Coalition, see www.anarchistfreethink.org/raza/main.html.

4. The literature on the history of Chicano Park is scattered and mostly nonacademic, with the exception of Delgado, "Turning Point"; Rosen and Fisher, "Chicano Park and the Chicano Park Murals"; and Cockcroft, "Story of Chicano Park."

5. City of San Diego, "Community and Economic Development Strategy, 2002–2004," November 18, 2004, www.sandiego.gov/economic-development/contacts/pdf/cedstrategy.pdf (accessed March 25, 2007).

6. O. Lewis, "Culture of Poverty."

7. Barrera, Muñoz, and Ornelas, "Barrio as an Internal Colony."

8. Joe Hughes, "Detectives Blame 'Little Punks' in Recent Spate of Deadly Attacks," *San Diego Union-Tribune*, January 4, 2003.

9. Leonel Sánchez, "Mural Gets New Life as Communities Revitalize," *San Diego Union-Tribune*, November 16, 2002.

10. Wilson, *Truly Disadvantaged*.

11. Moore and Pinderhughes, *In the Barrios*.

12. Thirty years after the Fair Housing Act, almost 3,000 tracts in the 2000 census reported extremely high poverty rates, meaning that 8.5 million people were living in ghettos, barrios, slums, or mixed slums. A *ghetto* is defined as a neighborhood that is at least 40 percent black; *slums* are at least 40 percent non-Hispanic white, and *mixed slums* do not have any predominant ethnicity. Blacks represent 50 percent, Latinos 24 percent, and non-Hispanic whites 22.5 percent of this marginalized population. Sixty percent of poor Latinos live in barrios and 32 percent in mixed slums. Even in cases where this increase

is linked more to demographic growth than to higher poverty rates, the percentage of Latinos living below the poverty line is still disproportionate to their share of the total population (8.1 percent in 1990); see Jargowsky, *Stunning Progress, Hidden Problems*.

13. Burns, Schlozman, and Verba, *Private Roots of Public Action*, 4.

14. Gurr, *Why Men Rebel*; Piven and Cloward, *Poor People's Movements*.

15. Meyer, Whittier, and Robnett, *Social Movements*.

16. Putnam, *Making Democracy Work*.

17. Davis, Mayhew, and Miller, *Under the Perfect Sun*.

18. Moore and Pinderhughes, *In the Barrios*.

19. Smith and Williams, *Gentrification of the City*, 18.

20. City of San Diego, "A Strategy for Updating the City's General Plan," General Plan, City of Villages, 2002, http://genesis.sannet.gov/infospc/template/mayor/goal3 .jsp; San Diego Redevelopment Agency, 2003, www.sannet.gov/redevelopment-agency/ index.shtml.

21. "Tienen que darse cuenta que aquí en una casa, viven dos o tres familias, para alcanzar pagar la renta, que no hay privacidad para nadie, que unos viven en garaje de casas, eso y que necesitamos apartamentos para gente de bajos recursos."

22. A District 8 elected official declared in 2002: "I want to beautify the community and I want people to know that the 8th District is really coming back" (Ray Huard, "Candidates in 8th District Have Common Goals," *San Diego Union-Tribune*, February 27, 2002); and "The plan is to rebuild San Diego's older neighborhoods into walkable villages where homes are close to shops, parks, and public transit" (Susan Gembrowski, "Activists Put Renewal on Agenda," *San Diego Union-Tribune*, April 24, 2002).

23. "Todo en San Diego está subiendo de precios, las casas, las rentas, antes pagabas $500 por dos recámaras, ahora son casi el doble, las renuevas, les echan la migra a la gente, y luego sube la renta un montón.... Yo tengo suerte porque compré mi casa hace casi 10 años. Pero la gente ya no alcanza para vivir aquí."

24. Yvette Tenberge, "Ballpark Dream Leaves Residents Homeless," *La Prensa San Diego*, July 13, 2001; "Renters Crying Foul Ball over Proposed Ballpark," *La Prensa San Diego*, July 6, 2001; Leonel Sánchez, "March to Put Focus on Rising Rents, Displacement," *San Diego Union-Tribune*, June 30, 2001.

25. "We are here, and we will not leave!" "Unity is strength"; "Unite with our community effort."

26. Pardo, "Gendered Citizenship."

27. Melville, *Twice a Minority*.

28. "¡Se sube mucho la renta! y luego no hay casas para gente de bajos recursos.... No es justo. Además aquí es una comunidad muy antigua, es una comunidad latina, para los Latinos, y no está bien que vengan los Americanos. Porque cada comunidad tiene su cosa, ¿no?"

29. Muñiz, *Resisting Gentrification*.

30. "Uno de los problemas más grandes es tener *affordable* housing, porque hay muy pocos affordable housing aquí. Yo creo que para que un niño salga bien en la escuela, tiene que salir bien su familia, porque si el niño llega sin comer, y sin casa donde dormir, ¿como es que crees que estudie en la escuela?"

31. Pardo, "Gendered Citizenship," 60.

32. "Batallamos largo porque no teníamos un lugar fijo donde reunirnos, la mayoría

de la gente perdía las reuniones, porque siempre íbamos cambiando de una casa para otra casa."

33. Miller et al., "Group Consciousness and Political Participation."

34. Anderson, *Imagined Communities.*

35. Nie et al., "Race, Ethnicity and Political Resources."

36. A linguistically isolated household is one in which no member fourteen years old and over (1) speaks only English or (2) speaks a non-English language and speaks English "very well." In other words, all adult family members have at least some difficulty with English (U.S. Census Bureau, 2000).

37. "Pero quiero vivir aquí porque es mi barrio. Si compro una casa, la compro aquí."

38. "Mis deseos ahora . . . es regresar allá . . . , me siento muy identificada por ser todos hispanos allá. . . . Allá, está el Bazar, está el Farmers Market, . . . se siente uno más identificado."

39. Social capital is also defined as being "all about the value of social networks, bonding similar people and bridging between diverse people, with norms of reciprocity. Social capital is fundamentally about how people interact with each other" (Dekker Uslander, *Social Capital and Participation in Everyday Life*, 3).

40. "Las señoras me dicen: vete a estudiar inglés en la escuela en la noche. ¡Tu puedes! Me dicen. Cuando termino el trabajo, a veces unas me llevan para la escuela. Es difícil, yo sola, con mi niño. Ellas me dicen, tu puedes, y yo voy."

41. "Lo que me gusta es que son muchas mujeres profesionales, y señoras de la comunidad . . . puedo estar tres horas en junta, y no me aburro, porque escucharlas a ellas y a sus diferentes puntos de vista, así es como me entero bien."

42. Tilly, *From Mobilization to Revolution.*

43. Norris and Inglehart, *Rising Tide.*

Chapter 9

1. For other testimonios, see Mario García, *Memories of Chicano History*; Gutiérrez, *Making of a Chicano Militant*; and Tijerina, *They Called Me "King Tiger."*

2. Balderrama and Rodríguez, *Decade of Betrayal.*

3. G. Sánchez, *Becoming Mexican American.*

4. Roberto Martínez, "The Border and Human Rights," unpublished manuscript, October 2002, p. 2.

5. The Chicano Federation is an advocacy and social-service community-based organization based in downtown San Diego.

6. Martínez, "Border and Human Rights," 3.

7. Santana High School is located in Santee, a community located in east San Diego County, fifteen miles east of downtown San Diego. The high school received national attention when a student shot and killed two students and wounded thirteen others there in 2001.

8. The so-called Youth Klan Corp was the youth component of the Ku Klux Klan, which was based in Fallbrook at that time. In the 1980s the KKK changed its name to the White Aryan Resistance (WAR) under the leadership of Tom Metzger.

9. Martínez, "Border and Human Rights," 4.

10. Ibid.

11. Interview with Herman Baca, August 23, 2002.

12. On November 6, 1986, Congress passed the Immigration Reform and Control Act of 1986 (IRCA). In its earliest form it was popularly known as the Simpson-Mazzoli bill, then the Simpson-Rodino bill.

13. Richard Louv, "The Mexican Migration," *San Diego Union-Tribune*, n.d.

14. The American Friends Service Committee is a national and international Quaker social-justice organization founded in 1917. It was a corecipient of the Nobel Peace Prize in 1947. The U.S.–Mexico Border Program, established in 1983, is based in downtown San Diego. It monitors and documents human and civil rights abuses in the border region.

15. Martínez, "Border and Human Rights," 6.

16. Ibid., 7.

17. Ibid., 8.

18. The U.S. Commission on Civil Rights office in Los Angeles sponsored both hearings before that body.

19. The Illegal Immigration Reform and Immigrant Responsibility Act of 1996 was a response by Congress to the 1994 bombing of the federal building in Oklahoma and was intended to target terrorists.

20. Operation Gatekeeper was launched on October 1, 1994, and was designed to push migrant crossings away from traditional crossing areas, such as San Ysidro, and into the mountains and deserts of California. As a result, hundreds of men, women, and children have died of hyperthermia, drowning, and accidents.

21. American Friends Service Committee, Abuse Report, February 1, 2002.

22. National Research Council report, "The Inequality of Justice: A Report on Crime and the Administration of Justice in the Minority Community," 1997.

23. California Rural Legal Assistance report, 2001.

24. *San Diego Union-Tribune*, March 30, 2002.

25. San Diego AFSC, "Introduction to Human Rights Report, 2001."

26. *Los Angeles Times*, July 19, 2002.

27. Immigration Law Enforcement Monitoring Project of AFSC.

28. Martínez, "Border and Human Rights," 12.

29. U.S. Commission on Civil Rights, *Who Is Guarding the Guardians?* 6.

30. The Raza Rights Coalition is a non-governmental organization based in San Diego.

31. Martínez, "Border and Human Rights," 13.

BIBLIOGRAPHY

Primary Sources

Alvarez, Luis L., April 25, 1978, SDSU Oral History Collection, SDSU Library, Special Collections

American Friends Service Committee Archive, Philadelphia, PA

Archives of American Art, Smithsonian Institution, www.aaa.si.edu

California Ethnic and Multicultural Archives, Special Collections, Donald C. Davidson Library, University of California at Santa Barbara

California Historical Landmarks Series, Bancroft Library, University of California, Berkeley

Celicio, Ermanie G. Interview, San Ysidro, November 15, 1982. SDSU Oral History Collection, SDSU Library, Special Collections.

City of San Diego, Planning Department

Documentos Para la Historia de California, Bancroft Library, University of California, Berkeley

Griswold del Castillo Collection, Chicano Studies Research Center, UCLA

María Ruiz de Burton Letters, H. E. Huntington Library, San Marino, CA

Mexican Files, Microfilm collection, Love Library, San Diego State University

Montijo, Joe. Video interview. Old Town History Project, SDSU, 1996

Moreno, Luisa, interviews, April 17, April 20, April 28, and June 2, 1971, by Carlos Larralde, copies in his personal archives

Office of Interpretive Services, California State Parks and Recreation, Sacramento, CA

Paul Taylor Collection, Bancroft Library, University of California, Berkeley

Provincial State Papers, Bancroft Library, University of California, Berkeley

Records of Shore Establishments and Naval Districts: Eleventh Naval District, National Archives Records Center, Pacific Southwest Region, Laguna Niguel, California

Robert Kenny Collection, Southern California Library for Social Studies and Research, Los Angeles

San Diego Historical Society, San Diego

Solis, Santiago. Rosita the Riveter Interviews, SDSU Special Collections. Love Library

U.S. Bureau of the Census. Thirteenth census, 1910, microform. Washington, DC, National Archives and Records Service, 1980.

Zoeth Skinnner Eldredge Collection, Bancroft Library, University of California, Berkeley

Secondary Sources

Acuña, Rodolfo. *Occupied America: A History of Chicanos.* 4th ed. New York: Longman, 2000.

Almaguer, Tomás. *Racial Fault Lines: The Historical Origins of White Supremacy in California.* Berkeley: University of California Press, 1994.

Almstedt, Ruth M. "Multiple World Views in a Diegueño Community." Master's thesis, Anthropology Department, SDSU, 1970.

Alurista. "El Plan Espiritual de Aztlán." *Documents of the Chicano Struggle.* New York: Pathfinder Press, 1971.

Alvarez, Robert Jr. *Familia: Migration and Adaptation in Baja and Alta California, 1800–1975.* Berkeley and Los Angeles: University of California Press, 1987.

———. "The Lemon Grove Incident: The Nation's First Successful Desegregation Court Case." *Journal of San Diego History* 22, no. 2 (Spring 1986): 116–35.

Anaya, Rudolfo A. *Bless Me, Última.* Berkeley: Quinto Sol Publications, 1972.

Anderson, Benedict. *Imagined Communities: Reflections on the Origin and Spread of Nationalism.* London: Verso, 1983.

Anguiano, Marco. "The Battle of Chicano Park: A Brief History of the Takeover." www.calacapress.com/cpsc/cpscbattleof.html. (Accessed March 8, 2007)

Anzaldúa, Gloria. 1987. *Borderlands/La Frontera: The New Mestiza.* San Francisco: Spinsters/Aunt Lute.

———, ed. 1990. *Making Face, Making Soul = haciendo caras: Creative and Critical Perspectives by Feminists of Color.* San Francisco: Aunt Lute Foundation.

Baca, Herman. "The Day the Police Rioted! Remembering 32 Years Ago!" www.azteca.net/aztec/cmora.html. (Accessed March 8, 2006)

Balderrama, Francisco E., and Raymond Rodríguez. *Decade of Betrayal: Mexican Repatriation in the 1930s.* Albuquerque: University of New Mexico Press, 1995.

Bancroft, Hubert Howe. *History of California.* Vol. 1, *1542–1800.* San Francisco: A. L. Bancroft and Co., 1884.

———. *History of California.* Vol. 2, *1801–1824.* San Francisco: A. L. Bancroft and Co., 1885.

———. *History of California.* Vol. 3, *1825–1840.* San Francisco: History Co., 1886.

Bandini, Helen Elliott. *History of California.* New York: American Book Co., 1908.

Barrera, Mario. *Race and Class in the Southwest.* Notre Dame: University of Notre Dame Press, 1979.

Barrera, Mario, Carlos Muñoz, and Charles Ornelas. "The Barrio as an Internal Colony." In *People and Politics in Urban Society,* edited by Harlan Hahn, 465–98. Urban Affairs Annual Reviews vol. 6. Beverly Hills, CA: Sage, 1971.

Bartletti, Don. *Between Two Worlds: The People of the Border.* Oakland, CA: Oakland Museum, 1992.

Bays, Sharon Arlene. "Women of the Valley of the Sun." Master's thesis, Department of Anthropology, University of California, Los Angeles, 1998.

Bennett, D. M. *A Truth Seeker around the World: From Hong Kong to New York.* New York: Liberal Publishers, 1882.

Berelowitz, Jo-Anne. "Las Comadres: A Feminist Collective Negotiates a New Paradigm for Women at the U.S./Mexico Border." *Genders* 28 (1998). www.iiav.nl/ezines/web/

GendersPresenting/2004/No40/genders/g28_lascomadres.htm. (Accessed April 15, 2006)

Bornemeier, James. "Study Paints Positive Picture of Immigration." *Los Angeles Times*, December 11, 1995, A3.

Bourdieu, Pierre, and James S. Coleman, eds. *Social Theory for a Changing Society*. Boulder, CO: Westview Press, 1991.

Brackett, R. W. *A History of the Ranchos*. San Diego: Union Title Insurance and Trust Co., 1939.

Brandes, Raymond S., trans. *The Costansó Narrative of the Portolá Expedition*. Newhall, CA: Hogarth Press, 1970.

———. "Times Gone by in California: Recollections of Señora Doña Juana Machado Alipaz de Ridington (Wrightington)." *Historical Society of Southern California* 41 (1959): 215–25.

"Breaking Out of Silence." In *Visión de la Mujer de la Raza*. San Diego: SDSU, 1976.

Brookman, Philip, and Guillermo Gómez Peña. *Made in Aztlán*. San Diego: Centro Cultural de la Raza, 1986.

Burnham, Linda Frye, and Steven Durland. *The Citizen Artist: 20 Years of Art in the Public Arena. An Anthology from High Performance Magazine, 1978–1998*. Gardiner, NY: Critical Press, 1998.

Burns, Nancy, Kay Lehman Schlozman, and Sidney Verba. *The Private Roots of Public Action: Gender, Equality and Political Participation*. Cambridge, MA: Harvard University Press, 2001.

Camarillo, Albert. *Chicanos in a Changing Society: From Mexican Pueblos to American Barrios in Santa Barbara and Southern California, 1848–1930*. Cambridge, MA: Harvard University Press, 1979.

———. *Chicanos in California*. San Francisco: Boyd and Fraser, 1984.

Carrico, Richard L. *Strangers in a Stolen Land: American Indians in San Diego, 1850–1880*. Sacramento, CA: Sierra Oaks, 1987.

Carrico, Susan Hunter. "Urban Indians in San Diego: 1850–1900." Master's thesis, Department of History, UCSD, 1984.

Castañeda, Antonia I. "Presidarias y Pobladores: Spanish-Mexican Women in Frontier Monterey, Alta California, 1770–1821." PhD diss., Stanford University, 1990.

Castañeda, Antonia I., Tomás Ybarra-Frausto, and Joseph Sommers. *Literatura Chicana: texto y contexto = Chicano Literature: Text and Context*. Englewood Cliffs, NJ: Prentice-Hall, 1972.

Castillo, Adelaida del. "Malintzin Tenépal: A Preliminary Look into a New Perspective." In *Essays on la Mujer*, edited by Rosaura Sánchez and Rosa Martínez Cruz, 124–49. Chicano Studies Center Publications. Los Angeles: UCLA, 1977.

Celardo, John. "Shifting Seas: Racial Integration in the United States Navy, 1941–1945." *Prologue: Quarterly of the National Archives* Fall (1991): 230–35.

Chávez, Leo. *Shadowed Lives: Undocumented Immigrants in American Society*. New York: Harcourt Brace Jovanovich, 1992.

Chávez, Patricio, and Madeleine Grynsztejn, curators, Kathryn Kanjo, coordinator. *La Frontera/The Border: Art about the Mexico/United States Border Experience*. San Diego: Centro Cultural de la Raza, 1993.

Cockcroft, Eva. "The Story of Chicano Park." *Aztlán* 15, no. 1 (Spring 1984): 79–103.

Cole, Martin, and Henry Wallace, eds. *Don Pío Pico's Historical Narrative*. Trans. Arthur P. Botello. Los Angeles: Arthur H. Clark Co., 1973.

Colston, Stephen A. "San Joaquin: A Preliminary Historical Study of the Fortification at San Diego's Punta de Guijarros." In *Fort Guijarros*, by Ronald V. May, Roy Pettus, and Stephen A. Colston. San Diego: Cabrillo Historical Association, 1982.

Cook, Shelburne F. "The Aboriginal Population of Upper California." In *The California Indians: A Source Book*, edited and compiled by R. F. Heizer and M. A. Whipple. Berkeley: University of California Press, 1971.

———. *The Conflict between the California Indian and White Civilization*. Berkeley and Los Angeles: University of California Press, 1976.

Cornelius, Wayne. "America in the Era of Limits: Migrants, Nativists, and the Future of Mexican–U.S. Relations." In *Conflict and Convergence*, edited by Carlos Vásquez and Manuel García y Griego, 371–98. Los Angeles: Chicano Studies Research Center/ Latin American Studies Research Center at UCLA, 1983.

Costo, Rupert, and Jeannette Henry Costo, eds. *The Missions of California: A Legacy of Genocide*. San Francisco: Indian Historian Press, 1987.

Crawford, James. "The Campaign Against 227: A Post-Mortem." *Bilingual Research Journal* 21, no. 1 (Winter 1998): 1–29.

Davis, Mike, Kelly Mayhew, and Jim Miller. *Under the Perfect Sun: The San Diego Tourists Never See*. New York: New Press, 2003.

Dekker, Paul, and Eric Uslander, eds. *Social Capital and Participation in Everyday Life*. London: Routledge, 2001.

Delgado, Kevin. "A Turning Point: The Conception and Realization of Chicano Park." *Journal of San Diego History* 44, no. 1. www.sandiegohistory.org/journal/98winter/ chicano.htm. (Accessed March 15, 2007)

Dittmyer, Scott. "Historical Study of the Neighborhood House Association." Master's thesis, SDSU, Department of Social Work, 1978.

Dubois, Goddard. *The Religion of the Luiseño and Diegueño Indians*. University of California Publications in Archeology and Ethnology 8, no. 3. Berkeley: University of California Press, 1908.

"Duvall's Log of the Savannah." *Quarterly of the California Historical Society* 3, no. 2 (July 1924): 118–20.

Eagen, Rev. Monsignor I. Brent. "San Diego de Alcalá." *Journal of San Diego History* 24, no. 1 (Winter 1978): 5–6.

Engstrand, Iris W. "The Occupation of the Port of San Diego de Alcalá, 1769." *Journal of San Diego History* 24, no. 1 (Winter 1978): 93–98.

Engstrand, Iris W., and Ray Brandes. "A Brief History of Old Town San Diego, 1821–1874." In *Old Town San Diego, 1821–1874: A Brief History and Descriptive Guide to Historic Sites*. San Diego: Alcala Press, 1976. Available online at http://history.sandiego.edu/ gen/OTSD/briefhistory.html.

Estrada, Leobardo F., F. Chris García, Reynaldo Flores Macias, and Lionel Maldonado. "Chicanos in the United States: A History of Exploitation and Resistance." *Daedalus* 110 (Spring 1981): 103–32.

Evans, William Edward. "The Garra Uprising: Conflict between San Diego Indians and Settlers in 1851." *California Historical Quarterly* 45 (1966): 340–46.

Exposición Homenaje Pablo O'Higgins—Artista Nacional, 1904–1983. Mexico City: Instituto de Bellas Artes, 1985.

García, Alma, ed. *Chicana Feminist Thought: The Basic Historical Writings.* New York: Routledge, 1997.

García, Eugene E., Francisco A. Lomelí, and Isidro D. Ortiz. *Chicano Studies: A Multidisciplinary Approach.* New York: Teachers College Press, 1984.

García, Mario T. "The Californios of San Diego and the Politics of Accommodation, 1846–1860." *Aztlán: International Journal of Chicano Studies Research* 6, no. 1 (Spring 1975): 69–85.

———. *Desert Immigrants: The Mexicans of El Paso 1880–1920.* New Haven: Yale University Press, 1982.

———. *Memories of Chicano History: The Life and Narrative of Bert Corona.* Berkeley and Los Angeles: University of California Press, 1994.

———. "Merchants and Dons: San Diego's Attempt at Modernization, 1850–1860." *Journal of San Diego History* 21, no. 4 (Winter 1975): 52–80.

García, Matt. *A World of Its Own: Race, Labor and Citrus in the Making of Greater Los Angeles.* Chapel Hill: University of North Carolina Press, 2001.

García, Richard A. *Rise of the Mexican American Middle Class: San Antonio, 1929–1941.* College Station: Texas A&M University Press, 1991.

García y Griego, Manuel. "The Importation of Mexican Contract Laborers to the United States, 1942–1964." In *Between Two Worlds: Mexican Immigrants in the United States,* edited by David Gutiérrez, 45–96. Wilmington, DE: Scholarly Resources, 1996.

Geiger, Maynard, trans. and ed. *Letter of Luis Jayme, O.F.M., San Diego, October 17, 1772.* Los Angeles: Dawson's Book Shop, 1970.

Gifford, E. W. "California Balanophagy." In R. F. Heizer and M. A. Whipple, *The California Indians: A Source Book.* Berkeley and Los Angeles: University of California Press, 1971.

Goldman, Shifra M. *Dimensions of the Americas: Art and Social Change in Latin America and the United States.* Chicago: University of Chicago Press, 1994.

Goldman, Shifra, and Tomás Ybarra-Frausto. "The Political and Social Contexts of Chicano Art." In *CARA: Chicano Art: Resistance and Affirmation,* edited by Richard Griswold del Castillo, Teresa McKenna, and Yvonne Yarbro-Bejarano. Los Angeles: Wight Art Gallery, UCLA, 1991.

González, Gilbert. *Chicano Education in the Era of Segregation.* Philadelphia: Balch Institute Press, 1990.

———. "Company Unions, the Mexican Consulate, and the Imperial Valley Agricultural Strikes, 1928–1934." *Western Historical Quarterly* 27 (1996): 5–10.

González, Ray. "The Myth of the Chicano Sleeping Giant." *California Journal* February (1979): 46–47.

Grebler, Leo, Joan Moore, and Ralph Guzmán. *The Mexican American People: The Nation's Second Largest Minority.* New York: Free Press, 1970.

Griffith, Beatrice. *American Me.* Boston: Houghton Mifflin, 1948.

Griswold del Castillo, Richard. "The Discredited Revolution: The Magonista Capture of Tijuana in 1911." *Journal of San Diego History* 26 (1980): 256–73.

———. *La Familia: Chicano Families in the Urban Southwest, 1848 to the Present.* Notre Dame, IN: University of Notre Dame Press, 1984.

——. *The Los Angeles Barrio, 1850–1890.* Los Angeles: University of California Press, 1980.

——. "The Mexican Problem: A Crucial View of the Alliance of Academics and Politicians during the Debate over Mexican Immigration in the 1920s." *Borderlands* 4 (Spring 1981): 257–58.

——. "The San Ysidro Massacre: A Community Response to Tragedy." *Journal of Borderlands Studies* 3, no. 2 (Fall 1988): 65–80.

——. *The Treaty of Guadalupe Hidalgo: A Legacy of Conflict.* Norman: University of Oklahoma Press.

——, ed. "A Brief Synopsis of San Ysidro's History with a Chronology of the Town's Most Important Events." San Ysidro: San Diego State University Community History Project, n.d.

Griswold del Castillo, Richard, Teresa McKenna, and Yvonne Yarbro-Bejarano, eds. *Chicano Art: Resistance and Affirmation, 1965 to 1985.* Los Angeles: Wight Art Gallery, UCLA, 1991.

Grugal, Donald M. "Military Movements into San Diego from the Mexican War to Statehood, 1846–1850." Master's thesis, SDSU, Department of History, 1950.

Guerin-Gonzales, Camille. *Mexican Workers and American Dreams: Immigration, Repatriation, and California Farm Labor, 1900–1939.* New Brunswick, NJ: Rutgers University Press, 1996.

Gurr, Ted. *Why Men Rebel.* Princeton, NJ: Princeton University Press, 1970.

Gutiérrez, David, ed. *Between Two Worlds: Mexican Immigrants in the United States.* Wilmington, DE: Scholarly Resources, 1996.

——. "Migration, Emergent Ethnicity, and the 'Third Space': The Shifting Politics of Nationalism in Greater Mexico." Rethinking History and the Nation-State: Mexico and the United States as a Case Study: A Special Issue *Journal of American History* 86, no. 2 (September 1999): 481–517.

Gutiérrez, José Ángel. *Making of a Chicano Militant: Lessons from Cristal.* Madison: University of Wisconsin Press, 1998.

Gutiérrez, Ramón. *When Jesus Came, the Corn Mothers Went Away: Marriage, Sexuality, and Power in New Mexico, 1500–1846.* Stanford, CA: Stanford University Press, 1991.

Harvard Civil Rights Project. "Race, Place and Opportunity: Racial Change and Segregation in the San Diego Metropolitan Area: 1990–2000," 2002. Available online at www.civilrightsproject.harvard.edu/research/metro/San%20Diego%20Paper%20 Part%201.pdf. (Accessed November 25, 2003)

Heilbron, Carl H. *History of San Diego County.* San Diego: San Diego Press Club, 1936.

Heizer, R. F., and M. A. Whipple. *The California Indians: A Source Book.* Berkeley and Los Angeles: University of California Press, 1971.

Herzog, Larry. *Where North Meets South.* Austin: CMAS/University of Texas Press, 1990.

Hewes, Minna, and Gordon Hewes, eds. and trans. *Indian Life and Customs at Mission San Luis Rey: A Record of California Mission Life by Pablo Tac, an Indian Neophyte, Written about 1835.* San Luis Rey: Old Mission, 1958.

Hughes, Charles W. "The Decline of the Californios: The Case of San Diego, 1846–1856." *Journal of San Diego History* 21, no. 3 (Summer 1975): 2–20.

Jargowsky, Paul A. *Stunning Progress, Hidden Problems: The Dramatic Decline of*

Concentrated Poverty in the 1990s. Brookings Institution Living Cities Census series. May 2003. Washington, DC: Brookings Institution. Available online at www.brookings .edu/es/urban/publications/jargowskypoverty.pdf. (Accessed March 15, 2007)

Johnson, Tim, ed. *Spirit Capture: Photographs from the National Museum of the American Indian.* Washington, DC: Smithsonian Institution Press with the National Museum of the American Indian, 1998.

Jones, Oakah L. Jr. *Los Paisanos: Spanish Settlers on the Northern Frontier of New Spain.* Norman: University of Oklahoma Press, 1979.

Jones, Sally Cavell. "The Battle of San Pascual." Master's thesis, UCSD, 1973.

Katz, Michael, ed. *The Underclass Debate: Views from History.* Princeton, NJ: Princeton University Press, 1993.

Keller, Gary D., ed. *Contemporary Chicana and Chicano Art.* 2 vols. Tempe, AZ: Bilingual Press/Editorial Bilingüe, 2002.

Killea, Lucy Lytle. "The Political History of a Mexican Pueblo: San Diego from 1825 to 1845." *Journal of San Diego History* 7, no. 3 (July 1966): 1–39.

Kroeber, A. L. "The History of Native Culture in California." In *The California Indians: A Source Book*, edited and compiled by R. F. Heizer and M. A. Whipple. Berkeley: University of California Press, 1971.

Langum, David J. "The Caring Colony: Alta California's Participation in Spain's Foreign Affairs." In *Southern California's Spanish Heritage: An Anthology*, edited by Doyce B. Nunis Jr. Los Angeles: Historical Society of Southern California, 1992.

Larralde, Carlos, and Richard Griswold del Castillo. "Luisa Moreno: A Hispanic Civil Rights Leader in San Diego." *Journal of San Diego History* 41, no. 4 (Fall 1995): 284–311.

Larralde, Carlos, and José Rodolfo Jacobo. *Juan N. Cortina and the Struggle for Justice in Texas.* Dubuque, IA: Kendall/Hunt, 2000.

Lee, Lawrence. "The Little Landers Colony of San Ysidro." *Journal of San Diego History* 21, no. 1 (Winter 1975): 26–51.

Lewis, Michael Andrew. "Ethnic and Racial Violence in San Diego, 1880–1920." Master's thesis, SDSU, 1991.

Lewis, Oscar. "The Culture of Poverty." In *On Understanding Poverty*, edited by David Moynihan, 187–200. New York: Basic Books, 1968.

Lipsitz, George. "We Know What Time It Is." *Centro Journal* 5, no. 1 (Winter 2002–03): 13.

Logan, John, Richard Alba, and Zang Wenqan. "Immigrant Enclaves and Ethnic Communities in New York and Los Angeles." *American Sociological Review* 67 (April 2002): 299–322.

López, Sonia. "Chicanas in the Student Movement." *In Essays on la Mujer*, edited by Rosaura Sánchez and Rosa Martínez Cruz, 16–29. Chicano Studies Center Publications. Los Angeles: UCLA, 1977.

López, Yolanda. "A Chicana's Look at the International Women's Conference." In *Chicana Feminist Thought: The Basic Historical Writings*, edited by Alma García, 181–82. New York: Routledge, 1997.

Lorenz, J. D. *Jerry Brown: The Man on the White Horse.* New York: Houghton Mifflin, 1978.

Lothrop, Gloria Ricci. "Rancheras and the Land: Women and Property Rights in Hispanic California." *Southern California Quarterly* 76, no. 1 (Spring 1994): 65–70.

Loumala, Katherine. "Dreams and Dream Interpretations of the Diegueño Indians of Southern California." *Psychoanalytic Quarterly* May (1936): 195–99.

Maciel, David R., and Isidro D. Ortiz. *Chicanas/Chicanos at the Crossroads: Social, Economic, and Political Change.* Tucson: University of Arizona Press, 1996.

Mariscal, George. *Brown-Eyed Children of the Sun: Lessons from the Chicano Movement, 1965–1975.* Albuquerque: University of New Mexico Press, 2005.

Martínez, Elizabeth. *De Colores Means All of Us: Latina Views for a Multi-Colored Century.* Cambridge, MA: South End Press, 1998.

Martínez, Pablo L. *A History of Lower California*, translated by Edith Duffy Turner. Mexico City: Editorial Baja California, 1960.

Mason, Bill. "The Garrisons of San Diego Presidio: 1770–1794." *Journal of San Diego History* 24, no. 4 (Fall 1978): 399–424. www.sandiegohistory.org/journal/78fall/garrisons .htm

Massey, Douglas, and Jorge Durand. *Return to Aztlan.* Los Angeles and Berkeley: University of California Press, 1989.

Mathes, Michael. *Vizcaíno and Spanish Expansion in the Pacific Ocean, 1580–1630.* San Francisco: California Historical Society, 1968.

Mazón, Mauricio. *The Zoot-Suit Riots: The Psychology of Symbolic Annihilation.* Austin: University of Texas Press, 1984.

McWilliams, Carey. *The Education of Carey McWilliams.* New York: Simon and Schuster, 1979.

———. *North from Mexico: The Spanish-Speaking People of the United States.* New York: Greenwood Press, 1968.

Melville, Margarita, ed. *Twice a Minority: Mexican American Women.* St Louis: Mosby, 1980.

Mesa-Bains, Amalia. "El Mundo Femenino: Chicana Artists of the Movement—A Commentary On Development and Production." In *CARA: Chicano Art: Resistance and Affirmation*, edited by Richard Griswold del Castillo, Teresa McKenna, and Yvonne Yarbro-Bejarano, 131–40. Los Angeles: Wight Art Gallery, UCLA, 1991.

Mexicans in California: Report of Governor C. C. Young's Mexican Fact-Finding Committee. Sacramento, CA: State Printing Office, 1930.

Meyer, David S., Nancy Whittier, and Belinda Robnett, eds. *Social Movements: Identity, Culture and the State.* Oxford: Oxford University Press, 2002.

Milkman, Ruth, and Kent Wong. "Organizing Immigrant Workers: Case Studies from Southern California." In *Rekindling the Movement: Labor's Quest for Twenty-first Century Relevance*, edited by Lowell Turner, Harry Katz, and Richard Hurd, 99–128. Ithaca: Cornell University Press, 2001.

Miller, Arthur, Patricia Gurin, Gerald Gurin, and Oksana Malanchuk. "Group Consciousness and Political Participation." *American Journal of Political Science* 25, no. 2 (1981): 495–511.

Monroy, Douglas. *Thrown among Strangers: The Making of Mexican Culture in Frontier California.* Berkeley and Los Angeles: University of California Press, 1990.

Montemayor, Roberto. "Border Divides the Best of Both Worlds." In *Southern California's*

Latino Community: A Series of Articles Reprinted from the Los Angeles Times, 29–33. Los Angeles: Los Angeles Times, 1983.

Moore, Joan, and Raquel Pinderhughes. *In the Barrios: Latinos and the Underclass Debate.* New York: Russell Sage Foundation, 1993.

Moraga, Cherríe L., and Gloria E. Anzaldúa, eds. 1981. *This Bridge Called My Back: Writings by Radical Women of Color.* Berkeley: Third Woman Press.

Morín, Raúl. *Among the Valiant: Mexican Americans in World War II and Korea.* Alhambra, CA: Borden Publishing Co., 1966.

Muñiz, Vicki. *Resisting Gentrification and Displacement: Voices of Puerto Rican Women in the Barrio.* Latino Communities series. New York: Garland Publishing, 1998.

Muñoz, Carlos Jr. *Youth, Identity and Power: The Chicano Movement.* London: Verso, 1989.

Nevins, Joseph. *Operation Gatekeeper: The Rise of the "Illegal Alien" and the Remaking of the U.S.–Mexico Boundary.* London: Routledge, 2001.

Nie, Norman, Sidney Verba, Kay Schlozman, and Henry Brady. "Race, Ethnicity and Political Resources: Participation in the United States." *British Journal of Political Science* 23, no. 4 (October 1993): 453–99.

Norris, Frank. "Logan Heights: Growth and Change in the Old 'East End.'" *Journal of San Diego History* 29, no. 1 (Winter 1983): 28–40.

Norris, Pippa, and Ronald Inglehart. *Rising Tide: Gender Equality and Cultural Change around the World.* New York: Cambridge University Press, 2003.

Oden, Frederick Bryant. "The Maid of Monterey: The Life of María Amparo Ruiz de Burton, 1832–1895." Master's thesis, History Department, USDUCSD, 1992.

Ortiz, Isidro D. "Latinos against City Hall: *Chicano Federation, Pérez vs. City of San Diego.*" In *Voting Rights and Local Government*, edited by Richard Santillán. Claremont, CA: Rose Institute, 1990.

Ortner, Sherry B., ed. *The Fate of "Culture": Geertz and Beyond.* Berkeley: University of California Press, 1999.

Owen, Robert C. "Indians and Revolution: The 1911 Invasion of Baja California, Mexico." *Ethnohistory* 10 (1963): 377–89.

Paez de Castro, Juan, James R. Moriarty, and Mary Keistman. "Cabrillo's Log, 1542–1543: A Voyage of Discovery: A Summary." *The Western Explorer: The Journal of the Cabrillo Historical Association* 5, nos. 2–3.

Panunzio, Constantine, and the University of California Heller Committee for Research in Social Economics. *Cost of Living Studies.* Vol. 5: *How Mexicans Earn and Live: A Study of the Incomes and Expenditures of One Hundred Mexican Families in San Diego, California.* University of California Publications in Economics 13, no. 1. Berkeley: University of California Press, 1933.

Pardo, Mary. "Gendered Citizenship: Mexican American Women and Grassroots Activism in East Los Angeles, 1986–1992." In *Chicano Politics and Society in the Late Twentieth Century*, edited by David Montejano, 58–82. Austin: University of Texas Press, 1999.

Paredes, Américo. *"With His Pistol in His Hand": A Border Ballad and Its Hero.* Austin: University of Texas Press, 1958.

Pattie, James O. *The Personal Narrative of James O. Pattie: The 1831 ed.* Introduction by William H. Goetzmann. Philadelphia, PA: Lippincott, 1962.

Paz, Octavio. *The Labyrinth of Solitude: Life and Thought in Mexico.* Translated by Lysander Kemp. New York: Grove Press, 1961.

Peters, Casey. "Peace and Freedom Party from 1967 to 1997." *Synthesis/Regeneration* 12 (Winter 1997). www.greens.org/s-r/12/12-05.html.

Phillips, George Harwood. "Indian Resistance and Cooperation in Southern California: The Garra Uprising and Its Aftermath." PhD diss., Department of History, UCLA, 1973.

Pitt, Leonard. *The Decline of the Californios: A Social History of the Spanish-Speaking Californians, 1846–1890.* Berkeley: University of California Press, 1966.

Piven, Frances, and Richard Cloward. *Poor People's Movements: Why They Succeed, How They Fail.* New York: Vintage Books, 1979.

Price, John. *Tijuana: Urbanization in a Border Culture.* Notre Dame, IN: University of Notre Dame Press, 1973.

———, ed. *Tijuana '68: Ethnographic Notes on a Mexican Border City.* Ethnology Laboratory Papers no. 1. San Diego: SDSU, Department of Anthropology, August 1968.

Proffitt, Ted D. III. *Tijuana: The History of a Mexican Metropolis.* San Diego: San Diego State University Press, 1994.

Putnam, Robert. *Making Democracy Work: Civic Traditions in Modern Italy.* Princeton: Princeton University Press, 1993.

Rivas-Rodríguez, Maggie, ed. *Mexican Americans and World War II.* Austin: University of Texas Press, 2005.

Roberts, Elizabeth Judson. *Indian Stories of the Southwest.* San Francisco: Harr Wagner Publishing Co., 1917.

Robinson, Alfred Robinson. *Life in California During a Residence of Several Years in the Territory....* New York: Da Capo Press, 1969.

Robinson, W. W. *Land in California.* Berkeley and Los Angeles: University of California Press, 1948.

Romo, Richard. *East Los Angeles: History of a Barrio.* Austin: University of Texas Press, 1983.

Romo, Terezita. "A Collective History: Las Mujeres Muralistas." In *Art/Women/California 1950–2000,* edited by Diana Burgess Fuller and Daniela Salvioni, 95–110. Berkeley: University of California Press, 2002.

Rosaldo, Renato. "Changing Chicano Narrative." In *Culture and Truth: The Remaking of Social Analysis.* Boston: Beacon Press, 1989.

Rosales, Francisco. *Chicano! The History of Mexican American Civil Rights Movement.* Houston: Arte Público Press, 1997.

Rosen, Martin, and James Fisher. "Chicano Park and the Chicano Park Murals: Barrio Logan, City of San Diego, California." *The Public Historian* 23, no. 4 (Fall 2001): 91–112.

Sánchez, George I. *Becoming Mexican American: Ethnicity, Culture, and Identity in Chicano Los Angeles, 1900–1945.* New York: Oxford University Press, 1993.

———. "Pachucos in the Making." *Common Ground* 4 (Autumn 1943): 13–20.

Sánchez, Rita. "Chicana Writer: Breaking Out of the Silence." In *Chicana Feminist Thought: The Basic Historical Writings,* edited by Alma García. New York: Routledge, 1997.

———. *Cochise Remembers: Our Great-Grandfather, Charles Henry Coleman.* San Diego: R and R Publishers, 2000.

———. "The Five Sánchez Brothers in World War II: Remembrance and Discovery." In *Mexican Americans and World War II*, edited by Maggie Rivas-Rodríguez, 1–40. Austin: University of Texas Press, 2005.

Sánchez, Rosaura, and Rosa Martínez Cruz, eds. *Essays on La Mujer.* Los Angeles: UCLA Chicano Studies, 1977.

Santillán, Richard. "Rosita the Riveter: Midwest Mexican American Women During World War II, 1941–1945." *Perspectives in Mexican American Studies* 2 (1989): 137, 138.

Segade, Gustavo V. "Identity and Power: An Essay On the Politics of Culture and the Culture of Politics in Chicano Thought." *Aztlán* 9 (Fall 1978): 87–97.

Shelton, Cynthia Jane. "The Neighborhood House of San Diego: Settlement Work in the Mexican Community, 1914–1940," Master's thesis, Department of History, SDSU, 1975.

Shipek, Florence, C. *Delfina Cuero: Her Autobiography: An Account of Her Last Years.* San Diego: Ballena Press, 1991.

———. "An Example of Intensive Plant Husbandry: The Kumeyaay of Southern California." In *Foraging and Farming: The Evolution of Plant Exploitation*, edited by David R. Harris and Gordon C. Hillman, 159–70. London: Unwin Hyman, 1989.

———. "Kuuchamaa: the Kumeyaay Sacred Mountain." *Journal of California and Great Basin Anthropology* 7, no. 1 (1985): 67–74.

———. *Myth and Reality: The Antiquity of the Kumeyaay.* Occasional Papers on Linguistics, No. 13, edited by James Redden. Carbondale: Department of Linguistics, Southern Illinois University, 1986.

———. "A Native American Adaptation to Drought: The Kumeyaay as Seen in the San Diego Mission Records, 1770–1798." *Ethnohistory* 28, no. 4 (Fall 1981): 296–99.

Smith, Jeffrey K. "The Healing Practices of Southern California Indians in San Diego County." Master's thesis, Anthropology Department, SDSU, 1984.

Smith, Karen J. "The Reclamation of the Imperial Valley, 1849–1916." Master's thesis, SDSU, Department of History, 1979.

Smith, Neil, and Peter Williams, eds. *Gentrification of the City.* Boston: Allen and Unwin, 1986.

Starr, Raymond G. *San Diego State University: A History in Word and Image.* San Diego: San Diego State University Press, 1995.

State of California. *Mexicans in California: Report of Governor C.C. Young's Mexican Fact-Finding Committee.* San Francisco: State Printing Office, 1930.

Stone, Clarence, and Heywood Sanders eds. *The Politics of Urban Development.* Lawrence: University of Kansas Press, 1987.

Takaki, Ronald. *Double Victory: Multicultural History of America in World War II.* New York: Little, Brown and Co., 2000

Talamante, Olga. "Notes from an Argentine Prison." *Vision de la Mujer* 1, no. 1 (1976): 8–13.

Taylor, Paul S. *Mexican Labor in the United States*, vol. 1. Berkeley: University of California Press, 1928.

Tays, George. "Pío Pico's Correspondence with the Mexican Government." *California Historical Society Quarterly* 13 (June 1934): 130–40.

Teisher, Arthur Jr. "The Rise of Na'at: The Garra Uprising as a Neo-Traditional Pattern of Indian Unrest in Southern California." Senior honors thesis, Department of History, UCSD, 1990.

Temple, Thomas Workman. "California's Birth at San Diego." *Academy Scrapbook* February (1953): 189–204.

Tijerina, Reies López. *They Called Me "King Tiger": My Struggle for the Land and Our Rights.* Translated by José Ángel Gutiérrez. Houston: Arte Público Press, 2000.

Tilly, Charles. *From Mobilization to Revolution.* Reading, MA: Addison-Wesley, 1978.

Toffelmeir, Gertrude, and Katherine Loumala. "Dreams and Dream Interpretations of the Diegueño Indians of Southern California." *Psychoanalytic Quarterly* May (1936): 197.

Treutlein, Theodore E. "The Portolá Expedition of 1769–1770." *California Historical Quarterly* 47 (1968): 295–310.

Tuck, Ruth D. *Not with the Fist.* New York: Arno Press, 1974.

Turner, Ralph H., and Samuel J. Surace. "Zoot-Suiters and Mexicans: Symbols in Crowd Behavior." *American Journal of Sociology* 62 (1956): 14–24.

Ubelaker Douglas H. "North American Indian Population Size, A.D. 1500 to 1985." *American Journal of Physical Anthropology* 77 (1988): 292.

U.S. Commission on Civil Rights. *Who Is Guarding the Guardians?* Washington, DC: GPO, 1981.

Valencia, Richard. *The Evolution of Cultural Deficiency Thinking.* Austin: University of Texas Press, 1995.

Véjar, Allen Olmstead, and Pablo Véjar, *Californios—One Portola Soldado de Cuera's Family in California (1769–1877).* San Francisco, CA: privately printed, 1989.

Vélez-Ibáñez, Carlos. *Border Visions: Mexican Cultures of the Southwest United States.* Tucson: University of Arizona Press, 1996.

Weber, David J. *The Mexican Frontier, 1821–1846: The American Southwest under Mexico.* Albuquerque: University of New Mexico Press, 1982.

Wilson, Julius. *The Truly Disadvantaged: The Inner City, the Underclass, and Public Policy.* Chicago: University of Chicago Press, 1987.

Wilson, Marjorie. "Legends of the Diegueño Indians." Master's thesis, SDSU, 1956.

Young, Iris Marion. "Five Faces of Oppression." In *Multiculturalism from the Margins: Non-Dominant Voices on Difference and Diversity*, edited by Dean Harris. Westport, CT: Bergin and Garvey, 1995.

Zavella, Patricia. "Engendering Transnationalism in Food Processing: Peripheral Vision on Both Sides of the U.S.–Mexico Border." In *Las nuevas fronteras del siglo XXI*, edited by Alejandro Alvarez Bejar, Norma Klahn, Federico Machon, and Pedro Castillo. La Jornada Ediciones, Centro de Investigaciones Colección: La Democracia en México. Mexico City: UNAM, 1999.

ABOUT THE CONTRIBUTORS

RICHARD GRISWOLD DEL CASTILLO is a historian who teaches Chicana and Chicano history at San Diego State University. His research interests have mostly focused on the nineteenth-century Southwest, in books such as *The Los Angeles Barrio, 1850–1880* and *The Treaty of Guadalupe Hidalgo: A Legacy of Conflict.*

MARÍA DE LA LUZ IBARRA is an anthropologist who teaches Chicana and Chicano studies at SDSU. She has written numerous scholarly articles about the lives of Mexican immigrant women who are domestic workers and is currently preparing a book manuscript about this subject, entitled "Borrowed Lives: Mexicanas and Intimate Care."

JOSÉ RODOLFO JACOBO is a graduate student at San Diego State University working on his PhD in education. His love of U.S.–Mexican border history has resulted in a number of important projects: a coauthored book entitled *Juan Cortina: A Struggle for Justice* and a co-edited book of poetry and photographs entitled *The Giving Gaze.*

EMMANUELLE LE TEXIER earned her PhD in political science and is associate professor at the University of Lille III (France) and member of the IMISCOE excellence network (International Migration, Integration and Social Cohesion in Europe). She became involved in researching barrio issues during her Fulbright scholarship, as a host fellow at the Center for Comparative Immigration studies at UCSD (2002–2003). She has published several articles and a book entitled *Quand les exclus font de la politique. Le barrio mexicain de San Diego, Californie* (Paris: Presses de Sciences Po, 2006).

ROBERTO MARTÍNEZ is a community activist and former director of the American Friends Service Committee in San Diego, responsible for monitoring and acting on human rights abuses against immigrants along the U.S.–Mexican border.

ISIDRO D. ORTIZ is a professor of Chicana and Chicano studies at San Diego State University. A political scientist, he specializes in the study of Chicano/Latino politics and educational policy and practice towards Chicanos. He is coeditor of *Chicanas/Chicanos at the Crossroads: Social, Economic, and Political Change* and *Chicano Renaissance: Contemporary Cultural Trends,* both published by the University of Arizona Press. He also served as coeditor of *Chicano Studies: A Multidisciplinary Approach.*

RITA SÁNCHEZ is a professor of Chicano studies and English at Mesa College who received her degree from Stanford University. She has had extensive experience in the arts, having co-owned and operated one of the first Chicano art galleries in San Diego and having organized a large number of art shows. Rita's research in family history has resulted in a book, *Cochise Remembers: Our Great-Grandfather, Charles Henry Coleman,* and in many articles on family history. She is also author of "The Five Sánchez Brothers in World War II," a chapter in *Mexican Americans and World War II.*

INDEX